£1·00
DC
Fub

Penguin Education

**Intonation**

Edited by Dwight Bolinger

Penguin Modern Linguistics Readings

*General Editor*
David Crystal

*Advisory Board*
Dwight Bolinger
M. A. K. Halliday
John Lyons
Frank Palmer
James Sledd
C. I. J. M. Stuart

D1253270

# Intonation

**Selected Readings**

Edited by Dwight Bolinger

Penguin Books

Penguin Books Ltd, Harmondsworth,
Middlesex, England
Penguin Books Inc, 7110 Ambassador Road,
Baltimore, Md 21207, USA
Penguin Books Australia Ltd,
Ringwood, Victoria, Australia

First published 1972
This selection copyright © Dwight Bolinger, 1972
Introduction and notes copyright © Dwight Bolinger, 1972
Copyright acknowledgement for items in this volume
will be found on page 456.

Made and printed in Great Britain by
Hazell Watson & Viney Ltd, Aylesbury, Bucks
Set in Monotype Times

To John Derrick McClure
*and the two links that bind us*

# Contents

# Introduction

There are two kinds of speech sounds, periodic and aperiodic, which is another way of saying musical sounds and noisy sounds. Both are indispensable, but their roles differ. Noisy sounds are mostly limited to the complexes that we call phonemes: the explosion of air when the lips are parted by which a [p] is partially identified, the particular grade of hiss that distinguishes an [f] from an [s]. Musical sounds are used in this way too; particular sets of overtones (called formants) make the difference between one vowel and another, [i] and [e] for example – the higher position of the tongue with an [i] creates resonances in the mouth that are not the same as with the lower position of the tongue for an [e] or an [a]; the positions do the same for the pulsations of the vocal cords that the stops do for the pulsations of an organ pipe – they change the quality. In addition, the mere presence of a musical sound distinguishes a [z] from an [s] – we call this 'voicing': a [z] is both voiced and noisy: an [s] is only noisy.

We are not accustomed to thinking of these uses of musical sound as really musical. They are too unlike our conventional notions of music. But language does make use of another part of the sound wave in a manner so like that of ordinary music that it is sometimes called the melody of speech. When we sing, most of our musical message is carried not by the overtones (which are what we use to tell one vowel from another) but by the fundamental. This is the tone that is identified musically as an A or a C or an F in such-and-such an octave. When we speak we use the fundamental too, and that is called intonation. It resembles music not only in its physical basis but in other ways as well – both have ties with emotion. The chief difference is that music is an art form and is highly elaborated; we insist on exact intervals and exact combinations, and we play all sorts of imitative and imaginative tricks with melodies and rhythms. Language cannot afford that degree of originality, for it has to be conventional; it has more important business than transmitting feelings, and this forces it to harness emotion in the service of meaning. It may be that the rising pitch on a question really reflects the speaker's inner uncertainty, or his excitement or interest in getting an answer; but questions are a grammatical category, and high or rising pitch is one way of telling them from statements.

What is a typical use of intonation in a language like English?

When a layman speaks of intonation he usually means one of two things: the total quality of the sound by which he can distinguish one dialect or language from another whether he understands what is being said or not, and the tone of voice to which he reacts more or less emotionally. The first includes much more than fundamental pitch, but this is easiest to sense and one often hears the comment that a speaker is talking in a sing-song (it is when the sing-song used by the speaker differs from our own sing-song that we are apt to be conscious of it). The second – the tone of voice – comes closer to being purely a matter of fundamental pitch; consider the different sensations one feels on hearing the 'same' sentence spoken in these three different ways:

Don't be                Don't be an                Don't be an
       an^(g^(r^y))              g^(r^y)                          g^(r^y)

The first is soothing or pleading; the second is assertive – it imposes the speaker's will, and is the way commands are usually made; the third is most likely to be explanatory – it could be in answer to 'How can I keep my blood pressure down?'

Yet language is a multi-storied edifice and even here things are not as simple as they seem. The soothing intonation may be overruled by a warning look – the speaker may be expressing something like 'I'm willing to be considerate about this but don't push me too far.' And the mandatory or assertive intonation may be sweetened by a smile. Gesture has the final say. Even within the intonation curve itself it is not just the way the pitch moves but what it moves over that counts. In the first of the three examples the distinctive fact is that the pitch goes down and then goes up; but one can easily invent examples in which this happens and there is almost no soothing effect at all:

                mon
He was
       a
              ster!

The pitch goes down on *was a* and up on *mon-*. The difference is that in *Don't be angry* the low pitch occurs on the most important word in the sentence, while in *He was a monster* it occurs on the indefinite article *a*. The low pitch in the middle suggests that the speaker is 'holding down' something, and it is obviously not the same to hold down something trivial as to hold down something important. Intonation, like everything else in language, is one instrument in an orchestra.

English is rich in the uses of fundamental pitch that are typified by those three examples. Many languages are poorer in that respect but richer in others. The sharpest divergence is between 'tone languages' and 'intonation languages'. The former use the fundamental as part of the system of distinctive sounds; a word in Chinese or Mazatec or Yoruba (to name three languages in different parts of the world) may differ from another word only in the fundamental pitch with which it is spoken. An 'intonation language' lacks this use of pitch but the term is really a misnomer because it has yet to be proved that any language is totally without the expressive uses of pitch that we normally associate with intonation. Pitch is like any other clearly audible characteristic of speech sound: it is there to be used, and almost certainly will be used, though in varying proportions for different purposes. Even in English it is possible for a change in fundamental pitch to make the difference between one phoneme – and hence one word – and another. A vowel following a voiced consonant tends to have lower pitch than one following a voiceless consonant; if the only difference between two consonants is that one is voiced and the other not, then we may hear the effect as much from the pitch of the following vowel as from the voicing itself – under some conditions, hearing *Zeke* and *seek*, the fact that the vowel in *seek* has a higher pitch may be a stronger clue than the voicelessness of the [s]. This use of tone has not become systematic in English as in the so-called tone languages, but it is available if needed.

The fact that English lacks 'tonemes' like those of Chinese does not mean that pitch in English is not layered, that is, that it cannot do more than one thing at a time. By merely changing the place where a pitch event occurs, without changing the event itself, we may make a distinction in word meanings at the same time that we produce a particular intonation contour with its own independent meaning. Take the two sentences *I don't want to run around* and *I don't want a runaround*. The same intonation – a fairly level pitch followed by an abrupt rise followed by a steep fall – may be used for both, with a meaning something like 'I assert this'. At normal speed they sound exactly alike except for the place where the rise and the fall occur – and the difference that this makes is not in the intonation (as one would find between 'I assert this' and 'I ask this') but in the words *run around*, where the rise occurs on -*round*, and *runaround*, where it occurs on *run*. The traditional view is that the 'stress' falls on a different syllable; but our clue to the position of the stress in this case is the behaviour of the fundamental pitch.

When it is not distinguishing word meanings or phrase meanings, a change in the location of the event may – still without changing the basic intonation – single out a word for special treatment. The two expressions *help yourself* and *serve yourself* are synonymous in referring to food, yet they are handled differently:

1. It's time to eat! Don't wait! Hurry up and serve yourself!
2. It's time to eat! Don't wait! Hurry up and help yourself!

In the second of these we have to put the jump in pitch on *-self*; that is what distinguishes *help oneself* in this sense from *help oneself* in 'Why does he do those things?' – 'He just can't help himself.' But in the first, if the jump is put on *-self* the meaning is 'Serve yourself, not somebody else' – the *yourself* becomes contrastive.

And when it is not doing either of these two things, the place where the event occurs may make an affective difference. This can happen when it does not matter which syllable of a word carries the stress and the speaker can put it where he pleases. The following was heard on a television commercial: *Do something about that mústache; I don't know why, but I can't get used to a bald-headed man with a mustáche.*

So a language which uses pitch in this way – an 'accent language' if we need a name for it – is not so very different from a tone language. Either is capable of adding an intonation system on top of its accent or its tone.

There is wide agreement among linguists on the units of sound that make distinctions in word meanings. There is no such agreement on the units of intonation. Some have argued that an intonation contour consists of a succession of levels, others that it is a succession of changes in direction. The disagreement reflects the difficulty of treating intonation independently of all the other events that tend to colour it. A classic example of complexity is the argument over 'question intonations'. We recognize questions as grammatical entities by such characteristics as inversions (*He is here; Is he here?*) and interrogative words (*He went there; He went where?; Where did he go?*). Is the intonation of a question to be counted as part of its grammatical identity? If it is, then we may have difficulty deciding what to do with a flip answer like:

Because I want
e
d to.

given to the question *Why did you do it*? It is an answer, hence it is not a question; yet the rising pitch seems to ask 'And what business is it of yours?' or 'What are you going to do about it?' We may have the same trouble with certain speakers, more numerous in some dialect areas than others, who in giving a long discourse raise their voices every so often, forcing their listeners to give some sign that they are paying attention – their sentences may be statements, but their intonation says 'Are you listening?' However important intonation may be to what a grammar classifies as questions, it seems to lead an existence of its own. The disagreements are the result of our knowing so little about that existence and what it means to language as a whole.

With no magic to deal with the mystery, the best we can do is sample as broadly as possible the probings that have been made at different points, by investigators with different points of view. How does intonation relate to grammar? to emotion? to music? What theories have been advanced to account for it? How does it bend to other forces, or how does it bend them? What are the differences and similarities from dialect to dialect and language to language? To provide some stimulating answers to questions like these was the purpose of bringing together the articles that follow. Little is settled but much is illuminated. The editor's main hope is that the reader will leave this volume with a deepened curiosity about what goes on when he hears or produces a stream of fundamental pitch.

# Part One
## Preliminaries

An introduction to the facts of intonation, rather than to the theories about it, requires a point of view. The one presented in the first article is that languages like English have an accentual system, which is more or less independent of the uses of pitch, to signal attitudes and divisions of the sentence, and that the latter have the form of configurations (rises, falls and sustains in various combinations) rather than of numbered phonemic levels. There are other viewpoints, as later chapters will show, but the advisability of separating accents (sometimes called stresses – but this term covers more than pitch contrasts) from the rest of intonational phenomena is pretty generally recognized. In any case it is useful to start with because it makes clear that there are layers that have to be treated separately.

An introduction to the facts also needs a word on how the physical data are gathered or at least verified. Until the latter part of the nineteenth century, estimates of the pitch curve of the voice depended on the human ear – even today many intonation studies demand no other instrumentation. A steady fundamental pitch can of course be determined by matching it with the known pitch of an instrument, but the normal fluctuating movements need a visual display if they are to be measured and analysed. In the second article Léon and Martin describe the kymograph, a primitive device for producing such a display, along with later instruments, capping their study with a description of their own highly sophisticated and marvellously graphic Melodic Analyser. It is too new to have been used in the experimental studies reported in this volume, but will profoundly affect future work by making it possible to examine large amounts of material without the need to make tedious calculations.

# 1 Dwight Bolinger

Around the Edge of Language: Intonation

Dwight Bolinger, 'Around the edge of language: intonation', *Harvard Educational Review*, vol. 34, no. 2, Spring 1964, pp. 282–93. Copyright © 1964 by President and Fellows of Harvard College.

The surface of the ocean responds to the forces that act upon it in movements resembling the ups and downs of the human voice. If our vision could take it all in at once, we would discern several types of motion, involving a greater and greater expanse of sea and volume of water: ripples, waves, swells and tides. It would be more accurate to say ripples *on* waves *on* swells *on* tides, because each larger movement carries the smaller ones on its back.

Suppose our view were limited to a few inches, and our awareness of the movement depended on watching the bobbing of a cork. We would be conscious of the ripples, but the rest might escape us as irregularities: sometimes the cork would execute its bob at a higher point than at other times, but those high and low times themselves would seem to be perturbed in unaccountable ways. Something to aid our limited view – a tracing, to measure the distance between peaks, or a clock, to measure the time as they passed, would help us to separate the overlying and underlying rises and falls. But even with a clear formulation of the four-tiered hierarchy of movement, our understanding would not be satisfied, we would not feel secure with it, until we had related each level to something beyond mere stirrings of seawater: the ripples with local breezes, the waves with gusts of wind, the swell with a distant storm, and the tide with the pull of the moon and the sun.

In speech (and in song – hence the name 'speech melody' to enforce the comparison), the ups and downs are those of the fundamental pitch of the voice, produced by the vibration of the vocal cords. Voice, purely as voice, plays many parts in communication. It provides the overtones that are the raw material for vowels; determines the difference between certain consonants and certain others, such as [s] and [z] or [f] and [v]; most importantly, it is what gives speech its power to ride over noise and carry long distances. Besides these roles – which, though they involve voice and hence tone, could almost as well be monotone – the fundamental pitch of the voice plays others that overlap in their physical manifestations like the motion of the sea. It has taken us a long time to separate the little ups and downs from the big ones; to tell where one stops and another begins; to identify other phonetic events, such as duration and loudness, that are associated with them; and to relate each to some separate function in communication. The work is far from finished, but enough is known so that no textbook on language can claim to be up to date if it fails at least to call attention to intonation as something whose differing forms from language to language has to be taught.

Yet intonation is not as 'central' to communication as some of the other traits of language. If it were, we could not understand someone who speaks in a monotone; and, in so far as our comprehension of written language is due to its being a faithful reproduction of speech, we could not read. We therefore must be wary of giving it undue attention just because it is something new.

How important *is* it? The answer depends on knowing how extensive the differences are between one language or dialect and another, and on knowing where the cost of misunderstanding comes too high. The place to begin is English.

I return to my analogy. The ripples are the accidental changes in pitch, the irrelevant quavers. The waves are the peaks and valleys that we call *accent*. The swells are the separations of our discourse into its larger segments. The tides are the tides of emotion.

The extremes – ripples and tides – are the easiest to describe and the least significant. The ripples are irrelevant by definition. If the first sound of an utterance is a stop consonant, say [d] as in the word *do*, the pressure of air that we build up behind it may be such as to heighten the pitch of the first part of the vowel at the moment of its release, which then drops slightly. Similarly, even when we aim at a monotone, the first part of an utterance drawing upon the bellows-like pressure from the lungs when it is strongest, is higher than what follows, unless we adjust other factors to compensate for it. These are involuntary changes in pitch, and there are many others. Indeed, since emotion affects us in so many ways, we can detect symptoms of it even here, as in the tremolo that goes with restrained tears or anger. We can even feign these symptoms, and it might seem that this makes them part of the communicative system. But somehow we discount those particular fakeries as insincere. The emotion that we deliberately put in, or that may be quite involuntary, and is yet respected as a genuine part of our message, takes a different form: an expansion and contraction of the total range of pitch. A surprised *oh*, an enthusiastic *yes*, or an indignant *no* reaches a pitch well above the average and may sweep to a pitch well below it; if the speaker is bored or indifferent or depressed, his range will shrink. Whether in response to a real stimulus or a pretended one – and here we dissemble outrageously and systematically – the effect is the same.

These facts are so obvious that I mention them only to dismiss them. The ripples and tides are probably much the same in all languages. We do not need to learn them in a foreign language (though, if we are learning the total culture, we might need to learn when to *repress* them – cultures differ in their concepts of decorum, in what outward manifestations of emotion are condoned). Our real troubles lie in the waves and the swells.

The waves, as the most abrupt *intended* movements on the bosom of pitch, depend on the relative gradualness of the rest. Ideally, by contrast, the rest is simply a level, inclined or flat, which we may think of as a reference line. Suppose we want to say *His brother was the one who cheated him*, and to emphasize just the word *brother*. This is how it comes out:

His <sup>bro</sup>ther was the one who cheated him.

Someone hearing this might respond with the question

His ther was the one who cheated him?
bro

The two sentences are virtually mirror images. In both, the syllable *bro*-juts out from the reference line, in the one by jumping up, in the other by jumping down. Here there happens to be a return to the same reference line; but sometimes the jump is from one reference line to another:

brother who cheated him?
It was his

What makes the syllable *bro*- prominent is its salience in pitch, to which is usually added a little extra duration and also, a good part of the time, some extra loudness. Languages that behave this way have an *accentual system*. They signal the *importance* of a word by accenting – giving pitch prominence to – one of its syllables. Picking just one syllable is for the sake of economy. The other syllables are needed for the swells, the larger movements of the reference lines, as we shall see later. For example, in a one-word sentence like the following, the single syllable is prominent, but the leftovers can tell us whether the sentence is a statement or a question:

Indis <sup>cre</sup> Indis <sup>cre</sup>
tions. tions?

Many linguists use the term *stress* for what I have been calling *accent*, or employ the terms interchangeably. I find it more useful to distinguish them, and accordingly I reserve *accent* for the syllable which actually *is* highlighted in a sentence – to show the importance of its word – and apply *stress* to the particular syllable in the word that gets the accent *if* the word is important enough to get one. In the word *fanfare*, the stressed syllable is the first; in *festoon*, the second. While there are certain rough tendencies, such as favoring an initial stress in nouns and adjectives and an end stress in verbs, stress in English can go anywhere.

There is an element of predictability, however, which is worth our attention because of its importance to rhythm as well as accent. What we can be sure of is that the stressed syllable, that is, the accentable one, will not be a syllable that contains a reduced vowel. In *fanfare* and *festoon* all vowels are full; except for arbitrary custom, *-fare* and *fes-* could be the stressed syllables. In *fancy* and *fatality* the syllables *-cy* and *fa-* contain reduced vowels, characterized by their loss of duration and their uncertain timbre. So it happens that a good part of the time the stressed syllable is unmistakable whether we accent it or not – in *formidableness*, for instance, only the first is stressed, because all the rest are reduced. We can schematize this system in three levels:

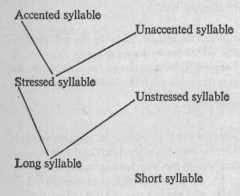

| | |
|---|---|
| Accented syllable | (Any stressed syllable *can* be accented; which ones *are* depends on the intent of the speaker.) |
| Unaccented syllable | |
| Stressed syllable | (All long syllables *can* be stressed. Only one, as a rule, actually is – this is an arbitrary trait of the language.) |
| Unstressed syllable | |
| Long syllable | (Long syllables contain full vowels; short syllables contain reduced ones.) |
| Short syllable | |

The first and last differences are audible; the middle one is not. Thus in *He's a shoe-box manufacturer*, said

      shoe-

He's a

          box manufacturer.

the syllable *shoe* stands out because it is accented, and *box*, *man-* and *-fac-* are distinguished by their length and the fulness of their vowels from *-u-*,

*-tur-* and *-er*. But without an accent, *-fac-*, even though it is the stressed syllable of *manufacturer*, does not stand out from *box* or *man-*.

I must warn the reader that this is not the analysis of English stress he is apt to find in textbooks. I offer it because I believe it is more accurate and because it more sharply distinguishes the role of pitch, limiting it to the topmost level, that of accent. And it has the further virtue of focusing on syllable types rather than talking about 'weak stress'. This is important in learning a language that either lacks the long–short dichotomy or has it only sparsely represented. Making students pace out a sentence in French or Spanish according to a fairly regular beat, instead of turning it into a fox-trot, is one way of mastering it. The smooth rhythm of successive long syllables (*Which fandango came first?*) is the exception in English, but is often the rule elsewhere.

Accentual systems involve more than singling out important words by accenting them. Accents and particular positions of accents become characteristic of sentences. When this happens, an adjustment may be called for between an accent for importance and an accent at some favored spot. We tend to favor the two extremes of the sentence (or, in longer sentences, the two extremes of each relatively independent phrase or clause), as if to announce the beginning and the end. There may be intermediate accents, but they are less prominent. This gives the sentence the shape of a bumpy suspension bridge:

```
          snow                    ear        to
The            generally comes        ly in Oc    ber.
```

Here the first accent is on *snow* and the last is on *-to-*, which stand as the pillars of the bridge. The roadbed is heaved up somewhat on the syllable *ear-*, and would be heaved up equally on other intermediate accents:

```
                                                        to
          snow                      ery  ear       month
The            generally comes  v        ly in the      of Oc
                                                        ber.
```

– but not ordinarily to the height of the terminal pillars.

It happens that in this example there is no conflict between the sentence accents and the accents of importance, and no adjustment is necessary. Or should we rather say that the language, by putting important things at opposite extremes, has already made the adjustment for us?

But if we rearranged things a bit, we might get

```
          snow                to
The            comes   ear
                          ly in Oc  ber, generally.
```

with *generally*, viewed as merely incidental, coming last. The accent of importance outweighs the tendency to put an accent at the end, and *generally* simply trails off. (This is not to rule out the possibility of its getting its own accent if it is an important afterthought:

The    snow  comes  ear ly in Oc to ber,  gen era l y.)

Nevertheless, though an accent of importance will always take command if there is a conflict, the tendency to put an accent at the end is often powerful enough to shift the *stress* of a word in order to have its way. I have recorded examples like the following from speakers in all walks of life:

It  tend ed to be in  flu enced.

– normal *influenced* becomes *influénced*. At the front end of the sentence the opposite happens, and one gets the strange pairs

I  ab solutely de ny it.  I de ny it abso lute ly.

A fair number of words (*absolutely, cannot, nearby, almost*, and others) permit this chameleonic shift of stress. It makes no difference to the importance of the word, of course, which syllable gets the accent, so long as one of them does.

And there is a special form of adjustment in which two syllables are accented. In answer to *What was that king's name?* the reply might come

It's  Neb uchad nez zar.

with the two accents of the sentence reduced to two accents within a single word.[1]

I have been speaking all along as if accent and emotion were separable, and have gone so far as to push emotion beyond the horizon and called it a tide, as distinct from the wave of accent. But jumps in speech are never far from jumpiness. An accent to show the importance of a word inescapably shows its importance for *us*; it is as if we meant to say 'This excites me', and left our hearer to infer 'It's worth getting excited about.' So we need not be surprised to find two significant emotional overtones in accent.

1. This illustrates the 'secondary stresses' which are, actually, the result of just such an adjustment: when we pronounce a word in isolation – say it as a 'citation form' – we make a sentence of it, and the secondary is a result.

One appears in the difference between an accent that jumps up from the reference line, and one that jumps down. The upward jump is unrestrained. The downward jump is the opposite. The restraint of the downward jump lends itself to many shadings – to express comfort, reassurance, doubt. In the following example the robust approval of the upward jump contrasts with the reservation of the downward jump: to the question *What do you think of it?* comes the reply

It's ni ce.   It's nice.

The other emotional overtone is simply the use of accents – often repeated accents in a single word (even a single syllable) to express great emphasis:

I ab so lute ly pos i tive ly wo n't.

The waves of accent need only be large enough to set off the accented syllable from its surroundings – this is why the effect could so easily be confused with loudness: the change in pitch was not radical enough for the hearer to sense its direction. The swells of separation are different. Their movement is necessarily wide. Indeed, the greater prominence of accents at the extremes of the sentence that we have just noted might better be put down as a manifestation of separation: the wave is there, but augmented by the edge of a swell that coincides with the sentence itself, to separate it from other sentences. 'Here', it seems to say, 'is where the sentence begins; and here is where it ends.'

Because interruptions are always jarring, the most conspicuous instance of separation is parenthesis. Once again the partners of pitch are duration – now in the form of a pause or of the kind of lengthening that substitutes for a pause – and loudness. The pitch level of the entire parenthesis is lowered, the volume is reduced, and the extremes are set off by pauses, though the advantage of relying more on pitch is that one needs to rely less on pause, and speech is accordingly not slowed down unnecessarily. In the following example, there is not only a lowering of the parenthesis itself, but a certain amount of raising in the environment of the parenthesis, to make the contrast all the clearer:

Be si des tim ber, its main re sources appear to be chi cle, a gummy

sub stance used large ly in chew ing gum, and oi l.

If it were not for the intervening parenthesis, the last two words, *and oil*, would have been at a considerably lower pitch (lower them here, and you appear to be saying 'chewing gum and oil'). Certain of the pitches of the main utterance overlap with those of the parenthesis – the range at our disposal is not wide enough to admit of a complete wrenching apart – but there is no mistaking the contrast in levels. The accents continue to appear where they normally would, but in the parenthesis they are flattened somewhat. Though it has nothing to do with the parenthesis, we can also see in this example the use of relative height for relative importance among the accents themselves, a characteristic of English that is still to be explored: the *-sides* of *besides* clearly carries an accent, but that of *tim-* goes higher.

More typical and far more frequent than separations for parenthesis, where the lowered pitch suggests a lower-ranking element of the discourse, are the separations that divide equal-ranking elements from one another. In their grossest form these are of two kinds: sweeping rises and sweeping falls. In

He took out his trust y k n i f e and slashed awa y.

the sweeping rise on *knife* separates the two clauses. The steep fall on *-way* separates the sentence from what follows, but there is not really the sharp division between an interior separation (rise) and an exterior one (fall) that this might suggest, since a fall could have been used in place of a rise:

He took out his trust y kni fe and slashed awa y.

As with accents, a greater or lesser breadth of movement may establish a hierarchy of importance. In

If I'm still aro u n d when you hear from him let me kno w.

If I'm still ar o u n d when you hear from him let me kno w.

the extent of the rises (with or without similarly differentiated pauses) tells whether the *when* clause is to be taken with *If I'm still around* or with *let me know*. Delattre calls these 'major and minor continuations'.[2]

2. See p. 168.

Simple rises for separation are common enough in English – for instance, they are almost always used with gnomic expressions like *Easy come, easy go, Out of sight, out of mind* – but they are apt to sound somewhat flip in ordinary discourse:

If he doesn't like<sup>it</sup> he knows what he can d o.

*(rise contour diagram)*

Simple rises – rises that once started do not drop back – are not only common, but are the rule, at least in French, Spanish and German, with no connotation of the gnomic or the flippant. So here we must be careful. The typical more nearly neutral shape in American English is different. In place of merely gliding up, it first goes up, then down, then up again but not very far – a rise–fall–rise:[3]

In the in<sup>ter</sup>i o r the snow generally comes ear ly in Oc to ber.

*(rise-fall-rise contour diagram)*

The shape is particularly noticeable when unaccented elements are added after the accent, prolonging the rise–fall–rise into a broad undulation:

In the in<sup>ter</sup>i o r prov i n c e s ....

*(rise-fall-rise contour diagram)*

3. This is a device that enables English to make a sharper distinction between questions and non-questions. The simple rise is used for all forms of incompleteness, including interrogation. The rise–fall–rise is incomplete, but its use in questions is extremely limited; in fact, it is used far less than is a straight fall:

Was it yes<sup>ter</sup> day that they came?

*(contour diagram)*

is a normal informed question;

Was it yes ter day that they c a m e?

*(contour diagram)*

would hardly be used except to repeat the speaker's own question as a sort of admonition, or to repeat the interlocutor's question in a kind of annoyed surprise. Where a separation comes in the middle of a question, the rise–fall–rise is avoided if what precedes is itself properly a question. Thus in *When you don't get exercise, do you have a good appetite?* the rise–fall–rise is normal on *exercise*; but when the clauses are reversed, it is not normal on *appetite*. It is normal between non-question alternatives (*I'll either read awhile, or I'll go to bed* – on *read awhile*), but not between question alternatives (*Will you read awhile, or will you go to bed?*).

The simple rise does more than mark a separation, of course. Since it is clearly set apart from the fall that marks the end of a statement, the rise signals a separation at a point of incompleteness. This leads to incompleteness at a further remove, though the kinship is still apparent:

If you $^{like}$ $^{i}$ $^{t}$ eat
it. $_{.}$  Do you $^{like}$ $^{i}$ $^{t}$ $^{?}$  Then eat
it.

The relationship between the incompleteness of the *if* clause and that of the question with *do* adds a third link between such clauses and questions, which are already tied together by the possibility of inversion (*Were I you* . . .) and by the sharing of *if* (*I don't know if* . . .: indirect question). Questions are of course the prime examples of unresolved utterances, whose resolution awaits their answers: there is no great difference, intonationally, between an unresolved clause and its resolution when in the mouth of a single speaker, and when in the mouths of two. But it must not be thought that the rise is a pure grammatical symbol for interrogation, for questions neither require it nor monopolize it. Other forms of incompleteness are of everyday occurrence. In the following, the aim is simply to leave the hearer in suspense, as if to say 'Imagine the consequences':

I'm $^{glad}$ that ice ages don't come $^{ev}$ $^{e}$ $_{r}$ $_{y}$ $^{cen}$ $_{tu}$ $^{r}$ $^{y.}$

In the next example, which is a petulant reply to *Why did you do it?*, the incompleteness implies 'What business is it of yours anyway?':

Because I $^{wanted}$ $^{t}$ $^{o.}$

And after a low-pitched accent the rise seems to imply merely an absence of assertiveness, which helps to give this contour its note of complaisance:

Don't
$_{wor}$ $^{r}$ $^{y,}$ I'll $_{help}$ $^{y}$ $^{o}$ $^{u.}$

The fall is typically terminal, but from literal 'conclusion' it has passed to a figurative 'conclusiveness' and may occur anywhere:

You must $^{nev}$ $^{nev}$ $^{say}$
$_{er,}$ $_{er,}$ things like that.

The deeper the fall, the more conclusive; just as, with the rise, the steeper it is the more inconclusive it is. As with accents, this proves once more how difficult it is to separate emotion from other functions of intonation. We are right when we stigmatize a monotone as 'lifeless'. Intonation is a half-tamed servant of language. The rise and fall can be thought of as grammatical signals of completeness and incompleteness, or as emotional gauges of tension and relaxation. Adding intonation, we turn each logical message into an act of will.

If this were a treatise on intonation, and not just a rapid survey to identify the uses of pitch and give enough examples to make the argument convincing, we could go on for a hundred pages more to consider the nuances of accent and separation. We would take into account the patterning of accents in ordinary commands, each lower than the last, like a mountain range flanked by descending foothills:

Let me have a look at that stethoscope.

We would compare the similar patterning, but differing pitch level, of questions introduced by interrogative words, and statements:

But how did you get home? I got home on the bus.

We would examine the ties between accents and grammatical constructions, such as the passive; or between separations and the use of extra words to make them possible, as in the following, which answers *Who would do it?*

John. or John would. John would. (*not* John.)

– where if we are positive, *John* is enough, but if we are tentative, and want a rise–fall–rise, the extra word is needed to cover the more complex undulation. The ramifications are legion.

## 2 Pierre R. Léon and Philippe Martin

Machines and Measurements

from Pierre R. Léon and Philippe Martin, *Prolégomènes à l'étude des structures intonatives,* Marcel Didier, Montréal, Paris, Bruxelles, 1970, pp. 85–97, 172–80. Translated for this volume by Susan Husserl-Kapit.

### The kymograph

One of the first measuring devices in instrumental phonetics was the kymograph described by Rousselot (1897–1908) in his *Principles of Experimental Phonetics.*

The principle of the apparatus (Figure 1) is simple. The sound waves of the word are transmitted by a rubber tube to a drum, which is caused

Figure 1  The kymograph of Rousselot (*Principes,* p. 1167)

to vibrate. A recording stylus mounted on the drum inscribes the vibrations on a sheet coated with lampblack attached to a cylinder revolving at a constant speed.

The drum, acting as a low-pass filter, fails to pick up the higher harmonics of the sounds of the word. The resulting curve brings out at most the first and second harmonics. A curve like that of Figure 2, rich in

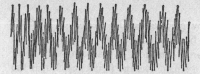

Figure 2  Curve rich in harmonics (made by oscillograph)

harmonics, becomes – when recorded on a machine as rudimentary as the kymograph – a trace like that of Figure 3.

Figure 3  Kymographic curve. The harmonics do not generally appear

A kymographic tracing therefore does not suffice to analyse the distinctive sounds of the word (its phonemes), but it is good enough to study the three prosodic parameters, duration, intensity and pitch. Following is a kymographic tracing of the sentence *L'horizon tout entier s'enveloppe dans l'ombre* (Figure 4).

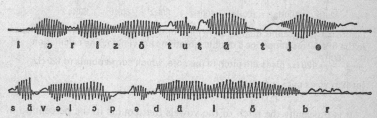

Figure 4  Kymographic recording of the sentence 'L'horizon tout entier s'enveloppe dans l'ombre'

*Duration.* This is measured in hundredths of a second. It can be easily calculated from a kymographic tracing when the speed of rotation of the paper is known.

*Intensity.* The amplitude of the resulting curve can be measured on a kymographic tracing by using an intensity metre. Given the inertia of the rubber membrane of the recording drum and the resulting frequency response, differences in intensity show up rather poorly on a kymogram. Rousselot calculated the intensity of sounds just by measuring the amplitudes in millimetres.

*Pitch.* Pitch can be determined by calculating the frequency of each phone. To do this it suffices to note how many vibrations there are during its emission. If the phone is of brief duration, say around fifty milliseconds, it is enough to allow for a single average frequency. But if the phone is long (for example a long vowel), it is necessary to average the frequency every fifty milliseconds so as to catch the possible changes in pitch, as in the example below (Figure 5).

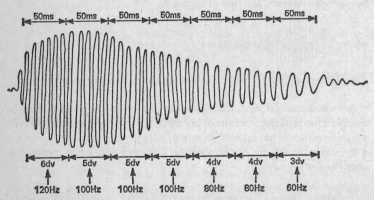

Figure 5 Kymographic display showing vibrations and frequency calculations. In the first 50 ms sequence 6 double vibrations are visible. The calculation $\frac{6 \times 100}{5} = 120$ Hz gives the pitch of the note, which corresponds to 120 Hz (or 120 cycles per second)

It is especially the pitch of the vowels that counts in the perception of intonation, and it is often pointless to compute the vibrations of the consonants, as some researchers have done.

One needs a good magnifying glass, good eyesight, and plenty of patience to make out the intonation even of a simple phrase by using this method, which phoneticians regularly employed in the heroic days of instrumental phonetics.

## Kymographic studies

Nevertheless, a good many important studies were carried out with the kymograph at the turn of the century – and not a few even of fairly recent date. Among the most important are the ones listed below:

BEACH, D. M. (1938), *The Phonetics of the Hottentot Language*, Heffer, Cambridge.

CAMA, K. (1939), 'A Study of the native Hindustani melody pattern and the acquired English melody pattern with special reference to the teaching of English in India', *Arch. Néerl. de Phon. Expér.*, vol. 15, pp. 103–10.

CANELLADA, M. J. (1941), 'Notas de entonación extremeña', *Rev. filol. esp.*, vol. 25, pp. 79–91.

DAAN, J. (1938), 'Dialect and pitch pattern of the sentence', *Proc. 3rd Int. Congr. Phon. Sci.*, Ghent, pp. 473–80.

GILI GAYA, S. (1924), 'Influencia del acento y de las consonantes en las curvas de entonación', *Rev. filol. esp.*, vol. 11, pp. 154–77.

MAACK, A. (1957), 'Verzerrungsfreie Melodiewinkel aus der Tonhöhenkurve', *Phonetica*, vol. 1, pp. 206–15.

MAGDICS, K. (1959), 'Intonation of the Hungarian settlers from Bukovina', *Acta Ling. Hafn.*, vol. 9, pp. 187–227.

MALHIAC, H. (1953), *Analyse et enregistrement de la voix parlée et chantée*, Société Générale d'Impression, Toulouse.

ROUSSELOT, P. (1924), *Principes de phonétique expérimentale*, 2e éd. Tomes 1 et 2, Didier, Paris.

SCRIPTURE, E. W. (1902), 'Studies of melody in English speech', *Philosophische Studien*, vol. 19, pp. 599–615.

SÉGUY, J. (1953), 'Un combiné magnétophone-électrokymographe en vue de l'analyse tonométrique', *Orbis*, vol. 2, pp. 518–20.

SÖDERGARD, O. (1957), 'L'intonation syntaxique en français', *Stud. Ling.*, Lund, vol. 11, no. 1, pp. 92–120.

WÄNGLER, H.-H. (1963), *Zur Tonologie des Hausa*, Schriften zur Phonetik, Sprachwissenschaft und Kommunikationsforschung (6), Akademie-Verlag, Berlin.

ZWIRNER, E., and ZWIRNER, K. (1936), *Grundfragen der Phonometrie*, Berlin.

## Oscilloscope and oscillograph

The oscilloscope makes it possible to represent the sound waves by a curve produced on the screen of a cathode ray tube, through the movement of a luminous spot created by the impact of electrons on a fluorescent coating. Thanks to the weak inertia of the moving elements – the electrons – one can examine the swiftest and most fleeting phenomena on the screen of an oscilloscope. Some instruments have a passband of 1000 MHz, i.e. a thousand million cycles per second. The frequencies of vocal sounds are between 0 and 10,000 Hz. It is therefore possible, even with a very inexpensive oscilloscope, to make very precise analyses in acoustic phonetics.

To get an *oscillogram*, one may either film the luminous spot or use a recording instrument called an *oscillograph*.

Figure 6, below, gives an idea of the richness of the oscillographic curve by contrast with the kymographic curve (Figure 4 above). The oscillographic curve makes it possible, theoretically, to study the timbre

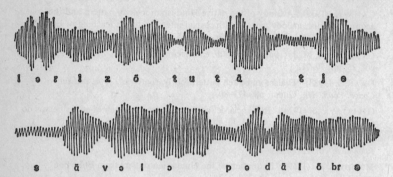

Figure 6 Oscillographic recording of the sentence 'L'horizon tout entier s'enveloppe dans l'ombre'

of the phones recorded. Actually, the analysis that has to be carried out is still too complex and for this kind of study another instrument is used, the spectrograph (see below).

In short, the use of the oscilloscope in experimental phonetics is the same as that of the kymograph where the purpose is to analyse the three parameters that are most important to the prosody: *duration, intensity* and *pitch*. But the oscillograph is superior to the kymograph in precision. It provides for more paper speeds (Figure 7). Higher speeds make it easier to count vibrations in order to study frequency. Finally, the scaling of the

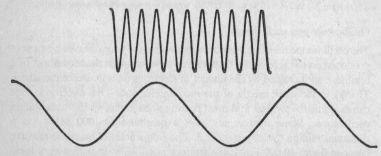

Figure 7 Two oscillographic recordings of the same sound with different speed settings (above, 100 mm/s; below, 1000 mm/s)

paper and the possibility of amplitude settings makes the calculation of amplitudes easier and safer.

## Oscillographic studies

The oscillograph is one of the most widely used instruments in modern phonetics laboratories, even though using it to measure pitch is as tedious as using the kymograph. It is hard to demarcate units, to pinpoint vibrations, etc.

Among modern studies whose authors indicate their technique of oscillographic analysis to investigate prosodic phenomena the following can be mentioned, among which that of Burgstahler and Straka (1964) seems both the most useful and the most clearly explained from a methodological point of view.

BOUDREAULT, M. (1968), *Rythme et mélodie de la phrase parlée en France et au Québec*, Les Presses de l'Université Laval, Québec et Librairie C. Klincksieck, Paris.

BURGSTAHLER, P. and STRAKA, G. (1964), 'Étude du rythme à l'aide de l'oscillographe cathodique combiné avec le sonomètre', *Trav. Ling. Litt.*, pp. 125–41.

DEVA, B. C. (1960), 'Psychophysics of speech-melody', *Z. Phon.*, vol. 13, pp. 8–27.

HOLDER, M. (1968), 'Étude sur l'intonation comparée de la phrase énonciative en français canadien et en français standard', in *Recherches sur la structure phonique du français canadien*, P. R. Léon (*Studia Phonetica I*), Didier, Montréal, Paris et Bruxelles, pp. 175–191.

JASSEM, V. (1959), 'The phonology of Polish stress', *Word*, vol. 15, pp. 252–69.

LEDEBOER VON WESTERHOVEN, L. F. (1938), 'Melodie und Tonbewegung im Niederlandischen', *Proc. 3rd Int. Congr. Phon. Sci.*, Ghent, pp. 489–96.

LÉON, P. R., and BALIGAND, R. A. (1969), 'Deux interprétations du "Pont Mirabeau", Étude du rythme et de sa perception', *Phonetica*, vol. 19, pp. 82–103.

MALMBERG, B. (1940), 'Recherches expérimentales sur l'accent musical du mot en suédois', *Arch. Néerl. de Phon. Expér.*, vol. 15, pp. 62–76.

PARMENTER, C. E., and TREVIÑO, S. N. (1930), 'L'intonation italienne', *Italica*, vol. 7, pp. 80–84.

PARMENTER, C. E., and TREVIÑO, S. N. (1932), 'A technique for the analysis of pitch in connected discourse', *Arch. Néerl. de Phon. Expér.*, vol. 7, pp. 1–29.

ROBINSON, L. (1968), 'Étude du rythme syllabique en français canadien et en français standard', in *Recherches sur la structure phonique de français canadien*, P. R. Léon (*Studia Phonética I*), Didier, Montréal, Paris et Bruxelles, pp. 161–74.

VARDANIAN, R.-M. (1964), 'Teaching English intonation through oscilloscope displays', *Lang. Learn.*, vol. 14, nos. 3–4, pp. 109–17.

## The spectrograph

The spectrograph is a much more versatile instrument for analysis than the oscillograph. Many technical descriptions of the machine and its use are to be found. The most important are those of Potter, Kopp and Green (1947) and Martin Joos (1948). This apparatus, marketed by the Kay Electric Company, is essentially a spectral analyser into which a recording (no more than 2·4 seconds long) can be fed to obtain a *spectrogram* representing the harmonics of the sound on a frequency scale of 0 to 8000 Hz (narrow-band setting, Figure 9). Intensity is shown by the greater or lesser degree of blackness of the harmonics on the spectrogram. The overall intensity is also shown by a linear or logarithmic amplitude display (see also the figure below).

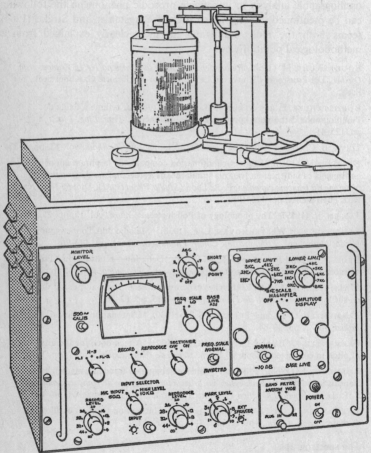

Figure 8

The spectrogram (Figure 9) reveals the arrangement of harmonics with their variations in frequency shown in the undulating movements of the horizontal lines. With a spectrum of this type the changes in intonation can be observed by following the curve of the fundamental. However, since

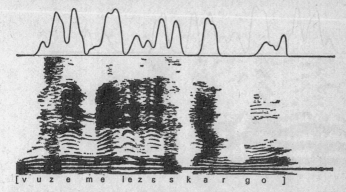

[v  u  z  e  me  lez ɛ  s  k  a  r  g  o ]

Figure 9 Narrow-band spectrogram of the sentence 'Vous aimez les escargots?' Duration is shown in ms on the abscissa, frequency (in this illustration) from 0 to 5000 on the ordinate. The jagged line at the top marks changes in intensity in db

the bottom line, that of the fundamental, has a comparatively low elevation and errors of measurement are liable to be serious, it is better to take some higher harmonic as the basis for measurement. In the sentence of Figure 9 it can be shown that the eighth harmonic, which is one of the easiest to follow with the eye, has the following values:

[vu   ze   me   le   zɛs   kar   go]
181  187  275  250  219  156  300

By measuring each of the other harmonics one can prove the simple relationship that exists among them. If the tenth is at 1500 the first (or fundamental) will be at $150 \left( \dfrac{1500}{10} \right)$, the second at 300, the third at 450, the fourth at 600, the fifth at 750, the sixth at 900, the seventh at 1050, the eighth at 1200, the ninth at 1350. If for any reason whatever (noise, filtering, etc.) the fundamental is absent from the spectrum of a vowel, one can always deduce its pitch from that of any two consecutive harmonics. By the same token it is advisable to calculate the frequency from the tenth harmonic, for example: the chances of error in measuring the fundamental are divided by ten.

There exists another type of spectrogram using a wider frequency scale. A frequency amplification is selected, say ten, and one obtains a spectrum ten times as wide for a given range of frequencies (the time scale does not change) (see Figure 10).

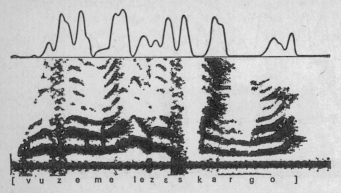

Figure 10 Spectrogram of the same sentence as Figure 9, showing the lower harmonics spread out

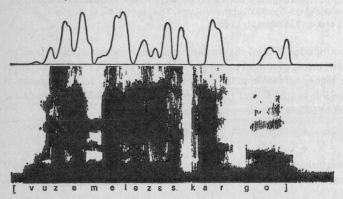

Figure 11 Wide-band spectrogram of the same sentence as Figures 9 and 10. It is comparatively easy to calculate the number of vibrations (by the vertical striations) of the low-pitched sounds but harder to measure the high ones.

## Spectrographic studies

Most modern phonetics laboratories have a spectrograph and the number of studies using it are quite numerous. Improvements in technique have greatly reduced the time required to make a spectrographic analysis. Nevertheless the procedure is slow and melodic analysis using the apparatus will be truly interesting only when it can be carried out in real time –

as is the case with melodic analysers (see the next section). If the spectrograph continues to be widely used for melodic analysis, it is mainly because of its reliability. With a little practice it is almost impossible to go wrong in calculating harmonic frequencies.

The following studies are analyses of prosodic phenomena, especially intonation; some contain explanations of the techniques used.

BOLINGER, D. L. (1951), 'Intonation: levels versus configurations', *Word*, vol. 7, pp. 199–210.

CRYSTAL, D., and QUIRK, R. (1964), *Systems of Prosodic and Paralinguistic Features in English*, Mouton, The Hague.

DELATTRE, P. (1961), 'La leçon d'intonation de Simone de Beauvoir, étude d'intonation déclarative comparée', *French Review*, vol. 35, pp. 59–67.

DELATTRE, P. (1963), 'Comparing the prosodic features of English, German, Spanish and French', *IRAL*, vol. 1, pp. 193–210.

DELATTRE, P. (1966a), 'Les dix intonations de base du français', *French Review*, vol. 40, no. 1, pp. 1–14.

DELATTRE, P. (1966b), 'A comparison of syllable length conditioning among languages', *IRAL*, vol. 4, no. 3, pp. 183–98.

DELATTRE, P., POENACK, E., and OLSEN, C. (1965), 'Some characteristics of German intonation for the expression of continuation and finality', *Phonetica*, vol. 13, pp. 134–61.

FANT, G. (1961), 'Sound spectrography', *Proc. 4th Int. Congr. Phon. Sci.*, Helsinki, pp. 14–33.

FAURE, G. (1961), 'L'intonation et l'identification des mots dans la chaîne parlée (exemples empruntés à la langue française)', *Proc. 4th Int. Congr. Phon. Sci.*, Helsinki, pp. 598–609.

HARDMAN, J. M. (1966), *Jaqaru: Outline of the Phonological and Morphological Structure*, Mouton, The Hague, cf. pp. 26–8.

JASSEM, V. (1959), 'The phonology of Polish stress', *Word*, vol. 15, pp. 252–69.

KALLIOINEN, V. (1968), 'Suomen Kysymyslauseen Intonaatiostav' (Remarks on the intonation of interrogative sentences in Finnish), *Virittaja*, vol. 1, pp. 35–54.

LEHISTE, I. (1961), 'Some acoustic correlates of accent in Serbo-Croatian', *Phonetica*, vol. 7, pp. 114–47.

LÉON, P. R. (1967), 'La joncture externe en français: nature et fonction', *Phonologie der Gegenwart*, pp. 298–306.

MALMBERG, B. (1961), 'Analyse instrumentale et structurale des faits d'accents', *Proc. 4th Int. Congr. Phon. Sci.*, Helsinki, pp. 456–75.

MUST, H. (1959), 'Duration of speech sounds in Estonian', *Orbis*, vol. 8, pp. 213–23.

REHDER, P. (1968), *Beitrage zur Erforschung der Serbokroatischen Prosodie*, Verlag Otta Sagner, Munich.

SAPON, S. (1958–9), 'Étude instrumentale de quelques contours mélodiques fondamentaux dans les langues romanes', *Rev. filol. esp.*, vol. 42, pp. 167–77.

SHEN, Y., CHAO, J., and PETERSON, G. (1961), 'Some spectrographic light on Mandarin Tone 2 and Tone 3', *Stud. Sounds*, vol. 9, pp. 265–314.

Pierre R. Léon and Philippe Martin 39

SHIMAOKA, T. (1966), 'A contrastive study on rhythm and intonation of English and Japanese with spectrographic analysis', *Stud. Sounds*, vol. 12, pp. 347–62.

SPEARS, R. A. (1966), 'A note on the tone of Maninka substantives', *J. Afr. Lang.*, vol. 5, no. 2, pp. 113–20.

SZMIDT, Y. (1968), 'Étude de la phrase interrogative en français canadien et en français standard', in *Recherches sur la structure phonique du français canadien*, P. R. Léon (*Studia Phonetica I*), Didier, Montréal, Paris et Bruxelles, pp. 192–209.

WEINREICH, U. (1956), 'Notes on the Yiddish rise–fall intonation curve', in M. Halle *et al.* (eds.), *For Roman Jakobson*, Mouton, The Hague, pp. 632–43.

WONG, H. (1953), 'Outline of the Mandarin phonemic system', *Word*, vol. 9, pp. 268–76.

## The melodic analyser of the University of Toronto

In very general terms, the system consists of a series of four Tchebycheff filters, ranging from 70 to 500 Hz, a computer program, and a sub-program for correcting such things as 'jitters' and 'misses'. Once the speech signal starts, the computer examines each channel to detect the location of the fundamental frequency. In other words the computer tries to detect in which channel the fundamental frequency is being filtered and, by comparing the values that have gone before and the values that come after the one that is being examined, it tries to be sure of extracting the fundamental frequency and not the second harmonic (James, 1970, p. 170).

The illustration shows the television screen of the analyser being used to teach intonation. The model pattern (upper half) like that of the

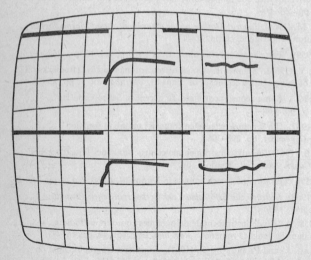

Figure 12

student's imitation (lower half) can be retained on the screen as long as desired. Either pattern can be erased at will. The fundamental pitch curve is produced on the screen in real time, i.e. is traced as the speaker speaks.

The following sections outline the results obtained with the Melodic Analyser.

## Vowels

The analyser responds perfectly to vowel signals, which are the elements of melodic perception. But it is superior to other analysers in that it always gives an accurate indication of the fundamental frequency. It is a known fact – especially with the vowel [u] – that the second harmonic is often more intense than the first. This explains the erroneous results in the response of classical analysers when it comes to analysing a sentence like *Vous nous avez tous vus dans la rue?*

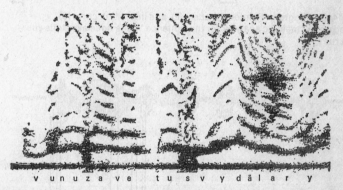

v u n u z a v e     t u s v   y dā l a r   y

Figure 13 Spectrogram of 'Vous nous avez tous vus dans la rue?'

By comparing the curves obtained for this last sentence as analysed by the spectrograph and as analysed by our apparatus (see below), we see that the response of the latter is in keeping with the curve obtained on the spectrograph.

## Noise

It is possible to distinguish background noise and consonant noise, both of which tend to cause erratic responses that interfere with vowel recording.

### Background noise

Our instrument, like all others making a partial spectral analysis, is perturbed by intense noise. A tape made of a conversation on a Paris street

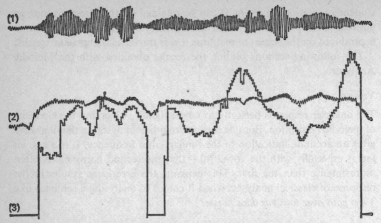

Figure 14 Oscillogram (1), intensity curve (2), and intonation curve (3) obtained on our melodic analyser for the sentence 'Vous nous avez tous vus dans la rue?'

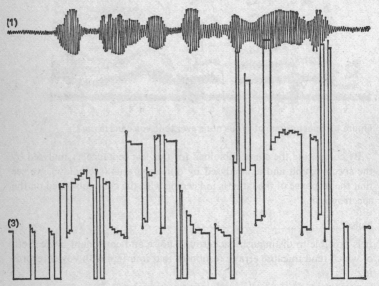

Figure 15 Fragment of a sentence taped at a high noise level. The intonation curve is perturbed

at a level of 8 db more or less above background noise produces an intonation curve that is difficult to interpret correctly. Here is an example:

With less intense noise, and given signals 20 db or more above background noise, our analyser is particularly resistant to interference. Here is a recording made in our laboratory at the same time that an adding machine, fan, etc. were operating:

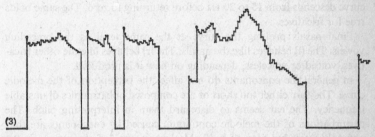

Figure 16  In spite of the noise (visible on curve 1), the intonation curve (3) appears clearly

*Voiceless consonants*

(a) Thus far we find that in *initial* position, voiceless fricatives do not cause any deviation from the general melodic curve. The stops, however, reveal a jump in frequency from 10 to 15 Hz.

(b) In the *intervocalic* position, voiceless consonants are characterized by an average jump in frequency of about 5 to 10 Hz.

(c) In *final* position, these consonants produce no perturbation of the curve.

*Voiced consonants*

(a) In *initial* position, voiced stops begin at a frequency of 10 to 20 Hz below the level of the following vowel.

The voiced fricatives show a concave pattern descending from 10 to 15 Hz below the level of the following vowel.

As for the nasals, [m], [n], [ɲ], they remain at the same level as the vowels. The liquids [l] and [r] begin from 15 to 20 Hz below the vowel curve.

(b) In *intervocalic* position, the voiced stops show the same pattern as in initial position, i.e. concave, from 5 to 10 Hz below the following vowel.

Voiced fricatives [v], [z], [ʒ], more periodic and sustained than the corresponding stops, are marked by a concave fall from 15 to 20 Hz.

The nasals, being the most periodic of all the consonants, as a rule blend smoothly in the melodic continuum of the vowels. Sometimes they are marked, however, by a slight fall from 5 to 10 Hz below the neighbouring vowels. The liquids [l] and [r] lower the curve, in general, from 5 to 10 Hz.

(c) In final position, the voiced consonants are plainly visible on the intonation curve. The stops [b], [d], [g], followed by a release or by a true schwa, show the same characteristic trough. When there is no release, the curve descends from 15 to 20 Hz before returning to zero. The same holds true for fricatives.

Final nasals prolong the curve at the same level as the preceding vowels. The [l] behaves like the nasals. The [r] behaves like the other fricatives, voiced or voiceless, depending on how it is produced.

In general the consonants do not affect the perception of the melodic curve. They are either too short or are composed of harmonics of unstable frequency. The ear seems to disregard them in interpreting pitch. The perturbations of the melodic continuum caused by consonants are thus not only weak but also of negligible importance for perception, in the analysis made by our apparatus.

Figure 17 shows the analysis of the sentence *Je n'ai pas très bien mangé hier soir*, as done by our analyser. The various interruptions of the curve that have been pointed out are readily visible.

### Octave shifts

Analysers currently on the market have to be readjusted each time the voice shifts octaves. This hampers any study of expressive style, where speakers generally use an expanded range, as in the sentence analysed below: *Est-ce que c'est beau?*

On a scale of 70 to 500 Hz our analyser permits all possible variations, as the preceding curve demonstrates. This flexibility makes it possible to analyse expanded ranges without difficulty.

### Sudden rises

In the case of a very rapid rise, neither the classical analysers nor the spectrograph reacts fast enough. In the example below, the same sentence

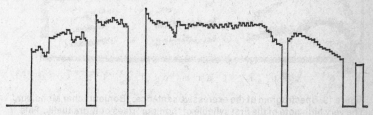

Figure 17 Oscillogram and intonation curve of the sentence 'Je n'ai pas très bien mangé hier soir'

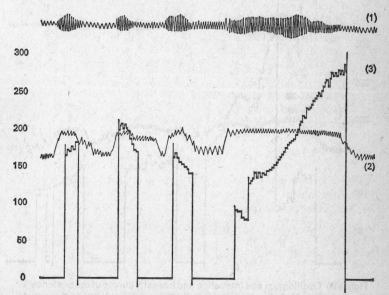

Figure 18 The curve (3) shows the melodic variations of the expressive sentence 'Est-ce que c'est beau?' A shift from 135 to 310 Hz can be seen

can be seen analysed on the spectrograph and on our analyser. The intonation has made an abrupt jump of 200 Hz in 100 ms. The spectrograph missed the analysis of this part of the curve but our analyser rendered it effectively.

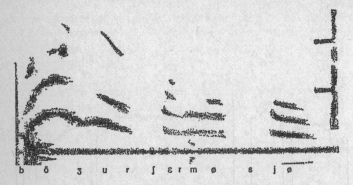

Figure 19 Spectrogram of the expressive sentence: 'Bonjour! cher Monsieur.' The very high note of the first syllable of 'bonjour' rises only gradually. This delay can be evaluated by comparing with Figure 20

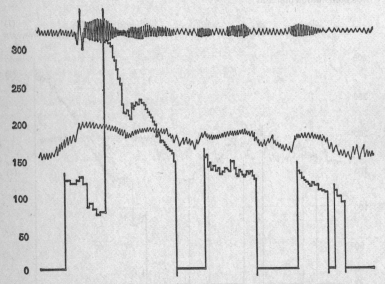

Figure 20 Oscillogram and intonation and intensity curves of the sentence 'Bonjour! cher Monsieur' on our analyser. This sentence is the same as that of Figure 19. The sudden rise shows clearly

## Precision

The scale of our intonation curve affords great precision. Even by taking the tenth harmonic, often difficult to read, or by using the 'scale magnifier', a spectrogram falls far short of the precision – down to one hertz – possible with our analyser.

Figures 13 and 14 show this difference clearly. Note the broad line of the spectrogram corresponding to the pass band of the narrow band filter with which one must estimate the frequency. This leads to a considerable lack of precision. All the slight variations of frequency within a vowel are lost.

To sum up: if our analyser is less resistant to background noises than the spectrograph, it is more precise and more sensitive to rapid changes of pitch, more reliable and more flexible than the other instruments of the same type currently in use.

*References*

JAMES, E. F. (1970), 'The speech analyser of the University of Toronto', in P. R. Léon, G. Faure and A. Rigault (eds.), *Prosodic Features Analysis*, Didier.

JOOS, M. (1948), *Acoustic Phonetics*, supplement to *Language*, vol. 24, no. 2.

POTTER, R. K., KOPP, G. A., and GREEN, H. C. (1947), *Visible Speech*, Bell Telephone Laboratories Series, Van Nostrand.

# Part Two
# Theory

The articles in Part Two can be divided into two halves. Those in the first half, by Pike, Trager and Stockwell, are typically American and represent chronological advances on the same base. The two in the latter half are not in this line of succession. Crystal's represents the British tradition, which it summarizes so thoroughly that no other representative is needed. Bolinger's advances a theory about a part of the field that has gone untreated up to now.

Kenneth Pike was the first American structuralist to attempt more than a programmatic treatment of intonation. He undertook, in his book *The Intonation of American English*, not only to give a thorough review of studies of English intonation done in England and America up to that time, but to examine in a coherent way all the factors – rhythm, pause, length, and stress, as well as pitch – that combine to make the prosody of the language. Other American linguists, notably Zellig Harris and Rulon Wells, held similar views, but with Pike the position of American structuralism on intonation was pretty well fixed. His approach still typifies the work done by the far-flung Summer Institute of Linguistics, and in modified form it is the one adopted by Trager and Smith (see pp. 83–6 below).

Pike established the 'level' approach to intonation. It differs from the 'contour' approach chiefly in that it regards relative heights of pitch as phonemic (that is, they bear the same relationship to intonational configurations as such phonemic entities as vowels and consonants bear to words). The term *contour* is used to refer to configurations, but the essential component is not the succession of movements (up, down, etc.) but the succession of levels, with movements being incidental to getting from one level to another.

Pike argued that intonational meanings are privative to intonation and are not to be confused with the syntactic uses to which they are put; he warned against insisting on 'question intonations' and 'statement intonations'. Intonational meanings were to be diligently abstracted from the meanings of words and syntactic constructions that occur with them and from their own particular manifestations at a given place and time. The chapter from Pike's book is given first because it is first in point of time and because it lays the foundation with a teacher's regard for presenting a difficult problem in a comprehensible way. One caution: the numbering system is the reverse of the one generally used by Pike's adaptors. Pitch 1 is highest, pitch 4 is lowest.

Probably the most influential treatment of English intonation has been that of George L. Trager and Henry Lee Smith, as it appeared in their 1951 study, *An Outline of English Structure* (Norman, Oklahoma). Within a few years it had been adapted to a wide range of grammars for classroom use – books as dissimilar as the *Roberts English Series* (1967) and the Pyles–Algeo *English: An Introduction to Language* (1970). It has the great pedagogical merit of lending itself to a notation that is economical to print and easy to interpret. But it has been just as influential in its theoretical impact, and has largely been accepted in generative-transformational treatments of intonation. Trager and Smith adopted much of the system developed by Pike. Their chief modification is the elaboration of the role of stress, and the formalizing of the pitches that occur at pause points. Where Pike marks a tentative pause and a final pause, with pitch behaviour conditioned by them (before a final pause, for instance, a pitch 4 will 'Tend to fade into silence while drifting downward' – see p. 70), Trager and Smith substitute terminal junctures (in Trager's article called contours), which are the intonational movements that punctuate the end of an intonation pattern; they are regarded as elements of the prosody in their own right: rise, fall and sustain. As with Pike, stress is regarded as an independent, but interacting, system, which is to say that if a rise in pitch and a perceived prominence (what we think of as 'loudness') occur at the same time, the pitch change is incidental to the stress. The study by Trager is an updating of the intonational part of the *Outline*.

Until very recently intonation was the chief item of unfinished business for the currently most vigorous approach to linguistics, that of generative-transformational grammar. An early exception was the article by Robert P. Stockwell, referred to in his new article written especially for this volume. Here he summarizes his former conclusions and goes on to review some recent work in the field which has been aimed at modifying the views on accent that were expressed in *The Sound Pattern of English* by Halle and Chomsky (1968). The reader will see how closely the latter still interlocks with Pike and Trager–Smith.

The British tradition is less revolutionary than the American.

Though both build on their own past, instead of successive revisions we find a continual broadening of essentially the same base. This is to be expected given the empirical and highly practical aims that have prompted the study of intonation in Britain. Large amounts of data have been examined – in the most recent studies great quantities have been assembled for the purpose – and systems have been strongly influenced by the need to publish materials for teaching English as a foreign language. David Crystal has made the most comprehensive study of English intonation to date. His work, the main chapter of which is reproduced here, is the best synthesis of the British approach, in which the concepts of 'nucleus', 'tune' and 'tone group' figure prominently.

Most descriptions of intonation have been at one or the other of the two extremes: atomistic or global. The atomistic description is one that looks for meaningless subunits which bear the same relationship to intonation that segmental phonemes bear to words; this is essentially the 'level' approach, with each level corresponding to a phoneme. The global description describes entire contours, giving their grammatical or attitudinal meanings; this is the 'tune' approach. The last article in this part, by Bolinger, takes a different tack: it adopts pitch *directions* as its units, which it assumes resemble gestures in the way they convey meaning, and looks at how the directions are combined and how they affect the parts of the sentence that are accented and the parts that are not. The latter – the unaccented syllables – have been pretty much ignored up to now, and in some treatments have been considered not to count at all.

*References*

HALLE, M. and CHOMSKY, N. (1968), *The Sound Pattern of English,*
    Massachusetts Institute of Technology.
PYLES, T., and ALGEO, J. (1970), *English: An Introduction to Language,*
    Harcourt Brace Jovanovich.
ROBERTS, P. (1967), *The Roberts English Series: A Linguistics Program,*
    Harcourt Brace Jovanovich.

# 3 Kenneth L. Pike

## General Characteristics of Intonation

from Kenneth L. Pike, *The Intonation of American English,* University of
Michigan Press, 1945, pp. 20–41.

### Constituted by sequences of pitches – intonation contours

Every sentence, every word, every syllable, is given some pitch when it is
spoken. Even a sound in isolation is produced by vibrations whose
frequencies constitute its pitch. There are no pitchless sentences.

Fluctuation in pitch occurs in the sentences of all languages. No language
uses a pure monotone. Once a person trains himself to listen for pitch in
speech he notices considerable fluctuation even in the voices of persons
reputed to be monotones.

The changes of pitch which occur within a sentence are not haphazard
variation. The patterns of variation, the rules of change, are highly
organized. Their intricacy is so great that, although one speaks his language with little effort, their analysis is extremely difficult and may induce
one to conclude that no actual organization or rules are present, but that
people use pitches by whim and fancy. In each language, however, the use
of pitch fluctuation tends to become semi-standardized, or formalized, so
that all speakers of the language use basic pitch sequences in similar ways
under similar circumstances. These abstracted characteristic sentence
melodies may be called *intonation contours*.

Intonation characteristics may be roughly divided into several types.
Some contours may be completely colorless in meaning: they give to the
listener no implication of the speaker's attitude or feeling. Since sentences
must be spoken with pitch, and pitch sequences become formalized, these
meaningless intonation contours represent the intonational minimum of
speech. They serve a mechanical function – they provide a mold into which
all sentences may be poured so that they achieve utterance. Nevertheless,
these mechanical contours may be very important for learning a language,
since failure to use them would immediately label a speaker as a foreigner
with a bad accent and hamper his freedom of style.

Other intonation characteristics may be affected or caused by the
individual's physiological state – anger, happiness, excitement, age, sex,
and so on. These help one to identify people and to ascertain how they are
feeling (unless, along with a 'poker face', they have a 'poker voice' which

does not reveal these facts, or departs from the anticipated norm in some way).

In English, many intonation contours are explicit in meaning. Whenever a certain sequence of relative pitches is heard, one concludes that the speaker means certain things over and above the specific meanings of the words themselves. A change of pitch contour will change the meaning of the sentence: thus, *horse?* and *horse!* are different.

A single contour is not necessarily exactly as long as a sentence. One sentence may have several contours, and a single contour may have several meaningful parts. This analysis will be demonstrated presently, but first, more detail will be given about problems of shades of meanings in the analysis of intonation contours.

## Accompanied by shades of meaning
*Contrasting pronunciations as evidence for different meanings*

Whenever an investigator finds a language in which a specific sentence can be pronounced in two, three, four, or more ways, he must investigate the reason for the different pronunciations. The different pitch sequences probably imply a changed relation of the speaker to the sentence, or of the sentence to its environment. It is improbable that much fluctuation will occur without an accompanying change of meaning. Languages which have mechanical intonation contours rather than meaningful ones would appear to have relatively little fluctuation: for example, Oto (an Indian language of Oklahoma) has a mechanical pitch contour in which stressed syllables of normal words have high pitch and unstressed ones lower pitch – and these relative pitch relationships seem not to be upset by emotional contexts; Oto has a few interjections, however, which can have one of several different pitch pronunciations, and these used in the proper context indicate the emotion or attitude of the speaker. In contrast to Oto, anyone who chooses to do so can pronounce in a dozen ways an English sentence such as *I am going to town today* (with surprise, exclamation, query or emphasis on different words); one must not assume that other languages are like English in intonation.

*Intonation meanings superimposed upon lexical meanings*
*(speaker's attitude)*

English words have basic, intrinsic meanings; these *lexical meanings* are the ones found in the dictionary. Frequently, the lexical meanings are very objective; for example, *horse* refers to an animal with four legs, solid hooves, and a flowing mane and tail. Sometimes the lexical meanings are less objective: for example, *try* does not refer to any single specific act, but rather to the undertaking of some task by choice. A word may have several lexical meanings: *horse* may refer to a mare, Percheron, supporting frame, knight (in chess), apparatus for vaulting, and so on; *try* may mean to make trial of, to experiment with, to afflict. When several meanings are possible to the one word, the particular meaning must be chosen which is pertinent ('makes sense') to the particular context in hand. Sometimes the context demands an interpretation in terms of metaphor or irony – or even falsehood. Nevertheless, all of the lexical meanings have this in common, that they are indicated only by the requisite consonants, vowels and stress, and a context where such a meaning is possible; in that sense, the lexical meaning is intrinsically a part of the word itself and not dependent upon extraneous phenomena such as pitch produced by emotion.

The intonation meaning is quite the opposite. Rather than being a stable inherent part of words, it is a temporary addition to their basic form and meaning. Rather than being carried by permanent consonants and vowels, it is carried by a transitory extrinsic pitch contour. Rather than contributing to the intrinsic meaning of a word, it is merely a shade of meaning added to or superimposed upon that intrinsic lexical meaning, according to the attitude of the speaker. Thus, to *horse*, may be added a pitch scheme indicating the speaker's surprise – i.e. *a horse!* (or the meaning could be given roughly in lexical form as *look at the horse about which I am quite surprised at its unexpected appearance*). In English, then, an *intonation meaning* modifies the lexical meaning of a sentence by adding to it the *speaker's attitude* toward the contents of that sentence (or an indication of the attitude with which the speaker expects the hearer to react). (See also, for further discussion of this point, p. 57–9.)

*Difficulty of isolating an intonation contour for analysis of its meaning*

In order to study his own intonation, a speaker needs to be able to repeat a sentence a number of times using substantially the same pitches each time, so as to compare the utterances and later study the effect of deliberate changes or substitutions in various parts of the sentence. Such repetition is difficult; the pitches appear elusive and ephemeral, and considerable practice is necessary before it can be done easily. The following imaginary anecdote will illustrate the problem: Paul was studying intonation, and noting any new contours which he heard at odd moments. One afternoon he said, very impatiently, *John, tell Mary that she has forgotten to go to the store; she will have to hurry to get there before it closes.* Paul noticed in his own speech something which he had not recorded previously; so he repeated the sentence for analysis. In turning to research, however, his impatience disappeared and he became introspective. In abandoning his impatience, he automatically dropped his impatient intonation contours, and, in becoming introspective, automatically substituted introspective intonation contours with slow forms, deliberate utterance, and resultant additional pauses and glides. Upon noticing these changes, Paul attempted to utter the sentence as he had done originally, and felt foolish since the simulated emotion of the intonation contours was not paralleled by actual emotion. Persisting in repetition, Paul suddenly could not be sure that he was repeating accurately, since the sentence now appeared somewhat queer and somewhat plausible simultaneously.

A phonographic or magnetic recording preserves a sentence without change, and is a decided help to analysis. There are difficulties involved, however: for best results, one must be able to hear a single sentence – not long paragraphs – repeated immediately, and this may be awkward to achieve. Further, once a faithful mechanical repetition is obtained, the normal non-significant variation of speech is lost, and attention is likely to ˙ ˙come focused on details which are not semantically of importance ˳ ˳en for shades of meaning; a phonetic transcription of these non-significant details obscures the picture of the actual systematic organization of the contours.

A musician has some advantage in hearing speech pitch, but must be careful not to lose all that value by falling into the error of trying to record absolute pitches and fixed intervals rather than relative phonemic pitch contrasts in which one pitch is higher than a second and so on, but neither is essentially related to any standard number of vibrations per second.

## Strength of meanings

An extraordinary characteristic of intonation contours is the tremendous connotative power of their elusive meanings. One might hastily and erroneously assume that forms which change so rapidly and automatically could not be semantically potent. Actually, we often react more violently to the intonational meanings than to the lexical ones; if a man's tone of voice belies his words, we immediately assume that the intonation more faithfully reflects his true linguistic intentions. Thus, if someone says, *Is breakfast ready yet?* the sentence is either innocuous or an insult according to whether it is spoken nicely or nastily – and if the insult is resented, the speaker defends himself by saying, *I just asked if breakfast were ready and she flew into a rage.* This illustrates the fact that the intonation contours, though fluctuating like the speaker's attitude, are as strong in their implications as the attitudes which they represent; in actual speech, the hearer is frequently more interested in the speaker's attitude than in his words – that is, whether a sentence is 'spoken with a smile' or with a sneer.

Usually the speaker's attitude is in balance with the words he chooses. If he says something mean, his attitude usually reflects the same characteristic. Various types of word play, however, depend for their success upon the exact opposite, that is, a lack of balance between content and intention or attitude. If one says something insulting, but smiles in face and voice, the utterance may be a great compliment; but if one says something very complimentary, but with an intonation of contempt, the result is an insult. A highly forceful or exciting statement in a very matter-of-fact intonation may, by its lack of balance, produce one type of irony. Lack of balance between intonation and word content may be deliberate for special speech effects.

## Principles and dangers in definitions of meanings

Once a particular intonation contour has been isolated, its meaning is determined by finding the least common denominator of the linguistic contexts or physical and emotional situations within which that contour occurs. If, for example, a low slightly rising contour occurs in utterances which are variously statements, queries, dependent clauses, and also occurs in the discussion of trees, children, algebra, atoms and cancer, while in each utterance the speaker is deliberating carefully on these items, then it is precisely the speaker's attitude of deliberation which constitutes the only contextual characteristic common to all of them. In this case, the low, slightly rising intonation contour must be defined as meaning a deliberate attitude of the speaker. As with words which may have two or more related lexical meanings, however, so with intonation contours one must sometimes indicate a central meaning with marginal variations from it.

For English, meanings of intonation contours are largely of this general type – *attitudes* of the speaker (or, occasionally, imputed by the speaker to the hearer). Most sentences or parts of sentences can be pronounced with several different intonation contours, according to the speaker's momentary feeling about the subject matter. These attitudes can vary from surprise, to deliberation, to sharp isolation of some part of a sentence for attention, to mild intellectual detachment. The lexical meanings and intonational meanings may coincide, as when one uses a deliberative intonation contour while saying the words *I'm still thinking about it*, or, as has already been shown, the words and intonation may be voluntarily placed in conflict for facetious purposes.

In analysing the meanings of intonation contours the chief danger of error – an error which has vitiated much work in the past – lies in the failure to get the common meaning from a large enough number of contexts. By abstracting the meaning of a particular contour just from a single context, or from contexts which are all grammatically or physically similar even although that contour actually occurs elsewhere in grammatically and physically diverse contexts, one tends to assume that the meaning is much more concrete than it actually is; this takes place when one includes in the definition of a contour the characteristics of the local context selected, whereas these characteristics would not universally appear with that contour if the sampling had been wider. Of these errors, the easiest to commit is to select phrases of a particular grammatical construction, demonstrate that a certain contour may appear on all of those phrases, and then claim that the contour in question means or indicates that grammatical pattern – in spite of available evidence that that contour could appear on other grammatical phrase types, or that the phrases used could receive any of a dozen other contours. In an attempt to escape the consequences of such a method, without abandoning it, one may try to define a contour several times over, first in one selected set of similar phrases, and then in another set, and so on; this can prove helpful as an intermediate step, but only if one afterwards carefully compares the various definitions to find the common item of meaning which is basic to them all, and then discards the characteristics limited to selected contexts and uses the universal meaning as the definition for all occurrences. Apart from such a procedure, the use of too restricted a context leads to great complexity by inducing multiple definition of contours, with a welter of rules for the types of contexts in which they occur; this is quite undesirable, since much of the complexity of rules postulated in this manner involves grammatical facts which for English have no innate participation in the meaning of the contours themselves.

The intonation system of English is decidedly intricate, and at best the analysis becomes highly involved in overlapping phenomena. In such a situation it is not surprising that an artificial complexity resulting from an over-detailed analysis of the context burdens the system unduly. By making the analysis cumbersome this is likely to lead to an unfortunate reaction of over-simplification in another direction, especially in the grouping into single units various formal differences of contour which may be minute, but are nevertheless semantically important. Thus, one may try to reduce all intonation curves into two, three or four basic tunes or melodies, and force all intonation phenomena to be described as mere deviations from them – or one may decide to ignore some of the deviations altogether, if they are rarely encountered in speech and are difficult to classify under the limited melodies set up as standard. Over-simplification of a different type – possibly combined with the preceding one – may consist in an attempt at predicting occurrence of contours by a grammatical rule-of-thumb. For example, popular non-linguistic tradition would seem to claim that there is a question pitch as distinct from a statement pitch; all questions are presumed to use the first of these two, and, as a corollary, the question pitch would not occur on statements. The evidence fails to support the assumption. There are many more contours than one for question and one for statement. Specifically, it was a marked surprise to me to find that there are many different contours which can be used on questions, and that for any contour used on a question I could usually find the same one used on a statement; likewise, for all – or nearly all – contours used on statements, I found the same ones used on questions. In other words, there appeared to be no question pitch as such. This type of evidence is responsible for the necessity of abandoning grammatical or lexical definition of contours; definition in terms of attitudes of the speaker has been utilized, instead, in this study.

Further problems in determining meanings may be mentioned briefly. The intonation contour may cover part of a sentence or a whole sentence; it is important to find in the sentences the key places which are most crucial to the formation of a meaningful contour. Furthermore, various types of intonation, such as the general pitch of the voice as a whole in contrast to the different pitches occurring within a single sentence, must be studied separately in so far as is possible. For instrumental studies of pitch, both of these cautions must be exercised, or measurements will be made of lists of items which are linguistically non-significant and not uniform; an instrumental analysis for linguistic purposes needs to be preceded by an analysis of contrasts of intonation which in turn demands careful attention to the characteristics which carry or control meanings.

### Distributed over phrases

An intonation contour is not limited to specific syllables or words, but may be spread out over as many syllables and words as are colored by the speaker's attitude. For example, an intonation contour which begins low and rises slowly could be spread over three syllables, as in (*He's*) *doing it?* or the entire rising contour may occur on a single syllable such as *Tom?* When a phrase becomes quite long, the contour may be subdivided, since a long contour is somewhat awkward to pronounce; sometimes contours may be spread over long sequences of syllables without being subdivided; at other times the stresses and arrangement of words cause even a five-syllable phrase to be divided.

When a falling or rising contour occurs on a single syllable, a *glide* is formed (see also p. 65), so that the entire contour may be actualized within that syllable, as in *Tom!?* (contour °4–1). When a falling or rising contour is spread over a number of syllables, the pitches tend to be fairly level on each syllable, but the rise or fall is accomplished by *steps* of pitch so that the pitch of one syllable is higher than the pitch of one preceding or following it, as in *ticket!?* (contour °4–1), and *Did you want him to buy it!?* (with the same contour, but heavy stress and low pitch on *want*, and high pitch on *it*).

## Compared to the tone of tone languages

The two most deep-seated characteristics of intonation are (a) the distribution of its contours over phrases, and (b) the addition of shades of meaning to phrases rather than the giving of lexical meaning to words. Both of these characteristics can be seen in contrast with a different type of pitch system in tone languages.

In a tone language the pitch of each syllable is basic to the word. Pitch contours are located on single syllables, not on groups of syllables. Every syllable has a pitch which is determined by the innate nature of the word itself (or occasionally by the morphology or by tone sandhi); no difference is observed in this principle whether the tone language has a tendency like Chinese toward monosyllablic morphemes and simple morphology, or like Mixtec (of Mexico) toward dissyllabic morphemes, or like Navajo (of USA) toward morphemes which may be part of a syllable – often a single consonant – or entire syllables in an extremely complex morphology.

Further, the tones of tone languages, with the consonants and vowels, form the actual words themselves so that no word exists unless its phonemic tone exists along with its sounds. As part of the innate structure of the word, the tone contributes its share toward carrying the basic lexical meanings of words. Just as the substitution of [m] for [b] can change English *bat* to *mat* and change the lexical meaning from a 'club used in baseball' to a 'fabric of plaited straw', so in Mixtec[1] the substitution of [t] for [ž] can change *žūkū* 'mountain' to *tūkū* 'different', and the substitution of [ˋ] (a low tone) for [˗] (a medium tone) can change *žūkū* 'mountain' to *žūkù* 'brush', while *žūkú* (with one high tone) is 'yoke' (a Spanish loan from *yugo*) and *žúkú* is 'non-domesticated'. Thus, the problem of defining meanings in a tone language is that of defining the lexical meaning of words – not first defining the lexical meanings as carried by vowels and consonants and then defining a shade of meaning added by superimposed pitch.

In addition to their lexical pitch, however, tone languages may have various types of pitches superimposed upon them. Thus, the general pitch of the voice may carry implications of anger, disgust, joy, and so on (for example, the Mixtec men occasionally run into falsetto in angry protest).

## Divided into parts

In order to describe an intonation contour it does not suffice to say that it is rising, or falling, or falling–rising. Even the simplest rise has a complex series of relationships to other contours, and complex internal structure.

1. For an analysis of the tones of Mixtec, and a procedure for the analysis of tone languages, see Pike (1948). For an analysis of Mixtec grammar, see Pike (1944). These investigations of Mixtec were conducted under the auspices of the Summer Institute of Linguistics during annual field trips from 1935 to 1952.

The size of the interval between beginning and ending points, the height of the beginning point relative to the general pitch level of the sentence, paragraph, conversation, or speaker's norm, the relation to timing, phrasing, stress and pause – these and other characteristics need to be described for the complete understanding of any contour.

## Four relative levels at contour points

The pitches of intonation are relative. The absolute pitch of a syllable – the number of vibrations per second – has no significance as such. The significance of pitches is determined by their height relative to one another. If in the phrase *John came here*, a speaker gives 400 vibrations per second to *came*, and 200 vibrations per second to *here*, then *came* may be high in relation to *here*; but if *came* has 400 and *here* has 800 vibrations per second, then *came* is low in relation to *here*; that is, highness or lowness or intermediate stages of pitch are determined by the proportionate relation of syllables or phrases one to another, and not by their exact physical measurement.

In English, four relative but significant levels (pitch phonemes) can be found which serve as the basic building blocks for intonation contours. These four levels may, for convenience, be labelled extra-high, high, mid and low respectively, and may be numbered from one to four beginning with the one which is extra-high; a fall from high to low would be a change from pitch level two to pitch level four.

This number is not an arbitrary one. A description in terms of three levels could not distinguish many of the contours – for example, the three contours beginning on low pitch and each rising to a different height. A description in terms of five or six levels would leave many theoretically possible contrastive combinations of pitches unused. The four levels are enough to provide for the writing and distinguishing of all of the contours which have differences of meaning so far discovered, provided that additional symbols are used for stress, quantity, pause, general height of the voice, general quality of the voice, and so on. In this paper, the contours dependent upon the four levels will first be described and then a brief description will be given of some of the further modifying speech characteristics.

The distance between the four levels of English is not mathematically fixed, uniform or predictable. It varies from individual to individual, and the individual varies his own intervals from time to time. For general purposes, and until instrumental studies can determine the average spread of intervals and their fluctuation, one may assume that the intervals indicated by the symbols in this paper are more or less equally distributed between high and low.

The pitch levels appear to be nearly or completely meaningless by themselves. It is the intonation contour as a whole which carries the meaning while the pitch levels contribute end points, beginning points, or direction-change points to the contours – and as such are basic building blocks which contribute to the contours and hence contribute to the meaning. Nevertheless, some generalization of usage can be made: there is a tendency for pitch contours which include a pitch of level number one (except for contours °1-2 and °2-1) to contain some element of surprise or unexpectedness; pitch two is possibly the most frequent level for normal stressed syllables, while pitch four is frequent for unstressed syllables at the end of falling contours, and pitch three for unstressed syllables elsewhere. These latter generalizations are suggestive as a mnemonic device, but have little technical validity, because a mass of exceptions (such as contour °3-2 with stressed 3, and °1-2 with unstressed two) indicates that they do not reflect basic intonational organization. A more legitimate and effective generalization can be made by gathering into groups those contours which have related form (for example, contours falling to pitch four) and meaning (for example, mild versus intense contrast or pointing). Once these groups are established, some interrelationships appear, but they do not allow for postulation of meanings for pitch levels as such since, for example, the meaning of a contour falling to pitch two has little in common with the meaning of contours rising to pitch two or falling from that level.

In determining the pertinent level or levels of contour, one does not classify the pitch of every syllable or part of a syllable, but only those points in the contour crucial to the establishment of its characteristic rises and falls; these may be called *contour points* (see also p. 59). In any rising or falling contour, two contour points are present: the pitch level at its beginning and the pitch level at its end. For a contour which first falls and then rises (or, very rarely, one which first rises and then falls) a third contour point is always present at the place where the direction of pitch movement changes. In the following utterances notice the contour points (the numbers will be placed approximately under them).

| Tom! | Tom!? | Tommy! | Tommy!? | Margaret!? | telephone number! | telephone number!? |
|------|-------|--------|---------|------------|-------------------|--------------------|
| 2-4  | 2-4-3 | 2- -4  | 2- -4-3 | 2- -4-3    | 2- -4             | 2- -4-3            |

In the first five samples each syllable had at least one contour point, so that the relative pitch of each syllable was important to the establishing of contours and their meanings. In the last two samples, there were more syllables than contour points. These extra syllables can be pronounced with intermediate pitches in a general descending scale, or with considerable variation in the amount of drop from syllable to syllable. There may be many more than four actual levels, but it is the contour-point levels which are pertinent to the system. Compare the differences in the following utterances, all of which have the same contour points (except that an immediate versus delayed drop or rise in pitch is occasionally significant):

```
    telephone  number!
    2  3+ 3     4+ 4
or: 2  3   3    3   4
or: 2  3   4    4   4
or: 2  4   4    4   4
```

## The contour points of primary intonations

It is at the ends of sentences that contours with the strongest meanings tend to occur. For example, many different contours, including 2-4, 1-4, 2-4-3, 3-2 can be given on the last word of *I want to go home*; usually their meanings will be stronger or more prominent than the meanings of additional contours occurring earlier in the sentence. (If the last words have their lexical stresses partially suppressed, and the first word receives a sentence stress, no additional contours are added, but the size of the contour is increased, and its placement on an example like *I want to go home* is changed.) These important contours which frequently appear at the end of sentences may for convenience be called *primary* types; included in this classification, also, are all other contours which are similar in structure, even though they may rarely occur in sentence-final position; furthermore, these same contours are still called primary when they appear earlier in the sentences instead of at their ends. Their structure will be described in the paragraphs which follow.

A stressed syllable constitutes the *beginning point* for every primary contour; there is no primary contour without a stressed syllable, and every heavily stressed syllable begins a new contour. In the following illustration there are five stresses and five primary contours; the beginning of the primary contour will be shown by the degree sign [°] before the number of the pitch level:

The 'boy in the 'house is 'eating 'peanuts 'rapidly.
3-    °2-3 3-      °2-3   3- °2--3   °2--3    °2-  -4

The syllable which receives the stress is usually one which would normally be stressed anyhow, that is, is lexically determined, like the first syllable of *table*, and *company*, or the second syllable of *regard*, and *receive*, or the third syllable of *implications*. For polysyllabic words, the place of normal lexical stress may be determined according to their pronunciation by themselves, that is, in isolation.

All monosyllabic words when pronounced by themselves have a stress and a primary contour. However, it is inconvenient to consider the isolated form of the word as the most basic one. A simpler statement of the stresses of the language as a whole is obtained when one assumes that the most basic pronunciation of the stress or lack of stress of a monosyllabic word is that which is found in a phrase of the normal type. By normal type, in this instance, is meant a phrase which does not suppress the regular lexical stress of any of its dissyllabic nouns, adjectives, main verbs, and the like, nor add special sentence stresses to those syllables which are usually unstressed. Thus, *The 'teacher is coming* is not a normal phrase, because the stress is partially suppressed on the word *coming*. Likewise, certain monosyllables are stressed in normal phrases, but others are without strong stress there. Thus, the phrase *The 'boy is 'coming* is a normal phrase, because the stresses are regularly retained on *boy* and *coming*, but the phrase *The boy 'is coming* is an abnormal one because the stresses are partially suppressed on *boy* and *coming* and one is added to the word *is*. Those syllables which regularly receive stress in dissyllabic words, and those monosyllables which regularly receive stress in normal phrases, may conveniently be said to be *innately stressed*, even though these stresses can be partially suppressed. In general, those monosyllables which are innately stressed are the nouns, main verbs (i.e. not in auxiliary position before other verbs), adjectives, interjections, indefinite pronouns, demonstratives, interrogatives, and adverbs of time, place and manner. Those mono-syllables which tend to be innately without stress include the personal and reflexive pronouns, auxiliary verbs and adverbs of degree.

Any syllable which is innately stressed is potentially the normal begin-ning point of a primary contour.

If a single contour is spread over several words, each with innate stresses, only one of the syllables is permitted to be very prominent. This extra prominence comes (1) from optional added intensity on the syllable at the beginning point of the contour and (2) from obligatory lessened intensity on the remaining innate-stressed syllables of the contour. (How-ever, the reduced stresses usually remain somewhat more intense than those syllables which have no innate stresses at all. A stress which is retained or added will be marked ['] if it is fairly strong or ["] if it is intensely and emphatically strong.) This effect may be heightened by the length of the prominent syllables. Notice the syllables lessened or heightened in prominence in the pronunciation of the following illustrations (as above, the beginning of the primary contour will be shown by the degree sign [°] before the number of the pitch level):

*He's 'coming today.*
   °2-      -4

*He "wanted to buy it (but 'couldn't).*
   °2-      -4- -3 4-  °2--4

*He* ʺ*wanted to invest in securities (but* ʹ*couldn't*).
　°1-　　　　　　　　-4- -3- 4-　°2-　-4

(In the preceding set of illustrations, the words *today*, *buy*, *invest* and *securities* have had their syllables with innate stress lessened in prominence, whereas *wanted* had its innate stress made even more prominent by emphatic stress.)

For special effects the beginning point of a primary contour may be placed on a syllable which is not innately stressed, giving stress and prominence to that syllable while the normal innate stress and prominence is removed from other syllables. Note the following sentence:

*I didn't say* ʹ*unvestigate, I said* ʺ*investigate; the word normally is investigate.*
　　　　　°1-　　-4-3　　　　°1-　　-4　　　　　　　　　°1- -4

An *ending point* completes a primary contour. If the entire contour occurs on a single syllable, the ending point is constituted by the second half of that syllable, with a pitch *glide* connecting the beginning and ending points. This is true for utterances such as

*boy, why? gone!?*
°2-4 °3-1 °1-4-3

The ending point may be an entire unstressed syllable, as in

*ticket? happy;*
°3--2　°2--4

or part of an unstressed syllable as in

*ticket? happy, investigate;*
°2--4-3 °2-4-3 °2-　-(3)-1

or part of a stressed syllable, as in

*There's the man.*
°2-　　　　-4-3

If the contour is composed of two or more syllables as in

*ticket?,*
°3--2

there is a *step* up or down between them.

A *direction-change point* occurs at the center of a small but important minority of the primary contours, when the pitch changes from falling to rising or (rarely) rising to falling. This point may occur on the central part of a single syllable, or the first part of a stressed or unstressed syllable, or on a complete unstressed syllable; compare pitch four in

*Tom,   ticket, syllable.*
°2-4-3 °2-4-3 °2--4-3

The central part of a contour may be relatively level, so that the change point optionally occupies one or more syllables, as in

*telephone number* or *telephone     number.*
°2-(4-4)-  -4- -3          °2-(3+-3)- -4--3

   The end of a primary contour usually coincides with the end of some word, as in

*He wanted to do it* or *Tom*  or  *Always.*
    °2-                -4       °2-4-3    °2--4

The end of the contour, however, does not have to occur on the same word with which it began – as the first illustration in the preceding series demonstrates.

   The end of every word is potentially the ending of a primary contour. A contour which contains several words may, under special conditions of attention, emphasis, and the like, be broken up into as many contours as there are words. Compare the following set of illustrations; more samples could have been constructed from the same sentence:

*He wanted to do it.*
    °2-               -4

*He wanted to do  it.*
    °2- -4         °2- -4

*He  wanted to do it.*
°2-4 °2-               -4

*He  wanted to do    it.*
°2-4 °2- -4         °2-4 °2-4

   A primary contour may end in the middle of a word under special emphatic stress, or if the word has two innate stresses, as follows:

 ¹*in*"*adequate*
°2-3°1-  -4

 ¹*sar*¹*dine*
°2-3 °1-4

¹*impli*¹*cation*
°3- -4 °2-4

Primary contours frequently begin in the middle of words, as in *in¹sipid*
                                                                    °2-4

(For the part played by the beginnings of words in the establishing of intonation boundaries, see precontours [pp. 67–8] and rhythm units [pp. 72–6 and pp. 79–81].)

*Precontours within total contours*

Immediately preceding the stressed syllable of a primary contour there oftentimes will be one or more syllables which are pronounced in the same burst of speed with that primary contour but which themselves are unstressed. These syllables may be called *precontours*, and depend for their pronunciation upon the syllables which follow them. They may constitute grammatically independent words, like *a, he* and *under*, or they may be parts of a word, as in *re(ceive)* and *invo(cation)*. In innate structure they may be lexically without stress, or their innate lexical stresses may have been partially suppressed. Notice the difference of grammatical and lexical type in the precontours of the following illustrations:

*the  ¹boy*
 3-  °2-4

*He  ¹said so.*
 3-  °2-  -4

*an interesting "house ( – "not  an interesting "barn)*
3-              °1-4        °2-4 4-        °2-4

The different precontours have meanings, but in general their implication of the speaker's attitudes is not so strong as that of the primary contours. As an illustration of distinctive precontour significance, notice that of the two following utterances the second portrays a much more insistent attitude than the first:

*I want to go home.*
3-              °2-4

*I want to go home.*
2-              °2-4

A primary contour with its unstressed precontour knit closely to it in pronunciation forms a single intonational unit, a *total contour*. In the illustration immediately above, the intonation of *I want to go* is a precontour, that of *home* is a primary contour, and the entire pitch sequence is a total contour. If a primary contour happens to have no precontour, it constitutes a total contour by itself. Thus, both of the following items are total contours:

'Tom did it.
°2-        -4

The 'man did it.
  3- °2-        -4

In succeeding examples, numerals which symbolize key points in a single total contour will be connected by hyphens; the precontour numeral will be followed by a hyphen, and parts of the primary contour will be joined by hyphens also, as in the first of the following samples; the second sample contains two total contours:

Good morning Tom.
  3-  °2--4-    -4-3

The   doctor bought a car.
  3- °2-4-3 4-       °2-4

Precontours usually begin coincidentally with the beginnings of words, as in *the     man*.
          3-   °2-4

### Related to pause and rhythm

Intonation contours are intimately related to pauses and to rhythm, as this section will demonstrate. Nevertheless, intonation must be kept distinct from these latter speech characteristics, since in many respects they are independent one of another. Pause and rhythm are closely dependent upon one another in some of their elements and usage, but in other ways are independent, and so must be handled as separate significant entities (that is, as different types of phonemes or morphemes; for a summary of these differences, in operation and contrast, see p. 82).

### *Pauses* (*tentative and final*)

When a person makes a cessation of speech, there is a *pause*. There are two significant types of pause (i.e. two pause phonemes or morphemes) – a *tentative* one and a *final* one; these may be symbolized by a single and double bar, [/] and [//], respectively, and have the meanings indicated by their labels.

Either pause type may vary in length; the tentative pause is usually shorter in length than the final one, but it is not always so.

The tentative pause has one very important alternate form: instead of a gap in the speech, a complete cessation, there may be a lengthening of the last sound or two of the preceding word. This length takes up the same time as the physical pause would have done; there is no confusion with the normal sounds which are relatively long, nor even with lengthening for emphasis, since the elongation for the equivalent of pause is accompanied by a considerable weakening of the strength of the sounds, and it is this weakness of sound plus the length which can substitute for physical pause in the tentative pause phoneme. (Phonetically, then, the sentence

*The   man     is here*
  3- °2-4-3: 3- °2-4//

has a prolongation of [n] but, phonemically, it has a pause, to be written thus:

*The   man     is   here*.)
  3- °2-4-3/ 3- °2-4

On a dictaphone record I once heard the following sentence:

*Listen for the syllables that have high   pitch  and heavy stress.*
°3--2:  3-      °2- -4-3: 3-        °2-2: °3  / 4-  °2--2:  °2-4//

In order to rewrite the sentence phonemically, one needs only to substitute single bars, or tentative pauses, for the colons indicating phonetic length.

The tentative and final pauses affect in different ways the material which precedes them. The tentative pause tends

(1) to sustain the height of the final pitch of the contour. A °2-4 contour, for example, before a tentative pause tends to end on one or more syllables on pitch four without drifting downward; there may prove to be an occasional slight drift upward, although never as much as is found in a rise from significant level four to significant level three. In addition,

(2) the tentative pause often affects the quantity of the preceding contour in various ways not as yet clearly defined. The syllable preceding a tentative pause is often longer than usual, sustained on a level pitch. At other times, it is the beginning point of the primary contour that carries length and so gives the clue to the presence of the tentative pause. On the other hand, the departure from the undefined norm may be in the opposite direction, and yet give related results: a very short ending often indicates that a tentative pause follows. The same person, repeating the same sentence, may utilize different means for similar results in various repetitions of the same sentence. In general, it may be that any departure from the normal length of the elements of a primary contour contributes to the recognition of a following pause as tentative, provided that the full height of the pitch is sustained at the end of the contour.

The final pause modifies the preceding contour (or contours) by lowering in some way the normal height of the end of the contour. If the contour itself ends in pitch four, then preceding a final pause it will tend to fade into silence while drifting downward; this is considerably different from the pitch of the same contour which has a somewhat level, possibly sustained, ending when it occurs in the middle of a sentence without pause, or when it occurs before a tentative pause. If the contour is a falling–rising one, the rise appears not to go quite so high as it does in the middle of a sentence without pause, or before a tentative pause. This conditioned lower height, of a °2-4-3 ending, is still markedly higher than the sustained end of a °2-4 contour preceding tentative pause (however, a person who has not had the difference called to his attention, by contrasting pairs, is likely to confuse a °2-4/ with a °2-4-3/ or even °2-4-3/; once it is pointed out, however, the contrast is usually obvious to him).

Compare the following words when they are pronounced as part of a series, and when they are the last of the group:

*Apples, pears,  oranges, plums, peaches.*
°2- 4-/  °2-4/  °2-  -4/    °2-4/  °2-  -4//

(*I bought some*) *pears.*
 3-              °2-4//

*I bought some plums.*
3-              °2-4//

The difference between tentative and final pause is sometimes heard in an exaggerated form in fiery oratory. With some public speakers, one can know for some time in advance – say three short phrases or more – that the speaker is coming to the end of a paragraph or section of his oration, by the 'running down' modifications of his intonation contours as the pitch is let down before such a final pause.

Of the two pauses, the tentative one tends to occur at all places where the attitude of the speaker includes uncertainty, or non-finality. It is found, then, in hesitation, and after almost all questions – although there seem to be a few exceptions when a person asks a question (with a falling contour) without wanting an answer, or when he assumes the answer to be certainly known. When a pause occurs after a rising contour, I have found only the tentative type, both after questions, and statements, or parts of statements (but occasionally I have found the final pause after a falling–rising contour). A pause in the middle of a sentence is usually a tentative one, but by no means always so. Notice the following illustrations of tentative pauses:

*I   think   I'll . . .*
3-  °2-   -3 /

*Well, I . . .*
°2-3/  3-/

*Has he gone?*
   4-       °3-2/

*Where has he gone?*
   3-           °2-4/

*He   bought   it?*
   3- °4-      -1/

*I   wanted to do it, but I couldn't.*
4- °2-                 -4/  4-   °2- -4 //

(Contrast: *I   wanted to do   it,   but I couldn't.*)
              4- °2-          -4- -3/  4-   °2- -4  //

"*Spanish is a* "*beautiful* "*language.*
   °2-4  / 4-    °2-   -4   °2- -4//

   The final pause occurs where the speaker's attitude, at the time of pause, is one of finality, and for this reason occurs most often at the end of statements. The final pause is limited in occurrence almost – but not quite – entirely to a position after a contour falling to pitch level four; occasionally it is found after °2-4-3, and further research may show it elsewhere. Since the tentative pause also occurs frequently in this position, it is principally here that the two pauses may be found in contrast. Compare the following illustrations:

*I'm going.* (Implying, possibly, *and that's that*)
4-   °2-4//

*I'm going* . . . (Implying, possibly, *if you do not dissuade me*)
4-   °2-4/

   (Occasionally one hears a speaker who seldom has either kind of pause within a space of a number of sentences. This forms an elaborate complex rhythm unit; for the analysis of such units, see pp. 76–9.)
   Frequently, pauses in the middle of sentences separate large grammatical units such as clauses, or separate smaller units in such a way as to contribute toward their internal unity. In the next illustration, a routine pause separates clauses; in the second illustration the pauses – in conjunction with unifying rhythm (pp. 79–81) and unifying level intonation – set off the unit *three plus two:*

*If* '*Tom goes,* '*I     will* '*too.*
3-  °2-   -4-3/ °2-4- -4-3 °2-4//

'*Two,     times* '*three* '*plus two,  is* '*ten.*
  °2-4-3/ 4-        °2      °1- -4-3/ 3-  °2-4//

It is after primary contours that pauses may usually be found, as in the previous illustrations. Hesitation forms, however, sometimes end without a primary contour, and have merely an unfinished precontour. In this event, a pause may occur at the end of an utterance in a place other than at the end of a primary contour, as in the following illustration:

*But he . . .*
  3-   /

Sometimes also, a tentative pause occurs in the middle of a primary contour. This tends to set off the second part, as some type of parenthesis, or form of address, as in the next illustrations. Notice that the second part of the divided primary contour has no strong stress and that potential lexical stresses are sharply reduced in intensity (see also p. 80):

*No,   Tom,* (*I do not.*)
°2-4-/ -4-3/  4-   °3-4//

*No,   he said.*
°2-4-/    -4 //

### Simple rhythm units (*stress-timed and syllable-timed*)

English sentences are spoken with recurrent bursts of speed, with long or short pauses or with intonation breaks between. A sentence or part of a sentence spoken with a single rush of syllables uninterrupted by a pause is a *rhythm unit*. The following utterances are usually spoken as single rhythm units: *the car*; *intonation*; *here it is*; *he said he would*; *a jumping jack*. The next group of utterances would tend to be broken into two rhythm units each: *I want to go but I can't*; *If he comes he'll buy it*; *every day is Pepsodent day*.

A rhythm unit which contains one, and only one, primary contour is a *simple rhythm unit*. Notice the one strong stress and the one primary contour in each of the following simple rhythm units:

*the  uni*'*versity*
  3-      °2- -4//

'*Robert must do  it.*
°2-              -4//

*The* '*manager is the one who purchased  it.*
  4- °2-                                            -4//

The timing of rhythm units produces a rhythmic succession which is an extremely important characteristic of English phonological structure. The units tend to follow one another in such a way that the lapse of time between the beginning of their prominent syllables is somewhat uniform. Notice the more or less equal lapses of time between the stresses in the sentence *The 'teacher is 'interested in 'buying some 'books*; compare the timing of that sentence with the following one, and notice the similarity in that respect despite the different number of syllables: *'Big 'battles are 'fought 'daily*.

(Controlled strictly and mechanically in poetry – and possibly partially so in some types of elegant prose – the recurrent stress timing is perhaps even more important than the number of syllables in iambic or trochaic groups, or the like. Evidence of this fact is seen in the esthetic satisfaction obtained by English speakers from some lines of poetry – such as *Break, break, break* – which do not have the full complement of syllables normally to be found in the scansion of other lines of the same poems.)

The tendency toward uniform spacing of stresses in material which has uneven numbers of syllables within its rhythm groups can be achieved only by destroying any possibility of even time spacing of syllables. Since the rhythm units have different numbers of syllables, but a similar time value, the syllables of the longer ones are crushed together, and pronounced very rapidly, in order to get them pronounced at all, within that time limitation. This rhythmic crushing of syllables into short time limits is partly responsible for many abbreviations – in which syllables may be omitted entirely – and the obscuring of vowels; it implies, also, that English syllables are of different lengths, with their length of utterance controlled not only by the lexical phonetic characteristics of their sounds but also by the accident of the number of syllables in the particular rhythmic unit to which they happen to belong at that moment. Compare the similar timing and stresses but variant number of syllables in the following pairs of illustrations:[2]

*The 'man's 'here.*
3- °2-4-3/ °2-4//

*The 'manager's 'here.*
3- °2-4-3    / °2-4//

*If 'Tom will 'I  will.*
3- °2-   -4-3/ °2- -4 //

*If 'Tom'll do  it 'I  will.*
3- °2-      -4- -3/ °2- -4 //

2. For this basic principle of the timing of rhythm units and for similar illustrations I am indebted to Daniel Jones (1956, §§886–90).

A single rhythm unit from such a sequence of units may be considered the regular or normal type. Because its length is largely dependent upon the presence of one strong stress, rather than upon the specific number of its syllables, it may conveniently be labelled a *stress-timed* rhythm unit (a phonemic type in contrast to syllable-timed units to be mentioned below, with both of them on a different level of contrast from the simple versus complex rhythm types).

Many non-English languages (Spanish, for instance) tend to use a rhythm which is more closely related to the syllable than the regular stress-timed type of English; in this case, it is the syllables, instead of the stresses, which tend to come at more-or-less evenly recurrent intervals – so that, as a result, phrases with extra syllables take proportionately more time, and syllables or vowels are less likely to be shortened and modified.

English also has a rhythmic type which depends to a considerable extent upon the number of its syllables, rather than the presence of a strong stress, for some of its characteristics of timing; in English, however, the type is used only rarely. In these particular rhythm units each unstressed syllable is likely to be sharp cut, with a measured beat on each one; this recurrent syllable prominence, even though the stressed syllables may be extra strong and extra long, gives a 'pattering' effect. The type may be called a *syllable-timed* rhythm unit (in phonemic contrast to the stress-timed type).

If the unstressed syllables are each made quite abrupt, the unit becomes somewhat *staccato*. If the unstressed syllables are more or less equally timed, and somewhat prominent, but glided or smoothed together, the general impression is that of a *spoken chant*. Consider the following sentence, in this latter style:

*Susie is a tattle tale.*
°2-2- °3- -1- °2--2- °3-3//   (Chanted with syllable-timed rhythm)

Words in a very close grammatical association are likely to belong to the same rhythm unit. Notice the grammatical relationship between the words in the following illustration:

*the boy*
  3- °2-4//

*He's gone.*
  3- °2-4//

*Come in.*
  3-  °2-4//

*It's a big one.*
3-   °2- -4 //

*Hit him.*
°2- -4//

*When is  it?*
   3- °2- -4/

Words which have no innate lexical stress tend to join that rhythm group preceding or following them with which they are grammatically most closely related, as the following illustrations demonstrate:

*I'm going to,  tomorrow.*
3-  °2-   -3/ 3-°2-4 //

*He  gave  it  to the man.*
   3- °2-  -3/ 3-     °2-4//

*Whom  did you tell it to  yesterday?*
   °2-3/  3-     °2-  -3/ °2-  -4//

The beginning of any simple or complex (pp. 76–9) rhythm¹ unit (but not a weak rhythm unit, p. 79) almost always coincides with the beginning of a word, as in

*the boy,*
   3- °2-4/ and so on.

The beginning of a simple or complex rhythm unit likewise tends to coincide with the beginning of a total contour, whether the total contour begins with a precontour or begins directly with a primary contour, as in

*the  boy*   and *Don't.*
   3- °2-4//      °2-4//

The ending of a simple or complex rhythm unit tends to end coincidentally with some word; they terminate, also, at the place where some primary contour is ending at the same time. Potentially, then, the beginning of any word may become the beginning of a simple or complex rhythm unit, and the end of a word may become the end of such units.

Optionally, a sentence may be composed of one or more simple rhythm units and one or more total contours, although the change of arrangement usually changes the point of attention. Compare the following pair of illustrations (in the second, two rhythm units and two total contours occupy the place of the one rhythm unit and one total contour of the first illustration):

*Jim has gone!*
   3- °2- -4 //

*Jim     has gone!*
°2-4-3/   4-  °1-4//

In traditional English orthography, a punctuation mark usually, but not always, represents (1) a pause, and, therefore, (2) the end of a rhythm unit; in addition, it sometimes gives (3) a partial indication of the attitude of the speaker – a fact which, in turn, conditions the stress placement, or degree of stress, or intonation placement, or specific intonation, or even the quality of the voice, or some combination of these. Punctuation marks are often supplemented by italics, or capital letters, and so on, to make the stress and intonation type and placement more specific.

## Complex rhythm units *(including syllables in double function; intonation breaks; parataxis; unification rhythm)*

Frequently – especially in fast speech – two or more simple rhythm units, each with one primary contour, may be coalesced into one large rhythm unit. Such a combination comprises a *complex rhythm unit*, and contains at least two primary contours with no pause between them; the loss of a pause between two simple rhythm units changes the combination into a single complex one. The complex unit, like the simple one, has just one rush of syllables without a pause, but contains two strong stresses instead of one. In the following pair of sentences, notice that the first contains two simple rhythm units, but that the second sentence has only one unit, which is complex.

*The* 'children of the community are 'interested.*
3-   °2-              -4- -3/ 4-  °2-      -4//

*The* 'children of the community are 'interested.*
3-   °2-              -4- -3 4-  °2-      -4//

In the middle of a complex rhythm unit, a borderline syllable may serve in a *double function*. These syllables are the precontours of following primary contours, but at the same time give the impression of changing previous level primary contours into falls or rises. Such a syllable may be recognized in the symbolism by the fact that a hyphen immediately follows it, to join it to the succeeding primary contour, but a second hyphen immediately precedes the syllable to join it to the preceding primary contour which is level and short. In the following set of illustrations, the first sample contains two simple rhythm units and two total contours with a pause between them. The second has one complex rhythm unit but with the total contours separated. The third has one complex rhythm unit with a syllable in double function between.

*a* ¹*book of* ¹*stories*
3- °2-3/ 3-　°2-4//

*a* ¹*book of* ¹*stories*
3- °2-3　3-　°2-4 //

*a* ¹*book of* ¹*stories*
3- °2-　-3-　°2-4 //

(A fourth type seems to be much less frequent; it has no down glide on the first primary contour which, nevertheless, is short but followed by a pause:

*a* ¹*book of*　¹*stories*.)
3- °2　/ 3-　°2-4 //.

Although in the preceding section the relationship of the beginning and end of a (simple or) complex rhythm unit to the beginning and end of words and total contours has already been discussed, a further point should be emphasized. Since two (or more) primary contours may occur in a complex rhythm unit, the first of these contours ends within the rhythm unit; this implies that the contour border medially does not coincide with the rhythm border in such cases. However, the contour ending constitutes an *intonation break*, in the middle of the rhythm unit, which is still capable of influencing the rhythm.

Potentially, an intonation break may occur after the end of any word at all, but the potential after a primary contour is much stronger than elsewhere. A slightly slower rate of utterance will often break a complex rhythm unit into two simple units, even without a marked change of the speaker's attitude or attention, simply by introducing a pause after the first primary contour. In general, pauses can be introduced elsewhere in the sentence only when the speaker changes his attitude or attention, or speed, or emphasis, quite sharply.

These characteristics contribute to the continued internal coherence and unity of a primary or total contour even when they become overshadowed by the rhythmic unity of a larger complex rhythm unit. The individual contour unity is further maintained within a complex rhythm unit by the tendency of the unstressed syllables (or words) to adhere more closely to the total contour of which they are immediately a part, than to other total contours in the same complex rhythm unit. Furthermore, the unstressed syllables of the precontour are more rapid than those of the ending of the preceding primary contour,[3] and this difference in speed

3. I am indebted to instrumental studies of Classe (1939, pp. 116, 127), for measurements which called this to my attention.

sets them apart. This coherence of the parts of a total contour is symbolized by the hyphens which connect their parts. Hyphens are not used to connect two total contours, except in the case of syllables in double function, which are precisely the ones which at times tend to eliminate a barrier between contours.

In the first of the following illustrations, for example, notice that the hyphen arrangement signifies an intonation break of organization between *go* and *but* even when no pause occurs there. In the second illustration notice the optional pause. In the third sentence the intonation at the end of the first primary contour is modified to adapt itself more easily to slow deliberate speed within the same essential pattern of attention. In the fourth sentence, the speaker's attention switches from the desire to himself and to the action; this change of attention is accompanied by an added pause, an added total contour, an added rhythm unit, changed place of stress and modified intonation types. The fifth sentence retains the intonation contours of the fourth, but combines them into a single, rapid (pauseless), complex rhythm unit.

*I* '*wanted to go but* '*couldn't.*
3- °2-        -4  4- °2- -4 //

*I* '*wanted to go but* '*couldn't.*
3- °2-        -4/  4- °2- -4 //

*I* '*wanted to go    but* '*couldn't.*
3- °2-        -4-3/  4- °2- -4 //

'*I    wanted to* '*go    but* '*couldn't.*
°2-4/  4-          °2-4/  4- °2- -4//

'*I    wanted to* '*go    but* '*couldn't.*
°2-4 4-          °2-4  4- °2- -4//

Rhythm-unit barriers, whether between simple or complex units, may have *grammatical significance*. Two items which are not related by the grammatical subordination of one of them to the other, or by a close linking together as parts of a favored construction (such as the two main elements of a clause – the subject and predicate), may nevertheless be considered parts of a single grammatical unit if they are both within the same simple or complex rhythm unit. This relationship constitutes a type of *parataxis*. In the following set of illustrations, the first shows two rhythm units, with two items grammatically separate; the second illustration shows the same two items grammatically united because of their inclusion within a single complex rhythm unit:

It's ten o'clock. I've got to go home.
3- °2- -3- °2-4// 4-         °2-4//

It's ten o'clock; I've got to go home.
3- °2- -3- °2-4 4-         °2-4//

It should be noted that the preceding illustrations each have the same intonation contours, but are distinguished by their rhythmic organization.

A complex rhythm unit may become very long and involved, and the paratactic relationships intricate, if the speaker happens to be of the type (fortunately very rare, for the effect may be unpleasant) who gives the general appearance of introducing no pauses for emphasis or grammatical separation unless or until he runs out of breath. The following passage illustrates this abnormal type; observe the rhythmic organization; in reading it no pauses or hesitation should be introduced:

He 'said he was 'going but he 'didn't do 'anything to get 'under 'way
3- °2- -4-     °2-4 4-   °2- -4- °2- -4 4-     °2- -4 °2-

 and he 'came to the 'door He 'stood there like a 'dunce He just 'watched
-4     °2- -4-   °2- -4- °2- -4 4-   °2- -4-   °2-4

'other people 'pack their 'things He 'didn't 'help at 'all.
°2-     -4 °2-  -4- °2-   -4- °2-4 °2-   -4- °2-4//

A certain type of complex rhythm unit has an implication of *unification*. It seems usually to be characterized (1) by the presence of two (or more) strong stresses, (2) by a relatively rapid rush of syllables joining them together, (3) and by the absence of pause. Further, in relation to intonation there appears to be a minimum of contour separation in the middle of the complex, and the first contour of the series is usually level. In combination with the intonation appropriate to the context it is often utilized to show grammatical unity, or unity within mathematical parenthesis, or the unity of a phrase label, and the like. Compare the following illustrations for the types:

He's a big man. (Contrast: a big   man )
 4-  °2 °2-4//         °2-3/ °2-4//

Three minus two,   times five, . . .
 °2 °2-2   °2-4-3/ 4-  °2-4-3/

The  Chamber of Commerce, is there.
 4-  °2--2  2- °2--4--3/  4- °2-4//

*Weak and curtailed rhythm units*
When a tentative pause interrupts a primary contour, the second part of the contour then is left between pauses, constituting a separate rhythm

unit. However, this second part of the contour either has no innate lexical stress, or its lexical stresses have been partially reduced (conditioned by their position in the total contour). The result, then, is the formation of a rhythm unit with no strong stress, that is, a *weak rhythm unit*. Two of the principal types of these consist of (1) an indication of the speaker, or (2) an indication of the person addressed. These types may be seen in the following illustrations:

'*This is the  one, the teacher said.*
  °2-        -4-/                    -4//

'*Yes,  George, it's* '*time to* '*go.*
  °2-4-/ -4-3  /  4-   °2- -3- °2-4//

The first part of the primary contour also constitutes a rhythm unit because it likewise occurs between pauses. This part, however, contains the prominent stress of the primary contour. It differs from a normal simple rhythm unit precisely because it does not include the end of the primary contour; for this reason, it may conveniently be called a *curtailed rhythm unit*. In the preceding set of illustrations, '*Yes* and '*This is the one* constitute curtailed rhythm units.

When a sentence, because of the speaker's hesitation, is interrupted before the beginning of a primary contour – that is, before any strong stress has appeared – the unstressed precontour constitutes a type of weak rhythm unit. Compare the following samples:

*Why . . .*
  4-/

*In the . . .*
3-  /

*If he had only . . .*
4-          /

Occasionally, also, the identification of a speaker is given in a short rapid unstressed precontour, or part of a precontour, with a pause between it and the quotation which follows. The first part of such an utterance produces a weak rhythm unit, as in the following sample:

*I  said –  I will* '*not  go.*
3-   / -3-      °2-4-/ -4//

Curtailed and weak rhythm units may occasionally be found under very special conditions of attention, contrast or emphasis, as in the following illustration in which a pause occurs in the middle of the word:

*I   said – Re- write.*
3-          °2-4-/-4//

Usually, however, no pause is found in this kind of emphasis within a word; rather the expression tends to be in a single complex or simple rhythm unit, as in

*I   said – Re- write.*
3-          °2-4--4//

*Summary of contrasts between pause, rhythm and intonation*

After the preliminary statement of the general characteristics of intonation contours, and the discussion of pause and rhythm, it is convenient to summarize the reasons why no one of these can be equated phonemically with either of the others:

An intonation contour as such cannot establish the nature and borders of a rhythm unit since

1. Some single contours are divided into two rhythm units (that is, into a curtailed one and a weak one, as in

*Tom   has gone ).*
°2-4-/ -4-  -4-3/

2. some single (but complex) rhythm units contain two or more intonation contours (as in

*The   doctor is here ).*
  3- °2-  -3 4- °2-4//

Pauses cannot be equated with the borders of intonation contours, since pauses may occur

1. at the borders of the contours (for example, between simple rhythm units, as in

*He's coming today ).*
  3-    °2-3 / 4-°2-4//

2. in the middle of contours (before a weak rhythm unit, as in

*Here, said  I  ).*
°2-4-/        -4//

3. May be absent from a junction of two contours (in complex rhythm units, as in

*Nobody came).*
°2-4-3   °2-4//

Although rhythm unit borders coincide with pauses, neither one causes the other, since a unit of speech identical in rhythmic timing may end in either of two pause types (tentative and final, as in

'I'll go ... and 'I'll go ).
°2- -4/          °2- -4//

In addition, a unit of speech divided by a certain pause type, and ended by that same pause type, may nevertheless be pronounced with two or more different rhythmic patterns. Note, for example, that a simple rhythm unit may be followed by a simple rhythm unit, or a curtailed rhythm unit followed by a weak rhythm unit, as in

Help! Catherine! versus Help, Catherine!.
°1-4/ °4-  -3/          °1-4-/-4-    -3 /

Note also that a further type of rhythmic contrast within controlled pauses occurs between simple and complex rhythm units, as in

Tom has gone  versus Tom has gone .
  3-      °2-4//          °2-3   4- °2-4//

A third type of contrasting rhythm, within a controlled-pause context, exists between stress-timed and syllable-timed units, as in

Tommie isn't here       (with syllable-timed rhythm) versus.
°2- -2-  °3-1- °2-2-°3-3/

Tommie  isn't here  (with regular stress-timed rhythm).
°2- -4   °2-4  °2-4//

References

CLASSE, A. (1939), The Rhythm of English Prose, Oxford University Press.
JONES, D. (1956), Outline of English Phonetics, Dutton.
PIKE, K. L. (1944), 'Analysis of Mixteco text', Int. J. Amer. Ling., vol. 10, pp. 113–38.
PIKE, K. L. (1948), Tone Languages, University of Michigan Press.

# 4 George L. Trager

## The Intonation System of American English

George L. Trager, 'The intonation system of American English', from *In Honour of Daniel Jones: Papers Contributed on the Occasion of his Eightieth Birthday, 12 September 1961*, edited by David Abercrombie, D. B. Fry, P. A. D. MacCarthy, N. C. Scott and J. L. M. Trim, Longman 1964, pp. 266–70.

In the system of linguistic analysis practised by the present author, the intonation system of English, whether American or any other variety, functions as part of the syntax, delimiting stretches of utterance – clauses – that are examined in order to determine their structure, that is, their syntactic structure. But the intonation patterns that make up the system are themselves composed of certain kinds of phonological elements. And it therefore seems appropriate to describe the various aspects of these phonological elements as the author and many of his colleagues use and interpret them.

It is the intention to make this description succinct, and no discussion of other interpretations and of criticisms is given, nor is there much bibliography. This is a presentation of a position, and a statement of conclusions. It is believed that it will be useful, since no similar statement that is up to date has yet been published anywhere.

1. In *An Outline of English Structure*, hereafter referred to as *OES* (Trager and Smith, 1951), we discussed pitch and terminal junctures in sections 1.71 and 1.72 (pp. 41–8), and in the discussion of syntax (sections 4.0 to 4.5, pp. 67–80) there was some treatment of intonation patterns. Shortly after the publication of *OES*, the group of linguists working on the preparation of English-teaching materials at Cornell University in 1952 and 1953 (and at various other places for some years following), and including such excellent observers as Welmers and Hockett, noted certain omissions and difficulties in our presentation. Smith and I immediately recognized the correctness of the criticisms, and made the needed restatements; these were not published as such, but have been mentioned or alluded to in various publications by Smith and others. A couple of years later Sledd pointed out, in personal communications and oral presentations, that still further details were unaccounted for. Again Smith and I were able to see how these fitted into the total picture, and to make a workable restatement. Since about 1957 Smith especially has extensively studied the use of intonation patterns in English as markers of the boundaries of syntactic units, and he has in various stages of completion a series of statements

about English syntax and semology, based strictly on phonologically bounded units. In this connection it is also pertinent to note that it has become possible to separate out paralinguistic pitch phenomena from those of language proper (Trager, 1958). It is our hope eventually to publish this material either in a series of articles or in the form of a total revision and expansion of *OES*.

2. In *OES* we accepted and started from the basic analysis of English pitch made by Wells (1945) and extensively applied by Pike (1945).

There are four pitch phonemes (in most American usage a distinctive phonological unit is called a phoneme whether it is a vowel or a consonant or a stress or a pitch or something else). We call these 'low' /¹/, 'middle' /²/, 'high' /³/, 'extra high' /⁴/. They are found to have allophones that vary in height in terms of the stress (primary /ˊ/, secondary /ˆ/, tertiary /ˋ/, weak /ˇ/ [or unmarked]) of the syllabic that they accompany. A detailed examination of such allophones is given in *OES*, 1.71, pp. 42–4. Other allophones, involving contour or direction (sustained, rising, falling) are found at terminal points (*OES*, 1.72, pp. 44–9) and involve the amount of segmental material covered by the pitch.

From the material presented in *OES*, the following statement of intonation patterns can be constructed (examples will be given in (3) below): American English intonation patterns consist typically of three pitches and a terminal contour. The initial pitch of the three is most often /²/, but may be any of the others. The central pitch accompanies the primary stress of a phrase or clause, is most often /³/ in all kinds of material – statements, questions, or the like, but is frequently /⁴/ when there is what is usually called emphasis, and may often be /²/ or /¹/. The final pitch is most often /¹/ at the ends of statements, /²/ at the ends of clauses that do not end sentences, /³/ at the ends of certain kinds of questions, but may be any one of the four. The final pitch is modified by the terminal contour, being sustained /|/, rising /||/, or falling /#/; sustained occurs most often in clauses that do not end sentences, falling in statements and interrogative-word questions, rising in other questions and in many non-final clauses. When a clause begins with the primary-stressed syllabic, there are only two pitches, the central and the final, the initial being absent.

The modification necessitated by the observations of Welmers and Hockett involved the possibility of a fourth pitch in a clause, appearing after the initial and before the central. It has become clear that this pitch, when it occurs, always accompanies the secondary-stressed syllabic nearest to the primary, or, if there is no secondary-stressed syllabic, it falls on the tertiary nearest the primary. Any of the four pitches can appear in this position, /²/ being most frequent.

Sledd's observations indicated that there are also clauses containing four pitches in which there is a pitch after the central one and before the final one. Again, it seems to fall on secondary-stressed syllabics, or on tertiary-stressed ones if there is no secondary, but there are instances where it accompanies weak syllables when there are no stronger ones present.

Putting all these statements together, we now say: an intonation-pattern contains five pitch positions, which we designate as $a$, $b$, $c$, $d$, $e$. No occurrence of all five is known, and we believe it is not possible; the occurring forms are $ace$, $abce$, $acde$, and, when the clause begins with a primary, $ce$ and $cde$. The primary stress always accompanies $c$. If a clause begins with a secondary, immediately followed by a primary, it may be asked whether the pattern is $ace$ or $bce$; we know of no way to answer this question as yet, but believe that $bce$ may well be the answer; of course, if the clause ends as . . . $cde$, then the pattern can only be, we hold, $acde$, since we do not believe that $b$ and $d$ can occur in the same clause. The clause ends in a terminal contour ($T$). The intonation-patterns are then of these forms:

$aceT$
$abceT$
$acdeT$
$bceT$
$ceT$
$cdeT$

Any of the positions may be filled by any one of the four pitches, and $T$ is any of the three contours. It is not known whether all the possible combinations occur; but a good many of them have actually been observed in material spoken naturally and recorded on tape.

In $OES$ the examples given implied that rather long stretches of material could be single clauses with one intonation pattern only. This is probably possible in continued discourse of an oratorical or other literary or technical nature, but we believe that in most ordinary speech the clauses are rather short, and that most long sentences contain many pre-final clauses ending most usually in sustained /|/.

3. A few examples may now be given. These are as ordinarily spoken by the present author.

$aceT$    $^2$Ì'm gôing $^3$hóme$^1$ #
         $^2$Ì'm gôing $^4$hóme$^1$ # (definitely not somewhere else)
         $^2$Ì'm gôing $^3$hóme$^2$|$^2$bùt Ì'll bè $^3$báck$^1$ #
         $^2$Àre yŏu gôing $^3$hóme$^3$ ||

$^2$Ì'm gôing $^3$hóme nôw$^2$ ‖ ... (doubtful, or reticent)

$^2$Whêre ăre yŏu $^3$góing$^2$|$^2$E$^2$lízabeth$^2$ ‖

$^2$Whêre ăre yŏu $^3$góing$^2$|$^1$E$^1$lízabeth$^1$ ‖ (less polite)

$^2$Whô(m) ăre yŏu $^3$cálling$^3$ #$^2$E$^3$lízabeth$^3$ ‖

| | |
|---|---|
| *abceT* | $^2$Ìt's ĭn $^2$châpter $^3$óne$^1$ # |
| | $^2$Hè's ă $^3$gôod $^3$bóy$^1$ # |
| | $^2$Hè's ă $^3$gôod $^2$bóy$^2$|$^2$but ... |
| | $^2$Ìt's ă $^2$lông $^2$stóry$^2$|$^2$ănd ìt'll $^1$bóre yŏu$^1$ # |
| *acdeT* | $^2$Ì'm $^3$góing $^1$hôme$^1$ # |
| | $^2$Ì'm gôing $^2$hóme $^2$nôw$^1$ # |
| | $^2$It's $^2$wón$^3$derful$^1$ # |
| *bceT* | $^2$Châpter $^2$Óne$^1$ # |
| *ceT* | $^3$Álways$^1$ # |
| | $^4$Néver$^1$ # |
| *cdeT* | $^2$Éat $^3$yôur lûnch$^1$ # |

A succession of short clauses:

$^2$Wéll$^2$ ‖$^2$Ì $^2$thínk$^2$|$^2$it'd bè $^2$àll $^3$ríght$^2$|$^2$tŏ $^3$gó $^1$nôw$^1$ #

4. This systematization is based on American English. We have heard enough other varieties, however, and have examined enough of the reported intonation data for them, to be convinced that the system set forth here holds for the whole of the English language. The seeming great differences in the way different kinds of English sound in respect to intonation are due, we believe, to different distributions and occurrences of the pitches and terminals, within the same system. Thus American

$^2$Whô's $^3$thére$^1$ #

and Southern British

$^3$Whô's $^2$thére$^1$ #

are different exemplifications of *aceT*.

### References

Pike, K. L. (1945), *The Intonation of American English*, University of Michigan Press.

Trager, G. L. (1958), 'Paralanguage: a first approximation', *Studies in Linguistics*, vol. 12, pp. 1–12.

Trager, G. L., and Smith, H. L. (1951), *Studies in Linguistics*, occasional papers no. 3, University of Oklahoma Press.

Wells, R. S. (1945), 'The pitch phonemes of English', *Language*, vol. 21, pp. 27–39.

# 5 Robert P. Stockwell

The Role of Intonation: Reconsiderations and other Considerations

A paper written specially for this volume.

In my article on this subject (Stockwell 1960) (written just weeks after my first exposure to transformational theory at the 1958 conference on English grammar at Austin, Texas),[1] two claims were made about intonation in grammar that I very soon came to believe were wrong:

1. (i) That the number of surface phonological phrases tends to correspond one-for-one to the number of deep sentences.

(ii) That choice among alternative intonation contours is on a par with choice among alternative category realizations within the base component: i.e. that one 'chooses' contours as one 'chooses' lexical elements.

There are several kinds of correlation between deep structure and intonation, but nothing as simple as (1.i). On the other hand, neither is intonation a simple function of surface structure, as was assumed by Chomsky and Halle (1968). A good deal of work of recent vintage – in particular Bresnan (1971; 1972), Downing (1970), Pope (1971), Lakoff (1972), Berman and Szamosi (1972) and Bolinger (1972) – has borne on the question of predicting the location and form of intonation contours from levels of deep or shallow structure (and to some extent surface). It is possible that the only aspect of intonation that is predictable from surface structure alone is the range of 'optional phrasing' possibilities (Bierwisch, 1966; Downing, 1970). The other matter on which I believe I was wrong, the choice of meaning differences between contours (i.e. where the difference is not a function of the location of the center of the contour, or of the presence *v.* absence of a contour, but in the actual form of the contour itself), has not received much subsequent clarification.

There were also claims in that early work which I see no reason to retract, though some of them need considerable elaboration:

2. (i) That there is such a thing as a 'neutral' or 'normal' or 'colorless'

1. At which Noam Chomsky presented the 'Transformational Approach to Syntax' that was immediately available in mimeographed form, subsequently published in Hill (1962) and reprinted in Fodor and Katz (1964).

intonation contour for any sentence, serving as a baseline against which all other possible contours are contrastable, and thereby meaningful.[2]

(ii) That it is an intrinsic property of certain transformational rules that they assign to their output an intonation contour (i.e. that not all contours are predictable from inspection of phrase-markers at the surface or any deeper level: that some contours are consequent upon the derivation itself).[3]

(iii) That what is relocated to form 'contrastive stress' is the center of the intonation contour: that the notion 'center of the contour' is a distinct notion within a correct theory of intonation. It should not be collapsed with the notion 'stress' that relates to levels of prominence lower than the major one of each phonological phrase.

(iv) That Prepositions and Personal Pronouns (and, I should have added, several other 'grammatical' or 'functional' classes, like Articles, some

2. It is true that coreferential noun phrases in a sentence require destressing of the second NP, in general, even if the second NP is not an ordinary pronoun: *I voted for Eisenhower even though I didn't much CARE for the general*. The phenomenon of anaphora is closely linked with those of stress reduction and contour-center location. In all such cases, I believe it can still be maintained that there is a 'normal' (non-emphatic) reading which includes, as part of the specification of 'normal', this kind of anaphoric destressing, and that further juggling of the contour center produces a reading which must single out for emphasis, by virtue of its contrast with the normal reading, some otherwise unpredictable item for stress/pitch highlighting (= emphasis).

3. By this I mean, for example, that the rules which perform such operations as inversion of subject and auxiliary to form questions must themselves ASSIGN the appropriate rising contour to their output. The rising contour cannot depend on deep structure, since the underlying form of yes–no questions and of information questions is identical: the difference depends only on where the WH- morpheme is attached (to an NP, either within an adverb such that *at what time → when, at what place → where*, etc., or to the conjunction *either/or* such that WH-*either → whether* in indirect questions, and is zeroed out of direct questions). Nor can the rising contour depend on surface inversion of subject and auxiliary, since the inversion also occurs with initial negatives: *Never have I met such a fool*. Besides the rising contour of certain interrogatives, it appears to me that part of the function of any rules that deal with coreference is, at the very least, to mark repeated coreferential items as [-Contour Center], or some such specification, so that the basic rule of normal contour-center placement, roughly 'Place the main stress (= contour center) on the last stressable item to the right', can apply correctly in the presence of non-pronominal anaphoric elements. There is at least one type of example, observed first (so far as I know) by George Lakoff and called to my attention in this connection by Mona Lindau, where the usual destressing of pronouns and other anaphoric elements is reversed: *Bill kicked JOHN, and then HE kicked HIM*. This is necessary because of the use of contrastive stress twice in the same sentence: *HE* referring to John in contrast to Bill, and *HIM* referring to Bill in contrast to John. Note that these can BE contrastive only by virtue of the 'normal' reading (for the same string in another context) *He KICKED him*, where *he* is Bill and *him* is John. The notion 'contrastive stress' entails, as I see it, a prior notion of 'non-contrastive' or 'normal' or 'neutral' contours.

Auxiliaries, Modals, Conjunctions, certain classes of Particles and Adverbs – in general, all classes which can enter into satellite 'clitic' relationships with Nouns, Verbs and Adjectives [though the matter is not simple: see Kingdon (1958, pp. 170–207)]) are obligatorily destressed (or never receive stress) and do not 'count', as it were, in computation of the center of the *NEUTRAL* contour.

I would like to consider these various claims in relation to subsequent research to see to what degree a coherent theory of intonation has been achieved and to what extent there remain areas largely unilluminated. To discuss them I will distinguish four kinds of questions:

A. The *REPRESENTATION* question: What is the most economical and realistic system of linguistic representation of the intonational facts (i.e. the total set of linguistically negotiable perturbations of pitch and rhythm)?

B. The *NUCLEAR-STRESS* question: On what basis, and to what extent, is the location of the contour *CENTER* to be predicted?[4] (A corollary of this question concerns the prediction of which items can be *de*-stressed. Destressing, and contour center marking, are two sides of the same coin.)

C. The *BOUNDARY* question: On what basis, and to what extent, are the intonational 'pauses' to be predicted? (By 'pause' I mean the

4. By contour center I mean the point at which the pitch contour sharply changes: the pitch skips up, or down. The center need not be the highest pitch level, nor the lowest, but only the point of (relatively) abrupt transition.

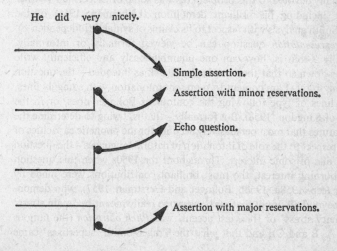

He did very nicely.

Simple assertion.

Assertion with minor reservations.

Echo question.

Assertion with major reservations.

boundaries between intonation contours, which do not correspond with silence, or absence of phonation, or 'breath groups'.) 'Pauses', in the sense here intended, are uniform perceptual realities, but they may not have uniform physical correlates either acoustically or articulatorily: perhaps timing.

D. The *MEANING* question: What is the range of meaning that can be differentiated directly or indirectly by intonational facts? (I shall not deal with this question here. I include within it and the previous one the matter of segregating out the endless variety of 'tone of voice' information that is not negotiated on a strictly linguistic basis. See Stockwell, Bowen, and Silva-Fuenzalida, 1956.)

## A The representation question

The greatest part of the literature on intonation prior to Pike (1945), as well as most of the literature produced in Europe to this date, has focused on the *meaning* question, and of course much of Pike's own work provided lively and insightful analysis of subtle contrasts in meaning that he believed intonation could differentiate. With Pike (1945), Trager and Smith (1951), and Chomsky and Halle (1968), the *representation* question received enormously more attention than it had before. This question naturally entails decisions about the relative weights of various acoustic parameters, in order to minimize the set of prosodic features required and arrive at an optimal phonemic representation. The most recent exemplars of this debate are Vanderslice and Ladefoged (1971). Lieberman (1967) was crucially devoted to this problem (as was some of Lieberman's earlier research, including his brilliant demolition (Lieberman, 1965) of the Trager–Smith analysis with respect to its claims of syntactic independence).

The *representation* question can be viewed formally or informally. Informally – that is, how can one unambiguously and efficiently write sentences down so that they can be read back as intended – the question is not important. I am content to represent intonation with squiggly lines, or with lines of type following the contour as Bolinger does, or in the manner of Kingdon (1958). But formally – that is, trying to determine the set of features that most persuasively account for the phonetic capacities of man, in respect to the role of intonation in natural languages – the question remains one of some interest. Throughout the 1950s when this question was of burning interest, the most brilliant contributions were made by Bolinger (esp. 1958a, 1958b, Bolinger and Gerstman, 1957), who demonstrated beyond all doubt that what everyone really meant by 'main stress' or 'primary stress' or 'heaviest accent' was *Pitch obtrusion* (the famous accents A, B and C); and that what the Trager–Smith 'superfixes' came down to (the famous *lighthouse keeper* examples) could be unambiguously rendered only by appropriate devices of *timing* ('disjuncture').

For reasons which remain mysterious to me, Chomsky and Halle persisted through their major opus in providing ingenious rules that are capable of assigning levels of stress far more finely differentiated than the four that Trager and Smith claimed. The impossibility of finding consistent perceptual correlates for putative contrasts between two (non-nuclear stress) versions of the *blackboard eraser, lighthouse keeper, British history teacher* types of examples has given Vanderslice (1970) rich ammunition for his amusing if sometimes pompous annihilation of the superfixes and their generative-transformational reflexes. Chomsky and Halle took the Trager–Smith data as given, and they undertook originally to show how these complex stress patterns were syntax-dependent.

The Trager–Smith four stresses still remain superficially intact in the latest foray (January 1971) of the Vanderslice–Ladefoged campaign. *Primary* is identified by them as the simultaneous features [+heavy], [+accent], [+intonation] – i.e. it is that accentable syllable which falls at the center of the intonation contour, which is what it always was in Trager and Smith (1951), in Hockett's modification (1958) of their notation, and in the various other treatments the analysis was given (Hill, 1958; Gleason, 1955; Stockwell, Bowen, and Silva-Fuenzalida, 1956; Stockwell 1962, Stockwell and Bowen, 1965). *Secondary* is [+heavy] [+accent] [−intonation] – i.e. 'full articulation with increased respiratory energy causing a pitch obtrusion', which is the same as primary except not at the contour center. *Tertiary* is [+heavy] [−accent] [−intonation] – i.e. everything that's left except the reduced vowels. *Weak* is the reduced vowels (or 'reduced timing', since there is not actual centralization in all instances). One of the Vanderslice–Ladefoged contributions is to point out that there are no viable stress contrasts between secondary and tertiary after the nuclear syllable ('nuclear syllable' is another of the many paraphrases for 'center of the intonation contour'): e.g. (3.i) = (3.ii) unless an optional disjuncture is inserted in (3.i) for just this purpose:

3. (i) He saw a *black* bird, not a *green* one. [Contrastive]

(ii) He saw a *black*bird, not a *crow*. [Compound]

But although they claim (correctly, in my judgement) that the four stresses cannot be used to resolve such ambiguities, they still require four levels of prominence, in all, for English: they transcribe the phrase *elevator operator* as (4.i) (=in Trager–Smith notation (4.ii), = in Chomsky–Halle notation (4.iii)):

4. (i) elevator      operator
   +a −+h−  +h−+h−

(ii) élevàtor òperàtor (TS would write *élevàtor ôperàtor*)

1 4 3 4   3 4 3 4                    1 4 3 4 2 4 3 4
(iii) elevator operator (CH would write *elevator operator*)

If we move the contour center to the left (as in *They MURDERED the elevator operator*), so that the one-stress on the first syllable is downgraded to secondary, then there are still two levels of prominence on this phrase, or any similar one. This is because English allows either full vowels or reduced vowels at the lowest stress level, as in pairs like *typhoon ≠ saloon, buffoon; citation ≠ legation*. The distinction can be made as a function of the 'heaviness' of the vowel – i.e. unaccented syllables can be heavy (have unreduced vowels) or light (have reduced vowels). This solution to the much debated four-stress *v.* three-stress question of the 1950s was adopted some years ago by Householder (1957) and by me in practical work (Stockwell and Bowen, 1965), though until Chomsky and Halle (1968) no one had stated the crucial rule which determines which vowels are reducible and which ones must remain unreduced – and it is THAT insight which is crucial to the Vanderslice and Ladefoged kind of solution.

The levels of prominence that we need to represent are, then, the following, given that vowel qualities are also represented (or predictable by rule):

5. *accented* (=*center of contour = nuclear stress =* Bolinger's *pitch accent =* Trager and Smith *primary =* Chomsky and Halle one-*stress = IPA strong = sentence stress =* Vanderslice and Ladefoged [+intonation, +accent, +heavy])

*Stressed* (=*non-nuclear accentable syllable =* Vanderslice and Ladefoged [−intonation, +accent, +heavy] = Trager and Smith *secondary =* Chomsky and Halle two- and sometimes three-*stress = word stress = IPA medial =* Bolinger's (1958b) 'morphological stress')

*Unstressed* (=everybody's weakest stress, universally acknowledged when the vowel is reduced, sometimes debated in examples like *refugee, canteen, portray, asbestos, typhoon, austere, effigy* where the relevant vowels are not reduced: these are the Vanderslice and Ladefoged [−intonation, −accent, +heavy] syllables, corresponding to Trager–Smith tertiary stress)

For the moment I take as established some version (the details are not important to the remainder of this discussion) of the Vanderslice–Ladefoged (1971) modification of the Chomsky–Halle (1968) rules for word-stress assignment. I think there are not many issues of great moment left under the *representation* question, because so much convincing work was accomplished between Pike (1945) and Vanderslice (1970).

## B The nuclear-stress question

In a recent paper by Joan Bresnan (1971) we have an insight which, if it is correct, is one of the most persuasive and explanatory insights into obvious and familiar data that the MIT school has come up with yet.[5] Whatever the difficulties that she still faces in making her proposal stick in detail (and there are several such, both ones that she is aware of and ones that have been, or shortly will be, pointed out to her by colleagues), the basic insight is so appealing that like some of Chomsky's first ideas about the role of transformations in grammar one feels it just *has* to be right. The relevant data has been around for so long that it's interesting to speculate on the way that scientific insights come about. Clearly, in this case at least it is not a matter of new data, nor even of a new observation about the grammatical relations to be found in the data. Stanley Newman (1946) cited such minimal pairs as

6. (i) I have INSTRUCTIONS to leave

(ii) I have instructions to LEAVE

and pointed out that *BREAD to eat* 'indicates a syntactic relation in which the noun is the logical object of the verb: that is, *breád to eàt* has a relationship with "to eat bread"', whereas in *a desire to EAT*, 'the verb stands in the relation of complement to the noun' (p. 179). One need not translate the preceding into the equivalent transformational jargon to come up with Bresnan's insight: namely, that the accentuation of *INSTRUCTIONS* in (6.i) and the de-accentuation of *to leave* occurs in the deep structure by the regular nuclear-stress rule at a stage prior to the transformation that lifts *INSTRUCTIONS* out of the lower

5. There will be some difficulty, for readers not closely acquainted with recent transformationalist literature, in following all details of the ensuing discussion. I have tried to state the arguments in such a way that a precise understanding of particular rules or terms is not necessary for the purpose of grasping their general import for the theory of grammar. Since this paper was conceived as an updating of my earlier views on the role of intonation in grammar (Stockwell, 1960), and since most of that updating depends on very recent work that has not yet filtered out into the generally available literature, part of what follows here has the flavor of a 'house paper'. For occupants of the house, so to speak, it may appear that I have oversimplified some arguments and even ignored crucial details; and for occupants of houses across the street, it may appear that I have forgotten how to talk any but the in-house language. I can only protest that my simplifications do not deliberately ignore substantive distinctions or consequences, and that I believed them useful and even necessary in order to communicate with the world outside.

sentence and drops it into the object slot of the upper one, into which position it carries along its accentuation; whereas in (6.ii) *LEAVE* is never moved away from its naturally accentuated position.[6]

Bresnan presents three classes of examples:

**7.** *Relative clause* (*v.* Noun complement)

(i) Mary liked the PROPOSAL that George left.[7]

*v.*

(ii) Mary liked the proposal that George LEAVE.[8]

**8.** *Direct and indirect questions* (fronting of stressed Noun *v.* fronting of unstressed Pronoun)[9]

(i) John asked what BOOKS Helen had written.

*v.*

(ii) John asked what Helen had WRITTEN.

(iii) Helen has WRITTEN something. [Contained in 8.ii.]

(iv) What has Helen WRITTEN? [Interrogative of 8.iii]

(v) Helen has written some BOOKS. [Contained in 8.i]

(vi) What BOOKS has Helen written? [Interrogative of 8.v]

(vii) The parable shows what SUFFERING men can create.

*v.*

(viii) The parable shows what suffering-men can CREATE.

6. The NUCLEAR-STRESS RULE (NSR) is a rule of Chomsky and Halle's (1968) that assigns heightened stress to the right-most stressable item in a specified domain – e.g. a phrase or sentence.

7. The phrase *the PROPOSAL that George left* is a Noun Phrase containing a restrictive relative clause: roughly 'a certain proposal which was left somewhere by George'.

8. The phrase *the proposal that George LEAVE* is the nominal equivalent of the sentence *Someone proposed that George (should) leave*.

9. It is assumed that (8.i) and (8.ii) have, as their underlying abstract form, something like

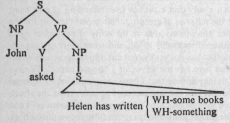

In order to derive the surface sentences from this structure, the object of *has written*, marked with WH-, must be moved to the front of the clause.

## 9. *Reduced relative clause* (*v.* Noun complement)

(i) Helen left DIRECTIONS for George to follow.
[i.e. 'directions such that George could follow them']

*v.*

(ii) Helen left directions for George to FOLLOW.
[i.e. 'directions to the effect that George should follow her']

Bresnan's claim is simply that relative clause formation and question formation are cyclical rules,[10] and that the nuclear-stress rule follows them *IN THE CYCLE* (not necessarily immediately – at the end of the cycle, before last cyclic and post-cyclic rules and of course before the next cycle up.) This device produces the right results by virtue of the peculiar way in which the NSR was formulated originally (as far back as Chomsky–Halle–Lukoff (1956), where it first appeared). The rule doesn't do what one might intuitively think a contour-center-marking rule *ought* to do, namely *add* a pitch-accent to the item that is singled out for the one-to-the-customer privilege (where the customer is a 'phonemic phrase' – i.e. everything between the two nearest boundaries of sufficient status to become intonationally-marked 'pauses'). Rather, the rule *subtracts* stress from the other items in the same phrase, and renders them thenceforth frigid and unresponsive to the possibility of becoming contour centers themselves. They can be weakened further, by subsequent applications of the NSR in higher (i.e. later) cycles – a weakening which is vacuous in terms of its effect on the prosodic qualities of the phonetic output, as already discussed under the representation question – but since the NSR is set up in such a way that it will only operate on items that already *have* maximum stress, they can't be strengthened and they therefore end up as destressed remnants to the *right* of the contour center (as in 7.i, 8.i, 8.vi, 8.viii, and 9.i above).

There are a number of aspects of the Chomsky–Halle formulation of the NSR that deserve comment; but if we ignore details of the rule itself and focus only on the Bresnan claim that the rule applies cyclically, the substantive content of her claim is that in normal, neutral intonation patterns the center of the contour is determined *By the sequential order of items in the deep structure*, such that if a stressable item is the right-most one subject to the NSR, then the stress that it receives is carried with it if it

10. Cyclical rules are, for the present purpose, transformational rules which apply in sequence to the lowest (most deeply embedded) sentence in a phrase-marker, and then reapply to the next higher phrase-marker, and so on. Some rules can be shown to be applicable only in the last or top-most cycle (such as Auxiliary Inversion, which derives *What* IS HE *doing?* from (*I don't know*) *what* HE IS *doing*), whereas others such as Passive Formation must be ordered among the cyclical rules.

is moved to the left by subsequent transformations: by placing the NSR after the cyclic syntactic transformations, Bresnan guarantees that rules within the cycle can move an item without changing the location of the contour center, but movement rules of the next cycle up, or post-cyclic or last-cyclic rules, *will* change the location of the contour center if they move that item to which the contour center has been assigned in the cycle.

Bierwisch (1968) has argued that constituents which are contour centers in the surface structure 'must be specially marked for that property in a very early stage in the syntactic derivation' (p. 177). His arguments had to do with anaphoric elements (with reduced stress consequent upon their anaphoric status within the context) and contrastive stress of various types. His arguments are therefore of a very different type from Bresnan's, even though he anticipates her conclusion, in this respect. It is remarkable how little has been accomplished subsequently in the study of the formal properties of contrastive stress. There is nothing comparable in detail or in conviction to the Chomsky–Halle kinds of proposals about the rules that govern the placement of neutral stress.

Bierwisch does not converge with Bresnan to argue for stress determination prior to surface structure in the case of neutral (non-contrastive) intonation patterns, but only for contrastive ones – or perhaps something more subtle, such as topic/comment marking. Emily Pope (1971), however, does converge by arguing that some syntactic rules that bring about deletions must *follow* rules which assign intonation contours; and the assignment of intonation contours, as she sees it, in turn depends on stress assignment. Her argument depends on contrasts like the following:

10. (i) Yes, happily. [= 'Yes, they are married happily.']

    (ii) Yes, happily. [= 'Yes, they are married, I'm happy to say.']

She claims that 'the process of intonation assignment is a mapping from surface-structure syntactic information to phonetic interpretations' (p. 72), and that it is a phonological phenomenon. I find some of her arguments less than persuasive, specifically (a) that intonation assignment depends on prior stress assignment, and (b) that intonation assignment rules 'take into account brackets but not labels' (p. 73), in that respect resembling the NSR, which she assumes to be a phonological rule *par excellence*. In respect to (a), I merely note that the only way in which intonation depends on prior stress assignment is for determination of the center of the contour; but *what* contour turns up (e.g. rising *v.* falling) in no way depends on the location of the center. It is quite likely that the contour, and its center, are altogether independent phenomena; the center perhaps depends on such factors as the NSR, emphatic stress marking, contrastive stress, or topic/comment marking; and the contour itself depends on factors sometimes very remote from the surface, such as degree of conviction with which an asserted belief is held ('He $^{ma}$y $_{be\ n}i^{ce'}$),' and at other times fairly close to the surface and obvious within the derivation, such as the yes/no interrogative rising intonation (which can be argued to depend either on the presence of some sort of trigger in the deep structure, or a deletable performative, or some special configuration such as WH-*either/or*, roughly 'WH-either he is going, or he is not going' as source of 'Is he going?'). The point is that Pope does not establish anything, in respect to the relation of intonation to the rules of stress assignment, beyond the claim that there is a one-to-one correlation between main stress and the center of an intonation contour: a fact which was not in dispute. There is ample evidence (e.g. Bolinger, 1958a) that the only way main stress is perceived is by virtue of the pitch perturbation that defines the center of the contour. In respect to (b), that intonation assignment rules operate only on brackets, ignoring labels, I follow Bierwisch (1966) in large part, though I believe but cannot demonstrate here in detail that the rules of optional phrasing – those rules which specify the location and form of intonational pauses that are not absolutely obligatory – require category labels to bring about correct downgrading to the status of 'clitic'. It will not be an absolute downgrading, but a relative and hierarchical one. For instance:

11. (i) I want to know how she BUILT it.

(ii) [Slower] I WANT to know HOW she BUILT it.

12. (i) I saw how quickly she BUILT it.

(ii) [Slower] I SAW how QUICKLY she BUILT it.

I take it that *how* in both (11) and (12) has the same node label above it: for (11) there is a deep structure containing 'She built it in some manner', and in (12) there is a deep structure containing 'She built it in a quick manner'. In both cases, WH-attachment to the 'manner' adverbial results in the form *how*. In both, a slowing down of the sentence introduces optional pauses and thereby two more intonation contours than appear in the corresponding faster version. Optional phrasing of this sort, as Bierwisch (1966) has demonstrated, is a highly regular phenomenon. It operates on the general principle that pauses must be introduced between higher ranking constituents before they are introduced between lower ranking ones. The principle has the important qualification that you ignore the ranking of any constituent that has been attached as a clitic, intonationally, to some other constituent. Thus in (11) and (12), the subject pronoun is attached as a clitic to the following verb. Therefore the slower version of the sentences does not introduce pause between the two highest constituents. Pronouns always look for a prop to support them. They are stressable only when the prop has been removed, or when they are contiguous with even less able-bodied categories (like prepositions or conjunctions), as in the phrase *between you and me*.

Returning now to (11.ii) and (12.ii), and considering examples like *between you and me* at the same time, it would appear to be impossible to state the conditions of optional phrasing without reference to category labels. Bierwisch has no examples of this type, and I am unable to make his rules (which make no reference to category labels) serve for these examples.

Pope's paper, then, sets out to show that there are phonological processes, namely intonation assignment, which must precede some syntactic transformations. If correct, this would provide another case like Bresnan's. Pope's claim that intonation assignment precedes some syntactic rules seems to be correct up to a point. There is no conceivable way in which the intonational contrast between (10.i) and (10.ii) could be assigned on the basis of surface syntactic information alone. The surface syntactic information is presumably identical. It follows either that intonation assignment is not a purely phonological process, or that in the course of the derivation of (10.i) and (10.ii) some tag is left behind (when the deletion occurs) to identify the contrast, or that intonation assignment is a phonological rule that applies before some syntactic rules (Pope's view). I think Pope has chosen the least persuasive of the three possible consequences of her evidence. I myself think the first alternative is correct. Some of the current leading MIT linguists like Postal, Ross and Lakoff are more likely to go along with the second alternative (of which a variant would be a so-called global or trans-derivational constraint). But I have no evidence to provide, yet, that would choose between the alternatives.

Even if Pope's arguments do not establish the position that phonological rules can be interspersed with syntactic ones, Bresnan's case, if solid, *would* do so. But her case is in fact a rather spongy one. Her evidence turns out to be either wrong, or internally so inconsistent that one has to reject any conclusion based on it.

In Kingdon (1958, p. 205) there are pairs like these:

13. (i) Introduce me to the man you were TALKING to.

(ii) I'll lend you that BOOK I was talking about.

One can dream up indefinitely many examples like (13.i) in which the non-contrastive contour center location is on the last accentable item of the relative clause.[11] All of them should be instances of *contrastive* stress, under Bresnan's hypothesis (cf. (7) above). George Lakoff (1972) has noted comparable examples (p. 286):

14. (i) Teddy is the only capitalist I would ever VOTE for.

(ii) Teddy is the only CAPITALIST I would ever vote for.

(14.i) is an especially persuasive counterexample because *capitalist* is not an obvious candidate for anaphora (and therefore unlikely to be destressed). Yet it is clear that (14.ii), not (14.i), is contrastive: it implies that the speaker would vote for any *non*-capitalist.

Counterexamples like (13) and (14), where Bresnan's hypothesis wrongly predicts that the last NP in the relative clause will remain the contour center after it is fronted, are reinforced by counterexamples to her second class of cases, the direct and indirect questions (8):

15. (i) He works for a chain of GROCERY stores.
What chain of grocery stores does he WORK for?
I asked what chain of grocery stores he WORKED for.

(ii) He established a new TRADITION.
What new tradition did he ESTABLISH?

or

What new TRADITION did he establish?

(iii) He bought a new dress for someone's WIFE.
Whose wife did he buy a new DRESS for?

It appears, in fact, that only a direct object allows a non-contrastive reading when it carries the contour center forward – and even that is not always obligatory, as in (15.ii). In (15.i) and (15.iii), the object of the preposition, even though at contour center when final, clearly cannot carry the contour center to the left, except contrastively. Lakoff (1972) has many examples like (15), and he has devised a particularly clever example which demonstrates that if an NP can be read ambiguously as direct object or prepositional object (within, e.g. a benefactive adverb), the direct object reading is preferred if the NP is fronted along with its stress, whereas the other

11. Bresnan's paper was the central subject of my seminar on English intonation in the winter quarter of 1970–71. During that seminar, my students – in particular Carol Lord – and I discovered these and other counterexamples. At the same time, and independently, George Lakoff in Michigan was writing the paper to which some of the following discussion is devoted. The degree of our convergence is apparent below. I am most grateful to him for his willingness to make the paper available to me prior to publication.

reading is preferred if the contour center is retained on the final accentable item:

16. (i) The men are competing for some countries.
[*ambiguous*: the countries may be their potential awards, or merely their sponsors]

(ii) What countries are the men COMPETING for?
[= Who is sponsoring the men?]

(iii) What COUNTRIES are the men competing for?
[= What countries make up the list of prizes?]

A similar, but less natural, example had occurred to us:

17. (i) The professor looked over a book.
[*ambiguous*: he glanced through it, or it was interrupting his direct line of vision]

(ii) What book did the professor look OVER?

(iii) What BOOK did the professor look over?

Such examples establish beyond any doubt that Bresnan's claim is too broad: it is not the case that final contour-center nouns carry the contour center to the left with them when they get fronted. They do so only if they are direct objects – and even then not always. Lakoff points to such examples as (18):

18. (i) Whose UMBRELLA have I taken?
[Predicted correctly by Bresnan's hypothesis]

(ii) Whose book did the reviewer CRITICIZE?
[Not correctly predicted; somehow the heavier verb affects the decision.]

(iii) Which CAR did he buy?
[Predicted correctly if we ignore Bresnan's own statement that NPs with *which* are not supposed to follow her prediction.]

(iv) Which car did the timid little clerk who works in our office BUY?
[I think that the neutral contour would have its center on *office*, which is what Bresnan would predict if you ignore her qualification about *which*; but Lakoff marks it on *buy*.]

Lakoff does not have any new light to cast on Bresnan's third class of examples (9). He notes that J. R. Ross in a class at MIT in 1967 made the correct observation about (19),

19. (i) John has PLANS to leave.

(ii) John has plans to LEAVE.

that in (19.i) *plans* is underlying direct object of *leave*, and that this fact somehow accounts for its stress. But this observation goes back at least to Newman (1946), as Ross was no doubt well aware even though it is not mentioned by Lakoff.

Lakoff's own solution (Lakoff, 1972) is apparently adequate to the evidence, though unsatisfying because it merely lists a set of curious facts within a global constraint[12] and provides no explanatory account of them. The constraint does, however, block a class of counterexamples to Bresnan's hypothesis which we have not dealt with so far, and which Lakoff was the first to observe:

20. (i) It is likely that he'll solve those PROBLEMS.

(ii) *Which PROBLEMS is it likely that he'll solve?

(iii) Which problems is it likely that he'll SOLVE?

[Bresnan introduces an irrelevancy here: she excludes examples with *which* from her predictions. But the example is just as damaging with *what*: 'What problems is it likely that he'll SOLVE?']

The Lakoff global constraint sets up three conditions under which an NP will be allowed to carry its contour-center-hood forward with it:

21. (i) In logical structure it is a direct object;[13]

(ii) In shallow structure it has no clause-mates following it;[14] and

(iii) In surface structure it is a clause-mate of its logical predicate.

It is condition (21.iii) which blocks (20.ii). Condition (21.ii) merely guarantees that it is final (and therefore subject to the NSR). And condition (21.i) is the fundamental condition that distinguishes those examples of Bresnan's which are valid from the classes of counterexamples cited in (13)–(18) above. It is also the condition that seems quite *ad hoc* and non-explanatory to me, though I have nothing better to offer.

Before leaving the nuclear-stress question, we should look again at examples like (6), (9) and (19):

12. A global constraint is one which applies across two or more stages of a derivation; i.e. one which is not statable as a constraint on the operation of a particular transformational rule, but must hold across several stages, even across intervening rules to which it is irrelevant. Since a constraint of this form enormously enriches the power of a grammatical theory (and thereby weakens the claims the theory can make), one allows it only in the face of compelling evidence.

13. By 'logical structure' what is meant is 'deepest, most abstract representation – hopefully corresponding to the logical semantic structure'.

14. 'Shallow structure' is that level of abstract representation that exists after all but last-cyclic and post-cyclic rules have applied. 'Clause-mate' has the apparent sense, namely 'constituent in the same clause'.

6. (i) I have INSTRUCTIONS to leave.

(ii) I have instructions to LEAVE.

9. (i) Helen left DIRECTIONS for George to follow.

(ii) Helen left directions for George to FOLLOW.

19. (i) John has PLANS to leave.

(ii) John has plans to LEAVE.

Unlike the other classes of examples, there is no quibbling about these. Furthermore, the Lakoff constraint (21.ii) does not hold for this class:

22. (i) I have INSTRUCTIONS to leave with Mary.

(ii) I have INSTRUCTIONS to leave on the airplane.

(iii) John has PLANS to leave here this afternoon.

And of course, since Lakoff's constraint (21.ii) merely formalizes the distributional fact which would allow Bresnan to apply the NSR to it, it follows that these examples are somewhat mysterious under either the Bresnan hypothesis or the Lakoff global constraint. Lakoff's constraint (21.i), that the contour center must be a direct object in logical structure, would appear to relate these examples to the ordinary relative clause and interrogative examples. But why does this class, alone, ignore clause-mates following it, any of which can be contour centers in other forms of the sentences:

23. (i) He left the instructions with MARY.
(cf. 22.i)

(ii) He left the instructions on the AIRPLANE.
(cf. 22.ii)

(iii) He left the plans here this AFTERNOON.

I can offer some weak evidence that the contour center of (6.i), (9.i) and (19.i) has nothing at all to do with having been an object of the lower verb in logical structure (and therefore nothing to do with cyclical application of the NSR). Consider sentences closely related to (9):

24. (i) Helen left DIRECTIONS, and George is to FOLLOW them.

(ii) Helen left DIRECTIONS. George can FOLLOW them (if he wants to).

(iii) Helen left DIRECTIONS (which George can follow if he wants to).

I think (24.iii) is closest to exemplifying my proposal: the low-pitch tag in (9) is the remnant of a fuller parenthesis: the entire parenthesis in (24.iii) would normally receive low pitch throughout – I think it is a separate contour with *follow* at the center, marked not necessarily by pitch obtrusion but by timing. If there are necessarily two contours in such sentences, *directions* would form the center of the first one (by the ordinary NSR), and the pitch drop would be a consequence of a parenthesis rule that is needed anyway – which may then, when truncated sufficiently, as in . . . *PLANS to leave*, appear to be a destressed final segment of a single contour.

## C The boundary question

Without pretending to do justice to a long and excellent dissertation (Downing, 1970), I can outline a hypothesis that has a great deal of generality going for it. The interest it has in relation to Bresnan and Pope is apparent from the following quotation (p. 204):

Although phonological phrase boundaries have only phonological effects, they must be assigned prior to the application of certain late transformational rules of the syntactic component. Therefore it must be concluded that independently motivated aspects of syntactic surface structure are not sufficient for the operation of phonological rules: some aspects at least of surface structure are determined exclusively by the necessity of providing input to the phonological rules that specify prosodic features . . .

Thus Downing adds to the clamor of Bresnan and Pope that intonation cannot be assigned from surface structure alone. He takes as the basis for his own position a claim of Emonds (1970) that 'a characteristic of root sentences is to be set off by commas' (8). Emonds's notion 'root sentence' is somewhat redefined by Downing, because Emonds's definition would include extraposed clauses, as in (25):

25. (i) It bothered him that she was intelligent.

(ii)

$$S_0$$
NP   VP   $S_1$

If root sentences are to be set off by commas (i.e. are to receive a separate intonation contour), (25) must be excluded. Downing's definition, then, is that a root sentence is not commanded by a VP node.[15] Given this definition, he inserts phrase boundaries, which indicate where the intonation contour will start and stop, at both ends of every root sentence. The rule that inserts these boundaries applies *after* the cyclic rules and *before* certain

15. The notion 'command' in this context means only that the given sentence is not dominated by a VP node nor a sister of a VP node.

post-cyclic rules. It works without any *ad hoc* quality to explain the intonational pauses in conjoined sentences:

26. (i) John bought the candy/and Mary ate it.

(ii) I told you that John bought the candy and Mary ate it.

In (26.i) the comma pause is (pretty much) obligatory – a fact which is explained by Downing's hypothesis, since the conjunction joins two root sentences. In (26.ii) no comma pause occurs, because the conjoined sentences embedded as object of *tell* are not root sentences. This is Downing's crucial observation; he then looks at other instances of obligatory pause, and tries to make them all fit the same hypothesis – a reasonable scientific procedure. One always wants to be absolutely forced by one's data to add any more machinery to the shop-full that one already has. In Downing's case, the procedure leads down an increasingly rocky and hazardous trail, however, and as he gets further away from basic conjunction, he becomes less and less persuasive.

The case beyond conjunction that looks best is adverb preposing, as in (27) (from Downing, 1970, p. 83):

27. (i) When John phones, the girls talk to him.

(ii) When John phones the girls, talk to him.

(iii) When John phones the girls talk to him.

(27.iii) is thrown in only to show that the comma pause, either way, truly *is* obligatory. But the natural order of these adverbs is final, and a pause is not obligatory:

28. (i) The girls talk to him when John phones.
The girls talk to John when he phones.

(ii) Talk to John when he phones the girls.
(?)Talk to $him_1$ when $John_1$ phones the girls.

But hold a moment: *is* it the case that any of the sentences of (28) can be spoken naturally with only one intonation contour? Downing thinks so; I think it is possible that the sentences are all two-contour sentences, with the second contour being a low-level one:

29. (i) The girls $^{TALK}$ to $_{John}$ / when he PHONES.

(ii) $T_{A_{L_K}}$ to $_{John}$ / when he phones the GIRLS.

If this is a correct observation – we will examine more data below – notice what would follow: there would be no need for insertion of phrase boundaries when the adverbial sentence is fronted. Each intonation pattern *has* a boundary in (29): what happens is that the intonation pattern *itself* is changed by the fronting rule, and Downing has interpreted this as boundary insertion:

30. (i) When he $PHONE^S$ / the girls $TALK$ to John.

   (ii) When he phones the $GIRL^S$ / $TALK$ to John.

We now have two questions: (a) by what device does Downing insert phrase boundaries when adverbial sentences are fronted (assuming that they do *not* have separate intonation patterns when they are not fronted)? (b) what kind of evidence will decide whether such adverbs have separate intonation patterns in their pristine (unfronted) state?

Downing's device is to formulate all the relevant transformations as attaching the fronted element by means of Chomsky adjunction rather than sister adjunction.[16] Thus:

31. (i)

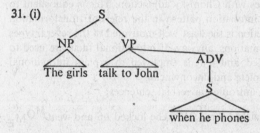

16. One of the central problems of 'classical' transformational theory is that of assigning a correct structure to the output of a transformational rule. In 'sister adjunction', a node is attached to the left or right of some daughter node (hence the term 'sister'). Thus in (31.i), sister adjunction would yield

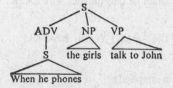

with the preposed adverb adjoined as left sister of NP. Chomsky adjunction, on the other hand, creates an additional node by COPYING the node which already dominates the node to which the moved item would be adjoined by sister adjunction, as shown in (31.ii), thus yielding an extra 'layer' of structure.

(ii)

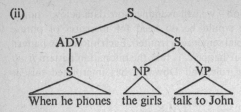

When he phones    the girls    talk to John

Quite simply, by Chomsky adjunction he turns a non-root sentence into a root sentence. He is of course honest about the *ad hoc* character of this device (p. 205):

'It is not possible to predict which particular transformations will employ Chomsky adjunction; rather it is necessary to specify Chomsky adjunction, sister adjunction, etc., as part of the structural change of each particular movement transformation. It appears in fact that individuals may employ different types of adjunction (as revealed in phrasing) in what is essentially the same transformation, e.g. in adverb preposing.'

It appears to me that the device is then circular as well as *ad hoc*: if you know from the surface output that you need a separate intonation pattern, set up the relevant rules with Chomsky adjunction. This is equivalent to *assigning* the separate intonation pattern in the relevant transformation itself. Chomsky adjunction is the least well-motivated of the several types of elementary transformations, anyway. If intonational facts are used to decide when it is needed, and if it is employed to explain intonational facts, the circle is complete and unconvincing.

Let us look at some unfronted adverbial sentences:

32. (i) When he had finished this $^{TA}S^K$ / he locked up and went $^{HO}M_E$

(Downing 1970, p.53 – intonation supplied).

(ii) He locked up and went $^{HO}M_E$ / when he had finished this TASK.

33. (i) Since you are an old friend of the $^{FA}M_I LY$ you have a

right to $^{KN}O_W$ (p. 53, intonation supplied).

(ii) You have a right to $^{KN}O_W$ since you are an old friend of

the FAMILY.

34. (i) Just as she fired the $^{PI}S_{TO}L$ Bill came into the $^{RO}O_{M}$.

(ii) Bill came into the $^{RO}O_{M}$ just as she fired the $^{PI}S_{TO_L}$.

35. (i) 'AM $_{I}$' Hilda SAID 'PREG$^{NANT}$?'

(ii) Hilda SAID, 'Am I PREG$^{NANT}$?'

These have been chosen to illustrate the following claims of mine: (a) that it is utter nonsense to suppose (with Chomsky–Halle, 1968) that the NSR can go right on applying cyclically and reducing the non-main-stressed items further and further – the limit of phrase length is rather narrow (the same point is made by Bierwisch (1968), though he apparently would go much further down the road of 1-2-3-4-5-6-7 stress reduction than I would, and he says nothing about the boundary limitation problem that is inextricably tied to the NSR-repetition problem); (b) that pitch-lowering (of the whole embedded contour) is obligatory with parenthetical items like (35.i), and this fact is not expressible as a function of phrase-boundary-insertion conventions;[17] (c) that the number of intonation contours, if you grant me level contours in (32) and (33), corresponds, in this class of examples, to the number of un-deformed deep sentences.

Of course, if (c) is correct, and can be extended (e.g. by rules which erase intonation patterns only under specified conditions with the transformations themselves, so that transformational rules do much the same thing in respect to intonation that they do in respect to other aspects of structure, namely reduce depth and eliminate structure in various ways – but not build or add structure), then one of my first hypotheses would be partially regenerated (see Stockwell, 1960). But a much wider range of cases has to be examined before such a claim can be supported, and I shall not do so here: I seek only to cast doubt on the kind of approach that Downing espouses, and encourage research in a less *ad hoc* direction.

It should be clear by now that we have not achieved a coherent theory of intonation in relation to syntax yet. But a great deal of interesting progress has been made, and intonation is, after several years of neglect, suddenly quite central again in syntactic discussions.

17. This observation has been made in the traditional literature on intonation repeatedly – I am not sure where I got it, though I owe it most recently to Peter Ladefoged in the seminar noted earlier.

## References

BERMAN, A., and SZAMOSI, M. (1972), 'Observations on sentential stress', *Language*, vol. 48, pp. 304–25.

BIERWISCH, M. (1966), 'Regeln für die Intonation Deutscher Sätze', *Studia Grammatica*, vol. 7, pp. 99–201.

BIERWISCH, M. (1968), 'Two critical problems in accent rules', *J. Linguistics*, vol. 4, pp. 173–6.

BOLINGER, D. L. (1958a), 'A theory of pitch accent in English', *Word*, vol. 14, pp. 109–49.

BOLINGER, D. L. (1958b), 'Stress and information', *American Speech*, vol. 33, pp. 5–20.

BOLINGER, D. L. (1972), 'Accent is predictable (if you're a mind-reader)', *Language*, vol. 48, pp. 633–44.

BOLINGER, D. L., and GERSTMAN, L. J. (1957), 'Disjuncture as a cue to constructs', *Word*, vol. 13, pp. 246–55.

BRESNAN, J. W. (1971), 'Sentence stress and syntactic transformations', *Language*, vol. 47, no. 2, pp. 257–81.

BRESNAN, J. W. (1972), 'Stress and syntax: a reply', *Language*, vol. 48, pp. 326–42.

CHOMSKY, N. A., and HALLE, M. (1968), *The Sound Pattern of English*, New York, Harper & Row.

CHOMSKY, N. A., and LUKOFF, F. (1956), 'On accent and juncture in English', in M. Halle (ed.), *For Roman Jakobson*, Mouton.

DOWNING, B. T. (1970), 'Syntactic structure and phonological phrasing in English', University of Texas dissertation, unpublished.

EMONDS, J. E. (1970), 'Root and structure-preserving transformations', MIT dissertation, unpublished.

FODOR, J. A., and KATZ, J. J. (1964), 'The structure of language', Prentice-Hall.

GLEASON, H. A. (1955), *An Introduction to Descriptive Linguistics*, Holt, Rinehart & Winston.

HILL, A. A. (1958), *Introduction to Linguistic Structures: From Sound to Sentence in English*, Harcourt Brace Jovanovich.

HILL, A. A. (1962), *Proceedings of the Third Texas Conference on Problems of Linguistic Analysis in English, 1958*, University of Texas Press.

HOCKETT, C. F. (1958), *A Course in Modern Linguistics*, Macmillan.

HOUSEHOLDER, F. W. (1957), 'Accent, juncture, intonation, and my grandfather's reader', *Word*, vol. 13, pp. 234–45.

KINGDON, R. (1958), *The Groundwork of English Intonation*, Longmans.

LAKOFF, G. (1972), 'The global nature of the nuclear stress rule', *Language*, vol. 48, pp. 285–303.

LIEBERMAN, P. (1965), 'On the acoustic basis of the perception of intonation by linguists', *Word*, vol. 21, pp. 40–54.

LIEBERMAN, P. (1967), *Intonation, Perception and Language*, MIT Press.

NEWMAN, S. (1946), 'On the stress system of English', *Word*, vol. 2, pp. 171–87.

PIKE, K. L. (1945), *The Intonation of American English*, University of Michigan Press.

POPE, E. (1971), 'Answers to yes–no questions', *Linguistic Inquiry*, vol. 2, pp. 69–82.

STOCKWELL, R. P. (1960), 'The place of intonation in a generative grammar of English', *Language*, vol. 36, pp. 360–67.

STOCKWELL, R. P. (1962), 'On the analysis of English intonation', *Proceedings of the Second Texas Conference on Problems of Linguistic Analysis in English*, ed. A. A. Hill, University of Texas Press.

STOCKWELL, R. P., and BOWEN, J. D. (1965), *The Sounds of English and Spanish*, University of Chicago Press.

STOCKWELL, R. P., BOWEN, J. D., and SILVA-FUENZALIDA, I. (1956), 'Spanish juncture and intonation', *Language*, vol. 32, pp. 641–65.

TRAGER, G. L., and SMITH, H. L. (1951), 'An outline of English structure', *Studies in Linguistics,* Occasional Paper No. 1.

VANDERSLICE, R. (1970), 'Occam's razor and the so-called stress cycle', *Language Sciences*, vol. 13, pp. 9–15 (Indiana University Research Center for the Language Sciences).

VANDERSLICE, R., and LADEFOGED, P. (1971), 'Binary suprasegmental features', UCLA Working Papers in Phonetics, vol. 17, pp. 6–24.

Robert P. Stockwell 109

# 6 David Crystal

## The Intonation System of English

Adapted from David Crystal, *Prosodic Systems and Intonation in English*, Cambridge University Press, 1969, pp. 195–252.

### The parametric approach

Intonation is viewed, not as a single system of contours, levels, etc., but as a complex of features from different prosodic systems. These vary in their relevance, but the most central are *tone, pitch range* and *loudness*, with *rhythmicality* and *tempo* closely related. Scholars have been anxious to restrict the formal definition of intonation to pitch movement alone (though occasionally allowing in stress variation as well); but when the question of intonational meanings is raised, then criteria other than pitch are readily referred to as being part of the basis of a semantic effect. This is a theoretically undesirable situation; either one adopts a relatively narrow definition of the phenomenon, and simplifies the formal description of intonation at the expense of the semantic, or one allows intonation a wider definition, with resultant increasing complexity in the formal stage, but an ultimately less involved semantic statement. The parametric approach in principle follows the latter course, but tries to do justice to the former by giving priority to those prosodic systems involving pitch movement (namely, *tone* and *pitch range*); in this way, one does not exclude features from other systems when these are made use of, along with pitch, to produce a given grammatical, accentual or attitudinal effect. Intonation, then, refers to a phenomenon which has a very clear centre of pitch contrast, and a periphery of reinforcing (and occasionally contradicting) contrasts of a different order. The point at which pitch contrast becomes completely subordinated to vocal or non-vocal effects of a different nature is the point at which intonation gives way to other communicational systems.

It has long been realized that, within the prosodic contrasts of English, some features are more noticeable and seem to carry more semantic 'weight' than others.

Some intonational categories are perceptually more distinct and linguistically more replicable than others, and this gradation seems to correlate with degrees of linguistic importance. It was shown (Quirk and Crystal, 1966) that, when native speakers were presented with the task of repeating an utterance, there was maximum agreement (84·8 per cent) over the location of tone-unit boundaries; agreement over tonicity (the placing of the nucleus within the tone group) was 81·6 per cent; onset location (the first prominent point in the tone unit) yielded an agreement of 77·3 per cent; and the exponent of nucleus (the nucleus syllable) an agreement of 74·4 per cent. Within the category of *tone* (the pitch movement of the tone group, not just the nucleus), it was clear that the polarity was most extreme between fall and rise, i.e. the distinction between these had clearest phonological status, and that the remaining nuclei tended to cluster into two groups, depending on whether they were more fall-like or rise-like. Rise-fall seemed to relate primarily to falling-type tones; fall–rise and fall–plus–rise to rising-type. Generalizing from these and other results, I would postulate a major division of nuclear tones into two types, *falling* (comprising simple, complex and compound tones, the final direction of pitch movement being downward in each case) and *rising* (again comprising simple, complex and compound tones, but the final direction of pitch movement being upward). The category of level tone retains an ambiguous status and must be discussed separately. Finally, from the ways in which native speakers reacted differently to the utterance they had as a model – particularly from their misidentifications and substitutions, which showed significant consistency – it becomes evident that what we are dealing with in intonational analysis is not a single system of contrasts increasing in delicacy until all contrasts are accounted for, but a 'system of systems', interacting in different ways, in different degrees at different places within the tone unit.

One thing emerges quite clearly: the most readily perceivable, recurrent, maximal functional unit to which linguistic meanings can be attached (in the present state of our knowledge) is the tone unit. It is the obvious place to start any examination of the English intonation system.

## The tone unit

To analyse English speech into a sequence of non-overlapping tone units means in effect to define their boundaries. In English there seem to be regular definable phonological boundaries for tone units in normal speech. Given that each tone unit will have one peak of prominence in the form of a nuclear pitch movement (as explained below), then after this nuclear tone there will be a tone-unit boundary which is indicated by two phonetic factors. Firstly, there will be a perceivable pitch change, either stepping up or stepping down, depending on the direction of nuclear tone movement – if falling, then step-up; if rising, then step-down; if level, either, depending on its relative height. This is due to the fact that the onset of each tone unit in a speaker's utterance is at more or less the same pitch level. The second criterion is the presence of junctural features at the end of every tone unit. This usually takes the form of a very slight pause, but there are frequently accompanying segmental phonetic modifications (variations in length, aspiration, etc.) which reinforce this. These phonological criteria suffice to indicate unambiguously where a tone-unit boundary should go in connected speech in the vast majority of cases.

There is a general agreement about the internal structure of the tone unit in English. Miminally, a tone unit must consist of a syllable, and this syllable must carry a glide of a particular kind. This is the obligatory element, and is usually referred to (in the British tradition) as the *nucleus* of the tone unit. The presence of a nucleus is what accounts for our intuition of 'completeness' at the end of the unit: if it is omitted, the auditory effect is one of 'being cut short'. Maximally, the tone unit may consist of three other segments: the head, the pre-head and the tail.

The *head* of the unit refers to the stretch of utterance extending from the first stressed and usually pitch-prominent syllable (or onset) up to, but not including, the nuclear tone. It consists of an unspecified number of stressed and unstressed syllables (at least one of the former).

The *prehead*, or pre-onset, refers to any utterance which precedes the onset syllable within the same tone unit. It consists of an unspecified number of unstressed syllables (at least one), but occasionally, under certain conditions, syllables with some slight degree of stress (not equivalent to the stress of the onset syllable, and never with pitch-prominence) may occur there.

The *nuclear tail* consists of an unspecified number of stressed or unstressed syllables (at least one of either) following the nuclear syllable, usually continuing the pitch movement unbrokenly until the end of the tone unit. In such cases, being wholly conditioned by the nuclear tone, the tail has no inherent linguistic contrastivity, and only degrees of stress may be distinguished within it.

We may now make a characterization of a tone unit's maximal internal structure as being:

Prehead   Head   *Nucleus*   Tail

the only obligatory element being the item in italics. A tone unit accordingly may be internally defined as a structure consisting of one of the following: P(rehead), H(ead), N(ucleus), T(ail); PHN, PN, HN, PNT, HNT, etc., summarizable as (P)(H)N(T), where brackets include optional elements.

## Tone

Every tone unit contains one and only one nucleus, or peak of prominence, expounded by one of a finite number of contrasting pitch glides or sustentions on the accentual syllable of the most prominent word. It has been called sentence stress, but this is misleading, as the tone unit is seldom co-extensive with a sentence, or even a clause. *Tone* may be seen from the point of view of its placement within the utterance (tonicity) and its directional type. Nuclear tones are divided into three main types: simple, compound and complex.

*Simple.* Here we include three types of unidirectional pitch movement, rising, falling and level, the centre of prominence being at the beginning of the glide. If there is a tail the direction of the pitch movement is usually sustained without change throughout. Any such distinction as that made between 'high' and 'low' varieties of simple tone is not thought of as basically a question of tonal selection, however, but as a combination of relative height from the *pitch-range* system plus pitch movement – falling tone plus relatively high starting-point or relatively low starting-point respectively. The 'high'/'low' distinction is thus primarily a matter of simple *pitch range*. The corollary of this is interesting; there are accordingly as many contrastive types of simple fall, let us say, as there are contrastive degrees of pitch height: as many as seven. This does not force us to distinguish systemically seven types of simple fall in English, however. In view of the fact that the simple *pitch-range* features may occur elsewhere in the tone unit than with the nucleus, but with the same contrastive force, and that the same pitch-range feature produces identical contrasts in different nuclear tones, it is clearly more economical to take the *pitch-range* contrasts separately. Out of seven possible simple *pitch-range* features, one is selected, within any tone unit, which determines the beginning-point of the tone. The 'meaning' of the tone, if one might put it crudely, is thus a combination of the 'meaning' of the simple *pitch-range* feature selected plus the 'meaning' of the nucleus.

Combining falling tone with the simple *pitch-range* system does not account for all the falling contrasts found in the data, however. There is a further independently varying possibility for falling and rising tones, namely, of co-occurrence with the complex *pitch-range* system.[1] If one examines the width of a nuclear tone in the data, three main types become apparent: the vast majority of the tones have a fairly consistent width, which we may call X; the remainder have a width perceptibly narrower or wider than X. There seems to be only one degree of widening and narrowing with any contrastive force in English. Once again, however, instead of calling ⟨ ,⟨ and ⌒ three 'different' nuclear tones within the tone system, it is better, in view of the fact that wide and narrow contrasts also apply to

1. The simple pitch-range system embraces the differences in pitch between one syllable and the next. The complex pitch-range system is the width of a tonal movement (widened, narrowed or monotone).

non-nuclear stretches of utterance, to postulate complex *pitch range* as a separate system. The majority of tones co-occur with the unmarked complex *pitch-range* feature X, and this may therefore be called the norm.

The same arguments apply to other nuclear tones. Restricting ourselves to the simple kinetic tones for the moment, we may summarize the possibilities of occurrence as follows (∅ stands for the unmarked terms in the simple and complex *pitch-range* systems):

| *Beginning-point* | *Range* | *Tone* |
|---|---|---|
| Relatively high ↑↑, ↑ | Wide (*w*) | Falling (ˋ) |
| Medium ↑, → | Normal (∅) | Rising (ˊ) |
| Relatively low ∅, ↓, ↓ | Narrow (*n*) | |

e.g. ∅ + ∅ + ˋ    ↑ + *w* + ˋ

↑ + ∅ + ˋ    ↑ + *n* + ˋ

∅ + *n* + ˋ

These discriminations are made without any reference to the ending-point of the nuclear glide. There are relatively few contrasts which can be made using the end-point compared with the range of contrasts elsewhere, partly because of the formal indeterminacy which exists at the end of a glide. It is usually immaterial how far a low fall falls, for example, this being largely a matter of physiological vocal range. It is the relative pitch height of the whole tone within the tone unit and the width of the tone which are linguistically the most important features, and the determining factor in this is the beginning-point of the glide.

One should note two further points, one phonetic, one functional. First, extra stress may affect a simple tone, particularly if it has a high beginning-point, to produce a tone which has a phonetic shape similar to a complex tone. ↑ˋ is often realized phonetically as ⁀ . This form is not normally confused with the complex tone, however, for one of two reasons: either the relative loudness of points within the pitch movement is clearly different in the two cases – ⁀ as opposed to ⁊ ; or the extent of the on-glide is much less – ⁀ as opposed to ⁀ . Secondly, some of the tones emerging from this classification are much more frequent than is normally supposed. A case in point is what one might call the high-mid falling tone ‾⁀ , which occurs often in the normal course of serious conversation. When a speaker is agreeing, usually non-committally (for example 'yes', 'hm', 'really'), to points being made in a discussion, his response-utterances tend to take this pattern.

*Level tone.* In English there is often (actually, in about 8 per cent of all cases) clear evidence of a tone-unit boundary, but no audibly kinetic tone preceding. In such a circumstance two courses are open: either one may classify the phenomenon as a further kind of head, or one may call one of the preceding level tones nuclear. The weight of evidence seems to force the second solution, for the following six reasons.

1. One of the level tones is always more prominent than the others, and equivalent to the prominence of kinetic nuclei; it does not seem possible to reduce this prominence and retain an acceptable tone unit. Also, the syllable on which it occurs is lengthened substantially, and there is a clear rhythmical break between what precedes and what follows.

2. This tone nearly always occurs on the last lexical item before the phonetic boundary, and is thus distributionally similar to kinetic tones.

3. If this tone occurs at the end of a subordinate or correlative grammatical structure, it admits of replacement by (usually) a rising-type tone. For example:[2]

```
            I |readily adMÌT this| - that |if you in'flict ‖corporal
'staccato'  PÙNishment|’ · with|in the qualifi'cations that I’ve
'lento'     de↑FĪNED| - ‘it is |going to · re'form · the THÙG|’ . . .
            |crimes of ↑vìolence| in |‖GÈNeral| - |‖decreased
            ↑MÁRkedly | · be|tween 'eighteen NĪNEty| and ‘|nineteen
'spiky'     'thirty FÒUR|’
```

Level here seems to be functioning as a 'marked' form of rise.

4. In non-subordinate structures the level tone has a range of meanings (boredom, sarcasm, etc.) quite distinct from the types of meaning carried by tone-unit heads, and very similar in force to other nuclear semantic functions.

5. A tone unit with a level tone of the above characteristics is acceptable to native speakers, and does not sound 'incomplete', such as would be the case if a kinetic tone had simply been dropped. Compare the effect of stopping after the word 'time' in the following pair of utterances: only the second admits a deliberate pause.

Once upon a time there were three bears

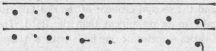

<hr />

2. Signs for tones: ˋ falling; ˊ rising; ˇ falling-rising; ˉ level. The first three are 'kinetic'. The ˈ sign before a syllable indicates stress but with no pitch contrast.

6. Level tone functions in relation to simple *pitch-range* features as other nuclei, though not of course to complex *pitch range*. A case can be made in fact for seeing level tone as an important functional gap-filler, i.e. a difference only in degree from the polarities of both fall and rise.

There remains the question of how far level tones may be grouped with rises or falls in any general kind of tonal classification. There is of course no real reason why they should be grouped with either, and when one examines their distribution with reference to a number of criteria, no clear answer suggests itself: level seems to hold an ambiguous position between the categories of rise and fall, and it would be unwise to force it into either. Level is clearly functionally rise-like: (a) in subordinate structures, as already mentioned, especially when preceded by a pitch step-up; (b) when it occurs as the exponent of the second element of the fall–plus–rise, i.e. as the maximal degree of narrowing that the rise can take (very frequent in public speaking, for example); (c) when seen from the point of view of its distribution with *pause* types. Level tones tend to be followed by pauses of much the same kind and range as rising tones do: rises and levels tend to have a majority of *brief* or zero pauses at tone-unit boundaries; falls generally have longer pauses. On the other hand, level tones seem to be more fall-like when one considers their distribution in respect of sequence of tones between *unit* pauses – in my data approximately 50 per cent of all falling-type and level tones occurred finally in a sequence, whereas only 25 per cent of all rising-type tones did. There are also various semantic reasons for not associating some occurrences of level tone with rising tones, for example the tendency to avoid the meanings of boredom or sarcasm in subordinate structures (where a rising tone might be used). On the basis of such evidence there would seem to be two distinct functions of level nuclear tone, one similar to the function of rising-type tones, the other similar to falling-type. Any phonological classification of level with either of these would clearly be artificial, consequently it is listed as a separate category of tone in this study.

*Complex.* Here I include all nuclei where there is a change in the direction of the pitch movement of a kinetic tone within a syllable, and only one maximum of prominence. (Contrast compound tones below.) The main categories are the fall–rise and the rise–fall, but both rise–fall–rise and fall–rise–fall occur. The first element of the ˇ and ˆ is phonetically more prominent than the second, and the second element of the rise–fall–rise and fall–rise–fall is phonetically more prominent than the third. The placement of the prominence varies somewhat: one finds both ⌒\ and ⌒\, ∪ and ∪ in English. All these tones fall under the rules for co-occurrence already described in relation to simple tone, but the exponent of markedness is different from simple tones, and there are slightly more possibilities for contrast. The phonetic form of the unmarked ˇ and ^, it is generally agreed, is $\cup$ and $\cap$ respectively (prominence not being indicated here), i.e. the beginning- and end-points are not on the same pitch level; and this relation is stable regardless of the pitch height at the beginning of the glide. As far as complex *pitch range* is concerned, the possibilities are increased by varying this final element. Thus the whole of the tone may be narrowed ($n^{\vee}$ ⌣, $n^{\wedge}$ ⌢), or with the fall–rise the second element only may be narrowed ($^{\vee}n$ ↴). Again, the whole of the tone may be widened ($w^{\vee}$ ↳, $w^{\wedge}$ ↱) or only one element (namely $^{\vee}w$ ↳, $^{\wedge}w$ ↱ and, very rarely, ∿).

*Compound.* These tones, also called correlative or binuclear tones, are combinations of two kinetic elements of different major phonetic types acting as a single tonal unit. The main types of compound are `+´ and ´+`. The two elements of a complex tone have in effect been separated to allow a larger stretch of utterance to fall under the semantic range of the nucleus. It is necessary to review the evidence in favour of taking a sequence of kinetic elements as a formal and functional unit. For this to be permissible at least four phonetic and distributional characteristics must be present.

1. The kinetic tones must display an 'endocentric' relationship, i.e. `ˋ, ^´, ˋ´, etc., but not ˋ, ´, ˇ, etc. 'Exocentric' sequences of tone units are interpreted as either separate or subordinate.

2. There must be no evidence of a tone-unit boundary between the tones. The syllables between the two kinetic elements must display an evenness of pitch pattern, continuing the pitch movement in a 'trough' or sustained arc from one to the other, for example ╲___╱ or ⌒ˋ . (This has the secondary effect of usually making the beginning point of the second element lower than what would be normal for the beginning of a new tone unit.) This internuclear stretch is rarely interrupted by a pause, but it may display some variation in pitch movement, so long as the general tendency is maintained. Similarly, it is rare to find the internuclear stretch (even when it is fairly long – say, of six or seven words) interrupted by the introduction or conclusion of a prosodic or paralinguistic feature, other than one which reinforces the 'trough' characteristic. In both types of tone there is a strong rhythmic unity between the elements, the internuclear syllables tending to be articulated relatively quickly in each case, and usually isochronously.

3. One element of the compound tone must be more prominent than the other, otherwise the analyst will tend to take the utterance as composing two separate tone units. The phonetically dominant element is usually the first. It is possible for *strong stress* to occur on the second element of a `ˋ⁺ˊ`, but here there tends to be a certain balance of *pitch range*, the first glide often being wider than the second. There is a stronger tendency for extra stress to occur on the second element of a `ˊ⁺ˋ`, not all such cases having compensating *pitch-range* characteristics: these must consequently be taken as exceptional from the point of view of tonicity.

4. Despite the phonetic prominence associated with the first kinetic element, it is the second which is the major functional element, and the basis on which the tone is classified. There is no formal confusion between compound and complex tones: the 'trough' characteristic of the former (*contra* the gradual rise or fall of syllables in the second element of the `ˇ` and `ˆ` respectively), its double prominence (*contra* the single peak of prominence in the latter), and its inability to weaken or suppress stresses after the first kinetic element, would seem to suffice to distinguish between all bidirectional nuclei. While admitting the existence of formal overlapping between complex and compound tones (i.e. an utterance whose phonetic shape was ambiguous as to whether it was an instance of one or the other), in the majority of cases in English it seems possible to identify a bidirectional nucleus as either compound or complex on phonetic grounds; the few examples of ambiguity which exist do not justify a theoretical treatment which takes them as variant forms of the one tonal category. Moreover, while from the semantic point of view it is well known that substantial overlap exists, and that this is probably greater than between any other two tonal types, it would be wrong to postulate any kind of semantic identity here, and suggest that `ˋ⁺ˊ`, let us say, is but a distributional variant of `ˇ`. While there are many cases where there is in effect 'tonal synonymy', for example,

I'm |sòrry about the ↑bóokcase| and I'm |sorry about the ↑bŏokcase|,

there are a large number of examples displaying clear semantic contrasts (as with |"yŏu don't 'know| (Well, who does, then!) *v.* |"yòu don't knów| (so why are you saying you do!); I |thòught it would ráin| *v.* I |thought it would rǎin|), and even where the semantic effect is basically the same in both cases, its distribution over the lexical items in the tone unit may be so different as to really demand a separate description (for example, the |màn said he'd ↑cóme| *v.* the |man said he'd ↑cŏme|). The phonetic and linguistic contrast between complex and compound tones thus seems sufficiently great to justify separate discussion.

## Nuclear tail

Syllables may follow the nucleus, to form a 'tail' of pitch movement. Tails in English are usually non-distinctive, their pitch-contours being automatically determined by the direction of the nuclear tone: in other words, they are not normally independently variable. But it would be wrong to deny any contrastivity at all to them, for occasionally linguistically significant variation may occur. Excluding level tone, where variation does not exist (any departure from level pitch movement in the tail being immediately interpretable as narrowed rising or falling), there are the following possibilities:

1. Tail continues the direction of the nucleus in an unbroken fall or rise, namely •. •⁰ This is by far the most frequent pattern. Stressed syllables in the tail are indicated with ' above and before a syllable, as illustrated below.

2. Tail begins by continuing nuclear direction, and then levels out. With falling tones, this may occur for two reasons: either it is an 'allotail' of type 1, due to one's articulating a fall near the bottom of one's voice-range and thus being forced to level out, or it is an attitudinally marked form of tail, communicating such a range of attitudes as irony, sarcasm or boredom. Stressed syllables in the tail are indicated with → above and before a syllable. Compare:

She's a |BÈAUTIFUL 'woman|    and    She's a |BÈAUTIFUL →woman|

With rising tones, flattening is rare. It may occur when one is near the top of one's voice-range, as with extremely puzzled questions using a 'high' rise, for example:

|WHÉN did you 'say that he was →coming|,

or when the tone is narrowed, for example:

|nWHÉN did you →say|.

Less than 10 per cent of all nuclei have tails with stressed syllables. This is a remarkably low proportion, and the generalization that tonicity falls on the last lexical item is therefore a most reliable one.

We may now summarize the English tone system in a single table:

Table 1 **Summary of English tone systems**

|  | Simple | Complex | Compound |
|---|---|---|---|
| Basic types | \ / ‾ | ˇ ˆ | \ + /    / + \ |
| Secondary types |  | ⋀ ⋁ | ˆ + /    ˇ + \ |
|  |  |  | \ + ‾ |
| Simple pitch range | ⇈, ↑ ↑, → + tone | ⇈, ↑ ↑, → + tone | ⇈, ↑ ↑, → + both elements |
| Complex pitch range | ∅, ↓, ↡   *n*\ *n*′ | ∅, ↡↓,   *n* + ˇ, ˆ, ⋀, ⋁ | ∅, ↓, ↡   *n*′ + \ etc. |
|  | *w*\ *w*′ | *w* + ˇ, ˆ, ⋀, ⋁ | *w*\ + / etc. |
|  |  | ˇ *n*, ˆ *w*, ˇ *w* | \ + *n*′   / + *n*\ |
|  |  |  | *w*\ + /   *w*′ + \ |

Frequency of occurrence for the basic types is interesting, the proportions (as percentages) in my data being as follows:

\    /    ˇ    \+/    ˆ    ‾    /+\

(51·2)   (20·8)   (8·5)   (7·7)   (5·2)   (4·9)   (1·7).[3]

## Classification of heads

The head of the tone unit is probably the most complex segment to describe, and probably least study has been made of it. It is that independently variable part of the tone unit stretching from and including the first stressed and usually pitch-prominent syllable (here referred to as the *onset*) and extending as far as but not including the nuclear segment. It is an optional element in the tone unit, but in fact it occurs in an extremely high proportion of tone units in English – about 70 per cent of the time in my data. Length of tone unit is closely tied to length of head, and in this respect – overall length – the head is the most variable element in the unit: in my data, instances of heads of one to thirty and more syllables (20+ institutional words) occurred.

The principle of description here is to delineate the contour of pitch movement over the head, by defining the pitch level of each syllable in terms of the level of the syllable preceding. The onset syllable is not of course defined in this way. This syllable is taken as given, being defined in

3. Cf. Quirk *et al.* (1964), where the proportions are \ 52·5, / 24·7, \+/ 9·3, ˇ 6·9, ˆ 3·9, ‾ 2·1, /+\ 0·6. Davy (1968) finds a significantly different pattern for conversation as opposed to reading, this is primarily due to the higher proportion of rising-type tones in the latter, namely:

for conversation: \ 58·7, / 16·1, ‾ 8·0, ˇ 7·4, \+/ 5·1, ˆ 4·2, /+\ 0·4;
and for reading: \ 50·2, / 24·6, ˇ 11·1, ‾ 5·5, \+/ 5·5, ˆ 2·1, /+\ 0·6.

a relatively absolute way for each speaker as being the pitch level towards which one automatically tends to return for the commencement of a new tone unit, unless a specific attitude requires *extra* pitch height or depth at this point to make its effect. Ascertaining the level of onset (or nuclear tone beginning, where there is no head) for each tone unit is in fact the only way in which general references to 'normal' pitch height of utterance can be made precise.

Head patterns in English are classifiable into two major types, *falling* and *rising*, the criterion in each case being how the head begins. The pattern at the beginning of the head may be reinforced or modified by the pattern in the middle, and the effect derived from the juxtaposition of these two will be in turn modified by the pattern at the end. The head is an extremely flexible segment, making available a wide range of linguistic contrasts. One cannot reduce all occurrences of head to two or three 'basic' types without a great deal of simplification and distortion.

I illustrate the following head patterns using a falling tone as nucleus, though of course any other tone would do equally well.

1. *Falling heads*. There are four main types, which I have designated A, B, C and D.

A. This head comprises a descending series of stressed syllables, usually with intervening unstressed syllables (these being optional); the stressed syllables are always *lower* than the preceding (stressed or unstressed) syllable. Typical patterns, transcribed in phonetic interlinear and tonetic transcriptions, are as follows:

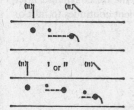 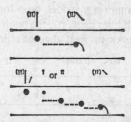

B. This head comprises a descending series of stressed syllables (with or without intervening unstressed syllables), some or all of which are *higher* than, or occasionally at the same pitch as the preceding syllable, but none of which is higher than the next previous pitch-prominent syllable or onset. These have been further classified into two types:
B1, heads with the beginning of the nuclear glide marked in *pitch range*;
B2, heads with the beginning of the nuclear glide not marked in *pitch range*.

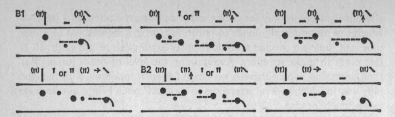

c. This head comprises a descending series of stressed and unstressed syllables, including any of the variations allowed under B, but with the additions that (a) if there are stressed syllables between onset and nucleus, the first must be lower than the onset, and (b) the nuclear tone must be substantially pitch prominent. A subclassification of these can be made depending on the direction of the pitch change which causes the prominence: C1, nucleus higher than the preceding pitch-prominent syllable; C2, nucleus lower than the expected normal step-down.

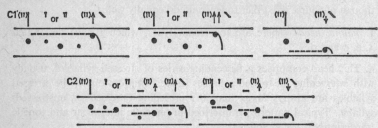

D. This head comprises a sudden drop following the onset syllable, after which two possibilities exist: D1, the pitch movement continues to fall; or D2, the pitch movement rises at some point.

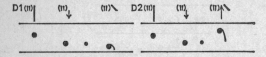

2. *Rising heads*. Two main categories of rising head may be distinguished, which I shall refer to as E and F.

E. This head comprises a rising series of stressed syllables, with or without intervening unstressed syllables, each stressed syllable being higher than, or occasionally at the same pitch as the preceding pitch-prominent syllable. Again, a twofold subclassification seems useful: E1, the beginning of the nuclear glide is marked in *pitch range*; E2, the beginning of the nuclear glide is not marked in *pitch range*.

 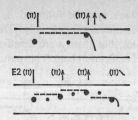

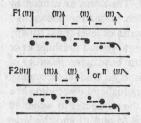 

F. This head begins with one or more rising stressed syllables, and then it ceases to rise. Pitch may then: F1, fall directly to a lower degree of pitch prominence (usually a booster, but occasionally a continuance or drop),

F1 (ll)| (ll)↑ _ (ll)↑ _ (ll)↑↘          (ll)| (ll)↑ _ (ll)↑ _ (ll)↑↓

F2(ll)| (ll)↑ _ (ll)↑ I or II (ll)↘        F3(ll)| (ll)↑ _ (ll)↑ _ (ll)↑ _ (ll)↑↗

the nucleus being optionally prominent; F2, fall ultimately (via a series of progressively lower pitch levels) to unmarked *pitch range* at the nuclear syllable; F3, fall as in F1 or F2 before returning to high pitch prominence (which may then continue as a 'secondary' rise).

3. *Falling–rising(–falling) heads.* The head begins by falling, as in the first category described above, then there is a change in the general direction of the pitch movement, as in the second category; this may then be followed by a further change in direction, as in the first category, and so on. There were few instances of this in my data, but examples collected suggest that a threefold subclassification may not be premature: G1, the first change in direction (which is the important one) may be a regular rise (including continuance) with pitch-prominent nucleus; G2, it may be extremely jerky, but still a general rising movement, and end with a pitch-prominent nucleus; G3, it may be jerky, as G2, but with the nucleus not pitch prominent.

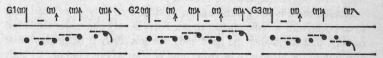

4. *Rising–falling(–rising) heads.* This is the reverse of category 3. The head begins by rising, then there is a change in the general direction of pitch

movement, which may be followed by a further change, and so on, theoretically continuing indefinitely. The nucleus may or may not be pitch prominent, but there were insufficient examples to justify even a tentative subclassification here. This pattern is referred to as type H.

The normal distribution of head patterns in English is much more complex than is normally allowed for, and the number of 'basic types' of head is also more than is usually pointed out. The norm as defined by Kingdon (1958, p. 3) is: 'An analysis of English intonation shows that this consists basically of a slowly descending series of level tones usually starting at or near the top of the normal voice range and finishing at or near the bottom.' However, if one examines the head types in order of frequency, it is clear that the majority do not display a gradual descending series in any sense. The only heads which are gradual and descending in a strict sense are grouped under A; but against these one has to weigh all the rising heads (E and F), the 'complex' heads (G and H) and the large number of heads which display incidental rises and drops throughout their length (B, C and D). A is certainly the most frequently occurring single *category* of head (about 30 per cent of all occurrences in my data), but this makes it a norm only in a very weak sense.

The reasons for this misemphasis on A-type heads would seem to be lack of study of spontaneous connected speech in the earlier period of intonation analysis. The 'ideal' stepping head may well be characteristic of some kinds of written English being read aloud, or of 'set' examples in a pedagogical context, but it is not common outside such contexts.

More prominence and precision should be given to the notion of 'accidental rise', i.e. the pitch-prominent marked features of simple syllabic *pitch range* which may occur throughout the length of a head – and which, incidentally, are not 'accidental' in any sense, nor do they necessarily rise. Their function seems twofold: to spread relative prominence over the words in the head, and to add prosodic variety to connected speech. They occur in about 80 per cent of all heads.

Finally, there is the question as to whether certain types of head tend to co-occur with specific nuclear tones. There is only one major tendency, namely, that the higher the head ends, the less likely it is for the initial direction of the nucleus to be rising, and vice versa. For example, C1 ends in either a high or extra-high booster, most often with ˋ, ˅ and ˋ⁺ ´, least often with ´, ˆ and ´⁺ ˋ; G3, where the nucleus begins low, co-occurs with rising heads frequently. Apart from this, the distribution of head types in respect of categories of nuclear tone shows no significant pattern.

### Preheads

The prehead of a tone unit comprises all syllables before the onset syllable. These are normally very few: in my data, the maximum number was five (four words). All such syllables are unstressed; the only occasion when a degree of stress is perceivable is when a noun, verb, adjective or adverb is brought into the prehead: it is then pronounced with slight 'inherent' stress, so that it is louder than the surrounding unstressed syllables, but it remains on the same pitch level as these, i.e. it is not pitch prominent.

The possibilities for pitch contrast are very limited: four areas of pitch height can be clearly identified and there is some evidence for distinguishing a fifth. The norm of prehead pitch is a level a little below that of the onset syllable, for example:

we should |LÌKE to|

The unstressed syllables may be level or may rise gradually towards the pitch level of the beginning of the onset syllable. This level is unmarked in transcription.

The remaining marked levels are as follows:

1. high prehead (for example ⁻the): the unstressed syllables are perceivably higher than the onset syllable, for example:

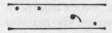

2. extra-high prehead (for example ⁼the): the unstressed syllables are very much higher than the onset, usually near the top of the voice-range, for example:

With high and extra-high, there is a tendency for the first syllable of the prehead to be perceived as accented, the pitch height overriding loudness as the main auditory cue to accent in this case. This is particularly the case when, of two unstressed syllables, one is normal and the other (usually the second) is high, for example: this ⁻is the |third . . .

3. mid prehead (for example _the): the unstressed syllables are heard as

being at the same pitch level as the onset; relative prominence is thus based mainly on loudness, for example:

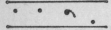

4. The remaining possibility is for an extra-low prehead (for example ₌the), where the unstressed syllables are below normal low level, for example:

Here the pitch of the prehead is very often lower than that of the end-point of the tone unit.

The grammatical structure of the prehead is largely predictable. The items which occur there are nearly always from the class of 'grammatical words' though non-grammatical items of certain types may be found. The grammatical constitution of the prehead is in fact restricted to combinations (subject to normal grammatical rules of order, which do not concern us here) of conjunctions, prepositions, pronouns, determiners and auxiliary verbs, with the occasional interpolation of an introductory adverbial, a parenthetic verbal group (such as 'I think'), or a part of a nominal group ('only', 'Mister').

### Inter-tone-unit relations

Tone units do not exist in isolation, but work in sequences in connected speech. As soon as tone units begin to be juxtaposed, one has to consider the question of what might be called 'tonal collocation', i.e. the extent to which the formal co-occurrence of tones displays predictable restrictions.

Most scholars have approached the question of tone-unit sequences from a wholly grammatical angle, first defining a grammatical structure, and then proceeding to an examination of the ways in which this structure carries a restricted range of intonation patterns. Clearly there are two sides to the problem, the grammatical and the phonological, but the latter point of view has been almost completely ignored. What are the recurrent patterns of tone-unit sequence in connected speech? Until one can give some answer to this question phonologically, one lacks the ability to assess the degree of prosodic 'uniqueness' of any given grammatical structure, and thus loses a great deal of the predictive power of the descriptive statements about co-occurrence which might be made. Phonological sequences of a fairly restricted type do exist independently of grammar, both within major grammatical structures and, less frequently, between structures, and one ought to be aware of the more important tendencies at work here before embarking upon any process of grammatical integration.

*Sequence of tone units*

To discover statistical preferences for the use of specific phonological sequences of tone units, it is first necessary to determine how to define the unit sequences to be compared. There are two possible approaches: one may arbitrarily take sequences in a fixed number (say in pairs, or threes), seeing what recurrent patterns exist, or one may utilize phonological features other than pitch as boundary markers, such as pause, or other prosodic features. Both these approaches are explored below.

The obvious place to begin was to take tone units arbitrarily in pairs ('di-sequences'), to see whether there were any significant tendencies. In view of the fact that quite a large proportion of the tone units in the data consisted of nucleus ($\pm$ tail) alone, attention was focused on the nuclear segment in the first instance, while not ruling out the possibility of other segments in larger units also having a recurrent sequential pattern. The question was asked: given a nuclear tone of type X, what is the probability of nuclear tone of type Y being the obligatory element in the next following tone unit? In other words, I was examining progressive influence of tone units on each other, not regressive (which does not seem to be linguistically relevant). To ensure total coverage, pairs of tone units (some 5000 in all) were studied in overlapping sequences, for example:

A—B
 B—C
  C—D, etc.

Final tone units in utterances (i.e. preceding a change in speaker or silence) were not taken as being influential in the same sense as within utterances: the relationship between intonation patterns at the end of one speaker and at the beginning of the next would seem to pose problems of a quite different order from those discussed here.

The general totals of frequency of co-occurrence were subjected to analysis using the $\chi^2$ test to assess degrees of statistical significance. This was to obtain some indication of the gradation of influence of tones upon each other by quantifying degrees of probability, so that one could say that X is *more* or *less* related to Y than to A, B, C, ... In this analysis, ^ and ' + ', and ˅ and ' + ' were grouped together, to give better frequencies of occurrence. ' as first element in a pair was omitted, in view of its general frequency: as it occurred in one out of every two tone units, genuine statistical tendencies for this category would have been obscured in a corpus of this size.

The following table shows the influence of the first tone on the second in my data in terms of a gradation of decreasing probability.

Table 2 **Gradation of progressive influence of tone upon tone in the data**

| | Tone 1 influences | Tone 2 | Probability (*of Tone 2 occurring as opposed to any other tone*) |
|---|---|---|---|
| 1 | ´ | ´ | 83·3 |
| 2 | ˇ | ˇ | 79·5 |
| 3 | ‒ | ‒ | 77·9 |
| 4 | ´ | ˇ | 68·4 |
| 5 | ^ | ^ | 67·0 |
| 6 | ´ | ` | 66·0 |
| 7 | ˇ | ` | 65·6 |
| 8 | ˇ | | 64·7 |
| 9 | ˇ | ^ | 63·9 |
| 10 | ´ | ^ | 63·3 |
| 11 | ´ | ‒ | 55·1 |
| 12 | ˇ | ‒ | 54·1 |
| 13 | ^ | ` | 40·7 |
| 14 | ^ | ˇ | 34·4 |
| 15 | ‒ | ` | 27·7 |
| 16 | ‒ | ´ | 26·7 |
| 17 | ^ | ´ | 25·3 |
| 18 | ‒ | ˇ | 17·8 |
| 19 | ^ | ‒ | 16·2 |
| 20 | ‒ | ^ | 5·7 |

Here the importance of 'tonal reduplication', the extent to which tones repeat each other in sequence, emerges very clearly: it is obvious that the main evidence for any notion of tone unit cohesion lies in the repetition of tones of the same category and not from a combination of tones of different categories. In particular, the dominance of the ' ´ + ´ ' sequence explains why this pattern has been given such frequent mention in discussion of intonation; moreover, it occurs over a wide range of grammatical contexts.

The nature of the decrease in probability of co-occurrence as one moves down the table is also illuminating, as it reflects the limitations of 'tonal cohesion' in English as a whole, by suggesting where the least important areas of mutual influence lie. There is a significant gap between the averages of pairs no. 12 and 13: above this point all probabilities are greater than 50 per cent; below this point there is a sharp drop to very low averages indeed. It is also significant that below this point the only tones which occur as first element in a sequence are rise–falls and levels: we may thus conclude that these tones exert least influence on following tones of any other kind, and that the linguistically more interesting tones that exert a general influence on anything which follows are the rise and fall–rise.

An extension of this method to longer sequences of tone units is of doubtful value because of the limitations of the corpus and the lack of grammatical perspective. As far as the first problem is concerned, it is clear that the longer the sequence, the more data one needs to obtain an adequate sample of all but the most frequently occurring tones. Even if one restricts one's attention to tri-sequences of tone units, one finds that the possible number of sequences is increased from 49 to 343 ($7 \times 7 \times 7$), and the scatter of sequences which occur less than ten times is substantial: in fact the only frequent tri-sequences are combinations of simple rise and fall, as one might expect – `\+\+\`, `\+\+/`, `\+/`, `\+/+\`, `/+\+\`, `/+\+/`, `/+/+\` and `/+/+/` (the latter being most frequent of all). There are certain interesting sequences of complex and compound tones, but these appear only as minor tendencies, and in fact it becomes simpler to list them than to classify them. Such patterns are in any case intuitively obvious.

Apart from this practical reason, the absence of any non-reduplicative sequences of three or more units' length in the present data is another reason for suggesting that the di-sequence approach is the most useful in this field. We might set up a hypothesis on this basis, therefore, that speakers tend to work with pairs of tone units, and that while TU1 has a direct influence on TU2, it has none on TU3; TU2 influences the choice of TU3 but not TU4; and so on. It is hoped on some future occasion to establish informant reaction techniques which would throw some further light on this matter. It is clearly an issue of central linguistic importance, relating as it does to the nature of the creative process in the production of language.

The other approach, that of using phonological features other than pitch to delimit sequences of units, is not at present very productive. For one thing there are so few of them. But the main reason for the inability of the analyst to extract useful information from phonologically defined longer sequences of tone units is that he has no guarantee that the sequences within each inter-pausal stretch, let us say, are in fact linguistically comparable. Between pauses there is a diversity of grammatical structures, and there is no way of knowing whether any occurrence of a tone is being used in a relatively abnormal way or not. Phonological analysis of tone sequences of any length is clearly of limited application, without a grammatical frame of reference of some kind. Without some means of grammatical delimitation and definition for longer sequences, it becomes impossible to draw any linguistic conclusions from the statistics. The longer the sequence the more one requires grammatical clarification of the structures 'carrying' the tone units. Otherwise, one is in danger of taking sequences as identical on the basis of a phonological surface structure, when in fact they perform totally different functions; for example, in the inter-pausal example, ′ ′ ` could be either two subordinate clauses plus a main clause, or a series of three sentences rapidly delivered – to take just two possibilities. At such a point analysis made without reference to grammar becomes artificial. Once the grammatical influence on longer sequences *has* been defined, however, it is then possible to go back and make a formal study of the non-grammatical residue of sequential information from a wholly phonological standpoint. A great deal more data than that used here would be necessary for this to be successful, and the only realistic way of approaching the problem would be via a computer. Further study of sequence of tones, therefore, or of other sequential parts of tone-unit structure, should not be made without reference to grammar.

## Theory of subordination

The theory of subordination presented here is essentially that outlined in Crystal and Quirk (1964). The primary characteristic of the subordinate tone unit is that its pitch contour, while having a complete and independent shape within itself, falls broadly within the total contour presented in the superordinate tone unit. It may precede ('preposed' subordination) or follow ('postposed' subordination) the superordinate nucleus, singly or in combination with other subordinate units having the same kind of systematization. To determine whether one of the two neighbouring tone units is superordinate (TU1) or subordinate (TU2), the following two criteria are used:

1. The nuclear type postulated as subordinate must repeat the direction of the nucleus in TU1, both nuclei being one of the two primary categories, fall or rise. If this direction is not similar, subordination is not possible, and the tone units must be treated as independent. Complex tones receive a treatment based on their potential relationship with one or other of the two main categories (see below).

2. The width of nuclear movement in TU1 must be greater than that in TU2. The range disparity between the nuclear tones is the main factor in determining the subordinate partner, degree of stress being secondary. The types of subordination reviewed below are based on the kind and degree of this disparity, which is perceived by comparing the starting points of the kinetic tones in TU1 and TU2. There are three main possibilities: either (a) TU2 will start and finish completely outside the range of TU1; or (b) there will be an overlap; or (c) TU2 will fall completely

within the range of TU1. It may well be necessary to take the latter two categories together, as little contrast seems to exist between them: they are closely correlatable in form and function, and the main contrast is undoubtedly between these and (a) above.

It is usual to find a correlation between an increase in pitch width and an increase in loudness, though this does not affect the decision as to the type of subordination involved. In my corpus TU1 was regularly more prominent than TU2, most of the difference being due to pitch increase or a combination of pitch increase plus stress. There were a few cases (about 10 per cent) where a subordinate unit (diagnosed by pitch width) had more prominence than the superordinate unit (though this was rarely due to *strong stress* or *high booster*). But since it is very much more usual to find subordination corresponding to reduced pitch width, reduced pitch range *and* reduced loudness, it seems reasonable to make the last two of these diagnostic in general, and particularly in the case of level nuclei, where pitch width is by definition inapplicable (see below).

A very similar situation existed for preposed subordination. Here, there was a greater variety of co-occurrences with *pitch-range* features within the subordinate unit (presumably because the unit occurs 'within' the head), but the same tendencies appeared here as above, TU1 being more prominent than TU2 in about 60 per cent of the cases.

Subordination would thus seem to be restricted in its occurrence to certain 'favourite' configurations of pitch/stress features. We may say that if the nucleus does not fall on the last lexical word of a phrase, and if the nucleus is pitch prominent in simple *pitch range* (particularly if it co-occurs with an onset or high booster) or if it carries strong stress, then it is highly probable that the final lexical item will be subordinate. It is rare for the subordinate nucleus itself to fall on the penultimate lexical item, or for other lexical items to occur between subordinate and superordinate nuclei – 70 per cent of all postposed subordinate units had no head, the nucleus occurring at onset position and any intervening utterance being a prehead (in about 20 per cent of cases) and/or a tail (in about 10 per cent of cases).

The development of the system of subordination may be represented in three stages:

1. The width of a TU2 unit (or units) occurs in a higher or lower pitch range in relation to the 'middle' range of TU1.

2. If TU1 is a fall, let us say, each of the positions of TU2 then allows at least one subordinate fall, whose range (as described above) either overlaps or falls within TU1, or falls outside of TU1. Similarly, it is possible to isolate eight categories of rise. A tonetic transcription is given along with

the interlinear ($e$ = 'extra-high', $h$ = 'high', $l$ = 'low' beginning-point of the subordinate tone)

3. But this is not yet the complete system, because each of the possibilities outlined in (2) has an alternative form with *narrow* pitch width. This narrowness may theoretically occur in all parts of the system, and results in a system of thirty-two types of subordination to distinguish all the variables within the rise and fall categories. In practice, however, not all of these numerous possibilities are realized with equal frequency. Some, indeed, are highly unlikely ever to occur, for example:

The most frequently occurring patterns in my data were those which approximate most nearly to a nuclear tail, namely:

but the following three patterns were also common:

But whereas a tail has little prominence and its only pitch movement is to follow directly that of the nucleus, the subordinate tone unit has a new pitch contour which always results in increased overall prominence as compared with a tail, and hence in a clearly different significance as well. At the most general level, for example, we may interpret the utterance: ɪ |TÒLD you [í |didn't *ln*WÀNT to| as carrying more information than: ɪ |TÒLD you ɪ 'didn't 'want to|, though the nature of this extra information remains to be defined. To illustrate this point further, we might consider a case like: how|èver [this may |bè]|, in the sense 'whatever the case may be . . .', which is different in meaning from: how|èver| this may |bè|, where the second tone is equivalent in width to (or wider than) the first and where there may be a longer pause following 'however': this has the effect of making the utterance an independent sentence, with the paraphrase '(well), this may be the case'.

There is one notational modification in the examples: the simple *pitch-range* symbols *e*, *l* and *h* relate the starting point of the subordinate nucleus to that of the superordinate nucleus, not to the pitch of the preceding syllable or segment-initiator. Thus in: it |wouldn't be [↑*h*ÁNY] ÚSE|, the *h* relates 'any' to 'use', and the ↑ relates 'any' to 'wouldn't'.

The basic patterns may be set out as follows (all examples being taken from the data):

A. *Simple subordination*, i.e. one TU2 either preceding or following TU1:

there |aren't mÀny 'murderers 'executed [in |THÌs 'country]|

this is |STÍLL [the |*e*LÁW]|  [WÒRLD] ↑ WÌDE|  which |[[*h*"ÁRE] tÉRMed]|

B. *Complex subordination*, i.e. more than one TU2 either preceding or following the TU1.

1. This is particularly typical of postposed TU2s, of which there are two types: (a) when the first subordinated unit (TU2) has another unit subordinated to it in immediate sequence (TU3), which is marked accordingly as if it were a fresh TU2 related to a TU1, for example:

this is |not o"BLÌGatory [Mr|*l*wÌLLiams [as you've sug|GÈsted]]]|

It is possible to have a fourth unit (TU4) subordinated to TU3 in like manner, but longer sequences do not seem to exist. (b) Where the first subordinated unit (TU2) has a second unit (and possibly a third) accompanying it in immediate sequence, which is formally equivalent to TU2 in pitch range and start, and which functions similarly to TU2 in relation to TU1. Such a sequence may be referred to as 'coordinate subordination', and referred to as TU22, for example:

David Crystal 133

I beʺ|LÌEVE that [|*In*BÒYS ʼunder ʼtwenty ʼone] [should |not be sent to

*In* PRÌSON]|

A TU22 may of course have a TU3 functioning in subordination to it,
for example:

e.g.: I be|LÌEVE [in de|tention *In*CÈNTRES] – ʻ[or |GLÀSS ʼhouses

ʺ[as they were |CÀLLED in the ʼarmy]]ʺ ʼ    *ʻlow narrow creakʼ*

                                            *ʺallegroʺ*

Only the first two of these patterns (TU1 + TU2 + TU3, TU1 + TU2
+ TU22) are at all frequent.

2. Complex subordination is rare in positions before TU1, there being
but three instances of this in the data; one example is as follows:

|only a . ə: a ↑FÈW MÓNTHS| |[ÀFTER . ə: [ ↑WÈLCOMING]]. with

enʺ↑↑THÙSIASM [of|FÌCIALLY]|

c. *Compound subordination*, i.e. one TU2 preceding and another following the TU1, as already illustrated in the preceding example. There were
few instances of this in the data.

d. *Compound complex subordination*, i.e. complex subordination both
preceding and following TU1 (which is highly unlikely), or complex subordination *either* before *or* after TU1 with simple subordination in the
alternative position. There is one such case in the data, of the following
form: TU3 + TU2 + TU1 + TU2.

Finally it is necessary to cater for the occasional complex tone (usually
only a fall–rise or rise–fall) which can enter into subordinate structure.
These nuclei (or the corresponding compound types) may occur as TU1,
in which case they must be repeated in TU2 in narrowed form, or be

followed by the relevant primary category (′ with ˇ, and ` with ˆ), to allow subordination to take place at all. The latter is by far the most frequent. In preposed subordination, a narrowed complex tone of the same type as TU1 may occur, or a simple tone which is of the same initial category as the phonetically most dominant element of the complex (or compound) tone, for example we may have the exocentric ′ + ˆ, or ` + ˇ, and not the endocentric ` + ˆ, or ′ + ˇ. The criterion of pitch width is still the deciding factor, though modified: the kinetic tone as a whole (and not merely its starting-point) is now considered in relation to TU 1. Thus ⌒ is subordinate to ⌒ and would in turn subordinate ⌒ . If this does not apply, it is still possible to infer subordination using the secondary criteria of reduced prominence (cf. above) and a lower or higher pitch-range outside the range of TU1. This would necessarily apply to level tones where, as we have seen, pitch-width is not applicable. For example:

the |ninety NÍNE [|point /NÍNE [per |CÈNT]]|

¹no refe↑rendum of [ ↑ÂLL] ᴵᴵ↑JÛDGEs|

the ap↑PEĀL [ma|chinery in the CŌURTS]]|

Levels may of course occur as TU2s, where the respective TU1s have kinetic nuclei; there the narrowness of *n* in TU2 has merely been carried to extremes, for example:

ᴵᴵBÝ [the |Home↑sĒcretary]]|

On the whole, there is no difficulty in deciding whether a sequence of tones is subordination or some other prosodic phenomenon, such as a sequence of unrelated units or a compound tone.

### References

CRYSTAL, D., and QUIRK, R. (1964), *Systems of Prosodic and Paralinguistic Features in English*, Mouton.

DAVY, D. (1968), 'A study of intonation and analogous features as exponents of stylistic variation, with special reference to a comparison of conversation with written English read aloud', University of London M.A. Thesis.

KINGDON, R. (1958), *The Groundwork of English Intonation*, Longman,

QUIRK, R., DUCKWORTH, A. P., SVARTVIK, J., RUSIECKI, J. P. L., and COLIN, A. J. T. (1964), 'Studies in the correspondence of prosodic to grammatical features in English,' in *Proceedings of the Ninth International Congress of Linguistics*, Cambridge, Massachusetts, 1962, Mouton.

QUIRK, R., and CRYSTAL, D. (1966), 'On scales of contrast in English connected speech', in *In Memory of J. R. Firth*, edited by C. E. Bazell *et al.*, Longman.

# 7 Dwight Bolinger

Relative Height

Dwight Bolinger, 'Relative height', from *Prosodic Feature Analysis*, edited by
Pierre R. Léon, Georges Faure and André Rigault, Marcel Didier, 1970, pp. 109–25.

## Summary

Not only is pitch a layer that interacts in complex ways with the other
layers of language; it is also layered internally. Four layers (according to
this theory) can be distinguished:

1. A rather highly grammaticized layer, including accents (syllabic prominence *per se*), terminals (rise, fall), and levels (parentheses, paragraph
and other discourse divisions).

2. A partially grammaticized layer, covering the behavior of accented
syllables in relation to reference points (which may include other accents).
This is the layer of 'controlled' affective meanings: the speaker conveys
his attitudes and along with them the information that they are part of his
message.

3. An ostensibly ungrammaticized layer, that of the behavior of unaccented
syllables. Here are the 'uncontrolled' affective meanings: the speaker
conveys his attitudes and along with them the information that they
override his message. But this of course is a message too – anything can be
faked. Hence the 'ostensibly'.

4. A genuinely ungrammaticized layer, that of levels dictated by emotion:
wide or narrow range, extra-high pitch, etc. These can be faked but are
less likely to be.

The paper concentrates on the second layer and the third.

Intonation cannot be analysed in a simple linear way. This is obvious from
certain types of embeddings in which the whole intonational scale is
reduced for a given stretch of speech, forcing that stretch to be interpreted
in contrast to the whole utterance. The clearest case is the parenthesis.
Within it we find normal syllable-by-syllable contrasts – a particular rise
in pitch may stand out and be interpreted as signaling importance within
the parenthesis – but the importance of the entire parenthesis is signaled
as low in the utterance as a whole. Example:

1. I $\overset{\text{some}}{}$ times won$_{\text{de}}$r,

when I have $^{\text{ti}}$me to $\overset{\text{pon}}{}$ der on such thi$^{\text{n}}{}^{\text{g}}{}^{\text{s}}$,

whether any of these efforts are really worth $\overset{\text{whi}}{}$ $l_{\text{e.}}$

(Pitch of *whether* slightly higher than *things*). If the *when* clause is put first, it has the same internal shape but comes up to the average level.

Parenthesis is not the only example of wheels within wheels. Another fairly obvious one might be called paragraph intonation. In a series of sentences each of which ends in a low pitch, one usually detects an overall lowering at the end, signifying the closing of a particular topic of discourse. If we can say that a downward movement of pitch signifies finality, then this represents finality imposed on finality. As with other kinds of embedding, there is probably no logical limit: one could have a complete-narrative intonation superimposed on a paragraph intonation superimposed on a sentence intonation. But there are practical limits. Intonational range is used up rather fast.

The third example of layering is the theme of this paper.[1] A pitch

1. The contrasts in pitch dealt with in this paper are not the ones that *produce* a pitch accent on a given syllable – abrupt, but not necessarily wide, departures from a reference line. Rather they are relationships *of* accented and unaccented syllables on a larger scale. For example, if we are in a wallpaper store and pronounce this sentence

I $^{\text{need}}$ a $\overset{\text{single}}{}$ ro$_{\text{ll.}}$

the dealer will understand us to mean just one roll; if we say

I $^{\text{need}}$ a $\overset{\text{sin}}{}$ gle ro$^{\text{ll.}}$

he will take us to mean that we do not want a *double* roll. In the first, *roll* is pitch prominent, in the second it is not, though there is very little difference in the overall shape of the contour. The properly intonational, as separate from accentual, contrast in pitch is illustrated by

I $^{\text{need}}$ a $\overset{\text{sin}}{}$ gle roll     I need a $\overset{\text{need}}{}$ a $\overset{\text{sin}}{}$ gle roll

in which the accentual contrasts are the same but there is an affective difference. Accentual differences are all-or-none. Affective, intonational differences are gradient.

movement like the one in figure 2 can be described as a rise–fall. In it there is a syllable (or possibly two or more) that is higher than its surroundings, and the height relative to that immediate environment we can suppose to have some kind of effect. In figure 3 there are two such rise–falls standing close together, and now we must ask how they influence each other. I propose that the most obvious effect is related to the tangent that is drawn from one peak to the next, and that there are differences between rising and falling tangents:

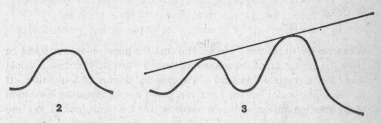

2                                                    3

For example, taking sentence number 4,

4. I'd *get* his con*sent* if I were you.

and putting it on 3 with a rising tangent, the consequences are not the same as putting it on a falling tangent. One thing we'll try to explore is the relationship between this tangent and a continuous pitch movement connecting the peaks, in this case giving 5 and 6 with rising and falling pitch respectively:

5. I'd get his con sent if I were you.    6. I'd get his con sent if I were you.

My first examples are with commands, which – when they contain at least two accents – regularly fall from the first to the last,[2] and contrast

2. Ambiguities may arise between the normal form of commands and that of question-answers if there are not enough syllables to give a full display. Thus *Beat it!* and *Get going!* are synonymous but the first has one stressed syllable, the second two. The first, in the shape

Beat it.

serves equally as a command delivered out of the blue, and as an answer to *What would you do if he threatened you?* The second would contrast, for these two situations, as follows:

Get go ing.    Get go ing.

with question-answers,[3] where there is a rise. So the command

7. Get a hair cut.

differs from the question-answer – which might come in response to the question *What do I have to do to look respectable?* –

8. Get a hair cut.

When we try to reverse these we find that the question-answer could be given the intonation of the command, though – precisely because it would *sound* like a command instead of the expected answer to a question – it would appear rude; but the command could not be given the intonation of the question-answer – I would not come into the room, look at you, and

3. Intonationally, the class 'statement' is both too broad and too narrow. It is too narrow because intonation is in the main indifferent to the grammatical form of an utterance. In the example, *Get a haircut. You can get a haircut. Get a haircut would be my suggestion*, etc. are all the same as answers to the question. It is too broad because intonation is concerned not with statements as statements but with different kinds of them. There are statements that come as observations having no connection with discourse, e.g. the remark that one might make to a motorist who carelessly splashes water with his car,

That wasn't a nice thing to do!

which is quite different from the answer one would give to an interlocutor's question *Why did you object?* –

It wasn't a nice thing to do

– a non-statement intonationally identical to this would be the petulant child's reply,

Because.

Even the notion of 'question-answer' needs to be modified, or at least to be interpreted in a special sense, because there are answers that do not exhibit an overall rise. For example, answering *When can I expect to hear from you?* it would sound strange to say *I'll see you in an hour* with the highest pitch on *hour* – it should go on *see*. 'Question-answer' can be interpreted to cover answers in which the speaker has in mind 'Does (will) my hearer wonder about the information I am giving him? To allay that wonder I will make a stronger appeal for his acceptance.' The majority of questions do imply the degree of wonder that calls for an overall rise in the answer.

say out of the blue *Get a haircut* with the intonation of number 8. We observe the same incongruity in

9. Let me give you a piece of ad$v_{i_{c_e}}$.     \*Get a $^{hair}$ cut.

So within the overall intonation of commands, what happens? I will use examples with enough syllables to give a good display. I might say

10. Hand me that little $^{pen}$ knife of yours.

Or I might say

11. Hand me that little pen knife of yours.

Number 10 has two peaks, the first higher than the second; number 11 is more or less continuous downmotion. Both are good commands, but they differ in their appropriateness to situations. With number 10 you would not be surprised if I took the penknife and went about my business. With the second, you would probably expect something more from me in the way of words or performance, e.g.

12. Hand me that little pen knife of yours.

Let's see what happens when I $^{trim}$ this a bit.

This contrast can be ignored for the moment, to consider again the main point: that the relative height of the two peaks has the same appropriateness to commanding as the continuous downmotion. It can be contrasted with the overall rise on a question-answer using much the same wording, for example answering the question *What did he do to help?*:

13. He $^{hand}$ed me that little $^{pen}$ knife of his.

– with two peaks, the second higher than the first; or, using a continuous rise,

14. He hand$^{ed}$ me that little $^{pen}$ knife of his.

There is a situational difference here too, but the main thing is the overall rise.

The same comparisons, with the same results, can be made with questions that use a terminal fall. But I don't want to overdo the examples.[4]

Thus far the only terminals used have been falling ones, and the only accents have been relatively high ones. There is also the contrary case, with rising terminal and accents that stand out by being lower than the reference pitch. We ask once again whether the tangent to two successive accents is comparable to continuous motion in the same direction.

Questions make the best examples, as they come most naturally with the terminal rise. We try two, in which the tangents go in opposite directions,

15. Is      thing                    16. Is      thing

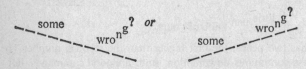

4. Questions of this type usually imply that the speaker already has part of the information he wants. Imagine that someone is planning to give a party but is not on good terms with the prospective guests. A friend asks

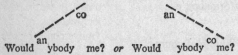

Listeners would probably interpret the first to mean that the speaker is just doubtful, and the second to mean that he is pretty sure no one will. If the two questions are asked with a continuous rise or a continuous fall, there is a difference, but the same implication of mere doubt as against negative assurance still carries through:

Similarly for interrogative-word questions with two peaks,

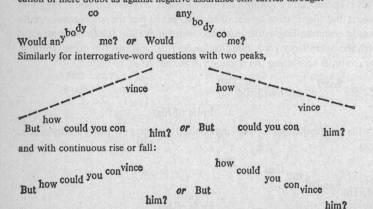

and with continuous rise or fall:

against two others, with continuous motion in place of the tangents:

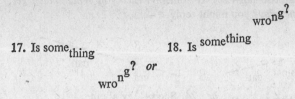

17. Is something wrong?    18. Is something wrong? or

The effect of the overall rise – however you want to describe it, perhaps a stronger appeal – is the same, and similarly the overall fall.

For a question-answer using the same configurations, we can imagine a child asking a question and a parent answering it as if to put the child back in his place. The child asks *What's this?* The parent answers

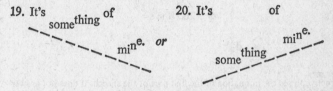

19. It's something of mine. or    20. It's something of mine.

The upmoving tangent in the second of these pretty clearly warns the child to mind his own business, despite the pseudo-sweetness of the inverted accents. Comparing these with continuous movement we get

21. It's something of mine. or 22. It's something of mine.

– again the warning stands out in the overall rise. The same comparisons can be made with commands.[5]

5. But there is a question whether these are really commands, intonationally speaking A person would not come into a room, put a package down on the table, and initiate a discourse with

I'm putting this down here.    *Please leave it alone.

Instead, he would end his speech with

Please leave it alone.

If the relationships hold for terminal rises as well as terminal falls, what about a terminal rise–fall–rise? If someone asks you *What shall I get Maude for her birthday?* you might reply

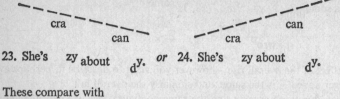

23. She's ˉˉ cra ˍ ˍ zy about ˍ ˍ can dᶠy. *or* 24. She's zy about ˍ ˍ cra ˍ ˍ can dᶠy.

These compare with

25. She's crazy aᵇout·can dᶠy. *or* 26. She's craᶻy a bout can dᶠy.

---

(It is instructive to see the intonation of the first part of the speech. It does not answer a question, but gives information that the hearer is expected to act upon, and has the intonation of a command. To say

I'm put ting this down he re.

would be inappropriate, though it would be normal – with *it* replacing *this* – in answer to *What are you doing with that?* The authoritarian tone of the two successive falls can of course be sweetened with gesture to any degree the speaker chooses. On the other hand, if the utterance came in answer to a question, e.g. *What shall I do with this?*, it might well take the shape

Just leave iᵗ a loⁿe.

and similarly if it doubles for a conditional clause, as the imperative so often does:

I'm putting this down heᵣe. Just leave it a loⁿe and everything will be fiⁿe.

'If you will leave it alone, everything will be fine.'

Once more the overall downmotions match, and the overall upmotions.[6]

The examples up to this point have been comparatively uncomplicated. They have involved two peaks at most, and the accents have moved in a uniform direction. Utterances are not limited to such rudimentary combinations, and may show not only more than two accents but also more than a single direction in which their pitches tend. Consider first a series of three peaks with a uniform rising tangent:

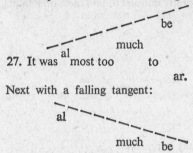

27. It was al most too much be to ar.

Next with a falling tangent:

28. It was al most too much be to ar.

These can be compared to the simple rise and simple fall:

29. It was almost too much to be ar.

6. In the previous examples the upmotion was given first. The last examples have the downmotion first. To do it the other way would have been to invite a contextual effect between the two examples, making 23 appear to refer to something already mentioned, as if the question had been *What shall I get Maude for her birthday? Would candy be all right?* This illustrates a difficulty with accents: when they highlight the utterance as a whole, or just the lexical items that carry them. Either interpretation can be given to either of the two-peaked utterances, though it would be less usual to have the higher of the two peaks second if it is the lexical item *candy* that is getting the attention and 'candy' has already been mentioned. The problem with which this discussion is concerned is not affected – overall downmotion and overall upmotion maintain their relationships. A better example of utterance accent as against individual item accent can be sought among idioms, where commonly the items lack individual significance. Thus *Look here!* as an idiom means that someone is being called to account – the word *here* does not mean 'in this place'. But it may be taken literally too. Either way the same accents and intonations can be used, and

Look he r el *and* Look he r el

contrast with each other in either sense.

*or*      al<sup>most</sup> too much to <sub>be</sub>

**30.** It was

                               **ar.**

With inverse accents there is a problem when more than two are joined by a tangent. It is possible though pretty unusual to join them on a falling tangent:

**31.** It was

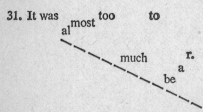

As for a rising tangent, I find it quite impossible:

**32.** *It was

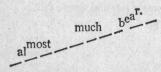

A fairer test is with questions, but the results are the same:

**33.** Is there

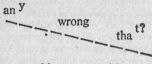

**34.** *Is there

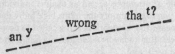

Nevertheless, the tangents and the steady movements can be compared as before. Example 33 can be compared to

**35.** Is there <sub>an</sub>y<sub>thing</sub> wrong with <sub>tha</sub> t?

There are of course more complex possibilities. In principle, it is likely that either normal or inverse accents can be combined in any order, though some sequences are unlikely. The commonest type of combination is the one in which inverse accents at the beginning of an utterance serve as a foil to high-pitched accents at the end. The tangent to the inverse accents can point in the same direction as that of the terminal rise, or in the opposite direction:

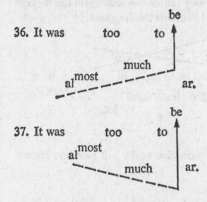

Whereas in number 37 there are two dimensions of contrast with the final rise, in that the accents themselves go down and the tangent to them also goes down, while the final accent rises, we also find a single dimension of contrast with only the tangent in contrast with the final rise:

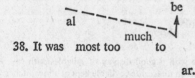

Other possibilities include an inverse accent between two normal ones, but this is unlikely unless the tangent rises:

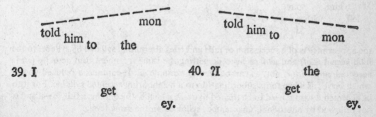

(Notice that 40 is not the same as 41, where *get* is unaccented:

```
        told
                    mon
41. I      him to get the
                            ey.)
```

They also include one or more inverse accents before two normal ones; the tangent to the inverse accents may fall or rise, but again the tangent to the normal ones generally rises. I combine the diagrams:[7]

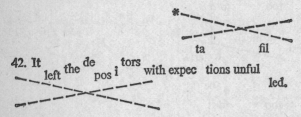

```
                 *
                    ta        fil
42. It     de    tors
      left the pos i   with expec tions unful
                                            led.
```

It seems unlikely, too, that three successive peaks will have the highest one in the middle

```
               get
        told         mon
43. ?I      him to  the
                       ey.
```

— unless the middle peak is on a word that is made prominent for its own sake, such as an intensifier:

```
            ter
         al         think
44. It was  most too rible to  about.
```

7. It is necessary to confect an example with a good display of syllables with reduced vowels to show the difference between an unaccented syllable kept at a low pitch to set off a following accent, and an accented syllable brought to a low pitch as an inverse accent. Thus looking at

```
                 ce
It    him    out
  left   with  a
                   nt.
```

the appearance is of a succession of falls and rises alternating syllable by syllable to the final accent. *Left* and *with* seem to be getting the same treatment. But actually *left* is accented, and *with* is not, as can be seen in example 42. It contains a reduced vowel, which serves as a cue to its subordination to a neighboring accented syllable. For it to be accented it would need to be treated like *left*, which both contains a full vowel and is not followed by additional, unaccented, syllables on the same level.

More examples could be added – in particular I could cite pitch directions that are broken between unaccented syllables:

45. I told him as simply as I could to be careful with money.

But these would only complicate the argument and would not, I think, affect what has been said about the dynamics of interrelated accents.[8]

8. The continued rise (or level) after an accent that is marked by being jumped up to, as on *told, sim-, could,* and *care-* in this example, is the criterion of what I have else-where termed Accent B, in contrast with Accent A, which is jumped down from, as here on *mon-*. An example of the same sentence with a succession of A accents:

I told him as simply as I could to be careful with money.

The behavior of the unaccented syllables after a B accent with reference to a following A accent makes a graded, but at the extremes a striking, difference in the attitude conveyed:

Just never you mind. Just never you mind. Just never you mind.

I don't believe him. I don't believe him. I don't believe him.

If I may attempt an exegesis of these three I will do it just in terms of the height of the accents relative to each other, since the implications of height above the reference line and height of unaccented syllables is dealt with in the text.

The overall rise carried by the mounting succession of accents in the first of each set of three intonations represents hearer-orientation. Indulging in what may be fancy but strikes me as close to truth, I would say that overall rise is a primitive alarm cry. It gives information that is useful to the tribe. The fact is that verbal alarms *are* always ex-pressed this way, and also that – as the examples have repeatedly shown – question-answers, which are oriented toward the person who asked the question, do the same. So do most questions, which are appeals to the hearer – they differ in their terminals sometimes, but not in their tendency to rise.

The overall fall of the third members of the two sets represents speaker-orientation. Things are settled. The speaker is assured, or speaking for his own benefit, or domi-nating someone. This is the regular intonation for commands. In the examples, *Just*

The best inference I can draw from the evidence I've given is that there is an intonational layer consisting of accented syllables and their relation to reference levels and to one another, which is independent of the changes in pitch that occur elsewhere. There is nothing remarkable in this, because it has been the custom to pretend that unaccented syllables did not matter, that their behavior was determined by that of the accented ones, except of course at certain pause points. But I think we must now go on and ask whether that is true, whether changes in unaccented syllables – while accented ones remain the same – affect the meanings of utterances.

Returning to examples 10 and 11, I recall suggesting that after 10 the subject might well be dropped, while after 11 – and this was expanded in 12 – something more would be expected. In 11, not to try to describe it in more definite terms, I think we can say that there is a sensation of being keyed up. This is even more noticeable in 25 and 26 as against 23 and 24. To take a fresh example, imagine someone being asked two questions: *As between dying and living as a cripple, which would you prefer?* and *How do you feel about living your whole life as a cripple?* Imagine being given two

---

*never you mind* means 'My time will come, you'll catch it no matter what,' and *I don't believe him* means 'Nothing will shake my personal doubt.'

The middle members have neither an overall rise nor an overall fall. The first accent is followed by a continuation of the rise, the second is approached by a fall. The attitude conveyed is a mixture of the first two, with the second predominating because it comes last. The meaning is something like 'This is suggested as something to be aroused about, but I am self-possessed about it.' It is typical of ho-hum exclamations (*Glory be, Well what do you know. If it isn't Sam Sneed*), things that may be important but whose importance the speaker dismisses,

```
               to                              to
          ing                          py
      noth                        hap
There's        wor          I'm          do
          ry about.                          it.
```

things of which the speaker disclaims responsibility, suggesting 'I don't care':

```
                          to
        the              same              or
     to              the
  go     dev      all                 it
He can          It's           m   Take   leave
         il.                   e.              it.
```

With this intonation an utterance like *Don't you worry* would not be said to placate the hearer about his own worries. It would be said either to mean 'You don't worry me' (*Don't you worry; I'll get you yet*) or 'You (or I) don't need to worry about any threat from X' (*Don't you worry, I'll take care of that big bully*).

The contrast between overall rise and overall fall is the theme of Maria Shubiger's article (1967). It contains many examples from British English.

answers to match the two questions, and then decide which would go best with which:

di
di
er
rath rath
46. I'd 47. I'd er
e. e.

If I can trust my own reactions, 46 fits the second question and might possibly be used with the first, but 47 is more than a bit unnatural with the second question. The first question poses a logical choice; the second calls for feeling. What signals the difference in the answers is the behavior of the unaccented syllable. I would like to characterize its function as that of showing *the speaker's involvement with the idea.* When his feelings get the better of him (or he wants to pretend that they do), the unaccented syllables maintain a high pitch.

What now of the effect of *raising* the pitch on an accented syllable? This is gradient and we can hike up it as much as we please. In place of 47 we can have

di
rath
48. I'd er
e.

I submit that the difference now is not the speaker's involvement with the idea, but rather the expressivity of his message. Where the sustained high pitch on unaccented syllables was as it were an uncontrolled factor, letting through the message the speaker's feeling about the idea, extra-high pitch on the accented syllable against a background of low-pitched unaccented ones is a controlled factor. It enables the speaker to underscore some fact of his message as new or surprising. It is as if lowering the pitch on the unaccented syllables – when everything prompts one to raise it – were saying 'Look, I'm in control of the situation; any raises I use are for my purposes.' This is crude, and I will restate it just as crudely: high pitch with a background of low pitch *serves* the speaker; overall high pitch *betrays* him.

I use the term 'controlled' rather than 'logical' because the meanings of intonation are too all-embracing to be confined to logicality. Nevertheless, cases of logical emphasis are the best examples of what I mean by 'control'. If in answer to *Why are you so partial to older people?* one heard

trust
un
are
young
49. The
worthy.

rather than

              trust

50. The $^{young}$ are un
                    worthy.

the logical contrast on *young* would be lost, and the speaker would seem to
have been carried away by his feelings.

As we range over more intonation patterns, the usefulness of the notion
of 'control' becomes more apparent. For the speaker has it within his
power to turn everything upside down. This is clearest with the inverse
accents, in which accented and unaccented syllables simply exchange
places – high-pitched unaccented syllables convey involvement, low-pitched
accented ones blunt the impact of whatever facts are reported or demands
made and the rising terminals remove any impression of assertiveness. So
these are used to reassure, to wheedle, to object without offence:

51. He $_{didn't}$ $_{mean}$ $_{i}$$^{t.}$     52. Wouldn't it be

                                        bet$^{ter}$ this $^{w}$ $^{a}$ $^{y?}$

We need, of course, a law of truth in intonation as we do in lending. A
reversal in which the normally uncontrolled is used in a controlled way
is a kind of falsehood. So reversed accents are apt to be taken as conveying
formalized, hence insincere, emotion. There are other similar cases.[9]

To summarize:

1. The height of an accented syllable by comparison with that of another
accented syllable produces the same effect regardless of the height of

9. For instance, putting exaggerated high pitch, extra length and loudness and
aspiration (or glottalization of vowels) including sometimes a rise–fall–rise, on a
normally unaccented syllable. The basis for this is seen in the type

     $^{c}$ $^{o}$ $_{u}$     do

How      l $^{d}$ you
              it!

in which accented *could* gets the treatment. It then is carried over to unaccented
syllables. The effect is one of great involvement checked by great restraint. Insincere
exclamations are especially common:

     $_{i}$ $_{n}$ the $^{wor}$        $_{d}$ $_{o}$ you $^{d}$        of my

What          How          Out
        ld!                o!       $^{w}$ $_{a}$ $_{y, sir!}$

intervening unaccented syllables. An overall rise contrasts with an overall fall.[10]

2. The height of an accented syllable contrasting with a following unaccented one conveys the impact of the message – its logical import, its informativeness.

3. The height of unaccented syllables conveys the involvement of the speaker. A return to low-pitched unaccented syllables implies control.

These effects combine. An utterance like

You shouldn't

                       r y.
                wor

has high involvement and no message impact – the whole purpose is to show the speaker's concern and minimize the importance of worrying. One like

                   wor
     shouldn't
You
                r y.

has no involvement and high message impact. It presents in a contrastive way the idea of not worrying. One like

     shouldn't wor

You
                r y.

shows both involvement and high message impact. These interpretations are still pretty hypothetical, but they are a stab at getting some kind of semantic interpretation of intonational elements independent of the particular utterances that they fall on (including utterance types like question and statement), and independent of the particular combinations, including both combinations with one another and combinations with other prosodic features, in which they occur.

10. See footnote 8 for my interpretation of this.

### Reference

SCHUBIGER, M. (1967), 'A note on two notional functions of the low-falling nuclear tone in English', *Eng. Stud.*, vol. 48, no. 1.

## Part Three
## Intonation and Grammar

Probably the most important grammatical function of intonation in the
language family to which English belongs is that of tying the major
parts together within sentences and tying sentences together within
discourse – showing, in the process, what things belong more closely
together than others, where the divisions come, what is subordinate
to what, and whether one is telling, asking, or commanding. Pierre
Delattre surveys these uses in French. His study is not only valuable for
relating intonation to grammar but also for revealing the underlying
kinship between the intonations of Western languages. What he has
to say about 'major and minor continuations', for example, can be
applied to English if it is seen in relation to other possibilities. English
has two ways of separating the clauses of a sentence. One of them is
much more the rule in English than in other European languages; it
consists in dropping the pitch at the break but then letting it rise slightly:

If he re$^{turns}$ both $_{of}$ $_t$h$^{e}$$^{m,}$ $_{re}$ fund the en$^{tire}$ a$^{mou}$

nt.

– the fall here is from *both* to *of* and the rise is on *them*. This intonation
is used when the speaker intends the first clause to be viewed as a new
idea. But if it only repeats what has gone before, then English tends to
use the same curve that Delattre describes for French. Imagine the
above example said in answer to the question *What do I do if he
returns both of them?* It would then probably be pronounced

If he re$^{turns}$ both $_{of}$ $_t$h$^{e}$$^{m,}$ fund the en$^{tire}$ a$^{mou}$
$_{re}$

nt.

– a simple rise all the way to the comma. This same intonation is
common on other expressions that are 'not new', such as folk sayings:

*Easy come, easy go; One for the money, two for the show; Ask me no questions and I'll tell you no lies.* Delattre was always as much interested in teaching as in experimenting and theorizing, and his treatment of French intonation has a clarity that is ideal for a textbook, drawing effectively and eclectically from both camps in the intonation controversy, the level camp and the contour camp.

A number of problems in syntax are easier to solve if it is assumed that at a level above the sentence itself there is a super-sentence meaning something like 'I assert this', 'I ask this', 'I order this', according to the mood of the speaker. Sometimes it is explicit: we can actually say *I assert that he did it* rather than just *He did it.* More often only a fragment of the higher sentence is there, usually in the form of a 'sentence adverb' such as *truly, generally, hopefully.* But usually in English no actual words betray its existence, and where the words are missing, intonation fills in. English uses numerous patterns for assertions, questions, commands and exclamations. It is not to be expected that all languages will make equal use of verbal signals on the one hand, and intonation on the other, for this purpose. In the second Reading Maria Schubiger shows how a favourite device in German, the modal particles, is paralleled by intonation in English.

The question of whether to be broad or deep plagues every scientist. The solution is to be both, but that is impossible in practice because no one has time. The formal grammar of the 1960s concentrated on the sentence as a self-contained structure and taught us much about it that we could not have learned otherwise. But it sacrificed the broader vision of the sentence in a community of sentences, or discourse. Of late this has begun to be remedied; such things as presuppositions, coreference, and presentatives are seen as linking sentence to sentence. An important use of intonation is to mark a relationship of this kind particularly between a sentence and the one that precedes it. Richard Gunter's article, published here for the first time, shows how the commonest of the intonation contours are used in this way, and incidentally has something to say about the reality of intonation phonemes. The notation used is that of Trager (pp. 83–6).

The part of grammar with which intonation cooperates most consistently is that of word order. When a sentence adverb is moved from the beginning to the end of a sentence, the intonation usually tells us so; hearing

The play end ed hap pi ly.

*rather than*

                      hap
          play ended
The
                 pi
                   l
                    y.

we are pretty sure that the meaning is the same as that of *Happily, the play ended*. But where intonation is most useful is with sentences in which the order of words cannot be changed – *Mary loves John* is not convertible to *John loves Mary*, as that would alter the meaning – and still the speaker wants to make a particular word prominent. The grammar does not permit him to do it by moving the word to a prominent position, for example to the end of the sentence; so he resorts to a change in pitch. This device is so common in English that it adds substantially to the impression of English as a language exceptionally rich in its use of intonation. An extreme example is

            want
   don't
I

              to tell him he isn't the kind of person I would care to spend the rest of my life with.

with everything after *want* at a low-level pitch – to convey the meaning that all of that is more or less understood from what has already been said, and the real focus of information is on what the speaker *wants*. In the last Reading, František Daneš surveys the possibilities and limitations of word order, and then shows how intonation makes up for deficiencies. His work is representative of the Prague School of linguistics, whose members have made 'sentence perspective' – how meanings and their communicative weight or importance are distributed along the length of a sentence – a principal concept in their theories of language.

# 8 Pierre Delattre

## The Distinctive Function of Intonation

from Pierre Delattre, *The General Phonetic Characteristics of Languages*, University of California at Santa Barbara, prepublication of Research Contract OEC-4-7-061990-0176, with the United States Office of Education, 1966–7, pp. 81–102.

Intonation is the salt of an utterance. Without it, a statement can often be understood, but the message is tasteless, colorless. Incorrect uses of it can lead to embarrassing ambiguities.

*Arrêtez le voleur!*  (Arrest the thief!)

could be understood as

*Arrêtez-le, voleur!*  (Arrest him, you thief!)

if the intonation curve does not keep falling until the very end.

*Vous l'appelez imbécile?*  (Are you calling him an idiot?)

might offend the listener and be heard as

*Vous l'appelez? Imbécile!*  (Are you calling him, you idiot?)

unless the rise of the curve increases to the end.

Distinctions of meaning that are due to differences in the intonation curves are not always so clear as the ones above, however. That is perhaps why two schools have appeared. For some, intonation is truly linguistic; differences of level and terminal shape in voice inflexions carry meaning. For others, intonation contours are not truly distinctive, they merely reflect the *attitude* of the speaker.

For the latter, between the encouraging statement

*Il est intelligent, celui-là.*  (He is intelligent, that one.)

said with a continuously falling pitch on *intelligent*, and the ironic one

*Il est intelligent, celui-là.*  (He is intelligent, that one.)

said with a characteristic rise on *lli* and fall on *gent*, an infinite number of *nuances* of meaning are possible, which all reflect differences of attitude but cannot be categorized into discrete units. To obtain linguistic changes of meaning would require some change at the segmental level:

*Il fut intelligent, celui-là.*   (He was intelligent, that one.)

*Est-il intelligent, celui-là?*   (Is he intelligent, that one?)

For the other school, every intonation contour has a distinctive function and can be classed in one of the families of contours often called pitch phonemes, or pitch prosodemes, or intonemes. Then,

*Vous sortez.*   (You are going out.)

with a falling contour, is meaningfully distinct from

*Vous sortez?*   (You are going out?)

with a rising contour, to the same extent as

*Vous sortez.*   (You are going out.)

with the pronoun preceding the verb, is meaningfully distinct from

*Sortez-vous?*   (Are you going out?)

with the pronoun following the verb.

Without taking sides with either school, we shall find ourselves closer to the distinctive-families point of view because we shall concern ourselves here only with the ten most frequent and most clearly defined intonations of French.

But first, to orientate ourselves and realize that a variety of pitch contours can play a role in communication, let us transform a few segmental sequences by exclusively changing the suprasegemental curves.

Everyone can hear what a gruesome meaning is given to the sentence,

*What shall we have for dinner, mother?*

when *mother* is said on a sharply rising intonation, instead of on a low plateau. Similar blunders can occur in French. Figure 1 offers a few examples of such transformation by pitch. Patterns 2, 3, 4 and 6 might result from a 'cannibal attitude'! 2 asks, 'Shall we eat mother?', 3 answers, 'Yes, we shall eat mother.' 4 explains that it is obvious, 'We shall eat mother (of course). Who else is there to eat?' In 5, the rising pitch, taking the place of the falling pitch of 1, changes the question to 'Are you asking me, mother, what we shall have for dinner?' And 6, not addressed to mother any longer, means, 'Are you asking me what we shall have for dinner? I am answering you that we shall have mother.'

Figure 2 offers another segmental sequence which lends itself to transformation by pitch. Examples 2, 4, 6 and 8 could again result from a touch of cannibalism.

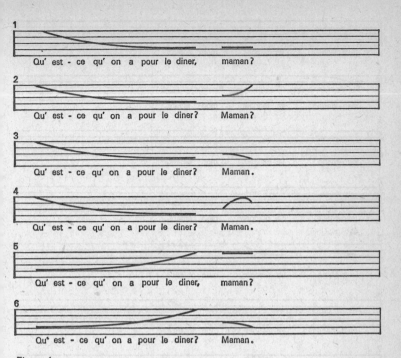

1
Qu' est - ce qu' on a pour le diner,    maman?

2
Qu' est - ce qu' on a pour le diner?    Maman?

3
Qu' est - ce qu' on a pour le diner?    Maman.

4
Qu' est - ce qu' on a pour le diner?    Maman.

5
Qu' est - ce qu' on a pour le diner,    maman?

6
Qu' est - ce qu' on a pour le diner?    Maman.

Figure 1

Figure 3 illustrates the tortures that can be inflicted upon a segmental sequence by varying the pitch contours. The question of line 1 is answered in seven different ways, all differently meaningful. And lines 9 and 10 present two more ways in which the same sequence can be understood.

Let us now see how order and objectivity can be found in this apparent labyrinth of intonation curves. It can be done by applying to the study of pitch contours the rigorous method of phonemic opposition in minimal pairs. This method yields the segmental phonemes of a language by substitution of *one* segment in a sequence. Thus, the oppositions of meaning: *épée, été, aidé, aîné, ailé, effet, essai, aisé*, show that, in French, the phones /p, t, d, n, l, f, s, z/ are distinctive consonant phonemes capable of producing a change of meaning; the oppositions: *pire, pure, pour, père, peur, port, part*, demonstrate that the phones /i, y, u, ɛ, œ, ɔ, a/ are distinctive vowel phonemes.

Similarly, substitutions of pitch curves should yield the distinctive *intonemes* of French. Illustrations of such substitutions are presented in Figures 4 and 5 by means of ten pairs of utterances.

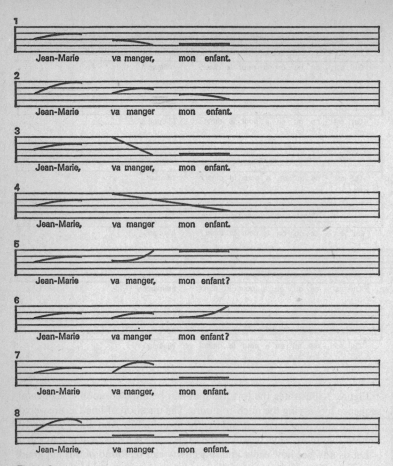

Figure 2

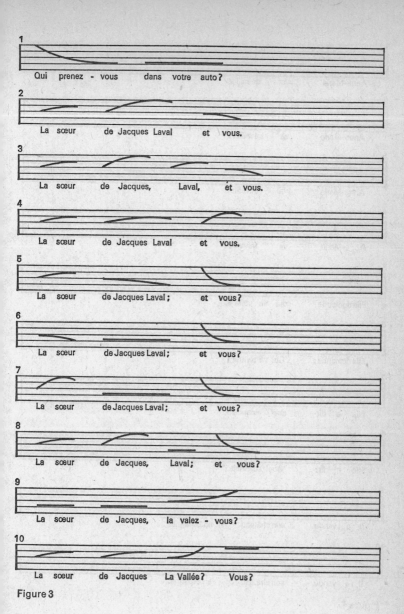

Figure 3

Pierre Delattre 163

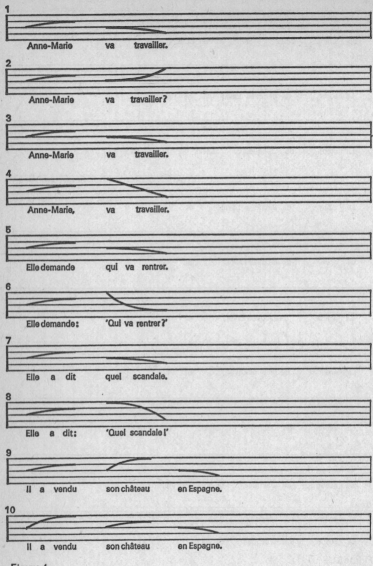

1
Anne-Marie    va    travailler.

2
Anne-Marie    va    travailler?

3
Anne-Marie    va    travailler.

4
Anne-Marie,    va    travailler.

5
Elle demande    qui va rentrer.

6
Elle demande:    'Qui va rentrer?'

7
Elle    a    dit    quel    scandale.

8
Elle    a    dit:    'Quel scandale!'

9
Il a vendu    son château    en Espagne.

10
Il a vendu    son château    en Espagne.

Figure 4

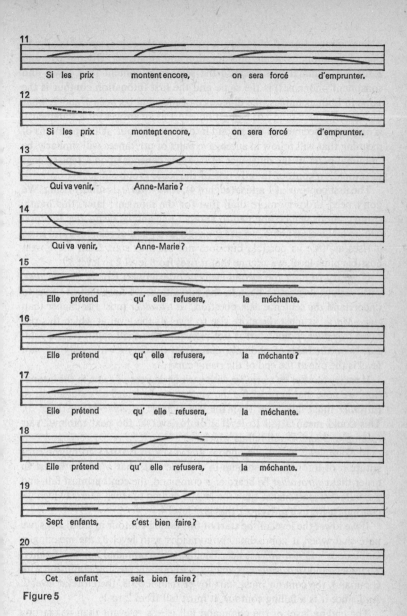

**11**

Si les prix montent encore, on sera forcé d'emprunter.

**12**

Si les prix montent encore, on sera forcé d'emprunter.

**13**

Qui va venir, Anne-Marie ?

**14**

Qui va venir, Anne-Marie ?

**15**

Elle prétend qu' elle refusera, la méchante.

**16**

Elle prétend qu' elle refusera, la méchante ?

**17**

Elle prétend qu' elle refusera, la méchante.

**18**

Elle prétend qu' elle refusera, la méchante.

**19**

Sept enfants, c'est bien faire ?

**20**

Cet enfant sait bien faire ?

Figure 5

In examples 1 and 2 of Figure 4, we oppose the expression of finality to that of question, by means of a question and an answer. Utterances 1 and 2 form a minimal pair because the segmental content (the vowel and consonant phonemes) is the same and the first intonation contour is the same in both examples; the difference of meaning between 1 and 2, what makes one understand 2 as a question and 1 as an answer (or a statement), is only a replacement of the second intonation contour. All oppositions of meaning that will follow in successive pairs of utterances will similarly be 'minimal pairs' if the difference of meaning depends upon a replacement of intonation contour in only one of the sense-group slots.

The first contour of 1 and 2 (Figure 4), *Anne-Marie*, is mildly rising. We don't need to know more than that for the moment; later, this lightly rising contour will be opposed to another one and its distinctive function will be made clear; here, we use it merely as a point of reference and since it rises as little as possible but does not seem to start from the lowest possible pitch level, we assume that it rises from level 2 to level 3.

If we try to utter the second element of examples 1 or 2, *va travailler*, with various degrees of RISE in the intonation, we note that in order to understand the sentence as a question, *va travailler* must rise higher than *Anne-Marie*; it must therefore rise to level 4; the level at which this rise of *va travailler* should start is not relevant – we shall call it level 2 arbitrarily on the basis of phonetic analysis of the curves – the only relevant level is the one at the end of the rising curve.

If we try to utter *va travailler* with various degrees of FALL in the intonation, we note that in order for the sentence to be heard as a statement, *va travailler* must fall lower than the last syllable of *Anne-Marie* (level 3). This could mean a fall to level 2 or to level 1; the next minimal pair (examples 3 and 4) will tell us which.

In examples 3 and 4, we oppose FINALITY to COMMAND by the substitution of intonation contours in a single slot, that of *va travailler*. In order that *va travailler* be heard as a command, the contour must fall, and the fall must start higher than the level-3 ending of *Anne-Marie* (which we continue using as a reference), that is at level 4.

If we lower the level of the start of this falling contour in small steps, we note that when it approximately coincides with level 3, the meaning is ambiguous – *va travailler* is heard neither as a command nor as a finality. To understand *va travailler* as finality, without any possible confusion with command, the contour must start lower than level 3, therefore at level 2. And since it is a falling contour, it must fall from 2 to 1.

The ending level of the command fall is less relevant than its starting level. We shall call it 1 because phonetically, it tends to coincide with the ending level of the finality contour (2-1).

In examples 5 and 6, we oppose FINALITY to INTERROGATION, also called 'information question' or 'falling question', by means of direct-discourse and indirect-discourse utterances. The change of meaning is accomplished by contour substitution in a single slot, that of *qui va rentrer*, the contour of the other slot and the whole segmental content remaining fixed. To take the meaning of interrogation rather than finality, the falling curve of *qui va rentrer* must start higher than the 3-ending of *elle demande*, therefore at level 4. The end of the fall is not relevant; it is arbitrarily placed at level 1 because it generally coincides with the end of finality, according to acoustic data.

It is interesting to note that the *qui va rentrer* of this sequence, in direct as as well as indirect discourse, could be said with a rising (2-4) contour. In that case it would not express interrogation. It would be the end of a question bearing not on *qui va rentrer* but on *elle demande*, even though *elle demande* could only have a 2-3 rise. The two terms of the opposition would then mean: *Is she asking who will return?* (indirect discourse), and: *She is asking:* '*Who will return?*' (direct discourse).

We have just described two contours which fall from level 4. There is one more, in French – the contour of exclamation (or at least its most typical realization, for exclamation enjoys more contour freedom than other expressions).

Examples 7 and 8 oppose finality to exclamation by means of an indirect-style utterance, meaning: *She divulged what a scandal had been caused*, and a direct-style utterance, meaning literally: *She exclaimed:* '*What a scandal!*' To be heard as an exclamation, *quel scandale* must start at a higher level than the 3-ending of *elle a dit*, therefore at level 4.

Acoustic analysis of the three falling contours whose distinctive functions have just been defined show regular, but small, differences among them. Those differences are schematized, on Figures 4 and 5, by a decreasing fall for interrogation, a straight fall for command, and an increasing fall for exclamation. However, those differences are too small to be perceived easily. Auditory tests of those pitch curves after the word content had been filtered out gave negative results with naive listeners; only trained phoneticians were able to distinguish among the three curves. For this reason we should perhaps call those three falling curves non-distinctive among themselves but only distinctive in regard to all the others. We can assume that, if sharper intonation differences among those three contours have not developed, it is because the grammatical differences are generally clear enough to require no prosodic help.

Whereas finality contours are falling, continuation contours are rising, in French. This is as it ought to be – one should easily hear, at the end of each sense-group, whether the sentence is concluding or continuing. But there are two different contours to express continuation in French. One rises higher than the other. The greater rise is called major continuation; the smaller one minor continuation. Examples 9 and 10 oppose minor continuation to major continuation. Here, however, a direct opposition of the types used in the preceding minimal pairs is not possible and we must have recourse to the next best procedure, which is a crossed opposition.

Minor continuation rises to level 3 and major continuation rises higher, therefore, to level 4. This difference of meaning between examples 9 and 10 demonstrates that a minor rise to level 3 and a major rise to level 4 have a distinctive value. When *il a vendu* rises to level 3 and *son château* rises to level 4, it is clear that the owner is returning from Spain, where he sold his castle (a castle that could well be in France). But when the contours are exchanged, that is, when *il a vendu* rises to level 4 and *son château* to level 3, it means that the castle he sold is in Spain (and the sale could have taken place in France). Obviously, the division into immediate constituents occurs after a major continuation rather than a minor one.

Examples of changes of meaning that are produced by exchanging the place of major continuation contours with that of minor continuation contours are common.

*Il a peint* (4) *la jeune fille* (3) *en noir* (1).

means that he made a portrait of a girl wearing black clothes.

*Il a peint* (3) *la jeune fille* (4) *en noir* (1).

could mean that he covered a girl with black paint.

*Il a demandé* (4) *qui écrivait* (3) *à sa fille* (2)?

means that he wanted to know who it was that wrote to his daughter.

*Il a demandé* (3) *qui écrivait* (4) *à sa fille* (1).

means that he asked his daughter to tell him who was writing.

Similar oppositions occur in English, but they are based on the place of stress more than on intonation contours.

*They decorated || the girl | with the flowers.*

is not the same as

*They decorated | the girl || with the flowers.*

But the main distinctive function of the major continuation rise is not made entirely clear by examples of crossed oppositions such as the ones given above. It appears even better in 'echelon' series of sense groups, as below.

*Si Anne-Marie* (3) *vient nous voir* (4), *on sera là* (1).
*Si Anne-Marie* (3) *vient nous voir* (3) *demain matin* (4), *on sera là* (1).
*Si Anne-Marie* (3) *vient nous voir* (3) *demain matin* (3) *pour le déjeuner* (4),
   *on sera là* (1).
*Si Anne-Marie* (3) *vient nour voir* (3) *demain matin* (3) *pour le déjeuner* (3)
   *sur la terrasse* (4), *on sera là* (1).

The function of the major continuation contour seems to be to unite several small units of meaning into one larger unit of meaning which does not end the sentence. Here, the rise to level 4 indicates that all the small sense-groups, from *Si Anne-Marie* to *sur la terrasse*, belong to the large unit of meaning which ends on the word *terrasse*.

Examples 11 and 12 (Figure 5) do not present an opposition. They are given to illustrate a peculiarity of the minor continuation contour, namely the fact that when it precedes a higher pattern (and only then) it can fall, as in example 12, as well as rise, as in example 11. It can fall when followed by a higher pattern, as in *si les prix*, but it must rise when followed by a lower pattern, as in *on sera forcé*. It should be noted, however, that minor continuation seldom takes that falling shape, and takes it for no other purpose, perhaps, than to break the monotony of repeated rising contours.

Examples 13 and 14 (Figure 5) oppose the question to the parenthesis. After falling contours, and after the contour of implication (example 18), parenthesis is expressed by a low plateau, close to level 1, in general. In example 14, to convey that the words *qui va venir* are spoken to Anne-Marie and not about her, *Anne-Marie* must all be said at the low level on which the interrogation *qui va venir?* had ended.

Examples 15 and 16 compare (rather than oppose) two different levels of parenthesis. After a falling contour, as in 15, the parenthesis plateau is low, but after a rising contour, the plateau is high, as in example 16. We note, then, that the parenthesis always takes the shape of a plateau, but the level of the plateau varies according to the contour that precedes. Since the level of the parenthesis plateau is thus conditioned, it can be said that the various levels of parenthesis are in complementary distribution.

The parenthesis plateau has many uses. It is most frequent as the second element in the structure of reduplication.

*C'est lui* (finality), *le voleur.*
*Qui le veut* (interrogation), *ce livre-là?*
*Je le connais* (implication), *votre ami.*
*Il est là* (question), *Jean-Marie?*
*Finissez-le* (command), *ce morceau.*

It is the intonation of the vocative:

*Entrez-donc* (command), *Monsieur.*
*Vous désirez* (question), *Madame?*
*Que voulez-vous* (interrogation), *Anne-Marie?*
*J'ai compris* (finality), *Jean-Pierre.*

It indicates a quotation:

'*Attendez-moi,*' (command) *dit-il.*
'*Il est fou!*' (implication) *s'exclama-t-il.*
'*Il est là?*' (question) *demanda-t-il.*

Examples 17 and 18 oppose *finality* to *implication.* The implication contour normally shows a quickly decreasing rise which ends with an embryo of a fall. The implied idea is generally not explicit, as in example 18; it is most of the time merely implicit, as in the next series of examples.

The contour of implication is used very frequently in everyday communication. To a question such as,

'*Il est arrivé,* (?) *mon ami?*'

one might answer with a series of implication contours, in order to reassure the questioner,

*Mais bien sûr . . .*
*Il est là . . .*
*Il vous attend . . .*
*Et avec impatience . . .*

If the implications were expressed, the contour of low parenthesis would be used:

*Mais bien sûr . . . voyons* (low parenthesis).
*Il est là . . . votre ami.*
*Il vous attend . . . le brave type.*
*Et avec impatience . . . croyez-moi.*

It is probably the first element of a grammatical reduplication that makes the best use of the implication contour:

*Je l'ai aperçu . . . votre ami.*
*Elle est connue . . . cette histoire.*
*J'en ai assez . . . de cette affaire.*

Implication can replace finality.

*J'ai vu Jean . . . (vous savez).*
*Il na' pas compris . . . (le pauvre type).*

It can replace command.

*Donnez-le-moi . . . (s'il vous gêne).*
*Qu'il parte donc . . . (puisqu'il n'est pas heureux).*

It can replace a question contour, the meaning being then radically changed to a request for approval.

*Vous viendrez . . . (n'est-ce pas)?*
*C'est bien vous . . . (qui l'avez fait)?*

It can even replace an exclamation, to lend a flavor of mystery.

*Quelle horreur . . .*
*Quel scandale . . .*
*Au secours . . .*

Finally, examples 19 and 20 show that it is not impossible to oppose minor continuation directly to another contour. But it takes a *tour de force* of homophony. If *sept enfants* is uttered on the low plateau of parenthesis, the phonemes (sɛtãfãsɛbjẽfɛr) are understood as: *Sept enfants, c'est bien faire?* But when *sept enfants* is given a contour of minor continuation, the same sequence of segmental phonemes is heard as: *Cet enfant sait bien faire?*

We mentioned earlier that the three contours that fall from level 4 are not clearly distinctive among themselves. Now looking back at Figures 4 and 5 we note that we also have three contours that R I S E to level 4: question, major continuation and implication. But those three are fairly distinctive among themselves, according to auditory tests given to naive listeners. In the figures, they are given schematized shapes which roughly represent their objective variations: for the question, an increasingly rising curve; for the major continuation, a decreasingly rising curve; and for the implication, a decreasingly rising curve with a slightly falling appendix.

To indicate the distinction by symbols, we add terminals to the levels as follows:

Question: 2–4₊
Major continuation: 2–4
Implication: 2–4_

In summary, of the ten intonation contours that emerge from our analysis by oppositions in minimal pairs, only seven are clearly distinctive:

1. Question (2–4₊)
2. Implication (2–4_)
3. Major Continuation (2–4)

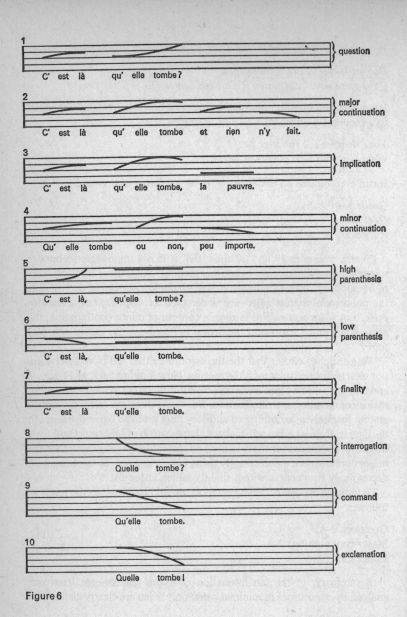

Figure 6

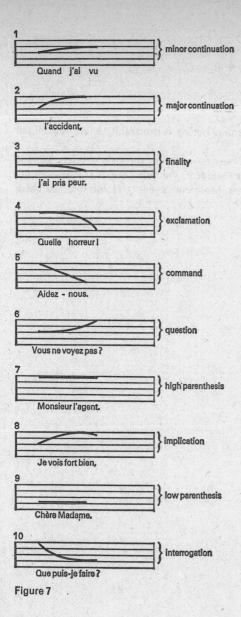

1   minor continuation
Quand j'ai vu

2   major continuation
l'accident,

3   finality
j'ai pris peur.

4   exclamation
Quelle horreur !

5   command
Aidez - nous.

6   question
Vous ne voyez pas ?

7   high parenthesis
Monsieur l'agent.

8   implication
Je vois fort bien,

9   low parenthesis
Chère Madame.

10   interrogation
Que puis-je faire ?

Figure 7

4. Minor Continuation (2–3)
5. Finality (2–1)
6. The two parenthesis (1–1, 4–4)
7. Interrogation (4–1)
   Command (4–1)
   Exclamation (4–1)

With the segmental phonemes (kɛltɔ̃b), it is possible to illustrate all ten contours (Figure 6).

We can also illustrate those ten contours through a brief dialogue (Figure 7): 'Quand j'ai vu l'accident, j'ai pris peur. – Quelle horreur! Aidez-nous. Vous ne voyez pas, Monsieur l'agent ? – Je vois fort bien, chère Madame. Que puis-je faire?'

# 9 Maria Schubiger

English Intonation and German Modal Particles:
A Comparative Study

Maria Schubiger, 'English intonation and German modal particles:
a comparative study', *Phonetica*, vol. 12, 1965, pp. 65–84; published by
S. Karger, Basel.

## Author's summary

After having established a certain parallelism between German modal
particles and English emotive intonation, the author examines in detail the
English tone patterns that can correspond to unstressed German *doch* in the
sense of 'By the way you talk one would think you didn't know.' It is
found that both the prenuclear tone and the nucleus can express this connotation, the former mainly by avoiding the neutral stepping head, the
latter by a preference for a rise–fall, in some cases a rise, instead of the
more neutral fall. Statements, commands and questions are passed in review.

The investigation of English intonation has reached a point where its
form has been explored almost to perfection, but where the various attempts to assess its function have resulted in a mosaic of partly concordant,
partly divergent opinions. Neither the description of French intonation nor
that of German – to mention only two languages the present author is
familiar with – has given rise to similar discussions. This is not only due
to the fact that the intonation of those languages has been investigated less
thoroughly than that of English – both American and British ('Received
Pronunciation') – but also to the less prominent part played by intonation
as sole bearer of subjective functions in these languages. In French there is
a wealth of turns of syntax, 'la syntaxe affective', unknown to English
(see Schubiger, 1935, p. 53); in German the so-called modal particles
largely perform this task.[1] Neither in French nor in German does this

1. The German particles have been treated – more or less summarily – by both
lexicographers and grammarians. Then comparisons with other languages have been
drawn. Arndt (1960) compares them with the similar Russian modal particles, Collinson
(1954) with the corresponding English means of expression. Although there are fewer
modal particles in English, locutional equivalents can be found in most cases. But in
the spoken language there is a strong tendency to do without them. This situation is also
reflected in the English translations of German works of literature. In the books
examined by Frau Pestalozzi-Schärli (n.d.) in her recent dissertation on *doch* and its
English (locutional) equivalents only 25 per cent of the *doch* particles have been
translated.

impair the role played by emotional intonation; but it is apt to make the grammarian by-pass this delicate subject, since he can base his description on locutional means of expression.

The present writer has on more than one occasion pointed to the semantic correspondence between German particles and certain English tone patterns (Schubiger, 1935, pp. 32, 36–8; 1958, pp. 44, 46). It is the purpose of this paper to make a further contribution to the subject. The great number of German particles, both simple and combined, makes it possible for the speaker to put into words practically every shade of feeling he wants to express. The elocutional means on which the English speaker heavily relies when urged to express his feelings, though just as expressive and differentiated, are much more elusive. At the base there is one of the two fundamental tone patterns: A nuclear fall (F) connotes finality, a nuclear rise (R) or fall–rise (FR) need of supplementation. With each sentence type one basic tone pattern can be considered neutral (R for general questions, F for all other sentence types), i.e. not connoting anything beyond what is expressed by the words, the other marked, i.e. conveying some additional meaning. The latter can only be gathered from the contents and context of the sentence. Roughly speaking, it can also be gathered from the sentence type. It has often been stated, e.g. that R instead of neutral F makes imperatives into requests and special questions into requests for information. The prenuclear patterns, too, can be either neutral or marked.[2]

It is interesting to note that when we set about assessing the meaning of the German particles, which, it would seem, was an easier task, we are faced with similar difficulties. The precise meaning of the particle can in many cases be gathered only from the contents and context of the sentence; and the various meanings often fall into groups that correspond to sentence types. Three examples will illustrate this.

2. 'Neutral' and 'marked' are terms the present writer has taken over from Halliday (1963). Hultzén (1959) speaks of congruous and incongruous use of F and R, the latter signalling that some qualification must be made regarding the utterance (p. 109) (see also Schubiger, 1958, p. 41: basic patterns and patterns with a specific connotation). What still remains to be analysed more closely, and can therefore not be taken into serious consideration in this paper, is voice quality. Voice quality is partly superposed on the melodic element (loudness, length, harshness or softness, etc.), partly a modification of the tone pattern itself: larger or smaller intervals, high or low average pitch (called voice quality and vocal qualifiers by Trager (1958)). Trager has made the closest tentative study of this subject, which he calls 'paralanguage'. Pike considers these phenomena under the title 'Modifications of contours' (1945, pp. 99–101). Catford (1964, p. 35) speaks of the paraphonological function of phonation in speech, as opposed to the phonological and the non-phonological one.

**1.** *nur*     *Imperative*

Hab *nur* keine Angst. Warte *nur*. Laß mich *nur* machen.

Tone of reassurance. With other voice-quality: threat (second sentence).

*Question*

Wie kommst du *nur* nach Hause? Doubt.

*Statement*

Ich muß mich *nur* wundern, daß er es aushält. Emphasis.

**2.** *doch*     *Retort*

A. Wieso kann Jacques denn so gut deutsch?

B. Er ist *doch* Elsässer. *doch* = as you should know.

*Exclamatory statement*

Der Hans ist *doch* ein Schlaumeier.

**3.** *schon*     *Reassuring statement*. Reaction to interlocutor's doubtful or worried utterance.

Ich werde *schon* aufpassen. Er wird *schon* darüber hinwegkommen. Die Firma wird es *schon* zahlen.

*Calculating statement*, pointing to a minimum requirement.

Ich werde *schon* aufpassen müssen. Drei Tage wirst du *schon* rechnen müssen. Zehn Franken wird's *schon* kosten. Wir werden's *schon* runternehmen müssen.

There is a similarity between German and English also in this: just as the basic function of the English intonation pattern is felt more or less distinctly, or has faded altogether, the originally notional meaning of the German particles has been eclipsed to a greater or smaller extent; e.g.

*English*

*It `isn't ˇbad* (= but it is not very good either).

Here the implication, expressed by the FR, is felt quite clearly.

*`Mind you don't ˇfall.*

Here there is no suggestion of something that might follow. The FR adds a warning note to the imperative.

*German*

Ist es *auch* wahr? (= You say it. But it is *also* true?)

Was der Kerl *auch* für Einfälle hat!

Here the notion of addition has disappeared altogether. The particle is purely emotive.

In consequence the insertion of a German particle or the use of a certain English nuclear tone is in some cases essential. English *It ˋisn't ˇbad* is notionally different from *It ˈisn't ˋbad*, German *Ist es auch wahr?* from *Ist es wahr?* In other cases – chiefly exclamatory sentences – one can make free use of these means of expression, their notional function having completely faded. There is no difference of meaning between

*German*: Bist du elegant! and Bist du *aber* (or *mal*) elegant!
*English*: ˉYou ˏare ˌelegant and ˉYou ˄are ˌelegant.

In view of this parallelism between German particles and English tone patterns it is tempting to compare the two means of expression in more detail. Yet within the scope of this article such a comparison can only cover a small and strictly limited section of the vast field. We shall make meaning our starting-point and consider rejoinders with the connotation: 'by the way you talk (or act) one would think you didn't know (or were ignorant of the circumstances)'. This kind of utterance lends itself to a comparison, because the connotation is in English nearly always expressed by intonation alone, in German by an unstressed particle, in most cases *doch*.[3] In English the tune with the nuclear F preceded by one or more low-pitched or gradually rising and therefore rather reduced innate stresses very often has the above connotation.[4] This is not surprising. Reduced innate stresses often denote that these items are not new to the situation; they also tend to give the utterance an unpleasant ring; e.g. *The ˌclock has ˌstopped aˋgain. I'm aˌfraid I've upˌset the ˋmilk* (O'Connor and Arnold, 1961, pp. 109–10, 120). Now by definition the particle *doch* we are here concerned with occurs in a sentence whose contents are not entirely new to the interlocutor. Moreover, unpleasant surprise, protest, censure easily colour an utterance which recalls to the interlocutor what he should know, or remember, or be aware of. Here are some *statements* with this tone pattern:

A. When can I have my typewriter back?

3. In his interesting book on the technique of translation Fritz Güttinger considers *doch* – together with *noch* and *bitte* – as one of the tests of a good German translation from the English: Indifferent translators do not make full use of this particle, which has no counterpart in English (1963, p. 148).
4. Allen gives both prenuclear patterns, saying that it is quite immaterial which we use, the rising trend being more usual when the introductory unstressed group is rather long (1954, p. 68). Kingdon, too, gives both patterns, the level prenuclear intonation being pitched very low (1958, p. 52). In O'Connor and Arnold (1961) the tone gradually rises from the first semi-stressed syllable to the beginning of the fall (pp. 17, 120). We shall here make use of both ways of marking.

B. *I ˌsent it ˌto you ˌthree `days aˌgo* (O'Connor and Arnold, 1961, p. 122).[5]
  Ich hab sie Ihnen *doch* schon vor drei Tagen zurückgeschickt.

(To somebody who seems to have missed our previous remark.)
*That's ˌjust what I `said* (Palmer, 1922, p. 73).
Das hab ich *doch* eben gesagt.

(To somebody who does not see an obvious equivalence.)
*That's the ˌsame `thing* (Palmer, 1922, p. 73).
Das ist *doch* dasselbe.

(To somebody impatiently waiting for breakfast.)
*I've ˌonly just got `up.*
Ich bin *doch* eben erst aufgestanden.

(To somebody suggesting an invitation to complete strangers.)
*We ˌdon't even ·know their natio`nality* (Jassem, 1952, p. 71).[6]
Wir kennen *ja* (or *doch*) nicht einmal ihre Nationalität.[7]

*ˌWillie is a `friend of mine; we ˌwent to `school toˌgether* (Frisch, 1962, p. 25).
Der Willi ist *doch* mein Freund; wir sind *doch* zusammen zur Schule gegangen (Frisch, 1959, p. 217).

*I ˌdidn't say a `word about your ˌmaking a ˌnoise when you ˌeat* (Frisch, 1962, p. 19).
Ich hab *doch* kein Wort gesagt, daß Sie schmatzen (Frisch, 1959, p. 213).

*But your ˌfifth (husband) was a `surgeon* (Dürrenmatt, 1962, p. 51).
Aber dein fünfter war *doch* Chirurg (Dürrenmatt, 1956, p. 50).

Carpenter (in despair):
*But they (the boards) are ˌmade to `measure* (Brecht, 1957, p. 24).
Aber sie sind *doch* nach Maß gemacht (Brecht, 1956, p. 38).

5. The specimen sentences with a reference to the source are drawn from two kinds of books: a) textbooks of Intonation, above all O'Connor and Arnold (1961), where all the utterances are set in appropriate contexts; b) German and English works of literature, mainly modern plays, and their translations. With (b) the passages where *doch* is not translated – or appears in the German translation without having a counterpart in the English original – where therefore intonation must express the connotation, have been marked by the present writer. It goes without saying that this marking is impressionistic, and that other variants would be possible, just as other patterns are often conceivable with the tonetically marked utterances of the textbooks. Non-impressionistic marking would have to be based on experiments, with a great number of subjects reading the same passage, a laborious task not considered necessary for this comparative study of two languages.

6. We had to construct this and a few of the following contexts, as most authors give only isolated sentences.

7. On the slight difference between *doch* and *ja* in the connotation here under scrutiny (Er ist *doch* krank/Er ist *ja* krank), the former having retained some of the adversative force of stressed *doch*, the latter merely reminding the interlocutor of something he knows, see Ehrke, 1926, p. 220.

Housekeeper (to Shen Te):

*I've ,no i·dea who you `are* (Brecht, 1957, p. 17).
Aber ich weiß *doch* gar nicht, wer Sie sind (Brecht, 1956, p. 27).[8]

If the surprise or protest is vivid, the prenuclear section can be modified in various ways. The rising movement is sometimes repeated, in which case the prenuclear stresses have their full weight. The pre-head can be pitched high or low; e.g.

(ˉ) *I've ,no i,dea who you `are.*

(ˉ) *We ,don't even ,know their natio`nality.*
*,Justice ,can't be `bought* (Dürrenmatt, 1962, p. 36).
Die Gerechtigkeit kann man *doch* nicht kaufen (Dürrenmatt, 1956, p. 32).

(ˉ) *But he ,wants to ,marry her to the `barber* (Brecht, 1957, p. 60).
Aber der will sie *doch* mit dem Barbier verheiraten (Brecht, 1956, p. 92).[9]

If the retort is chiefly a protest against the interlocutor's inconsistency, or similar contradictory attitude, the R nucleus is appropriate. The utterance verbalizes one element of the contradiction, the R nucleus implies the other. Here French *pourtant* renders the same meaning; e.g.

(To somebody who was pleased yesterday and is now complaining.)
*It was ,all ,right ,yesterday.* (So why complain to-day?) (Palmer, 1922, p. 78).
Gestern war's dir *doch* recht.
Tu étais *pourtant* d'accord hier.[10]

(To somebody reproaching us for inactivity.)
*I've ,done all I ,can.* (So why do you blame me.)

8. The connotation phoneticians have attributed to this pattern is remarkably uniform; O'Connor and Arnold (1961): querulous or disgruntled protest (p. 40). It is noteworthy that several of O'Connor and Arnold's drill sentences with this intonation (Tone-group 3) translate into a German sentence with *doch*; while none of the numerous statements with full prenuclear stresses (Tone-group 4) would in German suggest *doch*. Kingdon (1958): patient expostulation (p. 125). Jassem (1952): surprise, protest (p. 71). Palmer (1922): retorts (p. 73). Pike (1945) says of the rising pre-contour, which is relatively rare in American: protest (p. 68).

9. Also in German there can be a rising trend in the prenuclear part, which makes for greater liveliness, e.g. Aber ich,weiß doch gar nicht sie`sind (Collinson, 1954, p. 20). Though the description of German intonation is outside the scope of this article, there will be an occasional reference to it.

10. *Pourtant* is not essential. The rising intonation with equal intervals throughout is the main bearer of this connotation. The same pattern with a greater interval between the penultimate and the ultimate syllable is interrogative (see Coustenoble and Armstrong, 1934, p. 56).

Ich hab *doch* mein Möglichstes getan.
J'ai *pourtant* fait tout ce que j'ai pu.

(To somebody who has burst into tears.)
Stop crying. *You're ₁no ₁longer a ₁child.*
Schluß mit den Tränen. Du bist *doch* kein Kind mehr.

(To somebody complaining that he cannot enjoy the party.)
*You ₁weren't un₁happy on the ₁last occasion* (Palmer, 1922, p. 78).
Das letzte Mal hat's dir *doch* gefallen.

A. Don't let us joke any longer about ...
B. *We're ₁not ₁joking* (Frisch, 1962, p. 59).
Wir scherzen *ja* nicht (Frisch, 1959, p. 244).

(To the mate who went off to get wood-wool.)
What on earth is keeping you so long?
*₁Wood-wool is ₁easy enough to get ₁hold of* (Frisch, 1962, p. 39).
Holzwolle ist *doch* keine Sache (Frisch, 1959, p. 228).

La Hire: The wind is against him. Bluebeard: How can the wind hurt him at Orleans? *It is ₁not on the ₁Channel* (Shaw, 1936, p. 119). Orleans liegt *doch* nicht am Kanal (Shaw, 1925, p. 107).[11]

*Remark.* Sometimes this tone pattern, especially with negative or restrictive statements, does not so obviously point to an inconsistency. It

11. With this pattern, too, the connotations attributed to it by phoneticians are very similar: O'Connor and Arnold (1961): reproving criticism, resentful contradictions. Many of the drill sentences (Tone-group 6, esp. pp. 185–6) translate into a German sentence with *doch*. O'Connor and Arnold are handicapped by not distinguishing the low rise going up only a little and the low rise often reaching above the middle of the normal voice range. That is why they have to lump together the above connotations, which are expressed by a considerable rise, and 'reserving judgement, guarded', which has a lower rise (pp. 49, 169). Kingdon distinguishes the two types of rises by calling the one we are here concerned with 'emphatic low rise', with the connotation 'impatience or exasperation' (1958, p. 222). Some of his examples can very well be pictured in a context that in German suggests *doch*. Jassem, too, distinguishes the low-rising 'reserved' nuclear tone (1952, p. 76) from the full-rising one, which, when preceded by a low prenuclear tone, indicates 'surprise, bewilderment or protest' (pp. 75–6). Palmer also has the two rises, though his low rise, always preceded by a rising head, has not the same connotation as the low rise without head. He says of the one we are here concerned with that it is used with statements implying 'then why not ...'. Many of his examples are retorts of the *doch* type (1922, p. 78). Halliday likewise distinguishes the two rises, statements with the full rise being labelled 'contradictory, challenging, aggressive, etc.' (1963, p. 22). The present writer has resorted to a makeshift, speaking of a 'relatively high-rising low rise' (Schubiger, 1958, p. 44). Pike (1945) calls the low rise (4–3) deliberative, the high rise (4–1) deliberative + surprised, two attitudes, it would seem to the present writer, that are mutually exclusive. But to enter upon this question is outside the scope of this article.

chiefly connotes protest, criticism. Here, too, German *doch* is appropriate; e.g.

A. I shall have to sack him.
B. *You ₁can't do ₂that* (he is too useful) (O'Connor and Arnold, 1961, p. 49).
   Das darfst du *doch* nicht tun.


With R statements, where, contrary to F statements, the direction of the nuclear glide suggests on its own a subjective connotation, the nucleus can fall at or near the beginning, without blurring the *doch* connotation. The reduced stresses, if any, occur in the tail, where they are incorporated in the nuclear tone movement and do not of their own accord contribute to the expressive value of the tone pattern; e.g.

A. What a wretched week it has been.
B. *₂Yesterday was ·not a ·bad ·day* (O'Connor and Arnold, 1961, p. 173).
   Gestern war's *doch* ganz schön.

A. Sixpence, for that small amount.
B. *₂Sixpence won't ·break you* (O'Connor and Arnold, 1961, p. 173).
   Wegen Sixpence machst du *doch* nicht Pleite.

A. I don't think *we* ought to tell him.
B. *₂Someone's ·got to ·do it* (O'Connor and Arnold, 1961, p. 173).
   Jemand muß es ihm *doch* sagen.

A. Oh, I do wish I could go.
B. *₂I'm not ·stopping you* (O'Connor and Arnold, 1961, p. 173).
   ¹Ich halte dich *doch* nicht zurück.[12]

In addition to the emotive prenuclear intonation – or instead of it – a more emotional form of the nucleus can emphasize – or express – the *doch* connotation. A challenging or censorious attitude can be expressed by a rise–fall (RF) instead of a F; e.g.

A. Why didn't you tell me?
B. *You didn't ^ask me* (O'Connor and Arnold, 1961, p. 157).
   Du hast mich *doch* (or *ja*) gar nicht gefragt.

---

12. It is true that also utterances with an early falling nucleus can correspond to a German *doch*-sentence, namely when the words themselves suggest the connotation here under discussion; e.g. *I ˋtold you it was ₁foolish to ₁do it*. Ich hab dir *doch* gesagt, es sei unklug . . . . Compare with this the following utterance, where the words do not suggest that the interlocutor is reminded of what he knows already and where in consequence there is no *doch* in the German sentence: *I ˋtold him it was ₁foolish to ₁do it*. Ich hab ihm gesagt, es sei unklug. . . .

A. Don't close the door.
B. *But I ˌwasn't ^going to.*[13]
   Ich hab sie *doch* (or *ja*) gar nicht schließen wollen.

As the censorious attitude is expressed by the R F nucleus, there is no need of a prenuclear part with this connotation; the nucleus may occur quite early, with the reduced stresses in the tail; e.g.

A. Could you give me a tip every now and then?
B. Why should I? *Your ca^reer ˌdoesn't conˌcern me.*
   Deine Karriere geht mich *doch* nichts an.

A. May I have some more trifle?
B. *There ^isn't any ˌmore. You've ^eaten it ˌall* (O'Connor and Arnold, 1961, p. 157).
   Du hast *doch* alles aufgegessen.[14]

The F R instead of an early R is rather a down-toner than an intensifier.

| | |
|---|---|
| ˇ*Someone's ·got to ·do it.* | Jemand muß es *doch* tun. |
| ˇ*I'm not ·stopping you.* | ˈIch halte dich *doch* nicht zurück. |
| ˇ*I've no ·cause to be aˌfraid.* | ˈIch brauch *doch* keine Angst zu haben. |

are more mildly argumentative than ˌ*Somebody's got . . .*, ˌ*I've no . . .*, ˌ*I'm not. . . .*[15]

Also the R F R is possible, which tends to add a note of cheerfulness to the mildly argumentative F R; e.g.

(To a child afraid of bees.)
ⁿ*They won't ·hurt you.*
Die tun dir *doch* nichts an.

(To somebody warning us.)
ⁿ*I've said ·nothing ·wrong.*
ˈIch hab *doch* nichts Falsches gesagt.
ⁿ*Yesterday was ·not a ·bad ·day.*

13. This sentence is taken from Monfries (1963), Drill 34: 'Protesting answers and unjust commands', where the student is instructed to use RF throughout.
14. One of the labels O'Connor and Arnold (1961) attach to RF statements is: 'challenging or censorious' (p. 45). Kingdon says: 'mocking or impatient; in some cases protest against a false assumption' (1958, p. 221).
15. Cf. the down-toning effect of FR instead of R in flat contradictions, pointed out by O'Connor and Arnold (1961, p. 62): A. I can do it on Monday. B. *You ˌcan't* (as you ought to know perfectly well). *You ˇcan't* (and I am sorry that you should think you can). Kingdon (1958) gives the example: A. He hasn't taken them. B. ˋ*Yes he ˇhas* (apologetic).

The preceding FR and RFR utterances have in common the fact that the nucleus comes early, with the reduced stresses in the tail. The final rise often occurs on one of these potentially stressed post-nuclear words and gives it secondary prominence. In all these cases of intensified or toned-down English tone patterns the German particle is the same. The variants are mostly expressed, as in English, by elocutional means.

Many statements with one or more reduced prenuclear stresses followed by a nuclear rise, as exemplified on pages 180–81, have a FR or rather F + R variant, too. The F mostly occurs on a negative or restrictive element of the sentence. This pattern adds a plaintive or pleading note to the protest; e.g.

A. I do wish he'd mind his own business.
B. *But he was ˋonly ˌtrying to be ˌhelpful* (O'Connor and Arnold, 1961, p. 255).
Er hat uns *doch* bloß helfen wollen.

A. It's an absolute scandal.
B. *There's ˋno need to ˌget so worked ˌup aˋbout it* (O'Connor and Arnold, 1961, p. 255).
Du brauchst dich *doch* nicht so aufzuregen.

A. The amount of time one wastes there.
B. *You ˋdidn't ˌhave to wait ˌlong.*
Du hast *doch* gar nicht lange warten müssen.
Cf. *You ˌdidn't ˌhave to wait ˌlong* (O'Connor and Arnold, 1961, p. 185).

Here as elsewhere it is not always easy to keep FR and F + R neatly separate. Although slightly differing tone patterns have been claimed for them (Lee, 1956, p. 69), they are, to all intents and purposes, melodically identical. But while FR/*doch* takes us into the vicinity of concessive (limiting) *anyway, jedenfalls*; F + R/*doch* does not. It is purely emotional and could also be rendered by *really, wirklich*. Compare the following examples, all with similar wording, taken from O'Connor and Arnold (1961).

A. What a terrible waste of money!
B. *ˌYou ˋdidn't ·lose by it* (p. 174).
ˈDu hast *doch* nichts dabei eingebüßt.

A. I'm sorry about the mess.
B. *ˇYou ·couldn't ·help it* (p. 232).
ˈDu kannst *doch* nichts dafür.
Cf. *ˇyou · couldn't ·help it, ˋanyway.*
ˈDu kannst *jedenfalls* nichts dafür.

which in substance is not very different.[16]

A. Whatever made you pay him?
B. *It ₁couldn't be a₁voided* (p. 185).
   Ich konnte *doch* nicht anders.

A. Trust *you* to do something silly.
B. *I ˋcouldn't ₁help it* (p. 255).
   Ich kann *doch* nichts dafür.
   Cf. *I ˋreally ₁couldn't ₁help it.*
   Ich kann *wirklich* nichts dafür.
   which is about equivalent.[17]

The reaction of the speaker to his interlocutor's utterance or attitude can take the form of an *imperative*. Here the connotation is: 'By the way you talk (or behave) one would think you didn't know what was the obvious thing to do.' German *doch*, which here corresponds to French *donc*, is chiefly used in utterances which are a reaction to somebody's attitude or behaviour; while *eben* (Alemannic *halt*), French *eh bien*, appears in a rejoinder to an utterance; e.g.

(To a girl standing idly about.)
*₁Give me a ˋhand, Anna* (Frisch, 1962, p. 46).
Helfen Sie mir *doch*, Anna (Frisch, 1959, p. 234).
Aidez-moi *donc*.

(To somebody laughing at our ignorance.)
*You'd ₁better exˋplain it to me.*[18]
So erklär es mir *doch* (Frisch, 1959, p. 236).
Explique-le moi *donc*.

(To somebody out of breath and complaining of it.)
*₁Don't be in ·such a ˋhurry* (Brecht, 1957, p. 62).
Haben Sie *doch* nicht solche Eile (Brecht, 1956, p. 94).
Ne soyez *donc* pas si pressé.

A. I can't make a nosegay with one single flower.
B. *₁Try and ₁find an ˋother* (Palmer, 1922, p. 74).
   Such *eben* noch eine zweite.
   *Eh bien*, tâche d'en trouver une autre.

16. All the sentences followed by *anyway* that we have come across in the textbooks have a FR.
17. Kingdon marks F + R in the following way: *You ˋneedn't do ₋that. There ˋisn't a ₋better one;* for 'at times the rising tone falls on what may be considered to be the most important word in the utterance' (1958, p. 127).
18. Our own translation. The translator's version is unsatisfactory.

In English this kind of imperative often begins with *well*, corresponding to French *eh bien*, or ends with *then*, meaning *in that case*. In German it can begin with *so*, which also means *in that case*. However, these particles are not indispensable. The German particle *eben* and the English tone-pattern are the main bearers of the connotation; e.g.

A. The bus doesn't run on Sundays.
B. *Come by ˋtrain ˎthen* (O'Connor and Arnold, 1961, p. 125).
   So komm *eben* mit dem Zug.

A. I wish Ann didn't dislike me so.
B. *Well ˎdon't be so ˋrude to her in ˎfuture* (O'Connor and Arnold, 1961, p. 125).
   So sei *eben* in Zukunft etwas netter zu ihr.[19]

As with statements, the RF sometimes replaces the F, with a similar connotation; e.g.

A. This apple is not quite ripe.
B. *Take an^other one* (if you don't like the one you've got)
   (Kingdon, 1958, p. 231).
   Nimm *eben* einen anderen.

A. I ought to invite her.
B. *Well then in^vite her* (O'Connor and Arnold, 1961, p. 160).
   So lad sie *eben* ein.
   *Eh bien* invite-la.

A. This pen's useless.
B. *Well ˈtry a ^different one* (O'Connor and Arnold, 1961, p. 167).
   Versuch's *eben* mit einer anderen.

A. So far I haven't had time.
B. *ˈStart ^now, then* (O'Connor and Arnold, 1961, p. 167).
   So beginn *eben* jetzt.

The RF is especially appropriate with this type of imperative, because, like the German particle *eben*, it conveys that slightly mocking, detached

19. O'Connor and Arnold say of imperatives with this tone pattern 'critical surprise' (1961, p. 42). There are several other examples on page 125. As of statements, Palmer says of these imperatives: suggesting 'in that case' (1922, p. 74). With imperatives comprising at least two full stresses only, the pattern with a low nuclear fall is neutral. The pattern with a high fall links the utterance with what precedes and can have a similar connotation to the one discussed here with a low-pitched prenuclear tone sequence. Many of O'Connor and Arnold's drill sentences 137–9 translate into German imperatives with *doch* or *eben*. That the difference between the high and the low nuclear fall with imperatives applies also to American English may be concluded from Bolinger (1961, pp. 41–2).

attitude of somebody pointing to what the interlocutor should have hit upon himself.[20]

*Remark.* Imperatives with R do not, strictly speaking, belong here. They do not express an obvious consequence of the interlocutor's statement but connote sheer protest, like the statements with R mentioned in the remark on pages 181–2. That is why German *eben* is inappropriate here; e.g.

A. I'm going to sack him.
B. ˌDon't ˌdo ˌthat (O'Connor and Arnold, 1961, p. 191).
   Tu das *doch* nicht.

A. I'm terribly sorry.
B. ˌDon't aˌpologize (O'Connor and Arnold, 1961, p. 192).
Entschuldige dich *doch* nicht.[21]

With a F R these imperatives, like the corresponding statements, have a note of plaintive pleading (see O'Connor and Arnold, 1961, p. 249); e.g. ˋDon't ˌdo ˌthat. ˋDon't let it ˌget you ˌdown (O'Connor and Arnold, 1961, p. 259).

The reaction to the situation here under discussion, though it cannot be a real question, is sometimes cast in the interrogative form. Here the German particle is *denn*. With *special questions* the nucleus is a F or R F, with similar connotations as in the corresponding statements and imperatives: *what* questions correspond to statements, negative *why* questions in the present tense to imperatives; e.g.

(To somebody bothering us with his personal problems.)
ˌWhat's it got to ·do with ˋus? (Jassem, 1952, p. 71).
Was geht *denn* das mich an? = Das geht *doch* mich nichts an.

(To somebody refusing to believe in a person's identity.)
ˉWhat ˌelse can he ˋbe? (Frisch, 1962, p. 56).
Was kann er *denn* sonst sein? (Frisch, 1959, p. 241).

(To somebody complaining of his tight new shoes.)
ˌWhy don't you ˌwear an ˋold ˌpair?

(To somebody who has tried in vain to ring up a friend.)
ˌWhy don't you ˌwrite him a ˋletter?

20. O'Connor and Arnold say of RF imperatives 'shrugging off responsibility' (p. 48). Kingdon: 'impatient commands' (1958, p. 231).
21. As with statements, O'Connor and Arnold say of imperatives with this pattern: 'reproving criticism' (p. 532).

(To somebody perplexed by a predicament.)
ˌWhy don't you ^do something aˌbout it?

In German the imperative is much more appropriate here than the question form. The same holds good with French.

Zieh *doch* alte Schule an. Schreib ihm *doch* einen Brief.
Tu *doch* etwas in dieser Sache.
Ecris-lui *donc* une lettre.

*Remark.* There are many borderline cases, where one is in doubt whether the utterance is a real question or a veiled statement; for real questions, too, can have this intonation, which connotes surprise, often unpleasant surprise; e.g.

A. You must let me in. I've got a season ticket.
B. ˌWhy didn't you ˌsay so beˋfore (O'Connor and Arnold, 1961, p. 123).
Warum haben Sie das *denn* nicht gleich gesagt?
ˌWhat are you ˋtalking about? Von was redest du *denn*?

(To somebody who says that his guest does not like wine.)
ˌHow d'you ˋknow he ˌdoesn't ˌlike it?
Wieso weißt du *denn*, daß er ihn nicht gern hat?[22]

The surprise can also be caused by something or somebody catching our eye. The nucleus falls on the item that causes the surprise.

ˌWhat are ˋyou doing in the ˌPark? (Schubiger, 1935, p. 28).
Was tust *denn* du hier im Park?
ˌWhat did ˋshe ˌwant? (Schubiger, 1935, p. 31).
Was wollte *denn* die?[23]

Incidentally the last two examples point to another, more intellectual function of the German modal particle. When placed before a personal pronoun or similar normally unstressed word it indicates that this form-word bears a full stress. In the English corresponding sentences the context alone guides the speaker – or reader – in the placement of stresses. In

22. Many more examples are to be found in Allen's Exercise 70 (1954, pp. 73–4).
23. O'Connor and Arnold say that with special questions this pattern expresses a reaction to something very unexpected, and, for that reason perhaps, not immediately pleasing to the questioner (p. 40). With low head: 'somewhat unpleasantly surprised' (p. 109). Jassem says: 'surprise and protest' (1952, p. 71). Kingdon: 'mystification' (1958, p. 125).

print italics are often made use of, for instance in the above two sentences, both from Galsworthy's *Forsyte Saga*.

Here are some more examples:
Da kann *doch* 'ich nichts dafür.
*It's not ˅my fault.*

Was versteht *schon* 'die von Politik.
*ˌWhat does ˅she underˌstand of ˌpolitics?*
Da bin *wieder* 'ich nicht auf der Höhe (Eliot, 1962, p. 75).
*That's not ˅my line of ˌaction, you ˌknow* (Eliot, 1873, p. 186).
Aber wie kann *denn* 'ich Schmuck tragen, wenn du als die
Ältere keinen tragen willst? (Eliot, 1962, p. 20).
*But how can 'I wear ˅ornaments, if ˅you, who are the ˅elder ·sister,*
*will 'never ˅wear them?* (Eliot, 1873, pt. I, p. 13).

*General questions*, which in substance amount to statements, have an R nucleus; e.g.

A. Stop grumbling about it.
B. *Would ˌyou ·like your ·garden ·trampled over?* (O'Connor and Arnold, 1961, p. 181).
Wärst *denn* du beglückt, wenn man auf deinen Blumen herumtrampelte?

(To somebody worried about the Jones's opinion.)
*Does it ˌmatter what they ·think?*
Ist's *denn* so wichtig, was sie von dir denken?
Es ist *doch* egal was sie denken.

(To somebody wrongly blaming me.)
*Is it ˌmy fault that you have ·failed?*
Bin *denn* ich an deinem Mißerfolg schuld?

(To somebody exhibiting unmotivated surprise.)
*ˌIs it so ˌvery surˌprising?* (O'Connor and Arnold, 1961, p. 51).
Ist es *denn* so erstaunlich?[24]

The German particles being so very numerous and differentiated, while the tone patterns of English, at least in so far as they can conveniently be described, are less so, it is not surprising that also other German particles than *doch* correspond to the tone patterns treated in the preceding section. The difference of meaning, where not suggested by the contents and the context, is in English rendered by voice quality.[25] Here are some examples:

24. O'Connor and Arnold say that this pattern almost invariably expresses disapproval or scepticism (1961, p. 51).
25. See footnote 2.

1(a) `*Come ˌin*. Kommen Sie *doch* herein.
   `*Go ˌon*. Fahren Sie *doch* weiter.
   `*Cheer ˌup*. Nimm's *doch* nicht so zu Herzen.
   Here the adversative connotation is still felt to be present.

 (b) `*Come ˌin*. Kommen Sie *nur* herein.
   `*Go ˌon*. Fahren Sie *nur* weiter.
   There is no adversative element here. The tone is encouraging.

2(a) `⁓*I've said ·nothing ·wrong*. ˈIch hab *doch* nichts Dummes gesagt.
   Adversative element still present.

 (b) `⁓*That's a ·surˈprise for ·you*. Das ist *mal* (or *aber*) eine Überraschung
   für Sie.
   `⁓*Here's a thing you ·don't see too ·often*.
   Das ist *mal* etwas, das man nicht jeden Tag sieht.
   The adversative connotation has faded; both *mal* and the English
   tone pattern are solely expressive of emotion.

3(a) A. Why didn't you tell me?
   B. *You ˌdidn't ^ask me*.
     Du hast mich *doch* gar nicht gefragt.
   Adversative element still felt to be present.

 (b₁) A. There'll be about ten I suppose.
   B. *There'll be ^more* (O'Connor and Arnold, 1961, p. 157).
     Es werden *sogar noch* mehr sein.

 (b₂) A. Why didn't you inform me of this?
   B. It was strictly confidential. *I ˌdidn't ˌtell my ^husband*.
     Ich hab's *nicht einmal* meinem Mann gesagt.
   Here the R F can have a concessive connotation. With b₁ *more*
   could be replaced by *even more*; with b₂ *not* stands for *not even*.[26]

 (c) A. You seem to know this part of the country very well.
   B. *I've ^lived here for a ˌlong ˌtime*.
     Ich wohn *auch* schon lange hier.
   *Auch* has here a causal meaning, which in English is suggested by
   the R F.

4(a) *Does it ˌmatter what they ·think?*
   Ist's *denn* nicht egal, was sie denken?
   Es ist *doch* egal, was sie denken?
   The question amounts to a statement.

26. See the present writer's paper in the Proceedings of the 5th International Congress of Phonetic Sciences.

(b)  (Doctor to patient) *Have you been 'smoking a·gain?*
     Haben Sie *etwa (zufällig)* wieder geraucht?
     Auriez-vous (par hasard) recommencé à fumer?
     *Am I 'late?*
     Bin ich *etwa* verspätet?
     Serais-je en retard?

     (To somebody fumbling for his key.)
     *Have you for'gotten it?*
     Hast du ihn *etwa* vergessen?

     A. We had a meeting last night.
     B. *Should 'I have ·been there?* (O'Connor and Arnold, 1961, p. 219)
        Hätt ich *etwa* dabei sein sollen?

     A. Don't be so cut up about it.
     B. *Were 'you pleased?*
        Warst du *etwa* erfreut?

*Etwa* expresses a suspicion that the truthful answer must be yes (or no). In English there is often a high rise, i.e. a glide from a medium to a high pitch.[27] The suspicion may be a virtual certainty. That is also why some of the rhetorical general questions on page 189 could in German have *etwa* instead of *denn*.

Of all the German unstressed modal particles none, probably, has a greater variety of connotations than *doch*. We have here confined ourselves to one of its functions. In conclusion we will cast a brief glance at some other *doch*-sentences and their English counterparts.[28] With some current ones the English counterpart is a turn of syntax, e.g. the *doch* which makes a statement into a request for confirmation; e.g. Du hast *doch* die Fenster geschlossen? *You have ˋshut the ˎwindows, ˋhaven't you? Doch nicht etwa* with the verb in the future tense expresses apprehension; e.g. Er wird *doch nicht etwa* in den Teich gefallen sein. *'Don't 'tell me he 'fell into the ˋpond.*

The purely emotive, exclamatory *doch* has its counterpart in an English tone pattern with great pitch differences, either wide glides or wide jumps; e.g.

27. O'Connor and Arnold say that a high rise in general questions is light and casual (1961, p. 210). Jassem says that the high rise 'refers to a situation in which the listener is involved to a limited degree' (1952, p. 78). Also German *etwa zufällig*, French *par hasard* indicate that the speaker wants to make his question sound casual.
28. Schneider attributes to *doch* a variety of connotations, ranging from force of rhetoric to self-complacent assertion, and – in imperatives – anxious pleading or entreaty (1959, pp. 275–7). For a detailed study of the English locutional equivalents of German *doch* see Pestalozzi-Schärli (n.d.).

Du bist *doch* ein rechter Esel. ⁻*You* ˎ*are an ass.*
Das ist *doch* lächerlich. ⁻*That's ri*ˎ*diculous.*[29]
Es war *doch* wunderschön. ⁻*Wasn't it* ˎ*wonderful?*[30]
Das ist *doch* ein prächtiges Buch.
⁻*This is a* ˎ*lovely book*; or: ⁻*Isn't this a* ˎ*lovely book?*

29. It is interesting to note that even purely emotive *doch* has retained a trace of the meaning 'as you know': it is only appropriate in exclamatory sentences concerning something the interlocutor has had a share in.

30. Here a locutional and an elocutional means of expression are combined in English: the interrogative form, pointing, like *doch*, to a shared experience, and an emotional tone pattern. An exclamatory sentence about something new to the interlocutor cannot be in the interrogative form, nor can it in German comprise *doch*; e.g. You should have joined us; it was wonderful. Du hättest mitkommen sollen; es war wunderbar.

## References

ALLEN, W. S. (1954), *Living English Speech*, Longman.

ARNDT, W. (1960), 'Modal particles in Russian and German', *Word*, vol. 16, pp. 323–36.

BOLINGER, D. L. (1961), *Generality, Gradience and the All-or-None*. Mouton.

BRECHT, B. (1956), *Der gute Mensch von Sezuan*, Suhrkamp.

BRECHT, B. (1957), *The Good Woman of Setzuan*, trans. E. Bentley and M. Apelman, Grove Press.

CATFORD, J. C. (1964), 'Phonation types: the classification of some laryngeal components of speech production', *In Honour of Daniel Jones*, Longman, pp. 26–37.

COLLINSON, W. E. (1938), 'Some German particles and their English equivalents. A study in the technique of conversation', *German Studies presented to Prof. H. G. Fiedler*, Oxford University Press, pp. 106–24.

COLLINSON, W. E. (1954), *The German Language Today: Its Pattern and Historical Background*, Hutchinson.

COUSTENOBLE, H. N., and ARMSTRONG, L. E. (1934), *Studies in French Intonation*, Heffer.

DÜRRENMATT, F. (1956), *Der Besuch der alten Dame*, Arche.

DÜRRENMATT, F. (1962), *The Visit*, trans. P. Bowles, Cape.

EHRKE (1926), *Guide to Advanced German Prose Composition*, edited by H. F. Eggeling and K. Wildhagen, Oxford University Press.

ELIOT, George (1873), *Middlemarch*, in four vols., Blackwood.

ELIOT, George (1962), *Middlemarch*, trans. Ilse Leisi, Manesse.

FRISCH, M. (1959), *Biedermann und die Brandstifter, Spectaculum II*, Suhrkamp.

FRISCH, M. (1962), *The Fire Raisers. Three plays by M. Frisch*, trans. M. Bullock, Methuen.

GÜTTINGER, F. (1963), *Zielsprache, Theorie und Technik des Übersetzens*, Manesse.

HALLIDAY, M. A. K. (1963), 'The tones of English', *Archivum Linguisticum*, vol. 15, pp. 1–28.

HULTZÉN, L. S. (1959), 'Information points in intonation', *Phonetica*, vol. 4, pp. 107–20.

HULTZÉN, L. S. (1962), 'Significant and non-significant intonation', *Proceedings of the Third International Congress of Phonetic Sciences*, Mouton, pp. 658–661.

JASSEM, W. (1952), *Intonation of Conversational English*, Sklad Glowny: Dom Ksiazki.

KINGDON, R. (1958), *The Groundwork of English Intonation*, Longman.

LEE, W. R. (1956), 'Rise–fall intonation in English', *English Studies*, vol. 37, pp. 62–72.

MONFRIES, Helen (1963), *Oral Drills in Sentence Patterns*, Macmillan.

O'CONNOR, J. D., and ARNOLD, G. F. (1961), *Intonation of Colloquial English*, Longman.

PALMER, H. E. (1922), *English Intonation. With Systematic Exercises*, Heffer.

PESTALOZZI-SCHÄRLI, Annemarie (n.d.), *Die Wiedergabe des unbetonten* doch *im Englischen*, Diss.

PIKE, K. L. (1945), *The Intonation of American English*, University of Michigan Press.

SCHNEIDER, W. (1959), *Stilistische Deutsche Grammatik*, Herder.

SCHUBIGER, Maria (1935), *The Role of Intonation in Spoken English*, Cambridge University Press.

SCHUBIGER, Maria (1958), *English Intonation, Its Form and Function*, Niemeyer.

SHAW, G. B. (1925), *Die Heilige Johanna*, trans. S. Trebitsch, Fischer.

SHAW, G. B. (1936), *Saint Joan*, Tauchnitz.

TRAGER, G. L. (1958), 'Paralanguage', *Studies in Linguistics*, vol. 13, pp. 1–12.

# 10 Richard Gunter

Intonation and Relevance

A paper written specially for this volume.

Sentences are fairly easy to isolate in samples of human speech, and that fact leads linguists to make a great, unspoken assumption – that the sentence can be adequately treated in isolation. This assumption may be a convenience, but it is seriously misleading, for it tends to obscure important linguistic facts and relations.

A sentence usually occurs among other sentences; it is, in fact, usually connected to them in some way. A sentence is most closely connected to its *context sentence*, which is often the one just preceding. It is useful to say that a sentence is a *response* to its context, and is *relevant* to that context. These notions can be illustrated with the following two-line dialogue:

A (Context): Where is John?
B (Response): *2 He's in the 3 HOUSE 1*↓

In this dialogue, sentence A is the context for B. Conversely, B is a response to A and is relevant to A. This particular relevance may be called *answer to information question*. It arises from the fact that B follows A, and arises also from the facts of grammar, lexicon and suprasegmental phonology exhibited by A and B. Relevance is not something mystical; it is a product of the facts of sentences – facts that are clearly within the domain of linguistics. Relevance is, moreover, the phenomenon that permits humans to converse; thus it must be accounted of supreme importance in the working of language in human affairs. But it is clear that if we treat sentences like B in isolation, with their contexts stripped away, relevance evaporates. That fact alone is a powerful argument for the propriety of dealing with sentences in context, for without context there is no relevance.[1]

1. The word *context* has many meanings in linguistic discussion, and *relevance* is occasionally used by linguists in vague senses. But these notions, in the definitions given them here (introduced in Gunter, 1966) do not occupy much of the linguist's attention. For example, Bloomfield (1933, pp. 21–41) notes that an animal is capable of the familiar S – – – – → R; he adds that man is capable of the much more complex S – – – – → r ... s – – – – → R, in which s and r refer to speech as stimulus and response, so that one person may have a practical stimulus but through speech can

But an even more powerful argument is this: a context sentence acts as a floodlight upon the response, revealing details about that response, and clarifying its structure and meaning. The investigator who removes a sentence from its context shuts off that light; thus he may obscure the very facts that he is trying to understand. Some illustrations will show what is meant.

If we take an utterance like *3 John 1* ↓, we cannot discern much about its structure or meaning. But the moment we make it relevant to a context, the structure and meaning leap into focus, as in the following:

Context: *Who is in the house?*
Response: *3 JOHN 1* ↓

Instantly the observer sees that this response is elliptical, and that it has the underlying structure *3 JOHN is in the house 1* ↓. It is the context that allows this interpretation. But the very same phonetic sequence *3 JOHN 1* ↓, if taken in a different context, is revealed to have a completely different structure and meaning, as in the following:

Context: *Who did they see?*
Response: *3 JOHN 1* ↓

The full form of this response is *2 They saw 3 JOHN 1* ↓, a sentence in which the sequence *3 JOHN 1* ↓ is now the object. Again, it is the context that illuminates the structure and meaning of this response. Thus two examples of the utterance *3 JOHN 1* ↓ appear to be identical if taken in isolation, but different contexts allow us to see them as fundamentally different; indeed, those contexts compel us to do so.

Pronouns furnish another striking example of the same kind of interpretation in light of context. If we take a sentence like *2 He's in the 3 BARN 1* ↓, we can tell little about the meaning of the subject *He* except that its referent must be singular and male; but the moment we put this sentence in a dialogue as a response, we get further information:

Context: *Is John in the house?*
Response: *2 He's in the 3 BARN 1* ↓

---

stimulate another person to perform the practical response. What Bloomfield does not make explicit is the extended exchange of speech, which we might write as follows: S – – – – → r ... s ... r ... s ... r ... s ... etc. Such language ping-pong can go on indefinitely, and may be of two fundamentally different sorts: On the one hand there may be no relevance of one speech to the foregoing, as in the dual monologue of two actors on a stage, in which each speaks alternately, but neither is addressing the other; on the other hand there is true dialogue, in which each speech is relevant to the one that precedes it. The linguistic study of dialogue is the study of the devices that indicate relevance.

Now we know that *He* means *John*, and that piece of information is important; indeed, in a real conversation it might be crucial. Our usual way of talking about pronouns is all oriented to the speaker's point of view, the point of view of production. That is what leads us to say that a pronoun is a 'substitute' for a noun. But in understanding dialogue the point of view is quite different. The hearer must take a pronoun like *He* as a context signal that tells him something like this: Go back to the last singular, male noun in the context; that noun will be the meaning of this pronoun.[2]

Context may have an important bearing even upon the lexical meaning of an utterance. For example, if we isolate such an elliptical form as *3 WΛN 1* ↓ it is ambiguous, but a context may reveal with great precision the lexical meaning of this utterance, as in the following:

Context: *Do you mean they lost or won?*
Response: *3 WΛN 1* ↓

Or again:

Context: *How many fish did you catch?*
Response: *3 WΛN 1* ↓

Clearly it is the context in each of these dialogues that refines the meaning of the ambiguous sequence *3 WΛN 1* ↓.

For a final example of the way a context may floodlight the response, we may take such a sentence as *They are flying 3 PLANES 1* ↓. In isolation this sentence may be ambiguous, but it becomes quite clear in such a context as the following:

2. The rules for unravelling anaphora are really much more complicated than this illustration may seem to argue, as in such a dialogue as the following, for example:

Context: *John hit Bill.*
Response: *Did he hurt him?*

The pronoun *he* in this response clearly goes back not to the last context noun, but to the subject of the context sentence. Full context rules would have to allow for the parallelism exhibited by this response and context; there are other such complications. The behavior of these pronouns, and anaphora generally, suggests that the making of language and the understanding of language are quite different kinds of activity. The idea that pronouns are substitutes for nouns argues some kind of priority for the nouns – argues that somehow the noun exists first in the act of speech making, but is then supplanted by the pronoun. This implication is present in, for example, Lees and Klima (1963). It may be that these authors would deny that such an implication is intended, arguing perhaps that generative grammars are not models of either the speaker's acts or the hearer's. My point is that a hearer hears a pronoun first, and then is obliged to discover what it means by reference to its antecedent. Arguments about generative grammar should not be permitted to obscure this fact.

Context: *What are your friends doing?*
Response: *2 They are flying 3 PLANES 1 ↓*

Or in a different context:

Context: *What are those things?*
Response: *2 They are flying 3 PLANES 1 ↓*

The moment that *They* is identified as animate or inanimate through context, the structure of *flying 3 PLANES 1 ↓* also becomes clear. In fact, there seems to be no way to understand *flying 3 PLANES 1 ↓* except to determine first the meaning of *They*.[3]

Thus to inspect responses in their contexts reveals features of those responses that are not visible in isolated sentences. One of the features of English sentences that can be illuminated in this way is intonation.

The analysis of intonation that is widely known as the Trager–Smith system has served an important function: it has invited testing, and thus has stimulated linguists to gather new and interesting data for that purpose. But there is now widespread doubt that the system is adequate to organize the observations that it has made possible. The analysis is inadequate, or unsatisfying, in at least three ways. First, there is ground for doubt that the stuff of intonations is a set of discrete 'phonemic' pitch levels and terminal junctures. Second, even granting that the analysis into phonemes is correct in principle, there are not enough entities in the Trager–Smith inventory to go round, for there are intonations that cannot be written in the system at all. Third, the Trager–Smith analysis has never allowed us to see clearly what it is that intonation does in English – what it means. One may take an intonation in the abstract, divorced from words, and may try to assign a meaning to it, but that task is baffling. It is equally baffling to attempt to find connections between an intonation and the internal semantic or grammatical facts of the sentence with which that intonation occurs. Such connections are at best elusive, and it may be

3. The word *ambiguity* is itself sometimes ambiguous in linguistic discussion, for it expresses two notions that are easy to confuse. First, there is the notion that an isolated form like *flying planes* can have either of two constituent structures; second, there is the notion that a reader or hearer who actually encounters an expression like *flying planes* may not know which of its two possible constituent structures is meant. Ambiguity in the first sense may be fairly common in English, but ambiguity in the second sense is not very common except in the isolated sentences that linguists like to speculate on; for context usually makes it clear which of two possible constituent structures is meant in an expression like *flying planes*. A rather similar point is made in Lieberman (1967, pp. 103–10). This book came to my hands after this paper was written; thus I have not taken account here of its interesting assertions and conclusions.

that they do not exist at all. There are sentences that can take many different intonations; there are intonations that can occur with all sorts of sentences; and – most telling of all – there is no string of words that has one necessary intonation.

*A priori* it seems that we cannot confront the first two objections to the Trager–Smith system until we have somehow met the third, for until we know what intonation means we cannot say whether two intonations are phonemically the same or different; we cannot know what kinds of primitives intonations are built of, or what number of primitives there are, until we have understood which intonations mean the same and which mean different things. The most important question before us, then, is this: What is the role of intonation in English?[4]

This paper, though it falls far short of a complete answer to that question, does present conclusions about the role of *simple intonations* in one area of usage – the two-line dialogue, examples of which we have already seen above. These dialogues are made up of simple sentences like *John drank tea* and *John is in the house* and *The play was wonderful*. Every simple sentence of these three kinds has many forms besides the affirmative statement: each has question forms, elliptical forms, the negatives of these, and others. Several of these forms will be used in the illustrative dialogues to follow.

Simple intonations will be used with the responses of these dialogues. A simple intonation is one that accents a single syllable, as in *3 JOHN 1 ↓* or *3 NObody is in the house 1 ↓*. A *contour* begins with the accented syllable and continues to the end of the sentence; if there are syllables before the accent, as in *2 The play was 3 WONderful 1 ↓*, their intonation will be called a *precontour*. These definitions exclude any intonation like *3 JOHN 1 ↑ 2 is in the 3 HOUSE 1 ↓*, which accents two syllables, and is therefore not simple.

In all of the dialogues to follow, the first speech is a context, and the second is a response that is relevant to that context. The focus of attention is the response, for certain claims are to be made about the intonations that occur with responses. The claims to be supported are these:

1. The welter of different simple intonations that are possible in this usage can be reduced to a small number of significant sets of contours and a non-significant set of precontours.

4. My own ideas about intonation are directly indebted to: Pike (1945); Trager and Smith (1951); Bolinger (1961); Sledd (1960); Stockwell (1960; 1962). I am grateful to Dwight Bolinger for correspondence about the ideas expressed in this paper, and especially for his critical reading of an early draft of this paper. He saved me from many pitfalls, though all remaining errors are entirely my own.

2. These contours are not made up of discrete, phonemic pitch levels and terminal junctures.

3. In this usage an intonation means nothing in itself, nor is it dictated by the internal semantic or grammatical facts of the sentence with which it occurs. It may signal something about the emotional state of the speaker, but such 'expression' is a minor, unstable part of the intonation's meaning; the stable, testable meaning of an intonation in the present usage is the manner in which that intonation connects the response to the context.

The simplest possible English intonations are those that occur with monosyllabic utterances like *John*. In these intonations one is dealing only with accent and contour. The contours are short, since they cover only one syllable, and there are no precontours at all, since there are no syllables before the accent. Some of these intonations are given below in the Trager–Smith symbology. For reasons that will become clear in a moment, the intonations are arranged here in three sets. Each intonation should be imagined as spoken with a monosyllabic utterance like *John*:[5]

| A | B | C |
|---|---|---|
| 42 ↓ | 44 ↑ | 43 ↑ |
| 41 ↓ | 33 ↑ | 42 ↑ |
| 31 ↓ | 23 ↑ | 32 ↑ |
| 21 ↓ | 22 ↑ | 31 ↑ |
| 11 ↓ | 13 ↑ | 21 ↑ |

This representation deals in discrete elements of pitch and juncture. These elements are 'phonemes', with all the dogma and doctrine that the word implies. Thus the implication is present that each intonation is absolutely different from every other. For example, 41 ↓ and 31 ↓ are just as different from each other in signalling power as either is from, say, 33 ↑ or 32 ↑. But the behavior of these intonations in dialogue is distinctly

5. Trager and Smith did not, of course, use the terminal arrows in their original work; the original symbols for the terminal junctures were /|/, /‖/ and /#/. The reader will notice that nowhere in the present paper is there any use of the level arrow or any reference to the entity that it purports to represent. In fact, this writer does not believe that there is any such entity – none at least that is significant in the present usage. Suppose, for illustration, that we have a dialogue such as that below, with a response that in the Trager–Smith symbols might be written with a level arrow:

Context: *Who is in the barn?*
Response: *2 John 2 →*

The claim is that such an intonation would be interpreted either as high-rising or as low-rising, that is, it would be assigned either the meaning *Could it be John?* or the meaning *It is John.*

against this implication; for within one of the sets all the intonations behave alike. This fact should not be surprising, for all of the members of a given set closely resemble each other in that they share a gross shape: the members of A are grossly falling; those of B are grossly high-rising; those of C are grossly falling–rising. These gross shapes can be schematized with reference to a base line as follows:

Thus each set of intonations can be regarded as a *contour* with a recognizable shape, and each member of a set can be regarded as a *variant* of that contour. In a given dialogue, moreover, all of the variants within a contour signal exactly the same relevance, as in the following:

Context: *Who is in the house?*
Response: *3 J O H N 1* ↓ (Relevance: *Answer to information question.*)

This relevance remains intact with any variant of the falling contour, whether 41 ↓, 31 ↓ or 21 ↓. To be sure, each of these variants may seem to have its own flavor in this dialogue, but that flavor is emotional or expressive. In a given case it can be paraphrased with *This is all so dull* or *You're silly not to know that* or something of the kind. This emotional flavor is not very stable, however; as we shall see later it depends as much upon non-linguistic facts as upon the exact tonetic details of the intonation. What is important about these falling variants is that they all have the same gross shape. All signal the same relevance here; they all answer the question.

Turning to the high-rising contour and its variants, commutation again shows that all variants signal the same relevance, as in the following:

Context: *John is in the house.*
Response: *3 J O H N 3* ↑ (Relevance: *Reclamation.*)

Once again, each variant of the high-rising may have its own expressive overtones in this dialogue, and these overtones may range from faint surprise to incredulity, but they do not affect the relevance, which with every commutation of the variants continues to mean something like: *Indicate whether my response is indeed the item in the subject slot of your context sentence.*[6]

6. This paraphrase of the relevance at hand is one of the briefest; most such paraphrases are cumbersome, as in Gunter (1966). In the present paper I use simple glosses for each relevance, or merely names for kinds of relevance, such as *reclamation*, from Bolinger (1957).

Exactly the same kind of analysis can be made of the falling–rising contour and its variants in such a dialogue as the following:

Context: *Nobody is in the house.*
Response: *3 JOHN 1* ↑ (Relevance: *You forget John.*)

Yet again, commutation of the variants of the falling–rising contour over this response does not affect relevance: the variants 43 ↑, 32 ↑, 31 ↑ and so on all signal the same relevance here, though each variant may signal its own expressive overtones.

Thus the behavior of simple intonations in such dialogues argues that all intonational curves of a given gross shape mean the same, whatever their emotional coloring. To state the same conclusion in a different way, these curves are not made up of phonemic pitch levels and terminals as primitives. The important thing is the assignability of a given variant to its proper contour, of which it is merely one manifestation. At a stroke, then, a great reduction is made in the number of significantly different intonations in this usage; accordingly, a single writing can be used for each of the three contours. Hereinafter the writing 31 ↓ will be used for the falling contour, 33 ↑ for the high-rising, and 31 ↑ for the falling–rising.[7] Each of these writings stands for any of a large, but unknown number of variants that fall within each contour.

There is another aspect of this reduction that holds surprises for the experimenter who examines it for the first time. The two dialogues below will show what is meant:

Dialogue A
Context: *What did he drink?*
Response: *3 TEA 1* ↓ (Relevance: *Answer to information question.*)

Dialogue B
Context: *John drank wine.*
Response: *3 TEA 1* ↓ (Relevance: *Contradiction.*)

In the responses of both these dialogues the segmentals are the same, and both responses have the falling intonation. Now as has already been argued, either response can be rendered with any variant of the falling contour and that variant will fulfill the indicated relevance – *answer to information question* in A and *contradiction* in B. What is surprising – though it follows inexorably – is that one can render the first response

7. The difficulty of teaching a pitch-level scheme to classes of students first led me to the feeling that one is dealing with contours instead of discrete pitch levels. Students often grasp the contours quickly, but have endless difficulty marking the levels. There is some experimental evidence that practiced linguists have the same trouble (see Lieberman, 1965).

with some falling variant, then *switch that response bodily to the second dialogue, and it will then fulfill the indicated relevance in the second dialogue – contradiction*. The experimenter may sense a rather abrupt change in expression as the switch is made, but nothing will be lacking in the indication of relevance. Any falling variant will signal either of the two relevances; therefore, either response can be rendered with any variant of the falling, then switched to the other dialogue, and it will there fulfill the relevance indicated for that dialogue.

But context appears to have a powerful sway over our feelings about the very tonetic facts of a response contour; indeed, context seems to govern our very perception of those facts to a surprising degree. Perhaps the two dialogues below will make clear what is meant:

Dialogue C
Context: *Nobody is in the house.*
Response: *3 JOHN 1* ↑ (Relevance: *You forget John.*)

Dialogue D
Context: *John is in the house.*
Response: *3 JOHN 1* ↑ (Relevance: *Surely you don't mean John.*)

Here again both responses have the same segmental phonemes; and both employ the same contour. Any variant of that falling–rising contour will fulfill the indicated relevance in either dialogue; and again, one can render the response of one dialogue with a given variant of the falling–rising contour, then switch it to the second, and the relevance indicated for the second will be perfectly preserved.

The experimenters who attempt switch for the first time often express surprise and unwillingness to believe the assertions that have been made here. But they invariably accept those assertions after further practice with such experiments. Their doubts take two forms. The first is that the experimenter sometimes finds it difficult to believe that the variant in question does in fact remain the same, even when he himself is the utterer, and tries with all his might to keep that variant the same during the switch. The second doubt questions the assertion that an item switched from one dialogue to another truly fulfills relevance in the dialogue to which it is switched, or that it 'sounds natural'. Doubters are quite ready to believe when other performers are rendering the contexts and responses, but are not so ready when they themselves render the switched responses. For example, experimenters called upon to switch *3 JOHN 1* ↑ from Dialogue C to Dialogue D above will often feel the impulse to exaggerate the rise and fall of the variant as it is switched to D. They seem to feel dissatisfied with, say, the Trager–Smith 21 ↑ as a response in D; they feel impelled to make it something like the T–S 41 ↑. Yet curiously they are much readier to accept the 21↑ when it is rendered by someone else, especially if the response is accompanied by some gesture that seems to make it appropriate.[8]

The cause of these odd effects is hard to pin down, but perhaps it is this: As we have seen, an isolated sentence may not have a clear meaning or purpose in itself, but takes on an essence when supplied with a context to which it is relevant. The two become an organic whole, in which the response is suffused with the meaning of that whole. When we tear a response away from its context we cannot fully rid ourselves of the memory of that meaning with which it was suffused; but when others are performing contexts and responses, the onlooker is not so intimately involved in the matter, and tends to accept what he hears as perfectly normal exchange of speech. In short, the surprise that switch occasions in us has little to do with the exact tonetic facts of responses, but lies rather in the changing context, which frustrates our expectations and reveals to us that our perceptions are partly illusion tinctured with memory.

Switch bolsters the notion that relevance is a kind of constant, a more 'linguistic' notion than is expressiveness. We can divorce the two, and thus simplify the data that intonation presents – a desideratum that has long haunted the dreams of scholars. But to put expression aside and to proceed without it by no means allows us to say that expressiveness is unimportant, for it is important; it is all-pervasive in real conversation, and is thus a proper object of linguistic study. Also, it is complex in the extreme, seeming to defy every generalization that the investigator puts forward. One may think that he has found a stable expressive meaning for some variant, only to find upon further reflection that the generalization crumbles. For example, suppose that the response of dialogue A above is rendered with some low-pitched variant of the falling contour, say, T–S 21 ↓. Such a rendition seems colorless in that dialogue, certainly not unpleasant. Then the investigator may go on to note that when this response is switched to Dialogue B it suddenly seems to connote a smug assurance. Thus the investigator may think that he has discovered a law: 21 ↓ in Dialogue A is colorless, but in B is smug. But the generalization

8. The assertions made here about commutation, switch and the fulfilling of relevance rest upon two sorts of experimental procedure. The first is the monitoring of one's own performance: in studying switch, for example, one renders a dialogue aloud, then, holding in memory exactly the rendition of the response, the experimenter switches it to another dialogue. The second procedure involves at least three performers, A, B and C. A memorizes a response with a given intonational variant; B renders a context and A responds to it with his memorized item; then C renders a second context and A again responds with his memorized item. An observer, taking no active part in these renditions, stands aside and judges. Experiments with tape splices could be made, but I have not been able to carry out such experiments for want of the proper equipment.

crumbles when the investigator realizes that he has been assuming a gesture all the time. It is true that 21 ↓ may sound smug in Dialogue B; but imagine that it is rendered by someone who is tactfully correcting an error and the very opposite effect comes through.

The divorcement of relevance from expressiveness does not give us a ready way to handle expressiveness, which remains refractory and elusive in the extreme, influenced as it is by gesture and by the situation in which speech takes place; the divorcement merely allows us to proceed with the study of the way in which intonation marks relevance – a study that permits conclusions in which we can feel more confidence.

There are, then, two sorts of argument for the unity of all variants of a given contour: commutation of variants over some response in a dialogue leaves the relevance unchanged; and switch bolsters the notion that all variants within a contour are indeed the same. Thus are established three significantly different contours in the usage at hand.

But there is a fourth intonation that disturbs the harmony of this system. This is the *low-rising* contour, which can be written 11 ↑. This contour presents several problems. First, though it seems most to resemble the high-rising variants, it contrasts with them in the marking of relevance, as in the following dialogue:

Context: *Who is in the house?*
Responses:
(High-Rising)  *3 JOHN 3* ↑ (Relevance: *Could it be John?*)
(Low-Rising)   *1 JOHN 1* ↑ (Relevance: *Answer to information question.*)

The relevance to context marked by these two contours is clearly different in the two responses; the low-rising contour is therefore not to be grouped with the high-rising variants. Generally, the hearer need only perceive that a variant has a given kind of shape in order to assign that variant to its correct contour. But the hearer apparently must discriminate high-rising and low-rising contours by means of rather narrow tonetic details. This fact makes the low-rising contour seem oddly out of harmony with the rest of the system. But it is clear that the two contours signal different things in this dialogue, as indeed they do in others.

Further examination, moreover, indicates that the low-rising variants have, in one sense, much more in common with the falling variants, for in case after case low-rising and falling mark the same relevance in such dialogues as these:

Context: *What did John drink?*
Responses: *3 TEA 1* ↓ (Relevance: *Answer to information question.*)
*1 TEA 1* ↑ (Relevance: *Answer to information question.*)

Or in a different context:

Context: *Is John in the house?*
Responses: *3 YES 1 ↓* (Relevance: *Answer to yes–no question.*)
*1 YES 1 ↑* (Relevance: *Answer to yes–no question.*)

Thus the low-rising variants seem to serve as alternate forms of the falling in case after case. It is tempting, then, to subsume the low-rising variants under the falling contour, but two considerations militate against doing so: First, there is the stubborn fact that the low-rising is simply not shaped like the falling contour; second, there is the fact that the relevance-marking functions of the low-rising variants are rather sharply limited to the answering of questions; there are many functions that falling variants have that low-rising variants do not have.[9] One of these functions is recapitulation of the context, or of some part of the context. This relevance is a kind of assent to the proposition that the context makes. In the following dialogue, the falling variants fulfill this relevance in a natural way, but the low-rising variants sound odd or impossible:

Context: *John drank tea.*
Responses: *3 TEA 1 ↓* (Relevance: *Recapitulation.*)
*1 TEA 1 ↑* (Relevance: *???*)

In the following dialogue the falling variants fulfill the contradiction relevance, but the low-rising variants do not:

Context: *John drank tea.*
Responses: *3 WINE 1 ↓* (Relevance: *Contradiction.*)
*1 WINE 1 ↑* (Relevance: *???*)[10]

All of these facts considered, it seems best to set the low-rising up as a separate contour, equal with the others but eccentric in its distribution.

9. Dwight Bolinger in a personal communication suggests that the low-rising contour may sometimes mark questions, in which cases it fails to contrast with the high-rising contour in the relevance marked, as in the following:

Context: *Johnson wants higher taxes.*
Response: *1 SO 1 ↑*
*3 SO 3 ↑*

It may be that there are many such places in various kinds of dialogue where two contours mark the same relevance. In the cases I have isolated where contrast seems to be suspended, I have usually had great difficulty in coming to a firm conclusion.

10. There seem to be very few variants of the low-rising contour excepting those that differ in length. Perhaps the reason is that there simply isn't much pitch 'space' for the low-rising variants to wander in, since the lowest of the high-risings are just above the range of the highest of the low-risings.

We have to do, then, with four contours that can occur over mono-syllables in the usage under discussion. To summarize what has been said about them: Each of the intonations can be assigned to one of four gross shapes, or to state the matter differently, there are four contours, each with several variants; in a given dialogue a particular variant may have some distinctive expressive function, but expressiveness is elusive and unstable from dialogue to dialogue, and even appears to change in a particular dialogue when there are changes in the real surrounding situation or in the attitude of the speaker; linguistic meaning lies only in the shape of the contour, and that meaning is the way the contour connects the response to the context; these facts allow us to see that intonations are not made up of discrete phonemes of pitch and juncture. Finally, although the low-rising contour is somewhat eccentric in its functions, all of the contours can occur with any monosyllable in at least some function; moreover, any intonation that occurs with any monosyllable can be assigned to one of the four contours.

The four contours likewise apply universally to polysyllabic responses. This contention rests upon an assumption, to be sure, but that assumption is everywhere made in the literature on English intonation; study of the present usage, moreover, turns up no evidence against it. The assumption is this: longer contours like those on the right below can be equated with the shorter ones on the left below, which we have already dealt with over monosyllables:

|  | Shorter variants | Longer variants |
|---|---|---|
| (Falling) | 3 JOHN 1 ↓ | 3 JOHN is in the house 1 ↓ |
| (High-Rising) | 3 JOHN 3 ↑ | 3 JOHN is in the house 3 ↑ |
| (Falling–Rising) | 3 JOHN 1 ↑ | 3 JOHN is in the house 1 ↑ |
| (Low-Rising) | 1 JOHN 1 ↑ | 1 JOHN is in the house 1 ↑ |

Thus a contour like the falling, on this assumption, remains the same no matter whether it covers a single syllable or is stretched out to cover several. Dialogues like the following, in which the responses are longer and longer forms of the same underlying sentence, help to support this assumption:

Context: *Who is in the house?*
Responses: *3 JOHN 1* ↓  (Relevance: *Answer to information question.*)
*3 JOHN is 1* ↓  (Relevance: *Answer to information question.*)
*3 JOHN is in the house 1* ↓  (Relevance: *Answer to information question.*)

Or again:

Context: *John is in the barn.*

Responses: *3 JOHN 3 ↑*   (Relevance: *Reclamation.*)
*3 JOHN is 3 ↑*   (Relevance: *Reclamation.*)
*3 JOHN is in the barn 3 ↑*   (Relevance: *Reclamation.*)

Longer and shorter variants mark the same relevance in these dialogues.[11] This fact argues that the length of a contour has no meaning, and is simply an automatic concomitant of the number of syllables that the contour embraces. Longer and shorter variants are thus to be equally subsumed under the contour of which they are manifestations.

A given contour thus embraces much variety, yet *a priori* it seems certain that all the manifestations of a contour must remain within some range or set of limits; at least a given manifestation must be assignable to one of the four contours without error. Yet it is clear from a detailed study of contours and their variants that the latter are sometimes rather dissimilar. We have already looked at a few of the variants of, for example, the high-rising contour:

44 ↑

33 ↑

22 ↑

Such variants look like strata, each pitched at its own level. In the same way, we can visualize the bundle of falling variants.

But there are other variants of contours that seem to differ from each other not merely in pitch stratum, but in the manner in which they proceed from syllable to syllable. One of these variants of the falling contour, for example, is a smooth descent from the peak to the bottom of the fall, as in the following:

Context: *How was the play?*

Response: $WO_{N_{d_{e_{r_{f_{u_{l.}}}}}}}$

Another variant might be called the humped descent;[12] sometimes the hump comes in an unaccented syllable directly after the accent:

Response: $WON^{der}f_{u_{l.}}$

11. My Indiana University dissertation (1963) offers some experimental support for the contention that informants expand shorter contours to longer ones, at the same time that they expand and supply constituents to fill out elliptical forms.

12. This intonation came to my notice through Stockwell (1962). Stockwell attributes earlier discussion of it to James Sledd. I have not seen the Sledd work.

Sometimes the hump is included in the accent syllable:

Response:

WONderful.

All of these variants are clearly manifestations of the falling contour, for they all signal the same relevance in this dialogue, and they do so in other dialogues without exception. It is possible, in fact, to take a list of expressions that have the falling contour, render them with the smooth descent, and then translate them into a humped descent, as in the dialogue below, where it is clear that either the smooth or humped descent fulfills the relevance *Answer to information question*.

Context: *Who is in the house?*
Responses:

*Smooth descent*            *Humped descent*

JOHNny is in the house.

JOHNny is in the house.

BOB is in the house.

BOB is in the house.

It is even possible to translate a smoothly-falling variant over a mono-syllable into the corresponding humped descent:

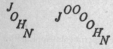

JOHN        JOOOOHN

The other contours also exhibit variants that differ in the manner of their procedure from syllable to syllable. For example, the high-rising contour has one variant that begins high and continues as a monotone to the end, where there is, at most, a barely perceptible further uprise at the very end; a second variant ascends stairstep fashion syllable by syllable to the very end, as follows:

Context: *The play was wonderful.*
Responses:

*Stairstep rise   Monotone*

$$WON^{der^{ful}} \qquad WON\,der\,f^{u^l}$$

These variants also seem to be fully interchangeable in any dialogue where either can serve to mark relevance. Yet both always signal the same thing, as both here signal the relevance *Is this what you said?* The same can be said for other variants of particular contours, so that ordinary variants that differ from each other in their pitch strata are equal in function to those that differ in their manner of proceeding from point to point.

But we have not quite done with variety in contours, for it is obvious that any variant of any contour must be actualized within the limits imposed by the segmental phonology of the material embraced by the intonation. (*Segmental phonology* must be taken here to include not only the consonant–vowel sequence, together with the distribution of stress and plus juncture, but syllable count as well.) Some aspects of the segmental material are necessarily registered in the manifestation of the contour. Consider merely that if the material contains a voiceless stop that fact will be registered by a break at that point in the intonation, however brief it may be; and if there are two syllables in the material – or twenty – that fact will also be registered in the intonation. Given such considerations, it seems inescapable that no two contours can be exactly the same unless the segmental material that they cover is also identical.[13]

When the accent of a simple intonation occurs on any syllable of the response after the first, the syllables before the accent bear a precontour, as in the sentences below, where the precontour is marked simply by the

13. The humming of intonations is a good pedagogical aid in the classroom; it is also useful in the analysis of one's own performance of intonation, especially when there is a question whether two intonations are alike or not. Humming has the virtue that it strips away all the consonants and vowels except *m*; also (as far as I can tell) it strips away plus-juncture. Humming preserves only the number of syllables, their length, volume and pitch. One can fill in a hummed intonation with several actual sentences, that is, match a string of words in some grammatical construction to the hummed intonation.

numeral 2. The precontour is to be understood as extending from that 2 to the accent:

*2 The play was 3 WONderful 1* ↓
*2 The play 3 WAS wonderful 1* ↓
*2 The 3 PLAY was wonderful 1* ↓
*3 THE play was wonderful 1* ↓

Precontours may thus be rather long, rather short, or non-existent; also they vary greatly in other ways. We have already seen some of the ways in which the variants of contours differ, but they are at least under the constraint that they must somehow stay within a range, for every variant must be assignable to its contour without error. But precontours are not under even this constraint, for they have nothing to do with the marking of relevance; consequently, they exist in many different patterns. A few of these are sketched in the following paragraphs.

First, the precontour may be level – a monotone on one or another pitch plateau. Below are three of these plateaus that seem to this writer possible and natural:

Context: *Where is John?*
Responses:

(low-level) *John is in the*
$$H \\ O \\ S \\ E_o$$

(mid-level) *John is in the*
$$H \\ O \\ U \\ S \\ E_o$$

(high-level) *John is in the H*
$$O \\ U \\ S \\ E_o$$

Another kind of precontour is the stairstep up, as in the following response:[14]

14. Stairsteps up are sometimes too rich in levels to be marked in the restricted inventory of Trager–Smith symbols, a fact pointed out by James Sledd in his review of Kingdon (1960).

Context: *Where is John?*

Response:

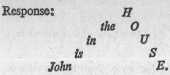

```
                    H
          the       O
     in             U
   is              S
 John             E.
```

Such stairsteps up can take many forms, depending directly upon the segmental material covered; that is, if the precontour is long, with many syllables, correspondingly greater variety is possible in the steps up. But even with the response above at least two other varieties of stairsteps are possible:

```
                  H
John is in the    O
                   U
                    S
                     E.
```

```
                H
John is in the  O
                 U
                  S
                   E.
```

There are many other sorts of pattern in precontours: there are stairsteps down, metrical effects, and much else, for precontours seem to wander even more extravagantly than do the variants of contours. The researcher who attempts to study precontours exhaustively can be so overwhelmed with their variety that he begins to doubt that they can be reduced to any system at all. But it is clear that precontours have nothing to do with the marking of relevance, which can be studied quite apart from the disconcerting variety of precontours.

There is, however, one kind of restraint upon variety in precontours, a limit that we have already seen in the variants of contours: in some way the precontour must reflect some of the facts of the phonological material that it covers. It must break momentarily at a voiceless stop, and it must register the number of syllables that it embraces. Given such facts, it may be that ultimately we shall be able to find order in precontours by making two assumptions: there is a limited number of patterns that precontours fall into, such as stairsteps, monotones and the like; and these patterns enjoy many sorts of actualization that depend upon the phonological material enclosed. For example, there may be only a small number of stairstep patterns, and the precise forms that these take would seem to be directly dependent upon the number of syllables available for the making of steps. Clearly, for instance, there can be only one step up if the precontour covers only two syllables. But it is plain that at the moment we do not know enough to make final pronouncements about the number and kinds of precontours.

This paper may have seemed to argue that two procedures are always easy to carry out:

1. The investigator can always decide whether an intonation is simple or not.

2. If an intonation is found to be simple, the investigator can always decide whether it consists of a contour alone, which can be identified as one of the four established, or whether it is one of those contours plus a precontour, the two being easily and neatly separable in such a way that the investigator can always assign the relevance-marking function to the contour alone.

In fact these procedures are easy to carry out in most cases, but in some cases they are not easy. It now seems proper to bring forward one of these difficult cases. This is the grossly falling-rising intonation that is said to be favored by some Englishmen for use with yes–no questions. This intonation also occurs among Americans with information questions, as follows:[15]

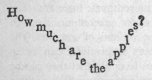

The same intonation sometimes occurs with statements, as follows:

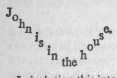

In isolation this intonation is difficult to mark. It gives rise to a series of questions: Is this intonation simple? If so, is the accent on *house*, so that the contour is low-rising and so that *John is in the* is all under a precontour that descends somewhat in the manner of stairsteps? Or is the accent on *John*, so that the entire intonation is a manifestation of the falling–rising contour?

15. This example is taken from Gleason (1964, p. 22). This item begins a dialogue, so that it has no overt context. Students often render it with the intonation under discussion, and the class then usually have difficulty marking it. The arguments that ensue are settled by professorial fiat, a kind of authority that must have settled many snch arguments over the past fifteen years.

Taken in isolation, examples of this intonation do not easily yield answers to these questions. The intonation is sometimes refractory even in the relevance relation to a context, especially in that relevance that can be called *denial*, in which the context is affirmative and the response negative, as in Dialogue A below, or the context is negative and the response affirmative, as in Dialogue B:

Dialogue A
Context: *John's in the house.*

Response: John isn't in the house.

Dialogue B
Context: *John isn't in the house.*

Response: John's in the house.

It is possible to render such responses so that they are unambiguous; but the point is that many actual occurrences of such responses are not easy to mark, for able students of intonation will disagree about them. Points at which scholars have difficulty in marking intonation deserve careful study, for the difficulties surely are of some theoretical importance. It may be, in fact, that the assignment of accent in the responses above is non-significant, that is, uncalled for by the language system; or perhaps the significance of accent placement is 'neutralized' in the denial relevance.

But considerable experimentation indicates that an ambiguous response of this kind, if switched to certain other contexts, is no longer ambiguous as to accent placement, the placement being revealed by the floodlighting effect of that new context. The investigator may, for example, switch the ambiguous response of Dialogue B above to Dialogue C below, where he will then hear the accent on *John*.

Dialogue C
Context: *Who is in the house?*

Response: JOHN is in the house.

But if switched to a different dialogue, the identical response may, through the same kind of *trompe l'oreille,* appear to present the accent on *house*:

Dialogue D
Context: *Where is John?*

Response: *John is in the HOUSE.*

A similar, and even more astonishing fact is this: the experimenter can render Dialogue C so that the accent is quite clearly on *John* in the response; then he can snip off the last three words of that response, *in the house,* switch those words and their intonation to Dialogue D, and will find that such a response in D will fulfill the relevance *Answer to information question,* and will sound quite genuine. These and other such oddities heighten the suspicion that context governs a great part of our perception of intonation, in which there seem to be few perceptual absolutes. Thus when a sentence is made in isolation we may have difficulty in deciding what the tonetic facts are; sometimes, as we have seen with the denial relevance, an intonation may remain ambiguous even when it does have a context.

Nor do difficulties end there in the study of English intonation, for there are usages, sentence types and complex intonations that have not even been touched in these pages. Scholars who have dwelt with these problems know that they are not all going to be solved tomorrow with a single flash of understanding. Indeed, it may be that English intonation requires not a single kind of explanation but several kinds; for it seems likely that intonation plays not a single role but many roles.[16]

But in the usage marked out for treatment in this paper, the role of intonation is clear: that role is the marking of relevance. Intonations that play this role must be studied over sentences in context, for only thus can we tell what significantly different intonations there are; only thus can we tell what they mean.

There are, in fact, four intonational contours that mark relevance. The four apply universally to English monosyllables; any intonation that occurs

16. Some forms, such as commands, often have no overt contexts; thus it seems unlikely that their intonations play the relevance role. Furthermore, it is prudent to remember that no sentence can be said without an intonation; it may be, therefore, that there are intonations that serve no purpose at all.

with a monosyllable in this usage can be assigned to one of these contours. The contours can be stretched to embrace several syllables, and may even have precontours before them. But the details of precontours, and even the details of the contours themselves, signal nothing but the emotional stance of the speaker. Thus a variant is not made up of discrete pitches and junctures, but merely has a gross shape which permits it to be assigned to its proper contour. In the usage at hand that contour is not a product of the internal facts of the sentence with which it figures, but is a context signal that binds the response to the context. Such context signals make dialogue possible.

## References

BLOOMFIELD, L. (1933), *Language*, Holt, Rinehart & Winston.

BOLINGER, D. (1957), *Interrogative Structure of American English*, Publications of the American Dialect Society, vol. 28.

BOLINGER, D. (1961), 'Contrastive accent and contrastive stress', *Language*, vol. 37, pp. 83–96.

GLEASON, H. A. (1964), *Workbook in Descriptive Linguistics*, Holt, Rinehart & Winston.

GUNTER, R. (1963), *Elliptical Forms of the English Transitive Sentence*, Indiana University microfilm.

GUNTER, R. (1966), 'On the placement of accent in dialogue: a feature of context grammar', *J. Ling.*, vol. 2, pp. 159–79.

LEES, R. B., and KLIMA, E. S. (1963), 'Rules for English pronominalization', *Language*, vol. 39, pp. 17–28.

LIEBERMAN, P. (1965), 'On the acoustic basis of the perception of intonation by linguists', *Word*, vol. 21, pp. 40–54.

LIEBERMAN, P., (1967), *Intonation, Perception and Language*, Cambridge University Press.

PIKE, K. L. (1945), *The Intonation of American English*, University of Michigan Press.

SLEDD, J. (1960), Review of Kingdon, *Language*, vol. 36, pp. 173–8.

STOCKWELL, R. (1960), 'The place of intonation in a generative grammar', *Language*, vol. 36, pp. 360–67.

STOCKWELL, R. (1962), 'On the analysis of English intonation', *Second Texas Conference on Problems of Linguistic Analysis in English*, pp. 39–55.

TRAGER, G. L., and SMITH, H. L. (1951), *An Outline of English Structure*, Battenburg.

# 11 František Daneš

## Order of Elements and Sentence Intonation

František Daneš, 'Order of elements and sentence intonation', *To Honour Roman Jakobson; Essays on the Occasion of his Seventieth Birthday*, Mouton, 1967, pp. 499–512.

In his paper 'Some universals of grammar' (1963), J. H. Greenberg[1] introduces the notion of DOMINANT ORDER of syntactic elements and explains (p. 76) that the 'dominance is not based on its more frequent occurrence' (a dominant order is not that alternative which is more frequent than its opposite, the 'recessive' order) but on the fact that the dominant order can always occur while its opposite is present only under specified conditions, i.e. in co-occurrence with another, 'harmonic', construction. These conditions are stated in terms of grammatical notions, such as verb, object, pronominal object, etc.

R. Jakobson, reviewing Greenberg's theory (1963), very aptly shows that in Slavic languages the 'recessive alternatives' to a 'dominant order' are numerous. The Russian sentence corresponding to 'Lenin cites Marx' may occur in six different variants, each representing another word order: SVO *Lenin citiruet Marksa,* SOV *Lenin Marksa citiruet,* VSO *Citiruet Lenin Marksa,* VOS *Citiruet Marksa Lenin,* OSV *Marksa Lenin citiruet,* OVS *Marksa citiruet Lenin.* It is worth noting that all the six logically possible orders may occur, even those three that, according to Greenberg, 'do not occur at all, or at least are excessively rare', namely VOS, OSV, OVS. Jakobson also points out that the conditions by which the occurrence (selection) of the different variants is regulated are not of grammatical character; one of the variants is 'stylistically neutral (unmarked)' while the other ones are experienced as 'diverse emphatic shifts'.

Jakobson's discussion contains two essential points, viz. the notion of the 'neutral order' and the suggestion that the order of sentence elements is also governed by some rules that are of a non-grammatical nature. Our following exposition tries to elaborate these two concepts on the basis of some ideas common in Prague-School linguistics.

1. Studying word order, one should always bear in mind two very important facts. First, the order of elements is a linguistic device (and a very elementary or primitive one) which operates on different linguistic levels and which will

1. Cf. also his paper for the Ninth International Congress of Linguists.

be employed for various intra-linguistic functions. Second, the intra-linguistic functions employ a set of systemic devices, and there is, in a given language, no biunique mapping of the set of devices into the set of functions; this means that to each function a subset of complementary devices is assigned, and vice versa.

1.1. Every utterance (i.e. every sentence taken as a unit of discourse or text (Hausenblas, 1964)) may be analysed (or represented), within the syntactic domain, on three different levels (cf. Daneš, 1964). The respective levels are: (1) the level of grammatical structure; (2) the level of semantic structure; (3) the level of thematic and contextual organization of utterance. On each level every sentence (utterance) may be analysed into its respective components and taken as a realization of the underlying abstract pattern. e.g.

|  | John | bought | a book |
|---|---|---|---|
| (1) | S | V | O |
| (2) | Ag | Ac | G |
| (3) | T | | C |

Explanations: S = Subject, V = Verbal Predicate, O = Object; Ag = Agent, Ac = Action, G = Goal; T = Topic, C = Comment.[2]

In languages like English the order of elements in the underlying patterns corresponds, as a rule, to the order of the respective words in the corresponding utterance. (Or, in other words, the fixed order of elements belongs to the constituent or even distinctive features of the pattern.) But there are languages in which the order of elements in the patterns is not necessarily fixed; it is not employed, or is only partially employed, as a grammatical device. This is often neglected especially by those scholars who base their generative scheme of linguistic description on English, as it has been aptly voiced by Dean S. Worth (1964). Let us now consider the order of elements on different syntactic levels in some detail.

1.2. On the grammatical level the rules of order are of three types: (1) functional rules; (2) concomitant rules; (3) weak rules. In each group the position of a sentence element is determined by its syntactic function, but in a different way.

In cases where the opposition between two syntactic categories is implemented (realized) by two different positions of the element in the sentence

2. The terms 'topic' and 'comment' have been introduced by Yuen Ren Chao (1959) and correspond to the terms 'theme' and 'rheme', used by some Czech scholars as English equivalents for V. Mathesius's terms 'základ (téma)' and 'jádro'. C. F. Hockett considers the 'bipartite structure' of a common clause as a language universal and calls them, too, 'topic' and 'comment' (cf. Hockett, 1963).

František Daneš 217

pattern (the order being thus a distinctive feature), the corresponding rules may be called 'functional rules' and the order of elements may be termed 'grammaticalized' (e.g. in English the pattern S–V–O).

On the other hand, in some instances the position of an element is 'fixed', and yet the violation of the rule fixing its position in the sentence does not lead to a different sentence (with other grammatical relations between the elements); the result will only be an 'ungrammatical' or 'less grammatical' form of the original sentence. The position of the elements in the sentence is then only a concomitant ('redundant', not distinctive) feature of their syntactic function. Such features do not belong to the system of the given language, but to its norm (the latter being, according to E. Coseriu, a commonly accepted, habitual, and traditional realization of the former).[3] Example: dependent genitive case follows its dominating noun in many European languages.

In the third case, a certain order of elements is 'usual'; any deviation from this order, permitted by the 'weak' rule and motivated by special non-grammatical conditions, is associated with the feature of 'non-neutrality' or 'markedness'. The possibility of 'inversion' is common, e.g. in some Slavic languages with the attributive adjective (the usual word order being there A N).

The fundamental distinction between these three types of grammatical word order, pointed out by Mathesius, has, unfortunately, been neglected by Greenberg;[4] thus, the latter scholar classes both English and Slavonic into the same common group II (S V O; cf. *o.c.*, 87 f.).

In languages with the so-called 'free' word order, we must consider a fourth possibility, i.e. a 'labile' order. In this case, the order of some elements of the pattern on the grammatical level is irrelevant; in utterances based on such a pattern, the position of the respective words vacillates according to non-grammatical conditions.

Languages may differ in the particular set of ordering rules (and in their distribution in different syntactic patterns), as well as in the functional loads of the rules.

1.3. It is obvious that in the above quoted Russian example (*Lenin citiruet Marksa* and its variants) the underlying grammatical pattern S–V–O contains neither a functional nor a concomitant fixed order. The variations of the word order may be due to a usual, or even to a labile, order. It seems as if the 'neutrality (unmarkedness)' of the variant *Lenin citiruet Marksa* were based on the fact that the underlying pattern S–V–O shows the usual

3. The significance of redundant features in linguistic structure was very aptly pointed out by R. Jakobson (cf. e.g., Jakobson, 1956). Such features are not operative as 'distinctors' but as 'identifiers' (cf. also Coseriu, 1952).
4. Cf. also some remarks of the present author (1965) and his earlier paper (1959).

order of elements. In other words, the unmarkedness of the given variant would follow from the agreement (correspondence) of the actual sequence of the particular words in the utterance with the order of the respective elements in the underlying pattern, while the other variants would be experienced as marked in consequence of the disagreement of both orders. Schematically:

|  | *Lenin citiruet Marksa* | | | *Lenin Marksa citiruet* | | |
|---|---|---|---|---|---|---|
| Actual sequence | S | V | O | S | O | V |
| Grammatical pattern | S → | V → | O | S → | V → | O |

(The sign → shows the usual order of elements in the pattern.)

But a deeper inspection shows that the matter is not so simple. Let us consider the following Russian examples; (a) *Rebjata kupalis'* (SV) and (b) *Nastala vesna* (VS), both of which must be intuitively and empirically considered as unmarked (the marked variants being *Kupalis' rebjata* and *Vesna nastala*, respectively). At the same time it is clear that both sentences are based on one and the same underlying grammatical sentence pattern; as both possible orders may (under certain, for the moment unspecified, circumstances) lead to an unmarked utterance, we must conclude that the order of elements in the underlying pattern is free (labile).

1.3.1. It remains to explain the conditions under which some sentences of this type are neutral (unmarked), and vice versa. If the explanation in grammatical terms has failed it must be sought for on the semantic level. Let us suppose that there are two semantic types of verbs, labelled, for this moment, X and Y, respectively, and that the verb *kupalis'* 'they-bathed' belongs to the type X, and the other, *nastala* 'she-came', to the type Y. According to our basic model of the three syntactic levels, we assume, in this case, two different *semantic* patterns underlying our sentences (a), (b), namely: (a) Ag → X, (b) Y → B,[5] with the usual order of elements. The respective tabular arrangement may be as follows:

|  |  | (a) *Rebjata kupalis'* (unmarked) | | *Kupalis' rebjata* (marked) | |
|---|---|---|---|---|---|
| grammatical | act. s.: | S | V | V | S |
| level | pattern: | S | V (labile order) | V | S (labile order) |
| semantic | act. s.: | Ag | X | X | Ag |
| level | patterns: | Ag → | X (usual order) | Ag → | X (usual order) |

5. B stands for a correlative term to Ag in the domain of Y.

|  | | (b) *Nastala vesna* (unmarked) | | *Vesna nastala* (marked) | |
|---|---|---|---|---|---|
| grammatical | act. s.: | V | S | S | V |
| level | pattern: | V | S (labile order) | S | V (labile order) |
| semantic | act. s.: | Y | B | B | Y |
| level | pattern: | Y → | B (usual order) | Y → | B (usual order) |

The matrices show that the marked (non-neutral) variants of the sentences are those which reveal a disagreement between the lines of actual sequence and of semantic patterns.

The significance of the semantic level for word order has not yet been sufficiently recognized and investigated. Nevertheless, the pioneering work of some Czech scholars (Firbas, 1953; 1961; 1962; 1964a; Adamec, 1963; 1966; Beneš, 1962; Novák, 1959; Pala, 1966; Uhlířová, 1966),[6] devoted to the contrastive analysis of English, Russian, and German with Czech, as well as some suggestions of other linguists (esp. Hatcher, 1956a, 1956b and Worth, 1964) have proved very promising. Thus, e.g. our semantic verbal category Y might be described as denoting 'existence' or 'bringing into existence (or upon the stage)' and its relevance to word order may be traced in different languages. Ascertaining relevant semantic categories and sentence patterns in various languages is one of the most important and interesting tasks of structural analysis.

The semantic category 'Y' is associated with additional linguistic means, the order of elements being only one of them. e.g. in English, where the order of elements is more grammatical than in Russian, this category will, in certain cases, be accompanied by a special construction, namely of the type 'there is (was) . . .'; e.g. *There were some new pictures on the walls.* Nevertheless, this construction involves an 'inversion' of word order as well (cf. Greenberg's 'harmonic construction'); instead of SV we have here 'there + VS'. It follows that in English, in the grammatical pattern S–V (distinct from the pattern S–V–O!), the order of elements S–V must be considered 'usual' (neither grammaticalized, nor fixed), allowing of the inversion, whereas the Russian equivalent (*Na stenach bylo neskol'ko novyx kartin*) is quite 'neutral' (unmarked).

The significance of the semantic structure of the sentence for the order of elements may be clearly shown on sentences rendering man's inner states and sensations. The person who is the 'recipient (R)'[7] of sensations, or 'bearer' of states, is expressed differently in different languages, by

6. For a survey of Czechoslovak studies, see Lapteva (1963).
7. The term 'Recipient' may be found in Jespersen (1969); the present author makes use of it in a somewhat modified meaning.

means of different syntactic patterns (cf. the following examples); nevertheless, in all our examples the phrase expressing R stands at the beginning of the sentence:

*Russian:*   *U Ivana bolit golova* ('With Ivan aches head')
          Adv.  V   S
*Czech:*   *Ivana bolí hlava*
         O   V   S
*English:*   *Ivan has headache*
         S   V   O

1.3.2. But it would be a false assumption to think that for every sentence there must necessarily exist a neutral (unmarked) form. e.g. whereas the Czech sentence *Zvoní telefon* (VS, 'The telephone rings') is experienced – in contradistinction to its variant *Telefon zvoní* (SV) – as fully neutral, its negative counterpart *Nezvoní telefon* and the variant *Telefon nezvoní* are felt as marked (although in different ways). The explanation should be looked for in the marked character of negation and in the different semantic value (position) of negative statements as opposed to positive ones.

On the other hand, there are some semantic types of sentences that may occur with a single order of elements only, even in languages with the so-called 'free' word order. Thus, in Czech sentences of the type *Lev je šelma* ('Lion is a beast'), i.e. in utterances that denote the placing of an individual into a class, the subject should precede the predicate.

1.4. So far we have analysed sentences in isolation, i.e. taken out of context and situation, as abstract structures. But these structures would be employed as concrete *utterances* in different contexts and situations. We should even admit that our above judgements concerning the neutrality of the particular sentences may have been sometimes more or less uncertain, influenced by possible contexts and/or situations. (The most 'uncontextual' sentences seem to be the generalized statements, such as 'Lions are beasts', 'Man is mortal', 'Dogs hate cats', etc.).

1.4.1. If we try to explain the different variants of the above-quoted Russian sentence 'Lenin citiruet Marksa', we come to the conclusion that the variations are motivated by their contextual (and situational) dependence and applicability (even the neutral variant clearly presupposes a certain context, or, more precisely, a certain class of contexts). In other words: every utterance points to a 'consituation' (to use Mirowicz's term).

Analysing the structure of utterance from this point of view, we state its bipartite pattern. The respective two parts may be defined from two different aspects. (a) Taking for granted that in the act of communication every utterance is, in principle, an enunciation or statement about something, we shall call the respective parts 'topic' or 'theme' (something that one is talking about) and 'comment' or 'rheme' (what one says about it). (b) Following the other line, linking up the utterance with the consitnation, we recognize that, as a rule, the topic contains 'old' or 'already known' elements, while the comment conveys the 'new piece of information'. Professor Vilém Mathesius, who elaborated these ideas (under the heading of the 'actual sentence bipartition' 'or functional sentence perspective'),[8] pointed out that as a rule, both aspects (the 'thematic' and 'contextual') coincide so that in most cases it is not necessary to differentiate between them. (In our rather sketchy account we shall use the terms 'Topic (T)' and 'Comment (C)'.)

1.4.2. The significance of this bipartition for the order of sentence constituents varies. 'Typically in Chinese, Japanese, Korean, English and many others, one first mentions something that one is going to talk about and then says something about it. In other languages, the most typical arrangement is for the Comment, or part of it, to precede the Topic . . . ' (see Hockett, 1963). Of course, such a general statement necessarily implies much simplification. It was Mathesius who – as early as at the beginning of this century – pointed out the fact that the order of sentence elements in every language is governed by a set of different factors (or, from another point of view, is operative in a set of different functions), the T–C bipartition being one of them only. The linguist has to ascertain the hierarchical ordering of these factors for different languages. Some decades later, Firbas drew attention to the fact that, on the other hand, the T–C bipartition employs a number of other linguistic means (the order being one of them only), namely lexical and grammatical devices (such as particles, articles, constructions) (Firbas, 1964b; 1966). Mathesius's line of thinking was followed by a number of Czech, Russian and other linguists in the analyses of different languages.

1.4.3. It is evident that in languages with the so-called 'free' order (i.e. in languages where the order of elements on the grammatical level is less grammaticalized and/or fixed), the order of the sentence components may, in concrete utterances, be employed for the purpose of signalling the T–C bipartition. This is the case, e.g. of Russian. How do these facts fit in with our model of the neutral (unmarked) order? It is easy to recognize that it is exactly the contextual bipartition that motivates the non-neutral (marked) order. Thus, in the Russian utterance *Lenin Marksa citiruet* we get the following matrix:

8. Cf., at least, his article (1929). Some Russian scholars use the term 'aktual'noe (smyslovoe) členenie' (B. A. Il'jiš, K. G. Krušel'nickaja, I. P. Raspopov).

| Syntactic levels | Actual sequence | | | Underlying pattern | | | Order | Agreement between 2 and 3 | Result |
|---|---|---|---|---|---|---|---|---|---|
| 1 | 2 | | | 3 | | | 4 | 5 | 6 |
| grammat. | S | O | V | S | V | O | labile | ○ | |
| semantic | Ag | G | Ac | Ag → Ac → G | | | usual | − | } marked |
| T − C[9] | | T | C | T → C | | | usual | + | |

From the matrix we learn that the usual order on the semantic level has been changed under the impact of the functional needs of the contextual bipartition. The resulting utterance links up fully with the given context (and in this sense it is not marked, but normal), and yet, if valued from the point of view of the linguistic system (i.e. as found in an isolated sentence), its word order will be experienced as marked.

1.4.4. Thus, by means of our matrix we can define a 'neutral sentence' as one which has no 'minus' sign in column 5. The linguistic interpretation of this statement is, clearly, that the functional needs of the T–C bipartition do not – in the case of the 'neutral sentence' – lead to the change (inversion) of a usual order.

In general, the explanation of the notion of 'neutral order' ought to be sought in the interaction (interrelations) of patterns on the three different syntactic levels. In patterns, some of their elements (or all of them) may be positionally bound, by a strong or by a weak rule. If, in the matrix of an utterance, all three levels are 'in agreement' (coordinated), such an utterance has a neutral word order. (The necessary condition is, of course, that at least one pattern contains a bound element. In utterances that do not fulfill this condition, the distinction between the neutral and the marked order is irrelevant.)

The notion of 'marked word order', on the other hand, implies the solution of a conflict between levels. The solution involves the existence of a hierarchy of levels and of some specific linguistic devices. There are two hierarchies: (a) hierarchy of different orders: (1) strong rules (i.e. grammaticalized order and fixed order), (2) weak rules (usual order), (3) free rules (labile order); (b) hierarchy of levels: (1) T–C level, (2) semantic level, (3) grammatical level. The means for solving conflicts are: (a) 'in-

9. The components T–C coincide, in different utterances, with different sentence elements or groups of them. While the former are only two in number (and often without a precise dividing line), the latter rank from one to a theoretically unlimited number.

version', in the case of weak rules; (b) sentence intonation; (c) particles, articles, lexical means, specific grammatical constructions; (d) selection of a different pattern.

1.5. At this moment we must answer two essential questions:

1. What happens when, in a matrix of the above type, a grammaticalized or fixed order appears?
2. Is the inversion C → T also possible (and if so, what would be the consequences)?

1.5.1. Question (1) may be demonstrated by the English sentence 'John hates Mary'. Its matrix contains the grammatical pattern S ⇒ V ⇒ O with grammaticalized order. This utterance fits in with a consituation where the topic of the discourse is 'John'. But in a different consituation, where the topic would be 'Mary' and the comment 'the hatred of John for her', the order of sentence elements should be changed. Column 2 (actual sequence) in the respective matrix would be:

| O | V | S |
|---|---|---|
| G | Ac | Ag |
| T | | C |

But the first (grammatical) line OVS is incompatible with the pattern S ⇒ V ⇒ O, showing the grammaticalized order. There are, generally, two ways of solving this problem: either to relinquish the possibility of rendering the T–C bipartition (in fact, there are differences in languages as to their 'sensitiveness' for contextual needs), or to use a different, more suitable grammatical construction. In the case of our English example, we can make use of the passive construction (in which words or phrases denoting Ag and G, respectively, are mutually replaced). The passive construction *Mary is hated by John* has the following matrix (in contrast to the active construction, the difference appears on the semantic level):

*Passive*

| S | Vpass | O |
|---|---|---|
| G | Ac | Ag |
| T | | C |

*Active*

| S | V | O |
|---|---|---|
| Ag | Ac | G |
| T | | C |

(Of course, we do not claim that in English the passive construction is the only possible solution of all cases. There are other means, such as the definite and indefinite article, sentence intonation, and others.)

1.5.2. In answering question (2), we shall consider the English sentence 'John is writing to his father'. If we take it as an answer to the question[10] 'What is John doing?', we should assign the topic value to 'John' and the rest of the sentence would form the comment of the utterance. This is the normal, neutral case, with T → C order. Now, imagine the same sentence as an answer to another question, viz. 'Who is writing to his father?' In this consituation, 'John' is felt as comment and the rest of the sentence as the topic of the utterance. Thus, the order of components would be inverse, viz. C–T, and the utterance experienced as marked, with emphatic coloring. The explanation of this shift must be sought for in the fact that in the respective matrix, in the last line of column 5, the sign 'minus' appears, due to the inversion of the usual order T → C.

At this point, the conclusion is not surprising, as it follows from our definition of 'neutrality'. But one must ask whether there is any formal device by means of which the shift in the contextual structure of the given sentence would be manifested (word order being, in this case, out of the question). In the domain of the *written* language, no such device would be employed and the respective alternative of the contextual structure of the sentence should be inferred from the consituation only. The *spoken* language, however, avails itself of a specific means for signalling the comment of the utterance, viz. the sentence intonation. This assertion seems to be of great importance and in the next section of our paper we shall outline the principal regularities between sentence intonation and T–C bipartition of utterance.

2. The functional diapason of *sentence intonation* (or, more correctly, of the intonation of utterance), as one of the prosodic features, is very wide and, as has recently been very aptly pointed out by Crystal and Quirk (1964, p. 12), the expressions 'prosodic' and 'paralinguistic' denote 'a scale which has at its "most prosodic" end systems of features (for example, intonation contours) which can fairly easily be integrated with other aspects of linguistic structure, while at the "most paralinguistic" end there are the features most obviously remote from the possibility of integration with the linguistic structure proper . . . ' The systemic functions of intonation contours are several (Daneš, 1960), one of them being simply to signal the T–C structure of utterance.

2.1.1. It appears that in many languages (perhaps in most, but we dare not,

10. The questions are used here in order to elicit a proper consituation.

for the present, make this a universally valid statement), the comment of the utterance would be associated with the center (nucleus) of the (terminal) intonation contour.[11] This means that in languages where, as a rule, the comment is placed towards the end of the utterance (cf. Hockett's semiuniversal), the centre of the terminal intonation contour (CI) should be located on the last stress-unit of the utterance. e.g.: *The train has* cŏme. *John hates* Mȁry. German: *Der Zug ist* gekȍmmen. Russian: *Prišel* pȍezd.

2.1.2. But as we have mentioned above, the grammatical rules of the English word order do not fully allow rearrangement of the sentence constituents according to the needs of the consituation (i.e. in accordance with the T–C structure). Thus, in the sentence *There were some pictures on the walls*, the phrase 'on the walls' does not evidently belong to the comment (the definite article signals the respective notion as already known); consequently, the CI would not be placed on the last stress-unit of the utterance, but on the last stress-unit of the comment of the utterance, particularly on the word *pictures*. A contrastive comparison with languages having the so-called 'free' word order appears to be very illuminating. Let us consider the following example (cf. Worth, 1964, p. 50):

|  | *Russian* | *English* |
|---|---|---|
| in consituation (a): | *Krovati stojali v jego* kȍmnate | *The beds were in his* rŏom |
| in consituation (b): | *V jego komnate stojali* krovȁti | *There were* bĕds *in his room* |

Thus in languages like English, the CI would often be placed on non-terminal elements of the utterance, while in others, as for instance in Slavic languages (conspicuously in Czech), the normal suprasegmental (prosodic) shape of the utterance (i.e. of the non-emphatic utterance in which no word is emphasized for contrast) is that with the CI in the last stress-unit. The supposition that the English sentence is only to a small degree sensitive to the needs of the context turns out to be not fully valid; the differences between languages lie mainly in the different means that are employed (as has been ingeniously pointed out by Firbas in connection with the use of articles).

I will adduce some other examples, in which the comment occupies a position very remote from the end of the utterance (so that a relatively very long terminal intonation contour arises): (1) '[They went to the river, but the water was so swift that the monkey was afraid. "Get on my neck", said

11. Some authors call this center 'the sentence stress' or 'the logical stress'.

the elephant, "I shall carry you . . .] I am not *afráid* to swim across a swift river" ' (Jassem, 1954). (The phrase 'to swim across a swift river', although standing at the end, conveys the notion which has been explicitly mentioned in the previous context and consequently belongs to the topic, not to the comment, of the utterance.) – (2) '[They've been cleaning them up the whole morning.] I've never *séen* such energy' (Lee, 1960). (The notion 'such energy' is implied in the preceding utterance.)

2.1.3. To sum up: While in Slavonic (especially in Czech) the variability of word order is compensated for by a rather uniform (automatic) location of the terminal CI, in English, on the other hand, the highly fixed word order is compensated for by a great variety of the possible positions of the CI in the utterance. In other words: in English it is rather the suprasegmental phonological structure that signals the 'functional perspective of utterance', i.e. the points of the highest communicative dynamism. Thus, we may conclude that the functional load of the two linguistic devices is different in various languages. (It is worth mentioning that the relatively high functional load of intonation in English shows itself in relation to other linguistic functions as well.[12])

2.2. Utterances conveying emphasis are governed by special rules. At least two classes of emphatic utterances should be distinguished: (1) emphatic utterances proper; (2) utterances with emphasis for contrast. In class (1) the emphatic feature characterizes the utterance as a whole, while in class (2) this feature is associated with one particular element of the utterance only.

2.2.1. The emphatic utterances proper are characterized by the inverse order on the contextual level, i.e. by the order C–T, and, consequently, by the onset position of the CI (this being located on the initial stress-unit of the utterance) on the suprasegmental phonological level; e.g.: *The* tràin *has come!* (in contradistinction to 'normal' *The train has* còme). In Russian: Pòezd *prišel!* × *Poezd* prìšel; and also (due to the 'free' word order) Prìšel *poezd!* × *Prìšel* pòezd. In German: *Der* Zùg *ist gekòmmen!* × *Der Zug ist* gekòmmen.

2.2.2. The emphasis for contrast is intended 'to show that a word is contrasted with another (either implied or previously expressed), or that a word introduces a new and unexpected idea' (Jones, 1956, p. 277). Bolinger has called such utterances 'sentences of the second instance' (1952). Contrastive emphasis may be rendered – according to circumstances – by a set of means: (a) word order, (b) a shift of the CI (it would be displaced from

12. Cf., e.g. the following statement of Halliday, McIntosh and Strevens: '. . . it is important to realize that spoken English makes extensive use of intonation to carry grammatical meaning' (1965, p. 53).

its 'automatic' (neutral) position, (c) a specific phonological form of the intonation contour. It is clear that in English the possibilities (b) and especially (c) are the most common, e.g.: *I sent a book to* hĕr (and not to someone else), the contrast having been achieved by means of the shift of the CI. (The normal form would be *I sent a* bŏok *to her*, according to the rule that in sentences ending with a preposition and a pronoun, the final pronouns are not stressed.) In addition to it, the contrast may be pointed out or modified by means of special intonation contours. Other examples: [*Look out, here comes a* cǎr.] *It looks like* ŏur *car. What are* yŏu *going to do? It was* extrĕmely *cold this year. I nearly* dĭd *forget it* (the emphasis is foregrounded by means of the construction with 'do' as well). Jŏhn *loves Mary* (and not George) = *It is* Jŏhn *who loves Mary* (with a special construction). *I* sǎw *the man coming along the road* (reassuring the person spoken to; a very long intonation contour). *I met her* fǎther (and not her mother or brother . . .); in this case the contrastive emphasis is rendered by means of a specific (emphatic) contour only, as the contrasting word is in the final position, so that the placement of the CI cannot function as a distinctive feature.

Many analogous examples might be easily adduced from other languages. German: *Ihr Bruder hat* lǎnge *auf Sie gewartet.* // *Ihr Bruder hat lange auf* Sĭe *gewartet.* / *Ihr* Brŭder *hat lange auf Sie gewartet.* (The normal form: *Ihr Bruder hat lange auf Sie* gewǎrtet (Essen, 1956).) Some Russian examples may be found in the book by Buning and Schooneveld (1961, see also Ebeling, 1958), Czech examples in the book on Czech sentence intonation by the present author (Daneš, 1957). It is exactly this contrastive emphasis that is often referred to as 'logical (sentence) stress'.

2.2.3. In addition, it is possible to use a specific non-terminal intonation contour for singling out the topic of the utterance; e.g. in English: *My* brŏther | *went to* Brĭghton (implying: 'as for my brother, he . . .'). *If it* succĕeds | *I shall make* . . .; in Russian: *Esli tebe* grŭstno |, . . .; in German: *Geheime* Sŏrgen | *sind eine schwere* Lǎst.

2.3. It has often been suggested that sentence intonation performs proper grammatical functions and lexical (semantic) functions as well. Undoubtedly, such examples, as:

1(a) *I didn't visit the* dŏctor | *because I was* ĭll.
 (b) *I* dĭdn't *visit the doctor because I was ill* (Lee, 1960).
2(a) *Please* wĭre | *if I am to* cŏme.
 (b) *Please* wĭre *if I am to come.*
3(a) *It is the* cŏuntry | *that suits my wife* bĕst.
 (b) *It is the* cŏuntry *that suits my wife best* (Schubiger, 1935)

evidently show the relevance of the suprasegmental phonological structure for the grammatical and semantic interpretation of such sentences. Nevertheless, it seems to us that the different grammatical and semantic interpretations are based on two different underlying T–C structures of the respective utterances. In other words: rather than saying that the intonation here works as a grammatical device (distinguishing, e.g. an object clause from an adverbial one, or determining the function of the conjunction), we should rather say that this is an accidental effect of two possible T–C structures of the given utterance. (e.g. in (2a) the 'if'-clause is marked as comment, whereas in (2b) it is the verb 'wire' that is signalled as an emphatic comment, while the 'if'-clause conveys a thing that is already known from the consitution.)

An analogous situation may be found in cases where sentence intonation seems to determine the semantic meaning of a word, e.g.:

4(a) *He also visited* Prăgue. ('He visited some other places and Prague additionally')

  (b) He ălso *visited Prague*. ('Others visited it, and he did so as well')

Fairly analogous examples may be adduced from other languages. But in all of them we shall find that the two different semantic interpretations of *also* (German *auch*, Russian *tože*, Czech *též*, etc.) are determined by the fact that in (4a) the adverb brings out the subsequent utterance portion as a new fact (comment), in addition to facts already known, whereas in (4b), with *also* bearing the CI, the situation is inverted.

Negative clauses seem to be a field especially favorable for the 'semantic intonation' in many languages. Cf. the following Czech utterances and their English counterparts:

5(a) *S každým* němluví. *He does not speak to* ănybody (with a falling-rising contour)

  (b) *S* kăždým *nemluví. He does not speak to* ănybody (with a falling contour).

The utterances (a) have the meaning 'he speaks only to some people', while (b) means, in an appropriate situation, 'he speaks to no one'. It is worth mentioning, however, that the meaning (a) is, in Czech, associated with the normal (automatic) form of the utterance, but the meaning (b) is signalled by de-automation, while in English the situation is reversed (it is the meaning (a) that is associated with a marked contour). Nevertheless, both languages have another feature in common: the semantic differences (a) and (b), rendered by intonation, depend, to a certain extent, on a favorable consitution; the respective intonational forms alone do not fully ensure that the utterance will be interpreted only in one of the two possible meanings, or, in other words, such utterances are not entirely un-ambiguous. But, at the same time, both languages have a pronoun, namely *nikdo, no one (nobody)*, which, in contrast to *každý, anybody,* is unambiguous, having the negative meaning (a) only (in accordance with the presence of the explicitly negative morpheme *ni-* and *no*, respectively).[13]

3. It is self-evident that any systemic linguistic description, whether generative or not, has to take into account all relevant facts about the most elementary and common linguistic devices, viz. the order of elements and the utterance intonation (cf. Halliday, McIntosh and Strevens, 1965, p. 73). And it seems to me that the generative scheme suggested by the MIT group is, in its recent form, scarcely able to account for them in a satisfactory way, mainly because its phonological component does not include the sentence intonation; besides, the position of the T–C organization, the systemic character of which is hardly to be denied, is yet to be stated. (Its considerable stylistic import does not, in essence, contradict the undeniable appurtenance of the T–C principle to *la langue.*)[14]

13. Cf. Vachek (1947). Klima, however, does not mention these facts in his paper (1964). A more detailed analysis of such negative clauses in Czech may be found in Daneš (1954).

14. Some remarks in Chomsky (1965) as well as a personal communication by the same author seem to inaugurate a possible attempt to incorporate the said facts into the new generative framework. As regards sentence intonation, an earlier study by Stockwell (1960) contains some valuable suggestions.

## References

ADAMEC, P. (1963), 'K úloze sémantiky ve slovosledu', *Slavica Pragensia*, vol. 4, pp. 297–300.

ADAMEC, P. (1966), *Porjadok slov v sovremennom russkom jazyke*, Prague.

BENEŠ, E. (1962). 'Die Verbstellung im Deutschen, von der Mitteilungsperspektive her betrachtet', *Philologica Pragensia*, vol. 5, pp. 6–19.

BOLINGER, D. (1952), 'Linear modification', *PMLA*, vol. 67, pp. 1117–44.

BUNING, J. E. J., and Schooneveld, C. H. van (1961), *The Sentence Intonation of Contemporary Standard Russian as a Linguistic Structure*, Mouton.

CHAO, Y. R. (1959), 'How Chinese logic operates', *Anthropol. Ling.*, vol. 1, p. 1.

CHOMSKY, N. (1965), *Aspects of the Theory of Syntax*, Harvard University Press.

COSERIU, E. (1952), *Sistema, norma y habla*, Montevideo.

CRYSTAL, D., and QUIRK, R. (1964), *Systems of Prosodic and Paralinguistic Features in English*, Mouton.

DANEŠ, F. (1954), 'Příspěvek k rosboru významové výstavby výpovědi', *Studie a práce Lingvistické*, vol. 1, p. 215.

DANEŠ, F. (1957), *Intonace a věta ve spisovné češtině*, Prague.

DANEŠ, F. (1959), 'K otácze pořádku slov v slovanských jazycích , *Slovo a Slovesnosk*, vol. 20, pp. 1–9.

DANEŠ, F. (1960), 'Sentence intonation from a functional point of view', *Word*, vol. 16, pp. 34–54.

DANEŠ, F. (1964), 'A three-level approach to syntax', *TLP*, vol. 1, pp. 225–40.

DANEŠ, F. (1965), *Proceedings of the Ninth International Congress of Linguists*, The Hague, p. 420.

EBELING, C. L. (1958), 'Subject and predicate, especially in Russian', *Dutch Contributions to the Fourth International Congress of Slavists*.

ESSEN, O. von (1956), *Grundzüge der Hochdeutschen Satzintonation*, Düsseldorf.

FIRBAS, J. (1953), 'On the communicative function of the verb in English, German and Czech', *Brno Studies in English*, vol. 1, pp. 39–68.

FIRBAS, J. (1961), 'On the communicative value of the modern English finite verb', *Brno Studies in English*, vol. 3, pp. 79–104.

FIRBAS, J. (1962), 'Notes on the function of the sentence in the act of communication', *Sborník prací filosofické fakulty Brněnské University*, p. A10.

FIRBAS, J. (1964a), 'On defining the theme in functional sentence analysis', *TLP*, vol. 1, pp. 267–80.

FIRBAS, J. (1964b), 'From comparative word-order studies. (Thoughts on V. Mathesius' conception of the word-order system in English compared with that of Czech)', *Brno Studies in English*, vol. 4, pp. 111–128.

FIRBAS, J. (1966), 'Non-thematic subjects in contemporary English', *TLP*, vol. 2, pp. 239ff.

GREENBERG, J. H. (1963), 'Some universals of grammar', in *Universals of Language*, Harvard University Press, pp. 58–90.

HALLIDAY, M. A. K., MCINTOSH, A., and STREVENS, P. (1964), *The Linguistic Sciences and Language Teaching*, Longman.

HATCHER, A. G. (1956a), 'Syntax and the sentence', *Word*, vol. 12, pp. 234–50.

HATCHER, A. G. (1956b), 'Theme and underlying question', Supplement to *Word*, vol. 12.

HAUSENBLAS, K. (1964), 'On the characterization and classification of discourses', *TLP*, vol. 1, pp. 67–83.

HOCKETT, C. F. (1963), 'The problem of universals in language', in *Universals of Language*, Harvard University Press, pp. 1–22.

JAKOBSON, R. (1956), *Fundamentals of Language*, Mouton.

JAKOBSON, R. (1963), 'Implications of language universals for linguistics', in *Universals of Language*, Harvard University Press, pp. 208–19.

JASSEM, W. (1954), *Fonetyka Jezyka Angielskego*, Warsaw.

JESPERSEN, O. (1969), *Analytic Syntax*, Holt, Rinehart & Winston.

JONES, D. (1956), *An Outline of English Phonetics*, Dutton.

KLIMA, E. S. (1964), 'Negation in English', in *The Structure of Language*, Prentice-Hall, pp. 246–323.

LAPTEVA, O. A. (1963), 'Čexoslovackije raboty poslednix let po voprosam aktual'nogo členenija predloženija', *Voprosy Jazykoznanija*, no. 4, pp. 120–27.

LEE, W. R. (1960), *An English Intonation Reader*, Macmillan.

MATHESIUS, V. (1929), 'Zur Satzperspektive im modernen Englisch', *Archiv für das Studium der Modernen Sprachen und Literaturen*, vol. 84, no. 155, pp. 200–10.

NOVÁK, P. (1959), 'O prostředcich aktuálního členění', *Acta Universitatis Carolinae, Philologica*, vol. 1, p. 10.

PALA, K. (1966), 'O nekotoryx problemax aktual'nogo členenija', *Prague Studies in Mathematical Linguistics*, vol. 1, pp. 81–92.

SCHUBIGER, M. (1935), *The Role of Intonation in Spoken English*, Cambridge University Press.

STOCKWELL, R. P. (1960), 'The place of intonation in a generative grammar of English', *Language*, vol. 36, pp. 360–67.

UHLIŘOVÁ, L. (1966), 'Some aspects of word order in categorial and transformational grammars', *Prague Studies in Mathematical Linguistics*, vol. 1, pp. 159–66.

VACHEK, J. (1947), 'Obecný zápor v angličtině a v češtině', *Prague Studies in English*, vol. 6, pp. 7–73.

WORTH, D. S. (1964), 'Ob otobraženii linejnych otnošenij v poroždajuščich modeljach jazyka', *Voprosy Jazykoznanija*, no. 5, pp. 46–58.

# Part Four
## Intonation and Emotion

It is no news to the average speaker that he betrays emotions by the tone of his voice. But how does he do it? Is it only the broad sweep of intonation that conveys fear, happiness, boredom, secrecy and doubt, or does the information lie partly in the squiggles or perhaps in other changes that have nothing to do with fundamental frequency? In the first article Lieberman and Michaels show that we do indeed depend on many factors for a sure identification, but that of those tested pitch contributes most.

The second Reading carries the analysis a step farther. It is concerned with how rather than how much. Uldall takes the presence of emotional meanings for granted and establishes connections between particular intonations and particular emotions. Her technique is that of the well-known semantic differential. She locates the intonation patterns in an 'emotional space' whose dimensions are the paired opposites of commonly sensed emotions that average speakers can recognize and talk about: pleasant–unpleasant, strong–weak, and authoritative–submissive.

The question of emotion is not a mere side issue where intonation as a part of language is concerned, for it is next to impossible to separate emotional meanings from grammatical ones. The first example that comes to mind when we want to illustrate the grammatical function of intonation is the rising pitch of yes–no questions. But is this purely grammatical? Such questions have a falling intonation about as often as a rising one, which proves that there is no true interdependence. A yes–no question then must have its rise for some other reason than the fact that it is a yes–no question. Is it because of an attitude – more uncertainty, greater curiosity? If so, that is suspiciously close to emotion.

# 12 Philip Lieberman and Sheldon B. Michaels

Some Aspects of Fundamental Frequency and Envelope
Amplitude as Related to the Emotional Content of Speech

Philip Lieberman and Sheldon B. Michaels, 'Some aspects of fundamental
frequency and envelope amplitude as related to the emotional content of speech',
*Journal of the Acoustical Society of America*, vol. 34, no. 7, July 1962, pp. 922–7.

## Authors' summary

Pitch pulses were electronically derived from the utterances of three male
native speakers of American English who each read eight neutral test
sentences in certain 'emotional' modes, i.e. as a question, an objective
statement, a fearful utterance, a happy utterance, etc. A fixed-vowel
POVO-type synthesizer was excited by these pitch pulses. The pitch
perturbations, or rapid variations in the fundamental excitation rate,
could be smoothed out and the POVO could be amplitude-modulated
with a signal derived from the original speech envelope amplitude.

Tapes were recorded and presented to separate groups of naive listeners
who categorized the emotional modes in forced judgement tests. Results
of the tests show that with unprocessed speech, the listeners were able to
correctly identify the emotional content 85 per cent of the time. When
only pitch information was presented, correct identification was made 44
per cent of the time. When amplitude information was added to the pitch
information, the identification rose to 47 per cent. Smoothing the pitch
information with a 40-ms time constant reduced the identifications to
38 per cent, while 100-ms smoothing reduced the identifications to 25
per cent. A 120 Hz monotone with amplitude information derived from
the original speech envelope amplitude resulted in 14 per cent identifications

## Introduction

The object of this experiment was to examine the contributions of fundamental frequency and of amplitude to the transmission of the emotional
content of normal human speech. With respect to the fundamental frequency, we particularly wished to see whether the perturbations of vocal
pitch, that is, the irregularities in the fundamental excitation rate, were
pertinent to the transmission of emotional information.

We used the techniques of speech synthesis in this experiment and synthesized acoustic stimuli that differed from one another only with respect

to particular acoustic parameters that exist in normal speech. These synthesized stimuli were then listened to and categorized by groups of subjects in terms of a set of emotional categories. If the presence or absence of a particular acoustic parameter causes a difference in the listeners' judgements of the synthesized acoustic stimuli, and if the presence of this particular parameter has been noted in the analysis of human speech, then we can state, with reasonable certainty, that this acoustic parameter is pertinent to the transmission of information and is an acoustic correlate of some phonetic or emotional event.

We wished, in so far as possible, to avoid subjective judgements, such as occur when informants are simply asked to state whether a particular tape recording sounds more natural than some other tape recordings. We therefore used categorization procedures.

**Experimental procedure**
*Emotional modes*

In an earlier study (Lieberman, 1961), a set of eight neutral sentences was recorded in an anechoic chamber by six male native speakers of American English. Each speaker was instructed to read each sentence with appropriate vocal modifications so that it could be identified as belonging to one of the following eight categories, or emotional modes: (1) a bored statement, (2) a confidential communication, (3) a question expressing disbelief or doubt, (4) a message expressing fear, (5) a message expressing happiness, (6) an objective question, (7) an objective statement, and (8) a pompous statement. Each sentence was read three times in each mode (see Table 1).

Table 1 **List of sentences used in the experiment**

---

1. The lamp stood on the desk.
2. They have bought a new car.
3. He will work hard next term.
4. His friend came home by train.
5. They parked near the street light.
6. We talked for a long time.
7. John found him at the phone.
8. You have seen my new house.

---

The twenty-four repetitions of each sentence were then placed in a random sequence and categorized by a group of twenty linguistically naive listeners in a forced judgement test to select the most identifiable utterance from each of the eight emotional categories for each sentence. A panel of trained observers then listened to the same set and rejected those utterances that they found to be unnatural or strained. On the basis of these criteria the best utterances of each of the eight emotional categories for each of the eight sentences of each speaker were selected.

For the present experiment we took from this selected set the utterances of three of the speakers, and again categorized the utterances in terms of the eight emotional modes with a new group of ten naive listeners. We then proceeded to isolate the frequency and amplitude information contained in the utterances of this tape recording.

*Preparation of test stimuli*

The first step was to make an intermediate tape for the generation of our test stimuli. With pitch-extraction circuits we derived a marker pulse on the leading edge of the amplitude peak of each fundamental period. We recorded these pulses on a dual-track tape with the original speech on the upper track and the derived pitch pulses on the lower track. The two waveforms were then simultaneously displayed by a tape-scanning mechanism on an oscilloscope. The errors in pitch extraction were then manually corrected with special erase and recording circuits on the tape-scanning device. Our derived pitch pulses were accurate to within 0·2 ms of the fundamental excitation. We used this tape to generate all of our synthesized waveforms. The derived pitch pulses were used to drive a POVO fixed-vowel synthesizer having formant frequencies of 750, 1100 and 2450 Hz and bandwidths of 70, 80 and 115 Hz, respectively. The output of the POVO was made asymmetrical with a diode and RC circuit, the better to approximate human sounds.

We subsequently made five different tape recordings, each varying the available acoustic parameters in a specific way. The first tape recording of synthesized speech made under these conditions used the derived pitch pulses of constant amplitude to drive the POVO. This essentially isolated all of the fundamental frequency information of our real speech input, removing all phonetic and amplitude information. The original speech waveform was recorded on the lower track of this tape recording and was critically compared with the synthesized waveform on the upper track in this and in all of our subsequent tape recordings.

On our second tape recording we included amplitude as well as fundamental frequency information. A 20 ms full-wave rectifying circuit was used to obtain the envelope amplitude of the original speech from the waveform on the upper track of our generating tape. The derived pitch pulses on the lower track of the generating tape which excited the POVO were then amplitude-modulated by this signal.

In our next tape recording we retained the amplitude modulation of the

POVO. However, we removed the pitch perturbations by converting the derived pitch pulses on the generating tape to an analogue signal, smoothing the analogue signal, and then converting the smoothed analogue signal into a pulse stream again. The block diagram for this operation is presented in Figure 1. The overall linearity of the frequency transformation is presented in Figure 2.

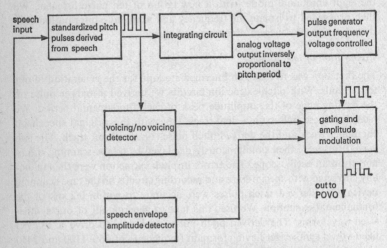

Figure 1 Block diagram illustrating pitch-smoothing operation. A train of standardized pitch pulses derived from our speech samples was inserted at the input. An integrating circuit produced an analog voltage inversely proportional to the pitch period and this analog voltage was smoothed and applied to the input of a pulse generator whose output frequency was voltage-controlled. A voicing detector operated a gate which insured that the POVO was driven only during the voiced intervals of the original speech signal. The envelope amplitude which amplitude-modulated the output pulses, was derived from the original speech signal.

We produced two tapes in which we excited the POVO with smoothed pitch, retaining full amplitude modulation. The smoothing time constants were 40 and 100 ms, respectively. The ouput-pulse generator, which excited the POVO, always returned to 100 Hz in the absence of voicing. The system is very similar to that used in some Vocoder pitch-synthesis circuits.

A final tape was made in which we set the output pulse generator to a constant 120 Hz and amplitude-modulated it, again deriving the amplitude information from the original speech on the upper track of our generating tape. This tape essentially isolated amplitude information from the

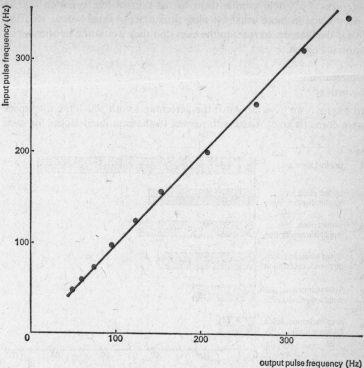

Figure 2 Calibration of pitch smoothing. The ordinate is the input-pulse frequency of Figure 1 while the abscissa is the output-pulse frequency of Figure 1 after smoothing.

pitch and phonetic information contained in the original speech. In the three latter tapes the output pulse generator was gated so that only the voiced parts of the utterances were synthesized.

*Listening tests*

Listening tests were conducted for each of these tapes with separate groups of ten naive listeners each. Each tape was presented to a group which had not heard any of the tapes before. By restricting our identifications to those obtained during the listener's first exposure to the stimuli, we minimized the chance that our listeners might be learning to identify the utterances by means of the idiosyncrasies of the speakers from whose utterances the pitch and amplitude parameters were derived. In a larger group of speakers these idiosyncrasies might well be ignored by the listeners who would ascribe them to the normal free variation that is encountered in more usual listening situations. In other words, we tried to get the listeners to react to the cues that they would use in listening to normal English.

## Observations
### General effects

In Figure 3 we have tabulated the percentages with which the utterances were correctly categorized with respect to the emotional modes for each

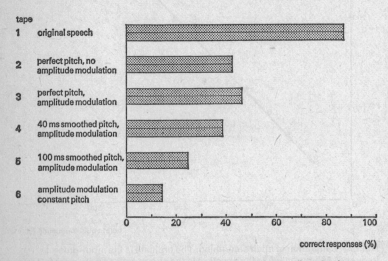

correct responses (%)

Figure 3 Percentages of correct identification of the emotional modes by separate groups of naive listeners for (1) the original wide-band speech signal; (2) perfect pitch pulses, derived from the original speech, driving a fixed POVO; (3) perfect pitch pulses driving an amplitude-modulated POVO, modulated with the envelope amplitude derived from the original speech; (4) pitch smoothed with a 40 ms time constant by the circuit of the block diagram of Figure 1; (5) pitch smoothed with a 100 ms time constant; (6) monotone at 120 Hz driving the amplitude-modulated POVO.

of our six tape recordings. Each run represents the responses of a different group of naive listeners on their first exposure to the test material. We note several effects. When the unprocessed speech was presented, 85 per cent of the modes were correctly identified. When we presented only pitch information, only 44 per cent were correctly identified. When amplitude information was added to the pitch information, the identification rose to 47 per cent. Smoothing the pitch information with a 40 ms time constant reduced the identifications to 38 per cent, 100 ms smoothing reduced the identifications to 25 per cent, while a monotone with amplitude modulation resulted in only 14 per cent identification, which, however, is still significant at the 0·006 level with respect to the results that would occur through chance guesses.

The following aspects of the data should be noted. First, fundamental frequency alone is not able to transmit full emotional information. Second, amplitude information plays a small though significant part in the correct

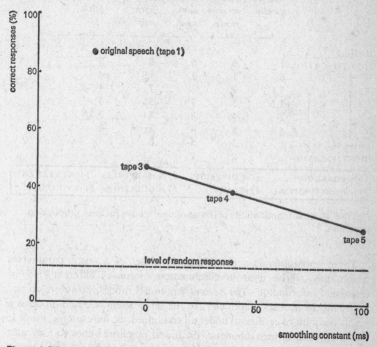

Figure 4 Effect of pitch smoothing on the identification of the modes. Tapes 3, 4 and 5 of Figure 3 are plotted. The stimuli on all three tapes had the same gross pitch range and the same amplitude modulation; only the fine structure of the pitch was varied.

recognition of emotions. Third, noting the results of tapes three, four and five, and recalling that all three had the same gross pitch range and the same amplitude modulation, we see that the fine structure of the fundamental excitation rate has a perceptible effect on the identification of the emotional modes (Figure 4).

Philip Lieberman and Sheldon B. Michaels 241

## Effects of emotional modes

In Figure 5 we have ordered the different emotional modes according to the frequency with which they were correctly identified for each of our processed tape recordings.

| | Tape (1) Original speech | (2) Perfect pitch, no amp. mod. | (3) Perfect pitch, amp. mod. | (5) 100 ms. smoothed pitch, amp. mod. | (6) Amp. mod., constant pitch |
|---|---|---|---|---|---|
| HIGHEST IDENTIFICATION | 1 | 6 | 6 | 6 | 7 |
| | 6 | 1 | 1 | 1,3 | 4 |
| | 7,8 | 7 | 3 | 7 | 1 |
| | 3,5 | 3 | 7 | 5 | 5 |
| | 2 | 4 | 8 | 4 | 3,6,8 |
| | 4 | 8 | 4 | 2 | 2 |
| LOWEST IDENTIFICATION | | 5 | 5 | 8 | |
| | | 2 | 2 | | |

1) is BOREDOM  3) is DISBELIEF  5) is HAPPINESS  7) is STATEMENT
2) is CONFIDENTIAL  4) is FEAR  6) is QUESTION  8) is POMPOUS

Figure 5  Relative identifiability of the emotional modes for each processing condition.

There apparently is a multidimensional set of acoustic parameters which may all be used in combination to convey different kinds of emotional information. The several emotional modes, however, do not utilize all the acoustic parameters to the same extent. Certain modes are highly resistant to confusion under all conditions, as, for example, mode 1, which apparently used phonetic, pitch and amplitude cues to a greater degree than the other modes. Other modes tend to be confused under most conditions, like, for example, mode 2. However, mode 4 seems to depend more strongly than the others on amplitude information, while mode 6 seems to depend more strongly than the others on pitch information.

## Effects of individual speakers

Individual speakers also seem to favor the use of different acoustic parameters for the transmission of the same emotional information. An example of this is seen in Figures 6 and 7.

## Speaker 1

| Response | 1 | 2 | 3 | 4 | 5 | 6 | 7 | 8 |
|---|---|---|---|---|---|---|---|---|
| 1 | 671 | 063 | 172 | 000 | 016 | 016 | 203 | 109 |
| 2 | 188 | 311 | 094 | 016 | 047 | 063 | 422 | 109 |
| 3 | 000 | 078 | 687 | 031 | 125 | 250 | 063 | 016 |
| 4 | 078 | 016 | 047 | 796 | 203 | 031 | 016 | 063 |
| 5 | 016 | 016 | 078 | 656 | 234 | 063 | 031 | 156 |
| 6 | 031 | 047 | 109 | 000 | 000 | 828 | 172 | 063 |
| 7 | 234 | 172 | 063 | 016 | 000 | 016 | 702 | 047 |
| 8 | 047 | 125 | 234 | 016 | 109 | 047 | 156 | 516 |

*Stimulus*

## Speaker 2

| Response | 1 | 2 | 3 | 4 | 5 | 6 | 7 | 8 |
|---|---|---|---|---|---|---|---|---|
| 1 | 843 | 109 | 063 | 000 | 000 | 000 | 172 | 063 |
| 2 | 047 | 296 | 203 | 094 | 219 | 000 | 297 | 094 |
| 3 | 000 | 063 | 483 | 094 | 141 | 391 | 047 | 031 |
| 4 | 016 | 031 | 172 | 546 | 219 | 016 | 031 | 219 |
| 5 | 016 | 141 | 188 | 078 | 296 | 031 | 281 | 219 |
| 6 | 000 | 031 | 078 | 078 | 094 | 953 | 000 | 016 |
| 7 | 266 | 141 | 047 | 000 | 000 | 031 | 749 | 016 |
| 8 | 016 | 219 | 125 | 031 | 031 | 000 | 078 | 750 |

*Stimulus*

## Speaker 4

| Response | 1 | 2 | 3 | 4 | 5 | 6 | 7 | 8 |
|---|---|---|---|---|---|---|---|---|
| 1 | 812 | 141 | 016 | 016 | 031 | 000 | 203 | 031 |
| 2 | 203 | 266 | 031 | 031 | 078 | 016 | 484 | 141 |
| 3 | 000 | 000 | 891 | 031 | 047 | 281 | 000 | 000 |
| 4 | 016 | 016 | 156 | 515 | 219 | 281 | 000 | 047 |
| 5 | 016 | 031 | 156 | 422 | 406 | 063 | 031 | 125 |
| 6 | 016 | 125 | 344 | 000 | 000 | 718 | 047 | 000 |
| 7 | 172 | 297 | 047 | 047 | 016 | 016 | 546 | 109 |
| 8 | 109 | 219 | 016 | 031 | 063 | 000 | 203 | 609 |

*Stimulus*

Figure 6 Normalized stimulus–response matrix for each speaker for tape 3 (in % $\times$ $10^{-2}$) (cf. Figure 3). The confusion matrices have the emotional mode that the speaker wished to convey arranged on the ordinates. The responses that these stimuli evoked in the listeners are on the abscissas. Note that speaker two's mode-5 stimuli were not confused with mode 4 as often as the mode-5 and 4 stimuli of speakers one and four.

Speaker 1

| Response | 1 | 2 | 3 | 4 | 5 | 6 | 7 | 8 |
|---|---|---|---|---|---|---|---|---|
| 1 | 280 | 188 | 344 | 047 | 063 | 000 | 250 | 078 |
| 2 | 266 | 171 | 156 | 078 | 016 | 172 | 328 | 063 |
| 3 | 078 | 188 | 344 | 078 | 109 | 266 | 156 | 031 |
| 4 | 047 | 016 | 250 | 202 | 266 | 172 | 078 | 219 |
| 5 | 047 | 016 | 359 | 156 | 344 | 172 | 047 | 109 |
| 6 | 063 | 156 | 156 | 047 | 031 | 578 | 219 | 000 |
| 7 | 563 | 109 | 078 | 047 | 047 | 047 | 281 | 078 |
| 8 | 141 | 094 | 313 | 016 | 375 | 063 | 094 | 154 |

*Stimulus*

Speaker 2

| Response | 1 | 2 | 3 | 4 | 5 | 6 | 7 | 8 |
|---|---|---|---|---|---|---|---|---|
| 1 | 423 | 234 | 078 | 031 | 125 | 000 | 281 | 078 |
| 2 | 172 | 233 | 172 | 094 | 109 | 063 | 344 | 063 |
| 3 | 031 | 063 | 312 | 016 | 125 | 531 | 125 | 047 |
| 4 | 047 | 047 | 297 | 312 | 250 | 125 | 047 | 125 |
| 5 | 047 | 125 | 313 | 328 | 063 | 109 | 156 | 109 |
| 6 | 031 | 047 | 266 | 063 | 000 | 734 | 031 | 078 |
| 7 | 406 | 281 | 078 | 031 | 109 | 031 | 283 | 031 |
| 8 | 219 | 250 | 219 | 063 | 031 | 047 | 250 | 171 |

*Stimulus*

Speaker 4

| Response | 1 | 2 | 3 | 4 | 5 | 6 | 7 | 8 |
|---|---|---|---|---|---|---|---|---|
| 1 | 345 | 156 | 109 | 000 | 078 | 125 | 328 | 109 |
| 2 | 156 | 219 | 156 | 109 | 063 | 047 | 328 | 172 |
| 3 | 000 | 047 | 405 | 094 | 250 | 313 | 094 | 047 |
| 4 | 016 | 016 | 344 | 170 | 297 | 313 | 031 | 063 |
| 5 | 016 | 063 | 250 | 172 | 453 | 109 | 078 | 109 |
| 6 | 078 | 172 | 219 | 031 | 031 | 547 | 141 | 031 |
| 7 | 359 | 297 | 016 | 031 | 078 | 031 | 329 | 109 |
| 8 | 297 | 297 | 094 | 063 | 078 | 031 | 313 | 077 |

*Stimulus*

Figure 7 Normalized stimulus–response matrix for each speaker for tape 5 (in % $\times$ 10$^{-2}$) (cf. Figure 3). Note that when pitch was smoothed, speaker two's mode-5 stimuli were more often confused with mode 4 than were the mode-5 and 4 stimuli of speakers one and four.

In Figure 6 the complete stimulus–response matrix has been tabulated for each speaker for the tape having perfect pitch with amplitude modulation. We note that for speakers one and four the listeners tended to make mode-4 responses to mode-5 stimuli. They did not confuse speaker two's stimuli in this manner. However, when we look at Figure 7 in which the matrices have again been tabulated for the tape having 100 ms smoothed

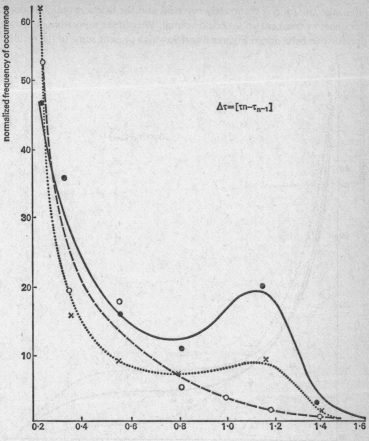

$$\Delta\tau = [\tau n - \tau_{n-1}]$$

Figure 8 Distribution of the absolute value of the difference between the durations of adjacent pitch periods[1] in ms for the mode-5 stimuli of each speaker. The difference in ms is plotted on the abscissa while the normalized frequency of occurrence is plotted on the ordinate. The data were obtained from our preliminary analytical study (cf. figure 1). Note that speaker two's distribution favors larger differences between the durations of his adjacent pitch periods. That is, he tends to have greater pitch perturbations for his mode-5 stimuli than do speakers one or four.

```
x··············x  speaker 1
●————————●  speaker 2      mode 5
○--------○  speaker 4
```

1. A pitch period is one cycle of glottal excitation ('vibration of the vocal cords'). As the fundamental is expressed in hertz (Hz or cycles per second), a fundamental of 100 Hz, for example, would correspond to a pitch period of $\frac{1}{100}$s or 10 ms. The pitch period is thus the inverse of the fundamental at any instant.

pitch, the situation is completely reversed and the listeners make mode-4 responses to speaker two's mode-5 stimuli. We can see a possible explanation for this behavior in Figures 8 and 9, which present some of the results

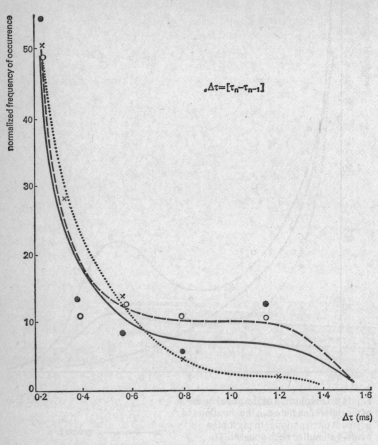

$$\Delta\tau = [\tau_n - \tau_{n-1}]$$

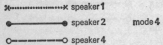

x·············x speaker 1

●————● speaker 2    mode 4

o————o speaker 4

Figure 9 Distribution of the absolute value between the duration of adjacent pitch periods in ms for the mode-4 stimuli of each speaker. Note that the mode-4 stimuli of speaker two are not differentiated from those of speakers one or four by a different distribution as are his mode-5 stimuli. Thus when the pitch perturbations were smoothed out more confusions between mode 5 and 4 occurred for speaker two (cf. Figures 6 and 7).

of the preliminary analysis of the pitch perturbations. In Figure 8 we can see that speaker two's distribution of the differences between adjacent periods favors greater pitch perturbations for his mode-5 stimuli than do either speakers one's or four's distributions. When the same plot is made in Figure 9 for mode-4 stimuli, the distributions of all three speakers are quite similar. Apparently speaker two's mode-5 stimuli are differentiated from his mode-4 stimuli through the presence of these perturbations. When we smooth out the fine structure of the pitch variations we remove the distinction between modes 5 and 4 for speaker two, causing the listeners to confuse the two modes.

## Stability of emotional categorizations

The results of the categorizations of the emotional modes by naive listeners on their first exposure to the stimuli were rather stable. As a check we ran the perfect pitch with no amplitude-modulation tape (cf. Figure 3) with two different groups of listeners. Both groups correctly identified the utterances 43·5 per cent of the time.

## Discussion
### Relevance of experimental results to less restricted speech signals

The level of correct identifications of the emotional modes in the data fell from 85 per cent to 47 per cent when we removed all phonetic information, retaining only pitch and envelope amplitude information. (By phonetic information we mean here any information directly related to vocal tract configurations or the spectral composition of the glottal excitation function, i.e. information that would be transmitted in the spectrum channels of a Vocoder or displayed in a narrow-band spectrogram. Roughly this is the information conveyed, in writing, by letters.) Since phonetic events play so important a role in the transmission of the emotional modes we might wonder whether pitch plays a secondary role in the presence of phonetic information and whether pitch information is immaterial or negligible in the presence of a correct and complete phonetic description of the speech material. Certain recent experiments suggest that this is not the case and that in the presence of phonetic information pitch still plays an important role in the transmission of emotional information and the enhancement of natural quality.

Abramson (1959) in an experiment with Vocoder-processed speech with a tone language (Thai), passed normally spoken Thai words, minimally distinguished by tone, '. . . through the Vocoder with the fundamental frequency of the buzz kept constant. No discriminations were made! With hiss alone, however, the results were better than in the natural whisper. We conclude that the features were present in the normal speech but that in the presence of the buzz listeners were set to hear pitch variations. Inspection of spectrograms suggests that tonal oppositions in Thai whispering lean on such concomitant features as changes in intensity, relative durations of vowels and small variations in formant frequencies'. Denes (1959) reported similar results for English intonation.

Kersten, Bricker and David (1960) reported on an experiment in which they used digital-computer processing to remove the pitch perturbations of sustained vowels spoken by two talkers. In A–B pairs, these processed samples were presented, together with the originals, to naive listeners who readily identified the machine-processed samples, which sounded noticeably mechanical compared to the originals.

It is therefore reasonable to infer that the results of our experiments, in which all phonetic information was removed, are relevant to more general speech transmission problems in which phonetic information is of course present.

## Conclusions

1. There is no one single acoustic correlate of the emotional modes of this experiment. Phonetic content, gross changes in fundamental frequency, the fine structure of the fundamental frequency, and the speech envelope amplitude, in that order, all contributed to the transmission of the emotional modes. Durational cues were not isolated in any stage of the experiment and therefore cannot be discussed.

2. The different emotional modes did not all depend to the same degree on all the acoustic parameters. Different speakers also favored different acoustic parameters for the transmission of the same emotional mode.

3. The fine structure of the fundamental frequency, that is, the perturbations in fundamental frequency, appears to be an acoustic correlate of the emotional modes. When these perturbations were smoothed out confusions between the emotional modes increased.

Most current systems of linguistic analysis of intonation seem incomplete in that they merely note gross changes in fundamental frequency, minimize the role of amplitude and phonetic variations, and entirely ignore the fine structure of the fundamental frequency. We have seen in this experiment, however, that these additional dimensions are responsible for a large fraction of the total emotional information transmitted in human speech.

## References

ABRAMSON, A. S. (1959), 'Vocoder output and whispered speech in a tone language', *J. Acoust. Soc. Amer.*, vol. 31, p. 1568.

DENES, P. (1959), 'Preliminary investigation of certain aspects of intonation', *J. Acoust. Soc. Amer.*, vol. 31, p. 852.

KERSTEN, L. G., BRICKER, P. D., and DAVID, E. E. Jr (1960), 'Human or machine: a study of voice naturalness', *J. Acoust. Soc. Amer.*, vol. 32, p. 1502.

LIEBERMAN, P. (1961), 'Perturbations in vocal pitch', *J. Acoust. Soc. Amer.*, vol. 33, p. 597.

Philip Lieberman and Sheldon B. Michaels 249

# 13 Elizabeth Uldall

## Dimensions of Meaning in Intonation

Elizabeth Uldall, 'Dimensions of meaning in intonation', from *In Honour of Daniel Jones: Papers Contributed on the Occasion of his Eightieth Birthday, 12 September 1961*, edited by David Abercrombie, D. B. Fry, P. A. D. MacCarthy, N. C. Scott and J. L. M. Trim, Longman, 1964, pp. 271-9.

[Editor's note: The first two paragraphs in the Reading as it appears here are the first two paragraphs of the Reading referred to as Uldall, 1960.]

It is clear that some kind of meaning is conveyed by the intonation of connected speech in both tone languages and non-tone languages. There is little agreement about the terms in which this meaning is to be described; every writer on the subject employs an open-ended supply of terms for this purpose. One kind of meaning conveyed is, however, clearly social and emotional rather than referential. Intonation can express social attitudes: speaker to listener: 'It wasn't what she said, it was the way she said it!'; to subject matter: 'Well, don't get in a temper with me; *I'm* not the Income Tax collector'; to the world in general: 'He sounds so arrogant', 'Don't whine!'

Attitude measurement seemed a promising technique by which to attempt to find out whether a group of subjects from the same linguistic community would in fact agree on the 'meanings' of intonations, and whether some few very general 'dimensions of meaning' in the emotional area could be extracted.

The experiment described here[1] consisted in offering to a group of subjects a number of sentences on each of which sixteen intonation contours had been imposed synthetically, and asking them to rate these on a set of scales consisting of opposed adjectives, with a view to investigating the attitudes or emotional meanings conveyed by the various contours (see Osgood, Suci and Tannenbaum, 1957). Professor Osgood's 'semantic differential' appears to be a suitable technique for investigating the emotional meanings of intonation contours, since it is precisely 'emotional meaning'

1. The work described here was carried out with the benefit of research funds from the Haskins Laboratories, New York, in connection with a grant from the Carnegie Corporation of New York.

I am much indebted to Dr Boris Semeonoff of the Department of Psychology of Edinburgh University for statistical advice.

which is strongly present in intonation, and with this aspect of meaning the semantic differential deals most successfully.

The fifteen subjects were speakers of American English, and the original recording on which the contours were synthesized was spoken by an American. The contours, shown in Figure 1, were the same as those used in an earlier experiment (Uldall, 1960). They were intended to cover all the kinds of variation which differentiate intonation contours, though of course nothing like all the possible combinations of variables were represented. The variables are:

Range: wide/narrow.
Pitch reached at end of contour: high/mid/low.
Shape of contour: one direction/with a change of direction.

Treatment of weak syllables:

(a) Continuing the line of the strong syllables.
(b) Rising above the line of the strong syllables.
(c) Falling below the line of the strong syllables.

The 'scales' used were the same as in the earlier experiment, with the addition of *authoritative/submissive*, *unpleasant/pleasant*, *genuine/pretended* (feeling) and *weak/strong* (feeling), so that the page on which the subjects were asked to rate each contour on each sentence appeared thus:

```
            bored — — — interested
            polite — — — rude
             timid — — — confident
           sincere — — — insincere
              tense — — — relaxed
    disapproving — — — approving
      deferential — — — arrogant
         impatient — — — patient
          emphatic — — — unemphatic
         agreeable — — — disagreeable
    authoritative — — — submissive
       unpleasant — — — pleasant
           genuine — — — pretended
              weak — — — strong
```

These terms were arranged with seven places between them; the subjects were instructed that the places next to the terms should be checked to indicate 'extremely' (bored or interested, etc.), the next place a little farther in from the terms to indicate 'quite' (bored or interested, etc.), the two places flanking the middle to indicate 'slightly' (bored or interested,

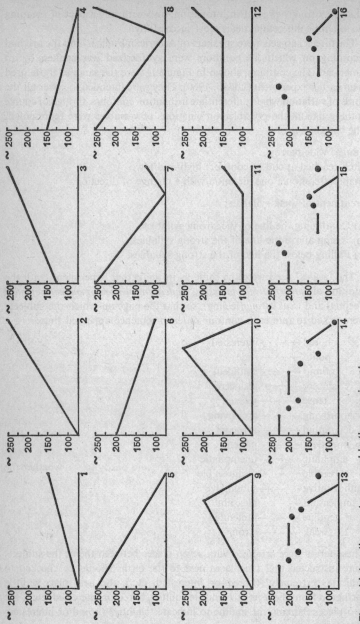

Figure 1 Intonation contours used in the experiment

etc.), and the middle space to indicate 'neutral' or 'neither' in relation to the scale under consideration.

The extra scales mentioned were added to the original ten in an effort to find more 'central' terms for the dimensions of emotional meaning which appear to be most strongly represented in intonation: 'pleasant/unpleasant', 'authoritative/submissive' and 'strong/weak' (feeling expressed). In the material on which the diagrams of A, B, C, D, E are based, three of the new scales were in fact used as being suitable characteristic terms in these dimensions. The addition 'genuine (feeling)/pretended (feeling)' was not successful; 'pretended' feeling must either not be expressed in intonation, or be a function of intonation in context; all the contours presented were rated as expressing 'genuine' feeling.

The four sentences were as follows:

A. Statement: 'None of the members are going.'
B. Yes-or-no question: 'Was it arranged at the meeting?'
C. Question-word question: 'What did he think they were doing?'
D. Command: 'Bring it along to the meeting.'

To these was added a nonsense-sequence:

E. ['soɯməvə 'paɪθərə 'zɛnɪŋ]

All of these sentences consisted of the same number and arrangement of strong and weak syllables. The real sentences were intended to be suitable as remarks between social equals. They were recorded by Dr Alvin Liberman of the Haskins Laboratories, New York. He found it necessary to speak them all on a rising contour in order that the final syllables should not be so low in intensity as to make synthesis difficult. The contours were 'applied' to the sentences by means of the Voback synthesizer.

Each subject took each test twice, some in the same order both times, and some in the reverse order. This was done partly in order to increase the number of judgements to be averaged, and partly to see whether the judgements appeared to be affected by the order in which the contours were presented: were the subjects judging the contours in relation to their whole experience of intonation, or in relation to the preceding contours? It is clear that the former is the case; the variability in judgement was more or less constant for each subject as a person, from two-thirds of a scale unit for the 'best' subject, to one and two-thirds scale units for the 'worst' one ('scale unit': the difference between e.g. 'slightly bored' and 'quite bored'). The average variation over all the texts was 1·12 scale units on test/retest.

These are larger 'errors' than Osgood found on test/retest for subjects judging word 'concepts' in similar tests: '... average errors ... always less than a single scale unit ... and for evaluative [pleasant/unpleasant] scales average about half of a scale unit' (Osgood, Suci and Tannenbaum, 1957, p. 131).

The contours themselves also varied in the amount of test/retest variability in the judgements made of them: e.g. contour no. 15 (raised weak syllables, final rise) is usually near the most variable end of a list of the contours arranged to show this characteristic. 'Raised weak syllables', though they certainly occur in American intonation, in the speech of men as well as women, are sometimes said to be a 'woman's intonation'. The variability of the judgements in this case may indicate that this contour was less familiar to the subjects than the other contours were, or that it was unfamiliar to some of the subjects.

There were also differences in the amount of variability on the various scale terms: the subjects were least variable on the scales expressing the 'pleasant/unpleasant' dimension, and most variable on those expressing the 'strong/weak' one. In other words, they were more consistent about their own reactions to the contours than about what they judged the 'speaker's' intention to be.

Factor analyses of the correlations between the various scales for each part of the experiment – A, B, C, D, E – were carried out with a view to extracting the main 'dimensions of meaning' conveyed by these intonations. As in the previous experiment, the 'pleasant/unpleasant' factor was by far the strongest. The grouping of the scale terms in the factor analyses made it clear, however, that this time the 'authoritative/submissive' factor came second and the 'strong (feeling)/weak (feeling)' factor third. This was the reverse of the earlier experiment, though there were some indications in the earlier one that the arrangement might not be the same for all four sentence types. It is possible that the uniform emergence of the factors on all the sentences this time is related to a larger and better choice of scale terms.

Two scales were chosen to represent each factor in the construction of the 'semantic space' diagrams (Osgood, Suci and Tannenbaum, 1957, p. 114), Figures 2a, b, c, d, e, which show the relations of the various contours to the three 'dimensions' and to each other. Subjects' scores (reversed where necessary) on *bored/interested* and *unpleasant/pleasant* were averaged to represent the 'pleasant/unpleasant' dimension; *authoritative/submissive* and *timid/confident* were averaged for 'authoritative/submissive'; and *weak/strong* and *emphatic/unemphatic* were averaged for the 'strong/weak' dimension.

The diagrams display, for each sentence-type and the nonsense-sequence, three dimensions: the right half of the diagram shows contours judged

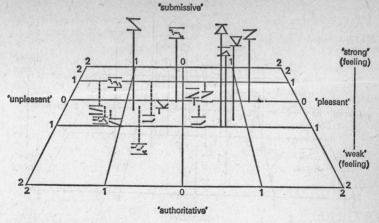

A: 'None of the members are going'

Figure 2a

'pleasant', the left half 'unpleasant'. The near half shows those judged 'authoritative', the far half 'submissive'. Solid lines rising from the point of intersection of these two scores show 'strong' judgements, the height of the line being proportional to the 'strength' of the feeling; dotted lines descending from the point of intersection of the first two scores show 'weak' judgements, with the length of the line showing how 'weak' the

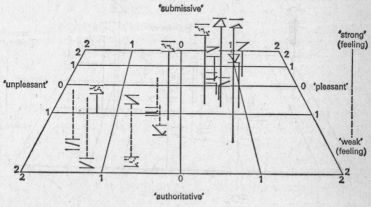

B: 'Was it arranged at the meeting?'

Figure 2b

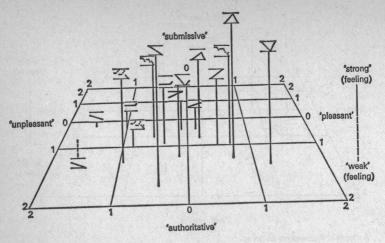

C: 'What did he think they were doing?'

Figure 2c

contour was judged to be. The contours are shown at the ends of the vertical lines.

Contours may thus be described by three terms: no. 8 is in all cases 'pleasant, authoritative, strong'; no. 4 is 'unpleasant, authoritative, weak' on the statement and both types of question, 'unpleasant, authoritative,

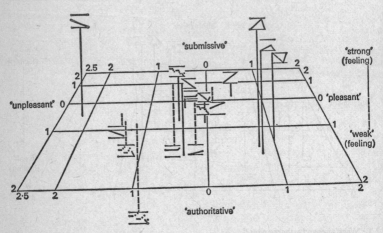

D. 'Bring it along to the meeting'

Figure 2d

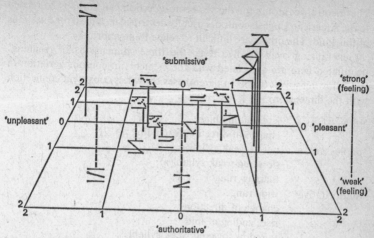

'submissive'

'strong' (feeling)

'unpleasant'

'pleasant'

'weak' (feeling)

'authoritative'

E. Nonsense sequence: (ˈsoʌməvə ˈpaɪθərɔ ˈzɛnɪŋ)

Figure 2e

strong' on the command. Where contours bear the same description in these terms, as e.g. nos. 8, 9 and 10, they may be near-synonyms in intonation, or it may be that they would be differentiated on some dimension of meaning not investigated.

The contours fall about equally into the 'pleasant' and 'unpleasant' sectors. Few contours appear in the 'submissive' sector; this may mean that there are few 'submissive' intonations, or it may be that 'submissiveness' is expressed less readily by intonation than by tempo or voice-quality, variations in which were of course expressly excluded from this experiment. The effects of context are also excluded, which may bear on the fact that fewer contours are considered 'weak' than 'strong'.

Figure 2c for the question-word question differs markedly from the others. Within the material of the experiment, it does not appear to be possible to be 'submissive' in asking this type of question, and it is difficult to convey 'weak' feeling. This is perhaps not a *phonetic* observation, but it is certainly of some linguistic interest.

The contours which are most nearly 'neutral' on the various sentence-types are as follows:

Statement: Final rises ending at mid pitch.
Yes-or-no question: Final rises ending high.
Question-word question: Final rises, ending high or mid.
Command: Final rises, ending high or mid.

The 'neutral' contours for the yes-or-no question can perhaps be related to the American English contours usually described as typical for questions of this kind. The others are difficult to relate to any norm.

Generalizing over the five tests, the three 'dimensions of meaning' postulated here are associated with the elements in contour variation in the following ways: (terms in parentheses show less consistent connection with the dimension)

| | |
|---|---|
| 'pleasant' | rises ending high |
| | change of direction [excluding no. 7] |
| 'unpleasant' | raised weak syllables |
| | (lowered weak syllables) |
| | (narrow range) |
| 'authoritative' | wide range |
| | change of direction |
| | rises ending at mid |
| | raised or lowered weak syllables |
| | (final fall) |
| 'submissive' | (rises ending high [excluding no. 8]) |
| 'strong' feeling | wide range |
| | change of direction |
| | lowered weak syllables |
| | (rises ending at mid) |
| 'weak' feeling | (narrow range) |
| | (raised weak syllables) |

The 'positive' ends of the dimensions are more easily characterized than the 'negative' ones.

Where the contours are rated differently on the different sentences, it can be seen that the less 'lively' a contour is, the more variable it is in meaning. The narrow-range 'smooth' contours nos. 1, 3, 4 and 6, vary most often from one sentence to another. The two rising contours, 1 and 3, vary on all three dimensions; the two falls, 4 and 6, are always very 'unpleasant', but can be 'authoritative' or 'submissive', 'strong' or 'weak'.

The more 'lively' the contour is, the more stable is its position in the 'semantic space' over the different sentences. Contours nos. 8, 9 and 10, involving wide range and a change of direction, always occupy the same sector of the space, the 'pleasant, authoritative, strong' one.

The less 'interesting' the intonation contour is, the more influential the sentence itself is in the judgement of the total effect, and vice versa.

## References

OSGOOD, C. E., SUCI, G. J., and TANNENBAUM, P. H. (1957), *The Measurement of Meaning*, University of Illinois Press.

ULDALL, E. T. (1960), 'Attitudinal meanings conveyed by intonation contours', *Language and Speech*, vol. 3, pp. 223–34.

# Part Five
## Intonation and Music

The melody of speech is the point at which music and language meet. A question that interests both musicians and linguists is how much one depends on the other. In Western cultures music conveys mainly a dynamic and emotional message. The dynamic suggests some kinship with rhythmic work and the dance. The emotional may well be related to Western uses of pitch in language, which as the articles in the last preceding section show are heavily freighted with emotive meanings.

George List's Reading approaches the question in a culture where it can be framed more precisely. Thai is a tone language. It distinguishes three relatively level ('register') and two moving ('contour') tones, distinctive for word meanings. When Thais sing are the melodic tones of the music made to conform to the linguistic tones of the lyric? List's answer is yes, in the main. The reader may entertain himself with some further questions: Is the music that accompanies a tone language more intellectual, or at least less emotive, than Western music? Is the difference between a music based at least partly on intonation and a music based on tone one factor in making us feel among friends with Hungarian or Finnish music and among strangers with the music of China and the rest of the Orient where tone languages are spoken?

If there is any connection at all between emotion and music, one expects the music of Thailand to differ from that of the English-speaking world. But what about differences *within* the latter? Is it possible that even dialectal differences are reflected in music? American and British English are rather good for making a comparison, as there are some pretty characteristic differences in their intonational preferences. In the second Reading, Robert A. Hall, Jr points out these differences and theorizes that they may account for the popularity of a typically British composer in Britain and his unpopularity elsewhere.

What the first two Readings do is demonstrate that since both musical melody and speech melody reside in the same human heads, they are bound to affect each other in some way. How deep the influence may go is another question: Thai tone is no more emotional, so far as we know, than the distinctive sounds of the vowels, and aspects of intonation that characterize one dialect as against another (specifically British and American English) need not at the same time convey a mood; these are more or less arbitrary associations. It is possible of course that embedded in music these same contrasts may take on an emotional tinge; but we ought to be able to put the question frontally. Fónagy and Magdics attempt to do so in the third Reading. Where language and music share the burden most intimately is in the direct transmission of an emotional message. Given that both do this, does each do it in its own way, or do they share the same means? The answer, to be valid, must be cross-linguistic; Hungarian is chosen, and contrasted with French, English and German. Not only are striking resemblances discovered between the means used by language and music, but also between Hungarian music and intonation and those of the three other languages. Since these are Indo-European and Hungarian is not, there has to have been either a wide sharing of culture or a close instinctive tie between emotions and melodic curves that points to a common origin.

A question remains, which is the extent to which musicians more or less consciously *put* the emotive devices of language into music, especially vocal music. The domain of music is that of all sound; a composer or a folksinger can choose to imitate the bleat of a calf or a roll of thunder. How much of the resemblance between intonation and music is artificial and how much springs from a direct welling up of joyous sound when one feels joyous, regardless of the medium?

# 14 George List

## Speech Melody and Song Melody in Central Thailand

George List, 'Speech melody and song melody in Central Thailand',
*Ethnomusicology*, vol. 5, no. 1, 1961, pp. 16–32.

Thai or Siamese is a tone language. In a tone language the relative pitch at which a syllable is uttered or the inflection given to it may be phonemic, that is, may affect the meaning of the syllable. For example, the syllable *kai* may have one meaning if uttered at a relatively high pitch, another meaning if uttered at a relatively low pitch, and a third meaning if uttered with an obvious downward inflection.

Thai therefore has what may be termed 'speech melody'. The intelligibility of any utterance of a speaker of Thai depends to a certain extent upon the accuracy with which he relates the pitch contour of this utterance with the pitch contours of the utterances surrounding it. In our Western culture we expect a coordination of speech accent and musical accent in song but we do not expect the melody of song to follow the intonation of our speech. In Thailand both speech and song have melodic contours. In what relationship do the two stand to each other? Is the musical melody subservient to that of the language or are the language contours modified to follow the musical contours? Must the contours of the music carefully follow those of speech so that complete intelligibility will be preserved or is the music free to construct its own melody independently of the melody of speech, the meaning of the language used then being understood by considerations of context? These are the questions to be considered in this article.

It should be added in passing that the length of single vowels is also phonemic in Thai. The same syllable uttered at a particular pitch or with a particular inflection and containing a short vowel has a different meaning than an otherwise similar monosyllabic utterance containing a long vowel. Thus in Thailand speech melody and song melody have both pitch and rhythmic characteristics. However, this discussion will be limited to the problems of pitch relations between speech melody and song melody. Temporal considerations will be omitted.

Thailand is divided into five cultural–geographical areas. The tones used in the dialects spoken in these five areas differ considerably in number and type. This analysis will be limited to the tonal system in use in Central

Thailand, the area surrounding Bangkok, the capital city. This Central dialect is also the official language of Thailand.

There is no great unanimity of opinion among speakers of the Central Thai dialect or among scholars who have studied it as to the types of tones used. However, the tones are generally considered to be five in number. Of these three are register tones and are referred to as middle, low and high. The other two are contour tones, one forming a descending contour and the other an ascending contour. The Thais use the terms just given to describe the register tones, middle, low and high, and these terms have approximately the same general connotations in Thai as they have in English. However, the Thais apparently have no commonly used terms to describe the contour tones (see Figure 1).

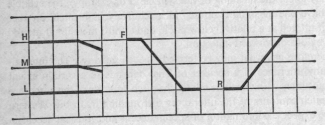

Figure 1

Figure 1 presents the schematic organization of the tones used in the Central Thai dialect as given by Haas (1956). The first tone is a high register tone with a slight downward inflection; the second, a medial tone with a very small downward inclination; and the third tone low and flat. The fourth – which the writer has designated falling – begins at the high level, holds this pitch momentarily, then slides down to the low level, and also holds this pitch momentarily. The fifth tone – which has been designated rising – presents a similar organization in inverse order.

The second tonal scheme, presented in Figure 2, was given to the writer by Swat Sukontarangsi, a graduate student at Indiana University and a native of Central Thailand. Swat has taught the Thai language to children in the schools in Thailand and to speakers of English in the United States. According to this informant this scheme is commonly used in teaching Thai to speakers of English. In this form the three register tones are presented purely as level or flat phenomena. The falling tone begins above the middle tone but below the high tone and then slides downward indeterminately. The initial and final points of the rising tone are also indeterminate.

In Thailand, as in many parts of the Orient, song or chant is used as a

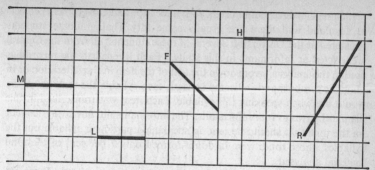

Figure 2

mnemonic device, the pupils using either chant or song in reciting their lessons. Figure 3 is an excerpt from the beginning of a recitation of the alphabet by a six-year-old pupil in the Bangkok schools. Although we may consider this to be song, or, at least, chant, the Thais refer to this genre as 'recitation'. They do not consider it to be song. The full alphabet consists of forty-four letters. This excerpt includes the first fourteen (see Figure 3).

Figure 3  Recitation of the alphabet

The numbers above the staff in Figure 3 refer to syllables, each syllable being held from one number until the following number. The actual sounds of the language have not been given since they are immaterial to this investigation. The capital letters found underneath the staff refer to the tones used in speech.

Indiana University administers both Education and Government projects in Thailand and there are usually some fifty Thai graduate students registered at the University. Several of these students, all from the Central area, acted as informants in this study.[1] Each listened to the recordings used in the analysis, wrote down the text of the item in transliteration or in phonetic symbols and indicated beneath each syllable the tone he or she would use when speaking this syllable. Each item was transcribed in this manner by two to four informants. The informants did not always concur on the tone that should be used in speaking a particular syllable but the syllables whose tones were in doubt formed only 7 per cent of the total material analysed.

In Figure 3, three such conflicts of opinion may be noted. These are indicated under syllables 12, 23 and 25. Three informants transcribed this item. Where two letters are found under a syllable the upper letter represents the opinion of two informants, the lower the opinion of one.

This little chant seems to follow quite closely the organization of tones given in Figure 1. Only three pitches are used. High is represented by $C^\#$, as in syllable 21; low by A, as in syllable 2; and the mid tone by B, as in syllable 7. The falling tone is represented by the pattern, $C^\# - A$, as in syllable 23; and the rising tone by the inversion of this pattern, as in syllable 3.

In considering syllable 23 to be associated with a falling tone the majority opinion of the informants is accepted and the minority opinion rejected. This procedure will be followed throughout the analysis. Syllables 12, 23 and 25 are therefore considered to be associated with the tone indicated by the upper of the two letters found below the staff.

In order to determine the degree of coordination found between the speech melody and the song melody in this example we shall compare the pitch level of speech and song of each syllable with that of the preceding syllable and with that of the following syllable. This type of comparison can be made with register tones only, since different opinions exist as to the relation of the initial and final points of the contour tones, falling and rising, to the three register tones and to each other. Following this method we see that although syllable 1 in Figure 3 is recited on the pitch $C^\#$, while the greater portion of the other mid tones in the example are recited on the pitch B, syllable 1 is in proper coordination with syllable 2 since $C^\#$, representing the mid tone, is higher in pitch than A, representing the low tone. The pitch of the tones in the Thai language is of necessity relative rather than fixed.

1. The informants were Kingkeo Attagara, Chalao Chaiyaratana, Sakon Changsanit, Swat Sukontarangsi and Kanda Thammongkol.

There is no syllable to consider preceding syllable 1. Syllable 2 is in proper relation to the preceding syllable 1. Syllable 3 cannot be considered since it is a contour tone. No judgement can be made concerning syllable 4 since it is preceded and followed by a contour tone. Syllable 7, on the other hand, can be compared with both the preceding syllable 6 and the following syllable 8 and coordinates with both.

Following this method we discover two sequences of non-conforming or non-coordinating syllables, 11–12–13 and 24–25–26.

Since opinions differ concerning the levels at which the contour tones begin and end we can judge their coordination with the musical contours only from the point of view of the direction in which they move. Since the three rising tones in this example are associated with an ascending musical pattern, and the one falling tone with a descending pattern, we judge them to conform.

We may thus conclude that of the twenty-eight syllables found in this excerpt, six do not exhibit full coordination of speech melody and song melody according to the method of analysis used. The degree of coordination exhibited is therefore approximately 79 per cent.

Figure 4 is a transcription of a recording of a recitation of the multiplication table by a group of children ages twelve to thirteen in the Bangkok schools. The excerpt covers two times one through two times twelve. Note that throughout this excerpt the single and level pitch, $F^\sharp$, in the song melody is associated with the tone contour, rising. The single or level pitch, $C^\sharp$, is associated with tone contour, falling, in two instances, syllables 25 and 41, and partially in a third, syllable 48.

After each informant had transcribed the text of each chant or song he or she was recorded speaking this text. In the spoken versions of this recitation the rising and falling aspects of the contours are carefully observed. According to the informants, in rapid conversation or recitation the high register tone is commonly substituted for the rising contour tone since the latter is the most difficult of the five tones to produce. There seems to be a similar substitution of the low register tone for the falling contour tone although this substitution does not seem to occur with equal frequency. Meaning is apparently then grasped by context. We must therefore assume that there are two acceptable forms of the rising tone and two of the falling tone.

One informant, Miss Chalao Chaiyaratana, has given the writer a more detailed analysis of the manner in which this substitution is structured. According to her observations, it is made only when the syllable has no assigned meaning when uttered with the substituted tone. Thus, the first syllable, *song*, has meaning when associated with the rising tone but not with the high tone. The high tone may therefore be substituted and the

Figure 4 Recitation of the multiplication table

meaning associated with the rising tone transferred to the previously
meaningless utterance at the high tone. Syllable 36, *yi*, has meaning if
associated with a falling tone, none if associated with a low tone. The low
tone may therefore be substituted for the falling tone. These are apparently
the common substitutions. This informant knows no instances, for
example, of the substitution of the mid tone for the rising tone.

Further evidence of the substitution of the low tone for the falling tone
will be seen in the last phrase of the recitation. Here the children differ in
their interpretation of syllable 48, *yi*. It is recited by part of the group in
the manner of syllables 14 and 29 and by the remainder in that of syllables
35 and 41.

Having accepted the substitution of the high and low register tones for
the rising and falling contour tones as a characteristic of Thai recitation,
and possibly speech, we find only two syllable sequences in this excerpt
which do not exhibit coordination of speech melody and song melody.
These are syllables 33–4 and 39–40. In these a change of tone from low to

mid does not produce a corresponding change of musical pitch. Adding these to syllable 48, in which the reciters themselves are inconsistent in the use of song pitches, we have five syllables out of the total of fifty showing lack of coordination. This excerpt therefore exhibits a 90 per cent coordination of speech melody and song melody.

The next transcription is also of a recording of a recitation in the Bangkok schools. The reciters were two young men in their late teens. Their recitation is of a series of poems in a rather complex classical form known as *klong*. In this case each poem contains only one stanza. The excerpt consists of one full stanza.

In Figure 5 note the downward glides from high tones in syllables 5, 9, 15 and 17. The glide at 15 is much more pronounced than the other three. This glide, at least, is not related to the necessities of speech tones.

Figure 5  Literary recitation, *Klong*

It is a form of intonation used as emphasis. Thus, intonation exists to some degree in Thai in addition to tone. The only other type of intonation apparently in common use is that of gradually dropping the general pitch level throughout a phrase or sentence and then returning to the original level as the next phrase is begun. This intonational practice does not seem to have affected the chants or songs analysed.

In discussing the relation of tones and intonation to chant and song in Chinese, Chao (1957) makes a distinction between 'chant' and 'sing-song'.[2] The term 'sing-song' is applied to a form used by vendors and by children in the lower grades in China and is characterized as a stereotyped form of

2. Chao's discussion is principally concerned with the Mandarin dialect which has four tones.

speech or recitation in which intonation plays no part. On the other hand, chanting of literary poems in the upper grades (a practice now dying out) apparently takes intonational phenomena into consideration. Although both Chinese 'sing-song' and 'chant' are improvised, only the latter requires training for proper rendition.

Since in the distant past the Thais migrated south from China and since some Thai groups are still found in southern China it is not surprising to find practices parallel to those of China. According to the Thai informants assisting in this study, the type of recitation used in the alphabet and the multiplication table is purely an aural tradition. The children receive no instruction in this type of recitation. The recitation of the *klong*, on the other hand, is taught in the schools.

In Figure 5 we find once more, in syllable 25, the substitution of the high tone for the rising tone, or, to state the matter more accurately, the use of the highest pitch of the song melody in association with the rising tone of the speech melody. Note that in both Figures 4 and 5 the highest pitch of the song melody is substituted for the rising tone. When a low tone is substituted for the falling tone, as in Figure 4, this low tone is the lowest musical pitch found in the chant melody.

The next example is an excerpt from traditional Thai classical song.

Figure 6 Song in classical style, 'Mountain Breeze'

This excerpt illustrates a phenomenon common to Thai song, the use of the nonsense syllable, *ey*, as a filler between sections of text. In the classical song continuants are also used. In this usage the enunciation of a syllable is completed and the singer continues for a brief period on the nasal, *ng*, before enunciating the second syllable. In Figure 6 nonsense syllables are indicated by a lower case *n*, the continuants by a lower case *c*.

The text of this poem is based on an ancient Javanese epic. Other texts have been set to the same musical melody. The tune also exists independently of text and is used as the basis of instrumental improvisation. Except in the case of the modern popular songs, the Thais claim not to compose new melodies but to utilize a stock of traditional tunes already in existence. They find no need to develop new melodies since the stock of pre-existing tunes seems quite adequate for their purposes. In setting a text to a pre-existing melody an attempt is made to select speech syllables whose tones coordinate with the contours of the musical melody. A number of Thais questioned over a period of several years have made statements similar to the above. This is apparently a fairly stable cultural point of view.

This approach to composition offers some parallels with traditional methods of composition used in China (Levis, 1937). Chinese musicians first composed their melodies as a generalized series of rising and falling contours plus reiterated pitches, using a special notation for this purpose. Words were then set to the composed melody in such a manner that speech and musical contours coordinated. Specific musical pitches were later selected from the various Chinese classical modes.

It is difficult to determine the degree of coordination of speech melody and song melody existing in this excerpt since the register tones are separated not only by contour tones but by nonsense syllables and continuants. Since the last two are meaningless, there are obviously no specific tones associated with them. The first five syllables coordinate well. Syllables 7 and 8, if not separated by a continuant, would certainly not conform. The mid tones of syllables 9 and 10 are separated by approximately a quarter tone. Later in the song are found falling tones associated with a descending and rising melodic arc and rising tones associated with the reverse contour. Since the poem is set to a pre-existing melody it is not to be expected that the degree of coordination would be very high.

In pursuing this study it seemed useful to secure some data possibly more objective than those established by the human ear, specifically, spectrographic evidence. Professor Fred Householder of the Indiana University Linguistics Program was kind enough to offer assistance in this direction by preparing spectrograph analyses of both the music and the spoken text of a short Thai lullaby. The informant learned this lullaby from her nurse, who had no formal education. Other Thais remember having heard the same lullaby as children but in varied forms. It can thus be assumed that this lullaby is a traditional folksong in the commonly accepted meaning of the term (see Figure 7).

Figure 7 shows a short section of the transcription of the song melody

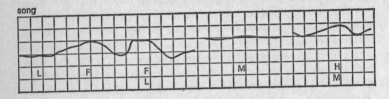

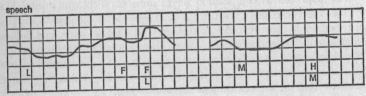

Figure 7 Lullaby, 'The Mother Crow'

in musical notation, the spectrographic transcription of the same section of the song, and the spectrographic transcript of the same section of the text when spoken rather than sung. The nonsense syllable, *ey*, is also used in this lullaby. It occurs at the end of this musical phrase but here has been elided. The nonsense syllable is not used in speech and therefore does not occur in the spoken version of the text.

Although the graphs of speech and song are remarkably alike throughout the lullaby, two principal differences can be noted. Rises are much more abrupt in song than in speech and the range of speech is very much greater than that of song. Each set of four short lines to the left of the song and speech graphs represents a range of an octave, divided into three approximate major thirds. The ranges of the song phrase and of the speech phrase as shown in the graphs in Figure 7 are as follows:

|       | Lowest pitch | Highest pitch |
|-------|-------------|---------------|
| Song  | $f^\sharp$  | $c^1$         |
| Speech | g          | $e^{\flat 1}$ |

The range of the song phrase is therefore a perfect fifth and that of the speech phrase a minor sixth. The total range throughout the song and spoken text shows a greater contrast.

|           | *Lowest pitch* | *Highest pitch* |
|-----------|----------------|-----------------|
| Song      | f              | $e^{b1}$        |
| Speech    | A              | $e^{b1}$        |

The total range of the song is thus a minor seventh while that of the spoken text is an octave plus a diminished fifth.

Again using the spectrograph Householder developed a schematic organization of the tones used in Central Thailand. These are shown in Figure 8.

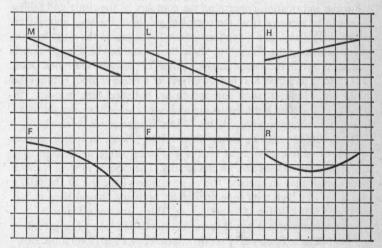

Figure 8

These graphs are averages of contours shown in a minimum of ten utterances and a maximum of forty. They are based on syllables both uttered in isolation and in context. The short lines to the left again represent the range of an octave, but divided into four minor thirds.

The schematic organization of tones based on spectrographic evidence differs considerably from that offered by Haas, Figure 1, or by Swat, Figure 2. The spectrograph shows that none of the register tones, mid, low, nor high, are level. Mid and low move down, high ascends. The difference in relative pitch between mid and low is quite small. The rising tone, it appears, does not actually ascend but dips and returns to approximately the same point. It is thus apparent why the Thais feel that the rising tone is the most difficult of the tones to produce.

Householder found two distinct forms of the falling tone, one a descending contour and the other, the only level tone of the group, appearing at the highest pitch. Thus there seem to be three forms of the falling tone in use, a descending contour, a low supposedly level tone, and a very high tone.

Should the initial half of the rising tone contour in Figure 8 be elided, the remaining part of the contour somewhat resembles the high tone. A similar elision of the first half of the falling tone would in turn produce a contour somewhat resembling the low tone. This may perhaps explain the use of high and low tones in rapid conversation and recitation to represent the rising and falling tones.

Further information concerning the contours of the rising and falling tones can be gathered from the complete graphs of the song and spoken text of this lullaby. The rising tone occurs four times in the song. In both speech and song the rising tone three times exhibits the dip and return contour shown in the spectrographic analysis of the individual tones. Once, in both song and speech, it takes the form of a rising contour without the initial dip. However, song and speech are not consistent in usage. In syllable 11 the speech shows the dip and return while the song shows an ascending contour only. In syllable 15 this relationship is reversed.

The falling tone occurs eleven times in the lullaby. In speech, almost without exception, there is at least a slight rise before the fall. In song this preliminary rise occurs less frequently. The descent in song is much more abrupt than in speech. The one example of the use of the falling tone as a very high level tone appears in both speech and song and is associated with syllable 15 in both cases. This is shown in Figure 9.

From this example it would seem that the falling tone when preceding another falling tone may take on the character of a high level tone. However, the matter is obviously not this simple. Two falling tones also appear in succession in Figure 7. Both are associated with descending contours.

The fact that the range of speech is larger than that of song is shown more clearly in Figure 9 than in Figure 7.

Two quite different methods can be applied in studying the degree of coordination of speech melody and song melody. The first would involve making spectrographic analyses of the recitations and song, and of their spoken texts, and comparing the graphs thus produced. The second would involve the transcription of the texts by the informants, transcription of the music in notation by the scholar, and the comparison of these results arrived at purely by ear. The results achieved by the first method would be acoustically accurate but not necessarily culturally valid. In the first place, it has been established that the human mind and ear make distinctions where the spectrograph makes none (Hockett, 1955). The reverse is of course obviously true. In the second place, although the Thai informants used in the analysis have a high level of education, they have in most cases only the

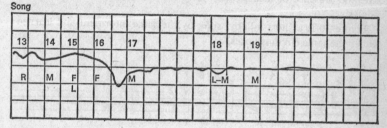

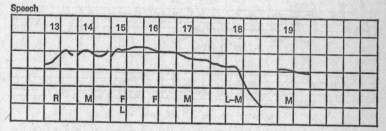

Figure 9  Lullaby, 'The Mother Crow'

most general concepts concerning the contours and relative pitches of the tones they speak. As far as can be determined, their conceptual pattern includes three register tones of contrasting levels and two contour tones, one descending and the other ascending. Although it is recognized that the rising tone is difficult to produce there is apparently no clear mental definition of its shape. This lack of a detailed awareness on the part of the informants of the mechanisms of their speech is not at all surprising. It is doubtful if many reading this article can make an accurate and detailed phonetic analysis of their speech habits in their own tongue. Is the reader, for example, aware of the circumstances under which he aspirates a 'p', and the circumstances under which he pronounces it without aspiration?

Again, it is impossible for the musicologist to either hear or to indicate in notation all the subtle differences in pitch which are registered by the spectrograph. Musical notation is, in itself, a generalization.

When a Thai utters what he considers to be a rising tone, he believes, he assumes, that he is producing an ascending contour. Whether this is the exact contour the tone takes acoustically is immaterial. When this syllable, using this tone, is sung to an ascending contour in song, the Thai has to his satisfaction achieved coordination of speech melody and song melody. And when the musicologist's transcription is sufficiently accurate to indicate the presence or lack of this type of coordination it suffices for his analysis.

Figure 10 is a short lullaby, sung by the same informant and learned under the same circumstances.

Figure 10  Lullaby, 'Boat and Rain'

Like many lullabies around the world this one has a refrain sung to nonsense syllables. In Thailand a type of hammock is often used as a cradle and the child is rocked by rhythmically pulling on strings attached to the cradle. This practice explains the rhythmic and almost metrical character of the song. It will be noticed that the refrain of nonsense syllables is organized sequentially but not the meaningful text. The sequence and the metrical organization may perhaps suggest Western influence but this little song shows perfect coordination of speech melody and song melody according to the method of analysis being applied.

The next example is a popular song of the present day which is based on a traditional classical melody. The informant who sang this song had heard it sung by her friends and on phonograph records issued in Thailand. The full song contains 29 syllables.

As will be noted in Figure 11, there were no differences of opinion among the three informants who transcribed this song as to the tones associated with the 29 syllables found in the text. Not only are the words set to a traditional tune but nonsense syllables are used to fill the musical phrase.

Figure 11 Popular song based on a traditional classical melody

However, coordination of speech melody and song melody is not nearly as high as in the recitations and the lullabies. Lack of coordination, for example, can be seen in Figure 11 in syllable sequences 4–5, 7–8–9 and 12–13.

Our last example is a highly acculturated popular song. The recording analysed is a copy of an unidentified commercial disc issued in Thailand. The song is sung by a female vocalist accompanied by a small orchestra of Western musical instruments and is cast in the common American popular song form of 32 measures of common time divided into four sections, $A^1$, $A^2$, B and $A^2$. Figure 12 represents the first eight measures, or $A^1$.

A detailed analysis was made of the entire 124 syllables heard in this song. Coordination of speech melody and song melody, as far as the register tones are concerned, is not very high. In Section $A^1$, shown in Figure 12, lack of coordination is found in syllable sequences 2–3, 5–6 and 19–20. In considering the contour tones a decision must be made as to whether syllables 24 and 26 are both acceptable as falling tones, and syllables 1 and 8 as rising tones. In the materials hitherto analysed the low level tone substituted for the falling contour has always been associated with the lowest musical pitch found in the entire item or excerpt. Similarly the high level tones substituted for either the rising or falling contours have been associated with the highest musical pitch found. This is not true in the melody of this popular song. However, a catalogue of the tones and as-

Figure 12 Acculturated popular song

sociated pitches occurring in this song shows that the high tone is most frequently associated with the pitch A, the low tone with the pitch F, and the mid tone with the pitch G. On this basis we accept the association of the pitch F with the falling tone and the pitch A with the rising or falling tone as proper coordination of speech melody and song melody.

The contour tones in this song show much more coordination than the register tones. This will be noted in syllables 4, 10, 14 and 17 in Figure 12. Contour tones found at cadence points seem to be coordinated with particular care (see Figure 13).

Figure 13 Acculturated popular song

The handling of the contour tones in the final cadences of A$^2$, syllables 59 and 124, is shown in Figure 13. Also the coordination at the cadence formula of the B section, syllables 89 through 94 is shown. In general, traditional Thai music seems to be cast in non-repetitive musical forms. This may be a reflection of the strong influence exerted on music by the tonal organization of the language. Language does not ordinarily fall into evenly balanced, repetitive groups. The triple repetition of the A section in this song would certainly tend to prevent perfect coordination of tones and musical contours. This is shown in Figure 13 in the tones associated with the melodic figure sung to syllables 17, 46 and 111.

The observations made may now be summarized. It has become obvious that not all genres of Thai song or recitation show the same degree of coordination of speech melody and song melody. Eight examples were analysed. The degree of coordination shown in each as determined by the methods of analysis used is shown below:

| Percentage | Item | |
|---|---|---|
| 100 | VI | Lullaby, 'Boat and Rain' |
| 90 | II | Recitation of the Multiplication Table |
| 79 | I | Recitation of the Alphabet |
| 78 | III | Literary Recitation, *Klong* |
| 78 | V | Lullaby, 'The Mother Crow' |
| 66 | IV | Song in Classical Style, 'Mountain Breeze' |
| 60 | VIII | Acculturated Popular Song |
| 59 | VII | Popular Song Based on a Traditional Classical Melody |

We can conclude, therefore, that in the central Thai culture there is a high level of coordination of the pitch elements of speech and song in the recitations or chants used in the public schools, whether traditional or improvised, and in folk songs such as lullabies where text and tune probably form one associated tradition. Less coordination is found in the classical song where the association of pre-composed texts and tunes presents much difficulty in achieving this coordination and where the frequent use of nonsense syllables and continuants tends to fragment the verbal phrase. Still less coordination is found in the present-day popular song, whether an acculturated imitation of a Western model or a setting of a new text to a traditional tune.

In answer to the questions posed at the beginning of this article, we can now conclude that in chant and song found in the traditional everyday life of the people of central Thailand, speech melody has played the most prominent role. Song melody has been subservient, and purely musical creativity operated within a small and limited sphere. In the artistic, aristocratic classical song musical creativity played a much greater role, utilizing meaningless syllables and continuants as a basis for this musical elaboration. As the imitation of Western styles has spread throughout the culture, coordination of register tones with the musical contours has tended to diminish in degree but the influence of the contour tones upon the musical line seems to have retained the greater part of its force.

The persistence of this last phenomenon, the highly acculturated popular song, as shown in Figures 12 and 13, is an excellent example of the strength and stability often shown by a largely unconscious cultural trait during the acculturative process. This cultural trait is apparently very strong among the singers of Central Thailand.

## Musical notation in figures

The music is written an octave higher than heard.

Two slurs, one above another, indicate a vocal glide or *portamento*. When the glide is found between two notes it is sung on the syllable of the first. When there is no note following the glide, the approximate pitch at which it ends is indicated by a grace note in parentheses. A glide into a note is indicated by a slanting arrow preceding the note and is sung on the syllable of the note.

A vertical arrow pointing upwards indicates that the note over which it is placed is sharp, but not more than a quarter-step sharp. A similarly placed arrow pointing downwards indicates that the note is flat, but not more than a quarter-step flat.

Wavy vertical lines indicate that the material placed between them is excerpted from context.

*References*

CHAO, Y. R. (1956), 'Tones, intonation, singsong, chanting, recitative, tonal composition and atonal composition in Chinese', *For Roman Jakobson*, Mouton, pp. 52–9.

HAAS, M. (1956), *The Thai System of Writing*, American Council of Learned Societies, Program in Oriental Languages, Publication Series B – Aids – No. 5, Washington.

HOCKETT, C. F. (1955), *A Manual of Phonology*, Indiana University Publications in Anthropology and Linguistics, Memoir 11, International Journal of American Linguistics, Bloomington, Chapter 5.

LEVIS, J. H. (1937), 'Chinese music', *Asia*, vol. 37, December, pp. 864–5.

*Recordings*

1. Recitation of the Alphabet, recorded by Howard K. Kaufman in Bangkok, 1953–4. Indiana University Archives of Folk and Primitive Music Tape No. 819.2.
2. Recitation of the Multiplication Table, recorded by Howard K. Kaufman in Bangkok, 1953–4. IU AFPM Tape No. 824.7.

3. Literary Recitation, *Klong*, recorded by Howard K. Kaufman in Bangkok, 1953–4. IU AFPM Tape No. 816.5.
4. Song in Classical Style, *Mountain Breeze*, sung by Nang Ootoomporn Uttara. Recorded by Priscilla V. Magdamo, Bloomington, Indiana, May, 1959, as part of class project, Music U 302, 'Recording and Transcription Techniques in the Study of Folk Music'.
5. Lullaby, *The Mother Crow*, sung and spoken by Kanda Thammongkol. From sound track of television film, *Music and Infancy*. Recorded by Indiana University Radio and Television Services, Bloomington, 1958.
6. Lullaby, *The Boat and Rain*, sung by Kanda Thammongkol. Recorded by George List, Bloomington, Indiana, December, 1959.
7. Popular Song Based on a Traditional Classical Melody, sung by Kanda Thammongkol. Recorded by George List, Bloomington, Indiana, December, 1959.
8. Acculturated Popular Song, copied in Bangkok from an unidentified commercial disc issued in Thailand, by Howard K. Kaufman. IU AFPM Tape No. 817.8.

# 15 Robert A. Hall, Jr

Elgar and the Intonation of British English

Robert A. Hall, Jr, 'Elgar and the intonation of British English', *Gramophone*, vol. 31, June, 1953, p. 6.

Elgar is very popular in England, and not at all popular elsewhere; in this respect, his case is similar to that of Fauré in France, or of Bruckner and Mahler in Austria. We have known this much for a long time; but why should it be so? On this point we have been offered various explanations, but all couched in terms of generalities and all basically unsatisfactory. During the 1920s and 1930s, a natural reaction against the late Victorian and Edwardian periods caused a certain amount of hostility to the more superficial aspects of Elgar's inspiration, which were identified with imperialistic bombast and with the overstuffed 'plushy' style of the turn of the century; but that attitude of disdain is rapidly passing, and Elgar is no more popular outside of England than before. Eric Blom, in the last chapter of W. H. Reed's *Elgar* (1959), suggests that it is 'likely to be merely a matter of an ancient tradition according to which "English music" is a contradiction in terms'; and yet, even nowadays, when Britten and Rubbra and Vaughan-Williams are well liked abroad, Elgar's music remains unpopular. Ernest Newman suggested ignorance of English culture as a cause: 'There is something in this most English of all composers that escapes all foreigners, no doubt because they have an insufficient acquaintance with the thousand years of culture and tradition out of which the mind of Elgar has flowered' (quoted by Porte, 1933, p. 98). Yet Verdi is beloved of many who know nothing of Italy, and the great German composers from Bach to Brahms are popular the world over. We are left with the vague feeling that Elgar is inexplicably unique, and that we can apply to all of his work what Daniel Gregory Mason said *apropos* of the 'Nimrod' variation (1918): 'It is a striking fact that the originality of the passage (for no one but Elgar could have written it) is due to subtle, almost unanalysable qualities in the mode of composition rather than to any unusual features of style.'

Can we find any more precise explanation than these 'subtle, almost unanalysable qualities' for Elgar's great popularity at home and unpopularity abroad? Purely musical analysis and attempted correlations with general cultural phenomena have not succeeded so far; perhaps we should look farther, in previously unexplored fields. One such area, in which relatively little work has been done to date, is that of intonation patterns in language. (We use the term *intonation* here in its linguistic sense, referring to speech-melody, the rise and fall of the voice in connected utterance; the term *inflection* is sometimes also used in this meaning, but linguistic analysts prefer to reserve *inflection* for grammatical variations of the type *man, man's men, men's* or *am, is, are*.) Ordinarily, in discussing language or thinking about it, we neglect intonation, because we take if for granted. There is a good reason for this, because intonation is perhaps the most deep-rooted and the least conscious of all aspects of linguistic behaviour. We learn the intonation patterns of our native language earlier, even, than its individual sounds, words or syntax; and when we learn a foreign language, we un-learn our native intonation with more difficulty than any other feature of our speech. There are differences in intonation, not only between languages but also between dialects of the same language (just listen to a Londoner and then to a Scotsman, or to a New Yorker and then a Texan).

Two of the most striking features of British-English intonation, which distinguish it from American English as well as from most European languages, are a wide range of variation in pitch and a predominance of falling patterns. The normal American's range of pitch is relatively narrow, as contrasted with that of British English; this is what gives the Britisher the impression that the American is speaking 'in a monotone', whereas the American thinks the Britisher is 'singing' rather than speaking normally. A falling pitch, from relatively high to relatively low, characterizes the end of a declarative sentence in both British and American English, and also a question beginning with an interrogative word, e.g. *Where are you going?* But in questions not beginning with an interrogative (e.g. *Are you coming?*) American English and most European languages use a sharply rising intonation, whereas British English has the same falling pitch that it has in *Where are you going?* (cf. Jones, 1964; Palmer, 1922). As a result, the British pronunciation of *Are you coming?* say, sounds decidedly strange and foreign to American and Continental ears; furthermore, the statistical pre-dominance of the falling pitch pattern in British English is increased by its use in this type of sentence.

Now let us turn to Elgar's music and see if it corresponds in any respect to these characteristics of British-English pitch patterns. We immediately notice that, as many observers have commented, Elgar's melodic line, in Mason's words (1918), 'shows a tendency to large leaps, often of a seventh, in alternating directions, giving its line a sharply serrated profile'. These leaps correspond exactly to the wide range of pitch variation in British-English intonation. Furthermore, we notice that a great many of his themes show a predominantly falling trend; think, for instance, of the main motives of *Falstaff*, the introductory theme of the *Introduction and Allegro*, the first subject of the Second Symphony, and a host of others. Even more significant is what Elgar does in working with material whose compass is of a more limited range, such as the 'Welsh' theme in the *Introduction and Allegro*. Here, as is well known, he was using a reminiscence of a tune he had heard in Wales, involving a drop of a minor third. He starts with his tune restricted to that interval; but as soon as he begins to develop it further, he goes off into his customary leaps and falling trend.

But there is even more direct evidence of the influence of speech patterns on Elgar's melodic invention. Reed tells, in his book on Elgar (1959, p. 75), how

he had a little habit of repeating some particular word or phrase that had taken his fancy. . . . The name of a place would please him in some way, and not content with repeating the word continually, he would set it to music, as for instance Moglio, the name of a village quite near to him when he was writing *In the South*. . . . Needless to say, the bars in the score of *In the South* marked with the word 'Moglio' are repeated in the music many times, just as he would keep saying it.

Reed's quotation from the score shows, furthermore, the characteristic downward curve of normal British-English intonation.

No wonder, then, that the English feel there is something peculiarly 'all their own' about Elgar, which the non-English fail to appreciate. According to our hypothesis, the phenomenon is due, at least in part, to his reflecting in his music the two most characteristic features of British-English intonation, its wide pitch range and its predominantly falling patterns. Since, however, we normally have a very hard time sorting out or even identifying features of intonation, the Englishman simply feels an 'instinctive' affinity to Elgar's music, and the non-Englishman feels its 'strangeness', both of them without knowing why. Our hypothesis, moreover, would give much fuller content to Elgar's somewhat mystifying remark that 'music was in the air all around you and that you merely had to grab what you wanted and as much as you wanted' (E. Blom, in Reed's *Elgar*, 1959, p. 179). This was not merely a vague expression of a 'curious mixture of humility and pride' (Blom); it would be perfectly natural for Elgar to speak this way, if he unconsciously found the major patterns of his melodic inspiration in the intonation of his native British English. Not only was it literally 'in the air all around him', whenever anyone spoke, but, even more important, since every human being speaks all the time to himself when he is 'thinking silently', Elgar had within himself and his own thoughts an inexhaustible source of his characteristic melody. This also explains Blom's remark (in Reed's *Elgar*, 1959, p. 178) that 'it is as though a composition had been for him (Elgar) like a slice of music cut from an invisible store' – just as, when we speak aloud, we are simply externalizing part of a continuing stream of internal, 'silent' speech.

The above are, of course, merely preliminary observations, intended to call attention to a correlation which deserves closer attention and more detailed analysis. There is a whole field for musicologists, as yet virtually untouched, in the comparison of melodic structure and linguistic intonation patterns. It would be worth our time and effort to examine the relation of (say) Fauré, Debussy and Ravel to French intonation, that of Bruckner and Mahler to Austrian intonation, and so forth. In this way, it might be possible to clear up some of the hitherto unsolved problems of popularity and reputation across national boundaries, as we have attempted to do here in the case of Elgar.

*References*

JONES, D. (1964), *Outline of English Phonetics*, Heffer.
MASON, D. G. (1918), *Contemporary Composers*, Macmillan.
PALMER, H. E. (1922), *English Intonation*, Heffer.
PORTE,. J. F. (1933), *Elgar and his Music*, Pitman.
REED, W. H. (1959), *Elgar*, Farrar, Strauss & Giroux.

Robert A. Hall, Jr 285

# 16 Ivan Fónagy and Klara Magdics

Emotional Patterns in Intonation and Music[1]

Ivan Fónagy and Klara Magdics, 'Emotional patterns in intonation and music',
*Zeitschrift für Phonetik Sprachwissenschaft und Kommunikations-forschung*, vol. 16,
1963, pp. 293-313.

We want to describe the melodic patterns of ten different emotions or
emotional attitudes chosen more or less arbitrarily. Our paper is based on
records of conversations, dramas, radio plays, as well as on experiments
made with actors on the one hand and on vocal and instrumental musical
compositions on the other.

The ten feelings or attitudes are as follows: (1) joy, (2) tenderness, (3)
longing, (4) coquetry, (5) surprise, (6) fear, (7) complaint, (8) scorn, (9)
anger, (10) sarcasm.

## Hungarian emotive intonation patterns

In Hungarian the pitch range is increased with *joy*. The level of the intonation pattern is raised approximately by a third. At the beginning of each
phrase (the stretch of speech ranging from stress to stress) the voice rises to
a higher level than in neutral speech, this rise is followed by a sudden fall
of a fourth or fifth, or possibly a third, and the succeeding level is either
preserved until the end of the phrase or turned into a very slightly descending line. In the case of animated joy the ending line of the phrases may
rise slightly (especially in women's speech). The voice never touches the
basic tone. In the case of mild joy the stressed syllables form a slightly
descending line in comparison with each other; the excited joy produces
a capriciously alternating level of stressed syllables. Joyful excitement
often turns originally secondary stressed syllables into main stressed ones.
The stresses of the phrases are approximately of equal force (independent
of the importance of the contents expressed by words). The distribution of
stressed syllables is arhythmical. The stress distribution as well as the
capriciously leaping intonation practically results in the breaking of the

1. We are grateful to János Ferencsik, chief musical director of the Hungarian State
Opera House, Bence Szabolcsi, academician, and József Ujfalussy, doctor of musicology
who helped us greatly in the selection of the musical material. Many thanks for the
critical remarks of János Maróthy, doctor of musicology. We hope our data, our
correct or incorrect statements will give an occasion for Professor Otto von Essen, the
excellent expert of speech melody, to enrich the phonetic literature with further
valuable studies.

sentence into pieces. The tempo is lively; the stressed syllables are generally sharp and clear; audible glides, 'portamento'-s, occur in stressed mono-syllabic phrases (Figure 1).

Figure 1

*Tenderness* is also expressed on a higher pitch level. The level does not fluctuate in this case. The stressed syllable keeps the phrase in a 'legato-arc', enclosing it so to speak; the melody of the phrase is very slightly descending and ends far above the basic level. Sentences consisting of more phrases show a gentle undulation of the pitch level (Figure 2). The tempo is

Figure 2

restrained, the loudness reduced. The articulation is extremely soft, often labialized and a little nasal. The voice sounds 'full'.[2]

*Longing* also brings about a narrow pitch range. The melody – generally after a short up-beat – begins to rise slightly on the stressed syllable. The stress is strong and 'embraces' the phrase (legato). After the stressed syllable the melody falls about one third, and ends in a gentle rise. Both the tempo and the loudness are restrained. The melody and stress curves run parallel until the stress minimum following the peak; from here on loud-

2. The influence of emotions on voice production had been previously investigated by means of tomographic records, cf. Fónagy (1962).

ness is more and more diminished while the melody rises (Figure 3). The voice production is breathy, sometimes turning into whisper. The innervation of the muscles taking part in the expiration is slightly increased in the course of the sentence.

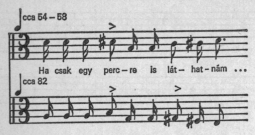

Figure 3

The melody expressing a *coquettish invitation* moves on the mid-level (or even lower). After an even, mostly 'melodic'[3] central part, the last syllable glides up about one third in an audible 'portamento' without any increase in loudness. The first syllable generally has a stronger stress accompanied by an up-glide. Despite the stress, the emphasized syllable is generally whispered. In the last syllable the voice often changes from a mid register into a head tone. The tempo is lively, the phrasing is staccato (Figure 4).

Figure 4

In *surprise* the voice suddenly glides up (or up-and-down) to a high level within the stressed syllable, then – according to the kind of surprise – falls to the mid-level (joyful surprise) or to a lower level (stupefaction) leaving the sentence melody unclosed. The beginning of the phrase bears a

3. An attempt to define 'melodicity' of speech and to distinguish the different grades had been made in a previous study (Fónagy and Magdics, 1964).

strong stress, the following syllables run down weakly. The tempo is restrained. The voice is breathy (Figure 5).

Figure 5

Among the different manifestations of fear, sudden fright and anguish will be mentioned.

The typical intonation form of *fright* is similar to that of surprise. The stressed syllable is likewise followed by a sudden fall, but the pitch range is essentially narrower in this case. The intonation form is on a lower level (it remains in the mid-zone), the unstressed syllables are arranged in a straight line, sometimes with a slight melodic rise (about a semitone) in the second part of the phrase. The tempo is lively, the loudness reduced. The voice is very breathy, often hoarse, the articulation is tense. Horror is generally pronounced in chest tone (Figure 6).

Figure 6

A prolonged state of fear, i.e. *anguish*, is first of all characterized by an extremely narrow pitch range. The melody of the stressed syllables rises about a semitone and returns to the mid-high level where it becomes, so to speak, paralysed (Figure 7).

The most characteristic manifestation of *complaint* is a more or less 'musical' intonation floating on one level and ascending a semitone at regular intervals. In the case of monosyllabic words, stress is accompanied

Figure 7

by an off-glide ('portamento'). The tempo is restrained. The stress distribution is as equal as the melody itself. More exactly, the melody ascends at rhythmic intervals, following the periodic contractions of the expiratory muscles. The voice production is normal, though the vocal cords are more compressed than necessary (Figure 8).

Figure 8

*Scorn* is reflected by a more or less even and finally slightly descending melodic line intoned on a very low level (Figure 9). The stressed syllables

Figure 9

are often lengthened; in that case the glide becomes audible. The loudness is reduced despite the high tension of the expiratory muscles. The vocal cords are compressed. The pharyngeal cavity is greatly narrowed. The articulation is tense but unrounded. The tempo is slow. Scorn is always sounded in chest tone.

*Anger* is generally expressed on a mid pitch-level and is characterized by a straight, rigid melodic line leaping up a fourth, a fifth or a sixth interval at the beginning of the phrases. The stressed syllables ascend frequently and rhythmically. Some syllables – which bear at best a secondary stress in neutral speech – appear with main stress in a hot-tempered dialogue (Figure 10). The voice production is often imperfect, breathy. Loudness is

Figure 10

not in proportion with the activity of the maximally tightened expiratory muscles. Articulation is also very tense. There is an equal tension in the laryngeal area.

*Sarcasm* is concentrated in the 'portamento' of the stressed syllables gliding to a low level in a 'wide arc'. The articulation is tense but illabial, the voice is compressed or grumbling, purring (Knarrton). The stressed syllables are lengthened (Figure 11).

Figure 11

## German, English and French emotive intonation patterns

The intonation forms reflecting emotions are conventional, bound to language and age. They can hardly be transplanted from one language into another, any more than melodic patterns having a grammatical function. Nevertheless this does not mean that the affective intonation forms are arbitrary. The arbitrary signs are necessarily conventional, but the conventional signs are not necessarily arbitrary (Fónagy, 1956). If a certain emotion is expressed by similar melodic patterns in non-related languages, then intonation must not be considered as arbitrary.

In order to control this suggestion we recorded (after having defined the situations) certain sentences spoken by two speakers of German, two of English and two of French, which sentences exactly corresponded to the above Hungarian sentences from the viewpoint of the emotion or attitude reflected.

*Joy* increases the pitch range in each of the three Indo-European languages, it is reflected in a higher pitch level, in a melody ascending frequently and at irregular intervals as well as in an irregular stress distribution. The stresses are approximately of equal force and are independent of the semantic importance of the words. The tempo is lively. Articulation is sometimes breathy (according to Trojan, 1952, p. 192, joy, exultation, is not characterized by a breathy articulation).

In French – in accordance with the oxyton tendency of stress distribution – the voice rises at the end of the phrases. So the joyful melody has in French sentences a crescendo character as against the descrescendo character of the Hungarian sentences. But if we do not directly compare the Hungarian and French affective speech, if we relate first the affective form

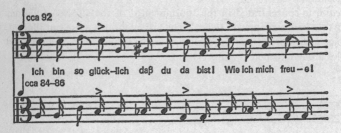

Figure 12

to the neutral form, enumerating the characteristic differences, the correspondences become obvious (Figures 12, 13, 14). In French the great lengthening of the stressed syllables plays an important part in the expression of joy. In Hungarian this possibility is limited by the phonemic character of duration.

The differentiative features of the Hungarian intonation of *tenderness* appear in the Western languages as well. The pitch level is higher than in

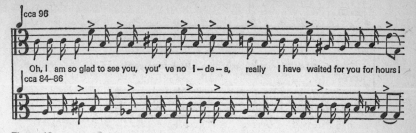

Figure 13

neutral statements. The pitch range is narrow. The stressed syllable 'embraces' the phrase even in the French sentence ('reposes-toi un peu'). In the long stressed syllables the off-glide ('portamento') is audible (especially in the English and German sentences).

Figure 14

The tempo is restrained, loudness sustained, the articulation is soft, slightly nasal, labial, the voice sounds 'full' (Figures 15, 16 and 17). All these correspond to Trojan's statements (1952, p. 178). A turn into head tone was not found in our Hungarian and foreign experiments.

Figure 15

Ivan Fónagy and Klara Magdics  293

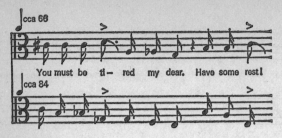

Figure 16

The melody configuration (cf. Bolinger, 1949) reflecting *longing*, namely, the slightly rising, descending, then at the end of the sentence gently ascending melody likewise appears in German, English and French. The

Figure 17

divergence of melody and stress distribution is as characteristic in these languages as in Hungarian. The pitch range is narrowed, the tempo is

Figure 18

restrained, the voice is breathy (Figures 18, 19 and 20). The increasing muscular tension – mentioned by Trojan (1952, p. 181, 'Taktgestalt $T <$') – is obvious.

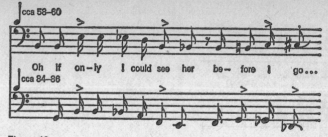

**Figure 19**

**Figure 20**

The stressed, nevertheless soft tertial up-glide of the last syllable characteristic of *coquetry* was never absent from the sentences. In the German sentence there are two up-glides (Figure 21). At the beginning of

**Figure 21**

the French sentence the melody makes a fourth interval step upwards, without 'portamento' (Figure 22). In the English sentence the melody rises three times in contrast to the neutral intonation, twice without 'portamento' and finally with 'portamento' (Figure 23). The dynamics of the

Figure 22

sentences are similar. The articulation of the stressed syllables is relatively tense, but loudness at the same time is suppressed, with voice turning into whisper. The change into head tone was clearly felt at the end of the English sentence and in the first gliding syllable ('sich') of the German

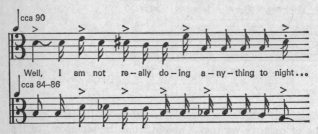

Figure 23

sentence. Trojan (1952, p. 182) does not mention a change into head tone in the case of 'luring' (Lockung).

*Surprise* increases the pitch range in the three Western languages too. In German and English the voice falls a fifth or a sixth interval from a high level (Figures 24 and 25). This sudden fall is to be found in French, but the

Figure 24

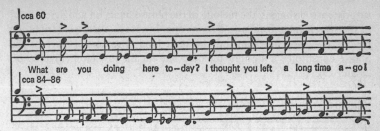

Figure 25

reversed movement, the sudden rise, is similarly frequent. In yes-or-no-questions surprise is reflected in an increase of the rising interval (Figure 26). According to Trojan, surprise (Verwunderung) is characterized by an

Figure 26

increase and decrease of tension and dynamics; he sees a relationship between the intonation of the yes-or-no question and that of surprise (p. 182 and ff.).

The intonation of sudden *fright* differs also in the Western languages from the melody of surprise in having a narrower pitch range, in the checking of loudness and speed and in its peculiar timbre. In the case of

Figure 27

surprise, astonishment, the melody of the phrase floats on a high level and in the last syllable it falls to a lower one. In speech expressing fright the melody does not stay long on the high level; the greater part of the phrase constitutes a straight melodic line on the low level (Figures 27, 28 and 29).

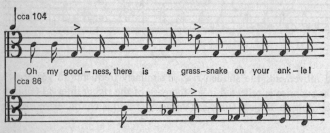

Figure 28

Figure 29

*Anguish* is characterized by an extremely narrow pitch range in the Western languages too; the stressed syllables ascend only one tone or a semitone from the rigid melodic line sounded on the mid-level (Figures 30, 31 and 32).

Figure 30

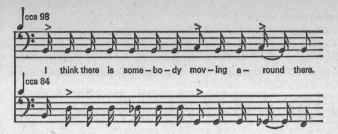

Figure 31

Figure 32

The intonation of *complaint* is built on the same principles as in Hungarian. The 'musical', 'smooth' melody is rhythmically interrupted by semitonic rises (Figures 33, 34 and 35). The laryngeal and pharyngeal muscles are tense.

Figure 33

*Scorn* is characterized by a narrow pitch range and a compressed or grumbled voice production, just like in Hungarian (Figures 36, 37 and 38). Trojan considers chest tone to be one of the most significant marks of

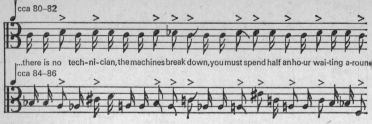

**Figure 34**

**Figure 35**

**Figure 36**

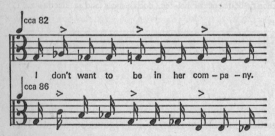

**Figure 37**

Figure 38

scorn (1952, p. 187). We did not come across breathy articulation (Trojan, l.c.) either in Hungarian or in the course of our foreign experiments.

Figure 39

*Anger* in German and English appears – as in Hungarian – in fourth, fifth or sixth ascending intervals of the stressed syllables, frequently interrupting the straight melodic line. In English there is an audible but

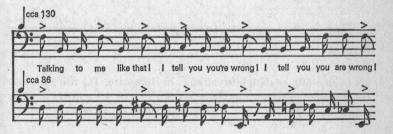

Figure 40

rapid off-glide within the lengthened stressed syllables (Figures 39 and 40). In French the voice ascends even an octave at the end of the phrase

Figure 41

(Figure 41). Trojan stresses the extremely strong dynamics of anger, the breathy voice production, the 'heavy' chest tone (which may sometimes change into head tone as a result of great tension, p. 188).

*Sarcasm* is felt in the checked, 'widely-arched', stressed off-glide, in the creaky voice as well as in the nasal timbre. The tempo is restrained. In English and French the 'portamento' is generally characterized by a wider

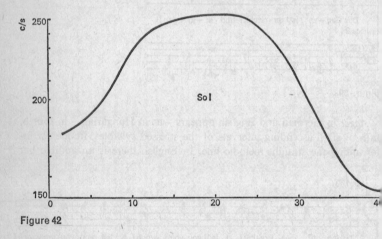

Figure 42

arc (with a fifth or sixth interval) than in Hungarian. The rising up-beat characteristic of sarcasm in German ('So!' Figure 42) appears to some extent in Hungarian ('*Úgy!*' Figure 43) (Figures 44, 45, 46).

### Emotional patterns in music

It seems that similar emotions, attitudes, are bound to analogous melodies in languages not interrelated. The musical signals of emotions may be considered as panchronic tendencies standing above languages and ages,

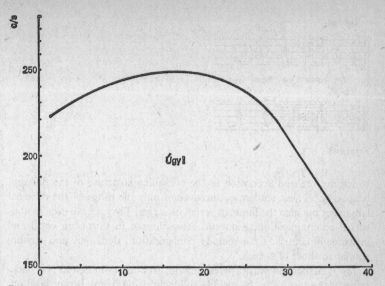

Figure 43

Figure 44

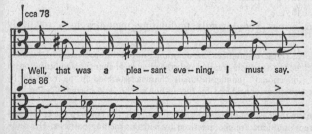

Figure 45

Figure 46

which are realized according to the prevailing structure of the different languages.[4] These tendencies surpass not only the range of the different languages but also the limits of verbal messages. They prevail even in non-verbal communication. Emotions are expressed in European vocal and instrumental music by a melody configuration, dynamics and rhythm similar to those of speech.[5]

*Joy* is associated with a lively tempo, with short motives. The backbone of the motive is the melody suddenly rising from a lower level (cf. Mattheson (1954) 'Ausbreitung unsrer Lebensgeister', p. 16). This rise, or surging upward, can be found even within the greater units as e.g. in J. S. Bach's *Whit-cantata* ('Mein gläubiges Herz, frohlocke!'), in the bass aria of the third cantata ('Empfind' ich Höllenangst und Pein, so muß im Herzen ein Freudenhimmel sein') in Handel's oratorio *Joshua* ('O had I Jubal's lyre!'), in the third movement (Das Wiedersehen) of Beethoven's sonata Opus 81a, *Les Adieux*, as the main theme, as well as in Schumann's wedding-song (*Helft mir ihr Schwestern*, Frauenliebe und Leben Opus 42). In the third act of Wagner's *Tristan* the slow series of ever-descending motives (Figure 47a) turns into the leaping melody of the shepherd's pipe announcing the good news (Figure 47b). Kurwenal's joyous exclamation seeing Tristan awaking in the third act ('Endlich! Endlich! Leben, o Leben!') is less stylized and stands nearer to the intonation of joy.

*Tenderness* brings about gently undulating melodies in a relatively

4. B. Chaitanya Deva, examining some emotional intonation patterns in Dravidian (Telugu), has come to the conclusion that only the pitch level changes significantly with emotion. No 'inflectional' (configurational) characteristics could be revealed by second degree equations considered by the author as the best means of expressing melody plots.

5. D. Cooke, on the basis of abundant musical material, has come to the conclusion that the different emotions are characterized by peculiar melody patterns. His book (1959), unfortunately, was not available to us at the time of writing this paper.

Figures 47a, b

narrow pitch range as e.g. in Orfeo's aria, from the first act of Monteverdi's *Orfeo* ('E più felice, l'ora Cheperte sospirai'), in Orfeo's aria from the third act ('Vi ricorda, o boschi ombrosi ...'); we recall the duettino number 7 of Don Giovanni and Zerline (*Don Giovanni* by Mozart, first act, Figure 48), or Zerline's aria number 13 ('wie ein stummes Lämmchen

Gib mir die Hand mein Le — ben, komm' in mein Schloss mit mir!

Figure 48

leiden ...', cf. Jouve, 1942, p. 111). Zerline's aria number 19, Don Giovanni's serenade, Wotan's farewell from Brünnhilde (*Die Walküre* by Wagner, third act, 'Der Augen leuchtendes Paar ...'), Pelléas's words spoken to Mélisande in the fourth act of *Pelléas et Mélisande* by Debussy ('Oh! qu'as tu dit, Mélisande ...'), Wozzeck entreats Marie to stay on with such a motif in the third act of Alban Berg's opera ('Du sollst da bleiben, Marie ...'). Embracing, gentle, legato melody curves reflect the tender feeling in Euridice's aria in the first act of Monteverdi's *Orfeo* ('Io non diro qual sia nel tuo gioir, Orfeo ...'), in Zerline's aria number 13 (*Don Giovanni*, first act: 'das kannst du nicht ...'), in Pamina and Tamino's duet (*Die Zauberflöte* by Mozart, second act, 'Tamino mein ...', Figure 49), in Brangene's affectionate words to her mistress (*Tristan und Isolde* by Wagner, first act, 'Herrin Isolde, trauteste Holde ...'), in Goulaud's words addressing Mélisande in the first act of *Pelléas et Mélisande* by Debussy ('Donne-moi tes deux petites mains').

Figure 49

These melody forms go far beyond the demonstration of tenderness in certain periods of European music. The so-called 'dolce' style is practically a general trend in rococo music.

The characteristic musical form of *longing* is a slightly descending, and at the end of the motive, a gently rising melody. The tempo is strongly restrained. Dynamics are first similarly restrained, then slowly increase, and at last – in contradiction with the melodic line – decrease again (cf. pp. 287-8, 294). This melody occurs in Orfeo's aria from the third act of Monteverdi's *Orfeo* ('Al mio languire . . .'), in Tamino's picture-aria (*Die Zauberflöte*, first act, 'Ich fühl' es . . .' cf. Ujfalussy, 1961), in the second movement ('Die Abwesenheit') of Beethoven's sonata Opus 81a in E flat major, *Les Adieux*, as a main theme, in Beethoven's song *An die ferne Geliebte*, in Schubert's song *Gretchen am Spinnrade* ('Sein Händedruck und ach, sein Kuß . . .'), in Schumann's *Träumerei*, in Brahms's song *O wußt' ich doch den Weg zurück*, in the kiss motif of Verdi's *Othello*,

Figure 50

in Wagner's Tristan-prelude (Figure 50). Mélisande sighs deeply as she sees her ring falling into the fountain in the second act of *Pelléas et Mélisande* by Debussy ('Elle est si loin de nous . . .').

*Coquettish* invitation, flirtation, luring, has a slightly descending, then with a last short (generally staccato) tone, ascending, musical form. Such motives accompany the offering and luring gestures of the girl in Bartók's *A csodálatos mandarin* (*The Miraculous Mandarin*), as e.g. when she lures the old cavalier, or later in her flirtation – first discreetly and then vehemently – pursued by the mandarin (Figures 51 a, b). This coquettish move-

a

b

Figures 51a, b

ment is 'softer', more playful and gentle in Susanne and the count's duet in the second act of Mozart's *Figaro* ('die sich gar schnell vergibt . . .').

A melody suddenly falling from a high level to a low one may express *surprise* in music too. Zerline expresses her astonishment in this way when she sees the abandoned Elvira asking for Don Giovanni's life ('Sie wünscht sein Leben?'); the same motif expresses her amazement at the news of Don Giovanni's damnation. This pattern occurs in Ottavio and Masetto's motif 'Che impesata' (cf. Ujfalussy). Golaud gapes in astonishment with a similar motif at the sight of Mélisande's beauty (first act of *Pelléas et Mélisande* by Debussy, 'O vous êtes belle!') and so with Bartók's Judith seeing the jewels in Bluebeard's castle (Figure 52).

Figure 52

The motif of surprise, amazement, very much resembles that of *horror*. After a sudden fall from a high level the melody grows rigid and moves between narrow limits. Horror is thus reflected in the monologue of Boris

Ivan Fónagy and Klara Magdics 307

tortured by visions (*Boris Godunov* by Moussorgsky, third act, Figure 53), as well as in Marie's alarmed cry ('Hilfe!', third act, second scene of *Wozzeck* by Alban Berg), or later, second act fourth scene, in Wozzeck's half-mad phantasies ('Der Mond ist blutig . . .').

Di — tja     o – kro —     vav – len — no — e     vsta – et'

Figure 53

Horror often turns into *anguish*; it becomes lasting as e.g. in Leporello's part when the statue appears in the door. The range of pitch narrows from a seventh to a second (*Don Giovanni*, second act, 'Ach nimmer oh möcht ich solche Gäste doch nimmer seh'n . . .'). That is how Papageno sings hearing about Sarastro's arrival (*Die Zauberflöte*, first act, Figure 54, cf. Ujfalussy); such a motif accompanies Varlam and Misajl's stealing out of

O     wär' ich ei – ne Maus,     wie  wollt' ich mich ver–ste–cken!

Figure 54

the forest in Boris Godunov (third act); with a similar motif Golaud lurks with his child in front of Mélisande's window (*Pelléas et Mélisande*, third act, fourth scene, 'Parle plus bas: Que font ils?'); Pelléas feels uneasy in his secret meeting with Mélisande (in the fourth act, first scene twice, 'J'entends parler derrière cette porte') or Mélisande hides in Pelléas's arms in the fourth scene of the fourth act ('Il y a quelqu'un derrière nous').

*Complaint* brings about a monotonous melody regularly ascending a semitone. The lamento choir of the *Psalmus Hungaricus* by Kodály is the stylized form of the Hungarian intonation form of complaint. The ascending emphatic tones embrace the lower unemphatic ones. The Lachrymosa of Verdi's *Requiem* as well as the lamento choir from the second act of Monteverdi's *Orfeo* ('Amor, Amor, Amor') reflect the paroxyton stress of the Italian language. The 'embracing' stress falls on the second syllable. The series of motives surges upwards (Figure 55). The monotonous melody of complaint is present in the first shepherd's part ('Oh, quanto è in vista Dolorosa . . .') in the second act of Monteverdi's *Orfeo*, in the first tenor's voice of the choir ('Quanto duol soffrir, ahimè!'), as well as in the

*Come un lamento*

Figure 55

orchestra accompanying Orfeo's wailing ('Tu se' morta...'). This lamenting melody appears in the orchestra when Donna Anna discovers her father's corpse (*Don Giovanni*, first act, cf. Jouve, p. 64), or when the statue appears in Don Giovanni's dining room (second act); Samuel Goldenberg and Schmuyle complain like this in Moussorgsky's *Pictures at an Exhibition*.

*Anger* in music is similarly characterized by upward leaps of fourth and fifth from a straight melodic line as e.g. in Ozmin's aria Number 3 (first act of *Die Entführung aus dem Serail* by Mozart), in Ozmin and Blonde's duet (second act), in Beckmesser's fuming part of the third act of *Die Meistersinger von Nürnberg* by Wagner (Figure 56). In Elvira's part in the

Aus sei – ner Schuster–stu–ben hetzt end–lich er den Bu – ben mit Knüppeln auf mich her.

Figure 56

first act of *Don Giovanni* ('Weh' dir Heuchler') the melodic line 'keeps level' under and above, interrupted by falls of fourth or fifth.

*Scorn* is expressed by a descending melodic line in a narrow range. Such a motif is sung by Elvira warning Zerline against Don Giovanni in the aria Number 8 of the first act ('Verachte was er spricht'). Wotan addresses Hunding in such a manner at the end of the second act of the *Walküre* (Figure 57). Golaud speaks about Mélisande with a like melody (*Pelléas*, fourth act, second scene, 'Vos longs cheveux servent enfin à quelque chose').

In a *sarcastic* melody the voice glides from a high register to low. The high tone is generally emphatic and punctuated. The portamento is replaced and provoked by the punctuated note and the following sudden fall. With such a motif Don Giovanni 'courts' Elvira in order to send her off

Geh' hin, Knecht! Knie — e vor Fri — cka: meld' ihr dass Wo–tan's

Speer ge — racht, was Spott ihr schuf.    Geh'!    Geh'!

**Figure 57**

with Leporello, to be able to make love to Elvira's housemaid (second act). This melody alone could reveal Don Giovanni's intention, if Elvira would not cling so firmly to her illusions. This motif is heard from Masetto addressed to the almost perfidious Zerline ('Wenn der gnäd'ge Herr wird sagen ...'); with such a melody Siegfried speaks to Mime in the second scene of the second act of Wagner's opera (Figure 58); Hans Sachs informs

...fängst du von Lie — be gar an!

**Figure 58**

Beckmesser with this motif that his trial song is not good enough to meet all requirements (*Die Meistersinger von Nürnberg* by Wagner, second act, 'er hält's auf die Länge nicht aus ...'), and inquires later after his health ('Herr Merker, sagt, wie steht's? Gut?'); the women mock the arrested guardsman, or the youngsters the 'mad Ivanovich' with such a melody in the third act of *Boris Godunov*; this is how Golaud speaks about Mélisande (*Pelléas*, fourth act, second scene, 'les donneraient à Dieu leçons d'innocence').

Despite the much greater (so to speak liturgic) restriction of the melodic formation of *folksongs* on the one hand, and of the relative independence of their texts and melodies on the other, certain emotions are reflected in the same way in our folksongs as in composed music and in speech melody.

Longing seems to be often accompanied by a descending and slightly rising motive in folksongs too ('Én Istenem add megérnem' ..., 'Visszanéztem félutambul ...', 'Álom, álom, mért nem jösz ...' ['My God, let me live to be with the one I love . . .', 'I looked back half way on my journey . . .', 'Dream, dream, why do you delude me . . .']' etc.). According to the statistics made on the basis of Kodály's volume (1960) a longing text was found with this motif in eleven songs while three songs expressing the same feeling showed other melodic solutions. In two cases other kinds of texts were accompanied by the 'melody of longing'.

The lamenting, plaintive melody is characteristic of popular mourning songs, and it appears in a great number of Hungarian folksongs ('Sirass édesanyám . . .', 'Árva vagyok, árva . . ., 'Istenem, Istenem . . .', 'A búbánat, keserűség . . .', 'Szegény Szabó Erzsi' . . . ['Mourn for me, my mother . . .', 'An orphan am I . . .', 'My God, my God . . .', 'The grief and bitterness . . .', 'Poor Erzsi Szabó . . .']" etc.). In Kodály's volume the melody of twenty-eight plaintive songs imitates the intonation of complaint, in nine songs the plaintive text is combined with other kinds of melody, and in two songs the lamenting melody accompanies texts of some other kind.

Tenderness is expressed by gently undulating melodies, slightly descending melody curves ('Repülj madár, repülj . . .', 'Árokparti kökény . . .', 'Fürjecském, fürjecském . . .', 'Zöld erdőben . . .' ['Fly, swallow, fly . . .', 'Blackthorn by the gully . . .', 'My little quail . . .', 'In the green forest . . .'] etc.), while quarrelling, anger are reflected in a melody ascending always on the same level ('Asszony, asszony, ki a házból . . .', 'Verjen meg az egek ura . . .', 'Verjen meg az Isten . . .' ['Wife, wife, leave my house . . .', 'May the Lord of Heaven damn you . . .', 'May God damn you . . .'] etc.). According to the statistics made on the basis of the Kodály volume the distribution of intervals in songs with tender and angry texts is as follows (cf. Table 1).

Table 1 **Distribution of intervals in Hungarian folksongs with tender and angry texts**

|  | Tender per cent | Angry per cent |
|---|---|---|
| first | 10 | 3 |
| second | 52 | 5 |
| third | 30 | 20 |
| fourth | 8 | 30 |
| fifth |  | 30 |
| sixth |  | 8 |
| seventh |  | 2 |
| octave |  | 2 |

## References

BOLINGER, D. (1951), 'Levels versus configurations', *Word*, vol. 7, pp. 199–210.

COOKE, D. (1959), *The Language of Music*, Oxford University Press.

DEVA, B. C. (1960), 'Psychophysics of speech melody', *Zeitschrift für Phonetik*, vol. 13, pp. 8–27.

FÓNAGY, I. (1956), 'Über die Eigenart des sprachlichen Zeichens', *Lingua*, vol. 6, pp. 67–88.

FÓNAGY, I. (1962), 'Mimik auf glottaler Ebene', *Phonetica*, vol. 8, pp. 209–19.

FÓNAGY, I., and MAGDICS, K. (1964), 'Das paradoxon der Sprechmelodie' *Ural-altaïsche Jahrbücher*, vol. 35, pp. 1–55.

JOUVE, P. J. (1942), *Le Don Juan de Mozart*, Freiburg.

KODÁLY, Z. (1960), *A Magyar népzene*, Hungarian Folk Music, Budapest.

MATTHESON, J. (1954), *Der volkommene Capellmeister*, 1739, Reiman, Basel.

TROJAN, F. (1952), *Der Ausdruck der Sprechstimme*, Vienna-Düsseldorf.

UJFALUSSY, J. (1961), 'Intonation, Charakterbildung und Typengestaltung in Mozarts Werken', *Studia Musicologica*, vol: 1, pp. 94–142.

# Part Six
## Universality

On the canvas that embraces all the languages of the world, is intonation
to be painted as a common theme or is it as arbitrary from language to
language as the connection between particular sounds and particular
word meanings? When we find two languages with numerous words
having similar meaning and similar sound – like French *rapsodie*,
*magique*, *tocsin* and English *rhapsody*, *magic*, and *tocsin* – our first
impulse is to assume a common origin somewhere, whether of the
languages as a whole or of some set of vocabulary that came to be
shared. The impulse seldom leads us astray; there is usually other
evidence to prove that the languages are related. If we have good reason
to believe that there is no connection in space or time between two
languages (short of the genesis of the human race itself), our impulse
then is to expect no similarity in the tie between sound and sense. It is
no surprise that the meaning 'level' is conveyed by *level* in English and
*p¹ing* in Chinese.

But suppose that against this background of no connection between
sound and word meaning that shows any kinship with English, we find
that Chinese uses pitch in a dozen or more ways that duplicate its uses
in English. It cannot be due to coincidence; the repertory of pitch
signals is not large enough – proportionately speaking it would be rather
like finding a thousand words in Chinese that match a thousand in
English, out of a total of a hundred thousand in each. With even 1 per
cent we would have to conclude that something about intonation must
transcend the usual language-specific connection between meaning and
form.

Part Six is only a sampling of a few languages where enough has
been published about their intonation systems to make comparison
possible. Nevertheless, the theme is unmistakable.

The first Reading, by Larsen and Pike, concerns Huastec. Neither
English nor Huastec is a tone language. Accordingly both are free to use
intonation for attitudinal meanings with a minimum of interference.
There is nothing to suggest that the two languages are even remotely

related in origin. The similarities that are found must then answer either to chance or to some inborn capacity of human speakers that is there to be unfolded in any language that encounters the right conditions. (A third possibility, that they are borrowed from Spanish which in turn resembles English, is hardly worth considering, given what is known about the tenacity with which languages cling to their intonation systems.) How closely Huastec matches English may be judged from the contours that Larsen and Pike describe. Here are four things to look for by way of hints:

1. The way the last syllable of *Johnny* is pronounced when calling from a long distance.
2. The way *Not so!*, *Never!*, and the like are pronounced for great emphasis, with a slide down on each syllable.
3. The way a question is asked when the speaker considers the whole idea absurd, e.g. *Who eats horse?*
4. The way a pitch rises for great surprise.

The system used for describing the intonation of Huastec is essentially that of Pike (pp. 53–82). The authors are researchers with the Summer Institute of Linguistics.

One of the areas of most intense linguistic activity – mainly on the part of the Summer Institute of Linguistics – has recently been that of New Guinea and surrounding territories. Alan Pence did fieldwork on the Kunimaipa language for eight months between 1959 and 1962. The second Reading gives his analysis of Kunimaipa, using Pike's system, like that of Huastec in the preceding Reading. Though this language is quite unrelated to either Huastec or English, the fundamental resemblances are nevertheless obvious. Questions and statements are typically distinguished by rising (or high) versus falling contours. Perhaps the most striking resemblance to the intonation of Western language is the contour described as 'mid high' (p. 334), which is approached from a high pitch, goes down, and then rises at the end. The meanings 'polite request, polite question' are carried by it. Compare the English.

```
     you
Do                        you
          it?   Would            me?
     like                  help
```

Point-by-point comparisons between the intonation of one language and that of another are few. The third Reading is Isamu Abe's comparison of English and Japanese, valuable for its proof of similarities far exceeding the reach of chance, recognizable in spite of being hedged in and warped by all the other complicated movements generally peculiar to one corner of the world, that each language has to make in its daily business of conveying a universe of meaning.

The fourth Reading, by Kerstin Hadding, compares some intonations in Swedish with related ones in English. Despite the complication of distinctive tone, the signalling of questions and statements in Swedish turns out to be strikingly similar to what is found in English. The method used by Hadding is as interesting as the results. She makes her comparisons by testing listeners with artificially produced intonation contours, which permit precise control of the parameters of pitch, duration and intensity. Both her Swedish and her American listeners reacted consistently when asked to judge the meaning of the contours and when asked to decide whether a given pitch movement was up or down.

The fact that the intonation of questions in Italian can be described by using 'tunes' that were devised for English says a great deal about the unity of intonation among Western languages. This may be due to the direct inheritance of a common intonation system from Indo-European. Or it may be due to the direct inheritance of a great deal else, which makes the daughter languages similar enough in other respects so that they perturb the universal traits of intonation in similar ways. More likely it is both. Whatever the reason, there is no mistaking the identities that one can discover in the fifth Reading, by Marguerite Chapallaz. A striking one is the interrogative-word question used 'Where an answer is courteously requested rather than insisted upon'. Compare the English and Italian:

When can you do it?     Quando potete far lo?

and contrast this pattern where the main accent occurs at the lowest pitch followed by a rise, with the peremptoriness of the one where the following pitch is lower and there is no rise:

When can you do it?

There are dissimilarities too, of course, especially in the timing of individual syllables. But the broad outlines are pretty much the same.

The general characteristics of intonation seem to be shared more broadly than those of any of the other phenomena commonly gathered under the label of 'language'.

# 17 Raymond S. Larsen and Eunice Victoria Pike

## Huastec Intonation

Abridged from Raymond S. Larsen and Eunice Victoria Pike, 'Huasteco intonations and phonemes', *Language*, vol. 25, no. 3, July–September 1949, pp. 268–77.

### Length

Vowel length is independent of stress and intonation. Long vowels contrast with short vowels in environments where both the stress and intonation are, within the limits of our perception, identical. In the two following examples the stress is on the first syllable (a raised dot indicates a long vowel): /bičow/ 'town', /bi·nom/ 'giver'; in these two examples the stress is on the second syllable: /cemθa·b/ 'being killed', /ce·mla·/ 'death'. The intonation of all four examples can be that of the narrative contour, in which case the pitches of the first two and those of the second two are alike.

Vowel length is not dependent on the position of the vowel in the word. Long and short vowels occur in all possible combinations in dissyllabic words (in the following formulae S indicates a short vowel, L a long vowel): SS /ʔat'em/ 'salt', /calam/ 'shade'; LS /bu·c'i?/ 'coward', /ʔe·yal/ 'boss'; SL /ciyo·k'/ 'chin', /ʔamu·l/ 'rubbish'; LL /ʔi·la·b/ 'seed', /ya·ni·l/ 'many times'. Likewise, all possible combinations occur in trisyllabic words: SSS /hilk'omač/ 'leftovers'; LSS /ʔa·šušlom/ 'field of garlic'; SLS /kʷ·ahi·lom/ 'widow'; LLS /hu·ču·k'čik/ 'blisters'; SSL /ʔalabe·l/ 'pretty'; LSL /bi·noma·c/ 'one who gave'; SLL /ʔuba·t'la·b/ 'game, plaything'; LLL /ʔe·la·šwa·y/ '(they) surely find each other'.

The following are words contrasting only in length: /ʔok'/ 'skull', /ʔo·k'/ 'head'; /cabal/ 'cooked corn', /caba·l/ 'earth'; /ʔu-nuhuw/ 'I sold (it)', /ʔu-nu·hul/ 'he is (or we are) selling'; /ʔin-t'okat/ 'I am clean', /ʔin-t'oka·t/ 'his cleanliness'.

Phonemically long vowels occur with one of two or more different phonetic lengths. The phonetically longer variety occurs in phrase-final syllables. The phonetically shorter variety occurs anywhere but phrase-final (a colon represents here a longer subphonemic variety than does the raised dot): /caku·l/ [tsaˈku:l] 'angry', /ya·ni·l/ [ya·ˈni:l] 'many times'. When these same words occur in a position other than phrase-final, they contain no vowels of the phonetically longer variety: /ʔit-caku·l šo·ʔ/ [ʔit·saˌku·lˈšo:ʔ] 'you are angry now', /ya·ni·l k'ale/ [ya·ˌni·lˈk'ale] 'he went many times'. That is, long vowel phonemes are phonetically longer in phrase-final position than elsewhere.

## Potential contour point

Intonation and stress are both described in terms of a point in the word which is designated as the *potential contour point*. This is located on the last long vowel of the word, or, if there are no long vowels in the word, on the first short vowel, regardless of the number of vowels in the word. In the following formulae of long- and short-vowel sequences, the syllable containing the potential contour point is in italics. Dissyllabic words: *S*S, *L*S, S*L*, L*L*; trisyllabic words: *S*SS, *L*SS, S*L*S, L*L*S, SS*L*, LS*L*, LL*L*; quadrisyllabic words: *S*SSS, S*L*SS, LL*S*L, etc.; monosyllabic words: *S*, *L*. (Proclitics and parts of compounds, in our transcriptions joined by a hyphen to the following word, are not reckoned in the location of a potential contour point.) Because of this difference in the placement of the potential contour point, a word that contains only short vowels sounds very different from a word with one or more long vowels, even though the intonation contour may be phonemically the same.

## Intonation: phonemic system

In Huastec conversation, a sentence may recur with a variety of pitch sequences. The difference in pitch from utterance to utterance is especially noticeable at the end of phrases. The pitches on which the successive syllables of an utterance are pronounced form characteristic sequences of contours. These contrast with one another, and are thus phonemically diverse. The pitch levels which compose the contours are pitch phonemes; there are at least three of these, and apparently no more than three. We symbolize them by accent marks over the vowel letters and the length dot: an acute for high pitch, a macron for mid pitch, and a grave for low pitch.

The contrasts between the levels cannot be analysed in terms of less than three; but further phonetic levels of pitch appear to be analysable as conditioned varieties of the three intonation phonemes. A mid pitch on a syllable in a phrase-final word is higher than a mid pitch on a syllable in other words, whereas a low pitch on a syllable in a phrase-final word is lower than a low pitch on other syllables. That is, there is a greater interval between a mid and low pitch in a phrase-final word than in other words.

In relation to the sentence as a whole, the intervals between the three phonemic levels depend upon the mood of the speaker. A tired or pouting person may talk with a low voice and narrow intervals, whereas an animated conversation may be carried on with wide intervals between the levels.

*Contour point*

Although each syllable is of necessity spoken on some pitch, the pertinent pitch sequences which contrast with other sequences begin on a *contour point*. That is, the contour point is the pertinent beginning point for a significant intonation contour. For the most part these contours begin at the last potential contour point in the phrase; such a point is here called a *routine contour point*. Certain other contours begin on a syllable other than the last potential contour point in the phrase; such a point is called a *special contour point*. Most of the significant contours are composed of a sequence of two phonemic levels; unless otherwise specified, one occurs at the routine contour point, the other at the end of the phrase. The pitches preceding the contour point, or between it and the phrase-final pitch, are predictable and therefore non-distinctive.

*The precontour*

This is the pitch sequence of the syllables preceding the contour point. It is predictable and therefore need not be symbolized in a phonemic transcription.

In fast speech, all syllables preceding the contour point (regardless of word boundaries) have mid pitch: //ʔuteyic koyo·c tana·ʔ ʔa·l an-k'imāˆθ//[1] [ˌʔūtēyītskōˌyō·tstāˌnā·ʔ·ˌā·lānk'ìˈmāˆθ] 'He drew near and rested there in the house.' In slower speech, word boundaries (here symbolized by spaces) are important. The rule for slow speech is that in every word, every syllable immediately preceding the potential contour point of that word has low pitch. The sentence already cited is pronounced [ˌʔūtēyīt-skòˌyō·tstàˌnā·ʔ·ˌā·lànk'ìˈmā·ˆθ]; compare also //ta·m in-elaʔ hum-pehač ʔo·w wēhàt// [ˌtā·mìnˌēlāʔhùmˌpēhātšˌʔō·wˈwēhàt] 'Then far away he found a cleared spot'.

*The intra-contour*

This is the pitch sequence which occurs on the syllables between the contour point and the end of the contour. It is predictable and need not be symbolized in a phonemic transcription.

Except for the intra-contour of the slurred contour (contempt contour), all intra-contours occur within one word. The long- and short-vowel sequences in which an intra-contour occurs are limited. In order to contain an intra-contour, a sequence must end in a short vowel and must contain three syllables or more; for if the sequence ended in a long vowel, both the beginning point and the end point of the contour would be contained in that vowel; and if the sequence consisted of two syllables of which the

1. Double slant lines enclose a transcription including pitch symbols.

second contained a short vowel, the beginning point of the contour would be on one of the syllables and the end point on the other. Of trisyllabic words, only words of the type SSS and LSS contain intra-contours, because they are the only words with the potential contour point on the first syllable. Of four-syllable words, only SSSS, LSSS, SLSS contain intra-contours. Words of five or more syllables are similarly limited.

The pitch of the intra-contour is the pitch of the lowest level of the contour, unless that lowest level is mid, in which case the intra-contour may occasionally and optionally vary to low. That is to say, if the contour is high–low, mid–low, low–low, low–mid, or low–high, the intra-contour is low. If the contour is high–mid, mid–mid, or mid–high the intra-contour is mid, optionally varying to low. We have no example of a high-high contour. Notice the intra-contours of these words: //ʔāhtitmàʔ// [ˈʔāhtìtˈmàʔ] 'singer', //ʔāhtitmáʔ// [ˈʔāhtītˈmáʔ] or [ˈʔāhtìtmáʔ] 'a singer, you say?', //ʔàhtitmā ʔ// [ˈʔàhtìtˈmāʔ] 'and a singer and . . .', //ʔāhtitmáʔ// [ˈʔàhtìtmáʔ] 'not a singer?!'.

### Intonation: morphological system

Certain connotations which are not expressed by morphemes composed just of segmental phonemes are added by means of ten or more different intonation contours. Each contour is a sequence of two intonation phonemes. Since these pitch sequences are not intimately related to specific lexical morphemes or sequences of morphemes, and since their meanings are various attitudes of the speaker superimposed upon the more concrete (and more stable) meanings of the words, we have analysed them as intonational features rather than as lexical tones. Each significant intonation contour is a single *intonation morpheme*, since it is meaningful as a whole and cannot be broken into smaller meaningful units.

Certain of the intonation contours will be first illustrated by a sequence of examples in which the word /ʔiba·/ 'no' contains the same segmental phonemes, but different intonation contours and different connotations.

//ʔibáˆ// (emphatic)
//ʔibāˆ// (matter of fact, without emotion)
//ʔibàˆ// (preoccupied, uninterested)
//ʔibáˇ// (called to a person a distance away)
//ʔibāˇ// (unfinished)
//ʔibā ˊ// (questioning: 'did you say no?')
//ʔibàˇ// (deliberate or thoughtful, with surprise)
//ʔˆībāˆ// (finality: 'absolutely not!')

This word 'no' shows how the several contours may be used with one word. Regardless of the contour, /ʔiba·/ still retains the lexical meaning of 'no'; but as the contours vary there are implications of different emotional attitudes on the part of the speaker.

*The narrative contour* is mid-low, varying to low–low. Semantically it is rather colorless, its chief characteristic being lack of emotion. It is used in both statements and questions. It is located on the last word of the phrase, beginning on the routine contour point and ending on the last vowel of the phrase. If the routine contour point falls on a phrase-final long vowel, the contour is a glide from mid to low. On a phrase-final monosyllabic word with a short vowel, the contour is a simple mid pitch.[2] Examples of the narrative contour on isolated words: S //hā?// 'water', L //?āˇč// 'grandmother', SS //bēšè?// 'badger', LS //hū·čùl// 'partridge', SL //colō^m// 'lace', LL //ya·nǐ^l// 'many times', SSS //wīk'aštè?// 'jail', LSS //?ē·yalčĭk// 'bosses', SLS //?ic'ā·màl// 'deer', LLS //?u·čāš·čĭk// '(they) speak to each other', SSL //tǒmkinē^l// 'marriage', SLL //?aki·-lā^b// 'carrying-shawl'.

The low–low alternant of this contour optionally occurs on words ending with a long vowel. This form of the morpheme is homophonous with the basically low–low intonation morpheme (see below): //halū^b// ∼ //halù^b// 'namesake'.

The narrative contour occurs more frequently than any other contour. In a certain text of 43 sentences by one informant, it is the only phrase-final contour used.

*The emphatic contour* (high–low ∼ high–mid) puts extra emphasis on the word on which it falls. The high-low alternant of this morpheme occurs on the last word of the phrase, beginning on the routine contour point: //hah yab in-le·? i-bú·rrò, ?in-le·? i-bíčìm.// 'He doesn't want a donkey, he wants a horse'; //tiwa? ne?ec an-kʷ'ahí·lòm// 'There goes the widow'.

The high–mid alternant occurs on a non-phrase-final word, beginning on a special contour point and ending on the final syllable of the same word. In this case another intonation contour, beginning on the routine contour point, is present in the same phrase: //?in-cémθā? an-?ìnìk// 'He killed the man'.

*The detached contour* (low–low) signifies that the speaker is preoccupied or uninterested or disdainful. It is used by the speaker when he is busy or thinking of something else, and in scolding children: //ka-t'aha? ?ancanà^?// 'Do it this way!'.

2. We neglected to check the form of the other contours when they fall on a phrase-final monosyllabic word.

*The call contour* (high–mid) is used (1) when shouting to or calling someone at a distance; (2) when the speaker is startled or frightened; (3) for emotional emphasis. When the routine contour point is on the phrase-final vowel (always a long one), there is a glide from high to mid. When the routine contour point is on some vowel other than the last, the contour-point vowel has high pitch and the vowels following it have mid: //hosé˘// 'Joseph!', //benhamí˘n// 'Benjamin!', //sá·rā// 'Sara!', //katarí·nā// 'Katherine!', //ka-met'aʔ an-ʔic'á·māl// 'Look at the deer!'.

Optionally this contour may be accompanied by a lengthening of the last vowel of the word (if that vowel is lexically short), with a consequent shift of the routine contour point to that vowel: //katarí·nā//. ~ //katari·ná˘// 'Katherine!', //tá·tā// ~ //ta·tá˘// 'Father!', //ka-met'aʔ am-bíčīm// ~ //ka-met'a am-bičí˘m// 'Look at the horse!'

One expression has been noted in which the entire contour falls on a non-final short vowel; with the occurrence of this contour that vowel is lengthened and the high–mid glide begins and ends on it: //ni-háyk'í˘ʔ// 'never!' //ni-há˘yk'iʔ// 'absolutely never!'. In this case the post-contour pitch is mid.

*The sequence contour* (low–mid) indicates that something is to follow. If the routine contour point is on some vowel other than the phrase-final one, the phrase-final vowel is mid and the contour-point vowel is low: //ʔàt'ēm// 'salt', //ʔà·šūš// 'garlic', //còcoblēk// 'a kick'. If the routine contour point is on the phrase-final vowel, the contour may be a glide from low to mid, or optionally a low pitch on the last vowel but one and a mid pitch on the last vowel. In the latter pronunciation the contour begins on a special contour point: //ce·mlà˘// ~ //cè·mlā·// 'death'.

This contour most frequently occurs before short pauses, where it connotes a sequence: //ʔin-le·ʔ an-ʔàhān, ʔan-bàkān, ʔani han-cābàl.// 'He wants a roasting ear, a tortilla and some cooked corn'. When the contour is used before a long pause it indicates that the speaker expects to say more.

*The hesitation contour* (mid–mid) is similar in meaning to the sequence contour but is less deliberate. Whether before a short or before a long pause, its connotation is that the sentence is unfinished: //ʔac'e·m an-ʔā·šūš// 'The garlic was wet—'.

*The question contour* (mid–high) is frequently used by someone repeating what another person has said. By means of this intonation he asks, 'Is that what you said?' Examples: //ʔic'í·lòm// 'playful', //ʔic'í·lóm// 'Did you say playful?'; //k'ale ya·nĭˀl// 'He went many times', //k'ale ya·nĭ ˂ l// 'He went many times, did you say?'.

This is also the intonation used when assent or dissent is expected from the one spoken to: //neˀec ta-ˀa·lim k'al an-tō·ˀól// 'Are you going fishing?', //k'aˀi·l an-t'ēlé ˀ// 'Is the baby hungry?'.

Where the routine contour point of this intonation morpheme falls on a phrase-final long vowel, the contour is a rising glide from mid to high. When the routine contour point falls on a vowel other than the last one, no glide occurs, but the pitch steps up to high on the phrase-final short vowel, not earlier: //čubaš in-t'ahā ˂ // 'Does he surely do it?', //kiθa·b an-ˀīθiθlomčík// 'Is the corn ugly?'.

The precontour preceding a question contour (p. 319) is more frequently spoken rapidly, with mid pitch, than slowly, with mid and low pitches: //ya·nic in-kʷi ˀyā·mál// [ˌyā·nītsīnkʷiˀiˈyā·mál], or, in slower speech [ˌyā·nītsìnkʷi ˀiˈyā·mál] 'He hunted a lot, you say?'.


*The unexpected contour* (low–high) is used when the speaker is surprised or startled, but is deliberating about what has happened or has been said. If the last vowel of the phrase is long, the contour is a glide from low to high; if the last vowel is short, the vowel of the contour point is low and last vowel is high: //haleˀ tin-ˀulal in-le·ˀ i-cànákʷ// 'Why does he say he wants beans?'. //ˀancana·ˀ in-t'aha·l a-halù ˂ b// 'Does your namesake do like this?'.


*The superemphatic contour* (mid–low mid–low) adds great emphasis. In the example we have given, it changes /ˀiba·/ 'no' to //ˀĭ˸bāˀ// 'absolutely not'; the short vowel in the first syllable changes to a long vowel. This contour seems to be more emphatic than the high–low contour. It requires two syllables; when the routine contour point is on the phrase-final vowel, this contour must of necessity begin on a special contour point.


*A contempt contour* (high slurred to low) has been noted in at least two examples. It starts with high pitch at a special contour point, located on the first potential contour point of the phrase, and steps down gradually to low. Each syllable of the intra-contour (pp. 319–20) is slightly lower than the preceding one. //hítaˀ kin k'apuw am-bičìm// 'Who eats horse?', //hánt'o ha-wašà·l// 'What are you looking at?'. The connotation of the first is contemptuous, disdainful; the second was addressed to a year-old baby.

No other intonation morphemes have been discovered. A high–high contour would appear to be theoretically possible within the system. Any others would have to be special types, like the one discussed in this section, or a combination of types, like the one in the last paragraph, or would force a different basic analysis.

## Summary

Huastec is considered to have phonemic vowel length because (1) certain minimally different words are persistently differentiated by length alone, (2) all the possible sequences of long and short vowels occur in words of two and three syllables, and (3) the differences in length persist in spite of intonation.

The pitch differences heard in Huastec are considered to be intonational (i.e. to constitute pitch morphemes) rather than 'word tones' because (1) there is no lexical pitch contrast between words of the same consonant-and-vowel pattern, and (2) the choice of a particular pitch sequence is determined by the attitude of the speaker, not by any lexical consideration.

In place of a system of contrastive lexical tones combined with some overlapping intonations, like that reported for the Maya of Yucatán, we have found in Huastec an intonational structure with a restricted number of morphemes, each composed of a sequence of pitch phonemes.

# 18 Alan Pence

## Intonation in Kunimaipa (New Guinea)

Alan Pence, 'Intonation in Kunimaipa (New Guinea)', Linguistic Circle of Canberra Publications, Series A Occasional Papers no. 3, Australian National University, 1964. Now *Pacific Linguistics*.

## Introduction

This paper concerns one aspect of the phonological system of the Kunimaipa language.[1] It is an analysis of a system of pitch signals which are distributed over phrases, and which add *shades of meaning* to utterances.[2]

In analysing this intonation, two ideas current in the theoretical work of Kenneth L. Pike have been of help. The first is the idea of hierarchy. Pike regards phonology as made up of basic building blocks (units) of various types. These form a series of levels which he organizes smallest to largest in a V-shaped display. The smallest unit is the phoneme. Phoneme units are distributed in such a manner as to produce syllables, and these in turn make up phonological words, and so on. The intonation of Kunimaipa fits into the total Kunimaipa phonological system at a mid level, which will be called phonological phrase.

The second idea found helpful came out in 1945 in Pike's treatment of American English intonation. This was the dichotomy he made between *precontour* and *primary contour*. In the current literature, the terms margin and nucleus are used (Pike, 1962). These terms indicate that we may expect to find in phonological systems, peaks of activity and troughs of activity. We may find peaks with certain characteristics, and troughs with differing characteristics. The terms prenuclear contour and nuclear contour are used

1. The main body of the some 8000 speakers of Kunimaipa live in the Goilala Sub-District of Papua; however, the dialect studied here is that spoken in the Bubu River area near Garaina in the Morobe District of New Guinea. This analysis is based on field work done in the area during 1961 and 1962 under the Summer Institute of Linguistics.

In this paper Kunimaipa is written in a practical orthography which represents twenty phonemes: p – /p/, s – /s/, t – /t/, k – /k/ (these have stop, affricate, and fricative variants, /k/ is backed before mid and low vowels); b – /b/, d – /d/, r – /ř/, g – /g/ (these have fortis stop and fricative allophones except for /ř/ which is either flap or trill); v – /ƀ/, j – /z/, l – /l/, h – /g/ (these have stop, affricate, and fricative variants, except /l/ which occurs as either [l] or [dl]); m – /m/, n – /n/, ng – /ŋ/; i – /i/, e – /e/, a – /a/, o – /o/, u – /u/.

2. Pike (1945) defines intonation in this way.

in this paper to designate trough versus peak activity, and the dichotomy has proved very useful in simplifying the description.

The total Kunimaipa phonological system is described in terms of a hierarchy of levels. On each level, units which occur are described in relation to the units with which they contrast, their internal modes of variation, and their distinctive distribution. Each level is seen as having units which are in turn distributed on higher levels. A full expansion of the system is seen in the example (extracted from text).

gi zagaɽ so got / e teagan ɬon / na egar oɽa eg//

'Going to inspect (the traps), he found no (game); they were still set.' The whole is a phonological sentence (//). It is subdivided into three phonological phrases (/), six phonological words (double space), and numerous syllables and phonemes. Pitch is marked by solid and broken lines; high pitch above the letters, mid pitch below the letters, and low pitch considerably below the letters. Solid lines indicate crucial pitch points; horizontal dotted lines indicate non-focal or fluctuating pitches.

In other examples a single syllable or segment may occur as the highest level of the system. The phoneme /e/ occurs as a syllable, and when spoken in isolation with intonation and other features e // 'yes', it is a phonological sentence.

Intonation is an independent system closely related to the whole hierarchy of phonological elements. It fits into the system at the level which we call phonological phrase (P-phrase), making this a very diverse part of the system.

Units of the Kunimaipa intonation system are primarily defined by pitch. The minimum units of the system are three pitch levels, the intonemes high, mid and low. These units combine into sequences which we refer to as *prenuclear contour* and *nuclear contour*. There are four contrastive types of prenuclear contour: stepping, rising, falling and level. There are ten types of nuclear contour: high, mid, low, high–low, high–mid, mid–high, mid–high–low, high–high–mid, mid–low and mid–low–mid.

A sequence of an obligatory nuclear contour preceded by one or more optional prenuclear contours is termed an intonation word (I-word). In the example, te pelavo sik 'at the wall', the first four syllables with their

pitch pattern constitute the prenuclear contour. The whole is an intonation word. Pitch is indicated by the solid and broken lines, mid first syllable, high syllables two through four, and low final syllable. The emic[3] content

3. By emic content is meant the content as the hearer would recognize it in terms of the system of the language. The /p/ in *Pay!* differs in pronunciation from the /p/ in

of this I-word is a stepping prenuclear contour followed by a low nuclear contour.

While the total system is described in terms of three level intonemes, in reality these registers are based primarily on occurrences of the nuclear contours. Though prenuclear contours are describable in these terms, in some respects they appear to function more directly as total contours (note above the contrast in the labels given to prenuclear *v.* nuclear contours) which coincide at some points with the levels of the nuclear contours.

Pike (1945, p. 70) notes a similar situation in English intonation in the 'descending stress series'. This is a unique contour in which there may be 'more stressed syllables or distinct pitches than can be fitted into four levels'.

The main points of contrast between the prenuclear and nuclear contours are: (a) prenuclear contour glides occur only across syllable boundaries (except that if the prenuclear contour consists of a single syllable, it may be gliding); nuclear contour glides may occur on one syllable or across syllable boundaries; (b) prenuclear contours may occur on long strings of syllables, nuclear contours occur on a maximum of two syllables; (c) sequences of up to four prenuclear contours occur unbroken by pause, pause usually occurs between sequences of nuclear contours or between nuclear contours and following prenuclear contours; (d) prenuclear contours occur at various pitch heights with no apparent contrast of meaning; a change of level in the nuclear contour area indicates a change of meaning.

Though it is the nuclear contour which is obligatory to the I-word, the prenuclear contour appears to carry an equally important meaning load in the system. For this reason the term prenuclear contour has been chosen, rather than one such as precontour which would understate this function.

This paper will describe first the prenuclear contours, then the levels and glides of the nuclear contours.

In gathering information on the Kunimaipa intonational system, about three and a half hours of taped text of various sorts have been used. Numerous examples of quoted speech are found in this text; thus it is felt that the analysis is made from widely representative data. In addition, informant elicitation has supported the conclusions drawn and added to them in certain respects. However, the treatment is not in any way exhaustive. Rare nuclear contour types may have easily been overlooked. Distributional limitations of the various types are only partially analysed. In

---

*Stop!*, but in spite of the phonetic difference a native speaker of English unhesitatingly labels both /p/. Similarly if a language has an intoneme of *low,* it will be recognized as *low* even though it may be a bit higher sometimes, or a bit lower. It is 'emically' *low.*

addition, since the analyst does not have a full command of Kunimaipa, it has been impossible to approach a complete description of the meanings of the various units.

**Prenuclear contour**

In the data analysed, four types of prenuclear contour have been noted: stepping (mid–high), rising (low–high), falling (high–low), and level (mid–mid). As implied above, the internal relationship between the pitches of a prenuclear contour is more important than pitch height itself.

The stepping prenuclear contour is basically a mid-pitch initial syllable followed by an optional high syllable, optionally followed by one or more syllables neutral in pitch. The contour has a meaning of normal or declarative statement. Figure 1 is a diagram of this contour.

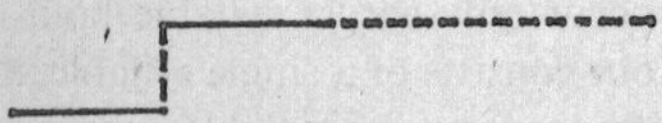

Figure 1 Stepping prenuclear contour

The first two syllables of this contour may be pronounced with low to mid or even low to high pitch. The third syllable (neutral in pitch) may be the same pitch as the second, slightly higher (the vowel /a/ tends to draw this pitch up), or slightly lower; additional neutral-pitched syllables usually decay in pitch. The final neutral-pitched syllable may be drawn up by a following intoneme. Neutral syllables may be very short, or even voiceless following /s/. A one-syllable statement prenuclear contour may be either a level mid pitch, a low to mid rising glide, or a mid to high rising glide. These patterns are considered allocontours since they appear to vary freely; however, more investigation at this point is needed. In the following examples, vertical stroke (/) divides the prenuclear contour from the nuclear contour. In parentheses following the lexical meaning is an indication of the intonational meaning of the contour which is being illustrated.

re /iparo /mot 'our things' (.)

da /ngasi /par 'a weapon' (.)

pim /gipijotanang /ma in 'with his vegetables, singly' (.)

ma/vat 'a red thing' (.)

a /ba /nap 'man' (.)

na /e nari me /no oh 'They used to kill others.' (.)

The rising prenuclear contour is basically a pattern which begins with a low (or occasionally mid) syllable and rises regularly on each succeeding syllable to a final high syllable. It has a meaning of incompleteness or sequence, and contrasts with the stepping prenuclear contour in that (a) it often begins lower, (b) the initial upstep is smaller, and (c) each succeeding syllable is higher in pitch than the previous. Figure 2 is a schematic representation of the rising prenuclear contour.

Figure 2  Rising prenuclear contour

Rising prenuclear contours occurring on one to three syllables may begin either low or mid, and those on two syllables often do not rise to high. Four or more syllable occurrences tend to rise the full low to high range, thus in longer ones the up steps between syllables are very short. This contour is often followed by a high nuclear contour, though most others may also occur.

reipa/ro\ /mot  'our things' (...)

rangi ./jah  'He lit it.' (...)

sapa/ne/puh  'He will go and' (...)

pop veir vi./iha/puh  'This one they covered and left, and' (...)

The falling prenuclear contour begins high and falls progressively throughout. Its meaning seems to be excitement. The contrast between this and preceding types is seen by comparing Figure 3 with Figures 1 and 2.

Figure 3  Falling prenuclear contour

In most occurrences of this type pitch drops with each syllable. However, in one example, each succeeding phonological word within the prenuclear contour is lower in pitch than the preceding; but within the word pitch rises slightly.

re̠ iparo/mot

okoh naek ̠am verevat am hohoranev hao/han

'Way down somewhere they came out and chanted' (!)

The level prenuclear contour is a sequence of mid- (or occasionally high-) pitched syllables. It has a meaning of suspense. It contrasts with the three other prenuclear contour types in that there is no significant rise or fall in pitch throughout. Figure 4 is a schematic representation of this type.

Figure 4 Level prenuclear contour

Careful listening to taped examples of this type reveals minute variation, up or down, from one syllable to another. This variation is without pattern, and does not affect the level character of this contour. The mid-level nuclear contour commonly occurs following this type; however, various others (low, high, high–low) have also been observed there.

reiparo/mot 'our things' (—)

aban pongariv tin /am 'two men, very carefully...' (—)

menaui/a kill chant (—)

ni vii /hoj 'You go on and put it.' (—)

In text, sequences of prenuclear contours occur without being interrupted by pause. In a preliminary check of the sequences of two which might occur, only the following were not found: stepping–falling, rising–falling, level–falling, level–rising, rising–level, and level–level. The rare falling and level prenuclear contours are, of course, even more rare in sequence. In the following examples, plus (+) indicates a break between prenuclear contours.

so/hot +ka hat +ro/pu\/vo
'We kept going up inside the mountain, and' (.), (.), (.)

gi/tahar +a/kah /vi ih 'Later they put him way up there.' (.), (.)

sa/or +vo/sihoi +reipa/ro /hoi

'. . . younger sisters and brothers, we all . . .' (.), (.), (. . .)

po͡ˌri  ǂkakam  /t͡ˈo͡ oh  'Those ones were pained.' (!), (—)

One- or two-syllable prenuclear contours are often ambiguous as to whether they are one type or another. A one-syllable contour with pitch in the mid to low area might be interpreted as either stepping, rising or level type. A one-syllable contour with pitch in the mid to high area might be interpreted as either stepping, falling or level type. A two-syllable contour rising from low to mid might be interpreted as either stepping or rising type. Three factors are considered in interpreting such occurrences: (a) the height of the pitch, (b) the size of the rise between syllables and (c) context. The first two are applied according to the contrastive features already given of each prenuclear contour type. Cases which are still ambiguous are interpreted as a type which would be likely to occur in the intonation context.

### Nuclear contour

There are ten types of nuclear contour: high, mid, low, high–low, high–mid, mid–low, mid–high, mid–high–low, high–high–mid and mid–low–mid.

Among the variants of the nuclear contours are those conditioned by their occurrence in the P-sentence. The final syllable of the P-sentence has fast decrescendo and drifts quickly into voicelessness. P-sentence medially (P-phrase finally) a syllable having a nuclear contour tends to have a more controlled dynamic. In addition to this conditioning, contours with final high and low intonemes at P-sentence boundaries tend to glide to extremes of the register.

### Placement

Each I-word has a nuclear contour. In most I-words this occurs on the final syllable; however, an occasional I-word has the nuclear contour spread over two final contiguous vowels. The distribution of such occurrence needs further study. At a P-sentence boundary in distinct or emphatic speech, the nuclear contour sometimes occurs on a final unstressed CV syllable. In the example, ro͡ˈ /pu 'a boy?', the high nuclear contour occurs on the final syllable whereas the prenuclear contour and P-word nuclear stress occur on the initial syllable. If the P-sentence ends with a voiceless variant of the vowel (which is intonationally non-pertinent), the nuclear contour occurs on the antepenult. Pause is not obligatory following a nuclear contour; however, only in rare cases is it omitted. Phrase stress (in contrast to P-word nuclear stress) does not occur. Degrees of emphasis are indicated by variation in general intensity, so that occasionally a P-word or P-phrase nucleus may be very loud, and occasionally very soft. The following examples illustrate the placement of the nuclear contour.

ha ito /kor 'doorway'

ti/na /e 'good thing'

je ire /vai 'tomorrow'

hasa /ha 'He went?'

ha /saha 'He went?' (with voiceless final vowel)

## Description

The high nuclear contour has a meaning of impending, incompleteness or normal question. It occurs following the stepping, rising and level prenuclear contours. It may occur on a final non-stressed CV syllable following the rising prenuclear contour. In this occurrence the contour is extra-high; elsewhere at P-sentence boundaries it is high rising; at P-phrase boundaries it is a level high pitch.

re /iparo/mot 'our things' (incomplete)

vat em vi /jat 'took, came, and left it, and' (incomplete)

pula ha/puj 'the flute's' (incomplete)

vat e/me/ngi 'You brought it' (incomplete)

ni vii /hoj 'You go on and put it.' (incomplete)

The meaning of the mid nuclear contour is unknown.[4] It occurs following the stepping, rising and level prenuclear contours, and has been observed to occur on a final non-stressed CV syllable. It is a mid-level pitch in all of its occurrences.

re iparo /mot 'our things' (meaning unknown)

pi ak epara /vah 'He, up at this place ...' (meaning unknown)

menge gi /puh 'We helped them and ...' (meaning unknown)

me tat sohot /het 'going along putting it ...' (meaning unknown)

4. Because of the distinctive use of this contour and the place which it fills in the system, it is assumed that a meaning contrast exists.

The low-nuclear contour has a meaning of normal or unemotional statement. It occurs most often following stepping prenuclear contours; however, it has also been observed following rising, level and falling prenuclear contours, and on a final non-stressed syllable. It occurs as a low falling glide or extra-low pitch at P-sentence boundaries. At P-phrase boundaries, it is a low-level pitch.

re/ iparo | /mot   'our things' (normal)

a | nga \/moh   'I am telling you all.' (normal)

me|napaj | /hat   'thinking to set (traps) . . .' (normal)

ema/ ha \ /puh   'they came and . . .' (normal)

pi | /ma   'his . . .' (normal)

a/ ngar a |/bu   'people' (normal)

The high–low nuclear contour has the force of an announcement. It usually follows a stepping prenuclear contour, but has also been observed to occur following rising and level. At P-sentence boundaries, this contour drifts quickly into voicelessness and the down-glide does not appear to terminate at any particular point. At P-phrase boundaries the end point is more obvious because of contrasting nuclear syllable dynamics.

re/ iparo/mo| t   'our things' (announcement)

na/ e   nari   me/no| oh   'They used to kill others' (announcement)

nga/ /ro|   'Child' (announcement)

hamal/ a/ho| p   'a big snake' (announcement)

hat  etet  he/ /je| i   'You all listen' (announcement)

The high–mid nuclear contour has (tentatively) a meaning of polite statement. It has been observed only following the stepping prenuclear contour.

re|iparo/mo| t   'our things' (polite)

ha|omaj  /to|h   'I'm about to speak' (polite)

ma|  moreg  /ha|om   'Or will I speak falsely.'   (polite)

The mid–low nuclear contour has a meaning of emphatic statement. It has been observed only following the stepping prenuclear contour. At a P-phrase boundary it stops at upper low rather than gliding to extra-low as it does at a P-sentence boundary.

reˈiparo ˈ/mot 'our things' (emphatic)

tuˈpumakih ˈ/heh 'He was in the men's house.' (emphatic)

jaˈ but tepat o ˈ/raej 'There is a money paper.' (emphatic)

/tooh 'They did it.' (emphatic)

The mid–high nuclear contour has meanings of polite request, polite question, or nonemphatic call. It occurs only following the stepping prenuclear contour. When it occurs on a final non-stressed CV syllable, it has either of the latter two meanings.

re ˈiparo ˈ/mo t 'our things' (polite question)

i ˈti ˈ/ha ˈv 'the firewood' (polite question)

haˈrangije ˈ/ngi 'You lit it.' (polite question)

eˈro ˈ/ma e 'Companion' (non-emphatic call)

The mid–high–low nuclear contour has a meaning of deep feeling such as intense sympathy or desire. It has been observed following only the stepping prenuclear contour. It usually occurs spread over a sequence of two contiguous vowels, but has also been observed on a single syllable. Because it may occur on one syllable, it must be treated as a contour of three intonemes.

reˈiparo ˈ/mo t 'our things' (feeling)

kˈivok ⁺v/elat ˈ/na n 'Fill a bag and give it to me.' (feeling)

poˈri ⁺ka ˈkam \/to o h 'Those ones had pain.' (feeling)

/po ˈv 'This' (feeling)

The high–high–mid nuclear contour is used as an intense or distant call. It occurs on a final non-stressed CV syllable or spread over two V syllables, and is often spoken in a falsetto voice. It has been observed following the stepping and falling prenuclear contours. Because it always occurs lengthened, it has been interpreted as a sequence of three intonemes, in contrast to the high–mid nuclear contour.

re¦iparomo/ta ¦‿ 'our things' (distant call)

vo¦nie/vui ¦‿ 'Voniev' (distant call)

e¦moopai ji tui tui ⁺ji¦lang lang -gio/gi¦

   call used when felling trees  (distant call)

va ̖ro ̸ ̸ae ¦‿ 'Varoa' (distant call)

The mid–low–mid nuclear contour is used as an excited sequence, both in listing items and as a type of hesitation. It has been observed following the stepping and level prenuclear contours. It occurs on the two final syllables of a P-phrase, either the stressed syllable and a CV syllable containing /a/, or two final contiguous V syllables, the second of which is /a/. When it occurs as a hesitation, it is often closed sharply by a glottal stop. The low to mid up-glide occurs on the final vowel, and often a mid to low glide occurs on the preceding syllable.

re¦iparo¦/mota‿'our things' (excited sequence)

u ̸e ̸/vora 'blood' (excited sequence)

api/rara 'sugar' (excited sequence)

pu ̸lahapu¦/pua 'the flute' (excited sequence)


## Implications

Having completed a study of this type, it is in order to ask what significance it has in the overall linguistic picture. There appear to be four main areas of usefulness:

1. No description of Kunimaipa phonology could be complete without a description of pitch signals.

2. In learning to speak a language, it is necessary to reproduce rhythmic and pitch patterns which are acceptable to speakers for whom the language is their mother tongue. While Kunimaipa is in no sense a major New Guinea language, and thus will not be learned by large numbers of non-indigenes, any further analytical work which is done in it will be furthered by an understanding and use of this system.

3. Various analysts are attempting to bring features of intonation in some way into their grammatical description. In a language like Kunimaipa where intonation obviously has a great deal of importance, a thorough analysis is absolutely necessary if intonation is going to be used with accuracy in the grammatical description. The importance of intonation, however, varies from language to language.

4. Though this study does not blaze any new trails in phonological analysis, it does show that a systematic approach to intonation is possible. This may help others struggling with the same problems.

*References*

PIKE, K. L. (1945), *The Intonation of American English*, University of Michigan Press.

PIKE, K. L. (1962), 'Practical phonetics of rhythm waves', *Phonetica*, vol. 8, pp. 9–30.

# 19 Isamu Abe

## Intonational Patterns of English and Japanese

Isamu Abe, 'Intonational patterns of English and Japanese', *Word*, vol. 11, no. 3, December 1955, pp. 386–98.

In the domain of pitch phenomena, Japanese has tone and intonation.[1] On the lexical level tone distinguishes the meaning of one word from that of an otherwise homophonous word. Intonation, on the other hand, is a phonetic manifestation (pitch being its instrument) of the attitude the speaker assumes toward the things spoken about or toward the auditor. It follows, therefore, that tone and intonation are functionally different from each other, in spite of the fact that they are characterized by the ebb and flow of pitch.

The analysis of *tone* in Japanese has a considerable history. There appear to be two kinds of approach – (1) static (or positional) analysis and (2) kinetic (or motional) analysis. Phoneticians favoring the first method posit a certain number of syllabic pitch levels and assign one of them to each of the component syllables of a word. The number of pitch levels is variously assigned – some prefer three, some two, some four, and the question as to how many pitch levels are most suitable is still going on. However, there is a tendency among some Japanese students of phonetics to favor two levels (high and low). Now, the advocates of the second view (i.e. kinetic analysis) maintain that intra- or intersyllabic movement of pitch is more vital for linguistic analysis than the positional analysis just mentioned. As early as 1927, Kooichi Miyata remarked that it is sufficient for tonal analysis to discover where in a given word there occurs a significant change in pitch between one syllable and another – i.e. a fall. He regarded other pitch phenomena characterizing the word as of but minor consequence. Quite recently Shin Kawakami questioned the value of the prevalent theory of level analysis. He states that 'it is impossible to think that there is such a thing as the height of a syllable. The important thing is to consider that there is only the height of a certain point of a syllable.' He thus describes various aspects of intrasyllablic tonal shift in an accent phrase. It is interesting to note, in passing, that Miyata's analysis

1. Japanese phoneticians usually refer to word tone as 'accent'. Throughout this paper, the term 'tone' will be employed in compliance with the customary European terminology, and to distinguish it from 'intonation'.

foreshadows the current phonemic approach now being experimented with in Japan. Shiroo Hattori (1954), for example, applies the term 'accent nucleus' to a syllable (he uses the term 'mora') which is or may be accompanied by another mora lower in pitch; e.g. in *Karakasa*, the second *ka* is high, and *sa* is low, so this *ka* constitutes the accent nucleus. He states, in effect, that one should consider the following two points to know the distinctive features of the accentual patterns of Japanese words: (1) Is there an accent nucleus? and (2) If it is present, on what mora will it be found?

These views have been quoted in order to show the general character of Japanese word tone. But the main concern of the present paper is intonation.

Intonation is very different from tone as we have just described it. Intonation may be said to have an 'emotive' function. Its purpose is to supply a delicate shade of meaning to the utterance upon which it is superimposed. It belongs to the field of 'expression' – being the reflection of the speaker's feelings or attitudes.

Tone and intonation often involve different aspects of pitch. Let us take up the word *ame* (rain). For comprehending the tonal structure of this word, all that is required is to notice that it has a perceptible fall in pitch between the element *a* and the element *me*. However, the absolute interval (i.e. musical range) of the fall is immaterial for tonal composition. Tonal value is a 'directional' value. And the so-called tonal pattern is an abstraction from the actually collected facts of similar directional compositions. On the other hand, the actual modifications of tonal range or the 'key' of tone is intimately correlated with problems of intonation. For example, when we say that a widened pitch range is suggestive of the speaker's heightened feelings – animation, anger, etc., or that a narrowed range expresses irony, indifference, etc., we are speaking of intonation. All this has no direct relation whatsoever to the composition of tone.

Japanese tone and intonation, both being pitch phenomena, overlap or clash in some instances. Nevertheless, it may safely be said that each has its own ground to maintain, as a general rule. Observe, for example, Kaku Jimbo's remark that 'sentence-intonation can never cause an inherent high pitch to become lower than a neighbouring lower pitch, or vice versa' (1925). Superimposed upon the word *ame* (rain), for example, a rising intonation merely *adds* a rising tail to the final syllable of the word. Superimposed upon the word *ame* (candy) (slightly rising tone), a rising intonation follows and elongates the direction of the word tone, bringing the last syllable yet higher. In any case, the intonational addition in no wise affects the basic tonal structure of these words. In a certain Chinese dialect, similar phenomena appear to occur. Chao observes that in the sentence *Zhege xao!* (It is decidedly good!) a falling intonation is not added simultaneously to the last syllable, but is joined on successively, after the word tone is completed – thus *xao!* (∿↓) (1933). (Be it noted that Japanese is not, strictly speaking, a tone language like Chinese, but similarities of this kind are still there.)

It has been hypothetically stated that intonation is emotional in origin – as it apparently is even now. Some phonologists are not inclined to treat intonation as an arbitrary system of signs. The late Arisaka, for example, maintains that there exist quite natural relationships between tunes and feelings. According to him, intonation is purely physiological; and for this reason, even if it has a number of qualities in common exhibited by its users, it is not a social system – and therefore, it is not a phonological system which is part of this social system (1940, pp. 128–31). Bally, on the other hand, asserts that 'on sait que, d'une manière générale, les intonations engendrées par l'émotion ne restent pas l'apanage du langage instinctif: elles pénètrent, sous une forme schématisée, dans la langue même; tous les idiomes possèdent une jeu varié de mélodies, fixées par l'usage et exprimant des sentiments déterminés' (Bally, 1935, pp. 126–7). There are some Japanese phonologists who, dissatisfied with the usual dichotomous classification (tone and intonation), claim that there should be recognized (1) tone (word accent), (2) intonation (natural and spontaneous speech melody), and (3) speech tune (conventionalized or idiomatic speech melody inherent in a given community) (e.g. Terakawa, 1945, pp. 305–7). Bolinger holds that intonation contains a few arbitrary uses, but they are embedded in a matrix of instinctive reactions; even the arbitrary uses may generally be assigned values consistent with the nervous interpretation (for instance, sentence fall occurs when the issue is settled, i.e. tension relaxes). Elsewhere, he claims that while much of our intonation is a cultural heritage and so 'learned' rather than 'natural', the correspondence of its meaning with nervous tension is too close to allow us to deny all physiological determination (1949; 1947). Perhaps this is a good way to look at intonation at this stage of analysis.

Prior to attempting too sweeping a conclusion about the real status of intonation, we consider it imperative first to state actual facts about the way intonations work in various languages. A comparison with each other, of the results thus secured, will provide us, we hope, with a somewhat more detailed and accurate picture of intonation as it is used in human speech.

Used in conjunction with an utterance, intonation modifies in a delicate manner the 'contents' (i.e. referential values) of that utterance or even supersedes them. It is worth mentioning that of late intonation has been given more attention than ever before for the analysis of sentence types. It is to be noted that the aim of an utterance is not always attained by unilateral means. The genuine purport of language for communication is expressed by a combination of a specific choice of lexical items (words), their proper arrangement (syntax), and sound. As an agglutinative language, Japanese possesses a large number of what may be called enclitic elements (particles being the most typical of them) – and some of these elements make intelligible the grammatical construction of an utterance, while others impart an emotional coloring to the expression. In fact, the latter are, in the minds of ordinary persons, a sort of 'visible' intonation. It may therefore be argued that, in some instances, the intonation would be allowed without much damage to meaning to play second fiddle so long as an adequate selection of words is made. Ryuuzaburoo Taguchi has observed that English contains varieties of spoken forms beyond mere words – and these are capable of expressing by vocal means diverse feelings like joy and anger. On the other hand, we have in Japanese such a vast field of emotional expression relying on 'phonogramic' words that we could, if we so desired, dispense with other devices of expression and might still be quite able to meet our communicative purpose. In effect, he appears to assume that in English emotional expressions are frequently formulated by cumulative means, while in Japanese they are mostly formulated by linear devices. Motoki Tokieda states, in effect, that 'if we had not developed in this language various types of word forms to indicate sentence structures, we would have developed other means of doing so – e.g. intonation' (1950, p. 357). He says we have a linear composition in *Darekakitaka?* (*ka* is a question particle, and we have a level low intonation at the end), but that we have a cumulative composition in *Darekakita?* (a question here signaled by a rising intonation). There appears to be much to be said for these statements as far as actual practice goes. It is true that Japanese is shackled with varieties of emotional and connective elements, and that we actually make conscious or unconscious use of them to suit specific needs. Unless actually pronounced, it would not be possible to determine, without a proper context to supplement its meaning, whether the expression *Darekakita* is a question ('Did somebody come?') or a statement ('Somebody came.'). The addition of the particle *ka* usually turns this into a question, with its accompanying falling intonation. (Compare this with Russian utterances containing the particle *li*.) However, it is equally true that *Darekakitaka* could be pronounced with a rising intonation as a normal question of this type. So it may safely be assumed that intonation, if it is employed at all, has a value of its own as a psychological pitch curve. This seems to be especially true of the English language. For example, the utterance *Is she happy?* is an interrogative sentence, yet different intonations could be superimposed upon it independently of its grammatical construction. Hans Kurath distinguishes (1) syntactical intonation, which expresses the syntactical relation between phrases, and (2) emotional intonation, which expresses the feeling or attitude of the speaker toward the idea expressed or the person addressed (1930). His statement that 'as a rule emotional and syntactical intonation do not clash, but the emotional intonation may run counter to the normal syntactical intonation and reverse it' appears to have some bearing on the question now under consideration. Here we recall a remark of Gardiner's that elocutional form (intonation) predominates over the locutional form (words) and that elocutional form provides the dominant clue to the special quality of a sentence (1932, p. 201).

Now we shall list some of the intonational patterns – if patterns they are – of some of the typical Japanese expressions. We restrict the examples to comparatively short ones to simplify the description. Then we shall compare their intonational patterns with those of their equivalents – or we should rather say 'near' equivalents – in English. *Sumisusanwa senseedesu.* 'Mr Smith is a teacher.' / *Tarooga kita.* 'Taroo came.' / *A to B too tasuto C ni narimasu.* 'A and B make C.' / *Moojiki haruni naru.* 'Spring will come round soon.' / *Amari ookuwa arimasen.* 'There is not much of it.' In ordinary expressions like these (i.e. 'colorless' statements made in a matter-of-fact way), the speaker usually finishes the utterance with a falling intonation. He simply has said what he has to say – no more, no less – and there naturally occurs a psychological pause sentence-finally, and physiologically, there comes relaxation, too. Nor would any particular implication be imparted to the whole expression. This is exactly what characterizes similar expressions in English. (Try this intonation on the above translations.)

The above examples would be given subtle emotional colorings by the addition of words (mostly particles), and this is what usually happens in animated conversation.

If a rising or a raised pitch is employed in such instances, probability is that the speaker is appealing (strongly) to the hearer or calling for the latter's 'participation' in or sympathy with his view or statement. Thus: *A to B too tasuto C ni narimasune* would be a reassuring remark or even a half question if pronounced with a rising intonation. Similarly: *Moojiki haruni naruyo.*

Again the rising intonation lacks that connotation of finality which is expressed by a fall in pitch. e.g. *Tabun.* 'Probably.' / *Iie.* 'No.'

We are capable of expressing a variety of implications in English merely by having rising intonations superimposed: e.g. *I'm not ˋdoing'anything.* (courteous refutation)/ *ˉIn a 'way.* (careful, deliberate statement) / *ˉThese things sometimes ˎhappen, you ˊknow.* (reassuring statement) / *You're ˉlooking for the ˎmoney, I sup'pose.* (doubtful statement).

Some of the above-mentioned examples may be changed to questions merely by the superimposition of a rising intonation. *Tarooga kita?* 'Taroo came?' / *Moosugu haruni naru?* 'Spring will come round soon?'/ *Tabun?* 'Did you say "probably"?' It appears that the formation of 'questions' by such means is often resorted to in various languages: e.g. Russian *vy student* (statement) and *vy student?* (question). I. C. Ward observes a similar phenomenon in the Yoruba language, too. Note that if the question is asked as a final alternative, one would not necessarily raise one's voice: e.g. 'Is it a banana?' 'No.' 'Is it a pear?' 'No.' *Dewa ringo (deshoo)?* ('Then, it's an apple, isn't it?')

The question particle *ka* is often used for interrogation in general and special questions, either with a rising or a falling intonation, but sometimes with different implications. In informal speech this *ka* is frequently dispensed with. Edwards's observation that interrogative sentences which do not contain interrogative words or *ka* are very rare is not true of the current usage. Compare the following examples: ('I can't tell a flatfish from a sole. Tell me . . .') *Korega hirame desuka?* (rise or sustained pitch) 'Is this a flatfish?' / ('Now I see the difference between a flatfish and a sole. So . . .') *Korega hirame desuka!* (fall) 'This is a flatfish, isn't it?' The English pattern *Is ˉthat ˊso?* is an ordinary question similar to *It ˊis?*, while *Is ˊthat ˎso?* would rarely be used for disagreement; it rather shows, almost invariably, astonishment but willingness to agree, as would *You ˊdon't ˎsay?* under the same circumstances. (The first example has a rise; the second falls.)

With reference to 'command–request' expressions, similar phenomena appear to be observable in Japanese and English intonation. The falling intonation would range from a frank informal request to even a brusque command; while the rising intonation would sound less informal, or would often afford a feeling of courteous request. However, too much 'appealingness' on the part of the speaker would work the other way round. It would then become too importunate a request, and would, in such an instance, sound hardly cordial. Try this on *Ohairinasai*. 'Please come in.' This may be pronounced with either a falling or a rising intonation.[2] It would seem

2. If the expression *Ohairinasai* is pronounced with a falling intonation, the 'fall' following the 'accented' element occurs between *sa* and *i*, and the final *i* carries the voice further down to the bottom (falling intonation). If a rising intonation is superimposed upon this identical expression, the voice glides up from *sa* to *i*, instead of rising from *i*, as might be expected. (This is an example of temporary tonal disturbance.) The reason may be that here *sai* is treated as a monosyllable. If *Ohairinasai* is an echo-question, we notice a fall between *sa* and *i* before the voice rises sentence-finally.

that a genuine command that calls for immediate obedience is invariably pronounced with a falling intonation. (A bark would hardly be accompanied by an appeasing tone!) Compare *Kaere* (or *Kaereyo*) 'Go back' or *Koi.* 'Come here'. (fall) with *Kiotsukete okaeri.* (Lit.) 'Be careful and go back' [May be said to a child on parting] (fall or, more often, rise). Similar usage appears to obtain in English expressions of this type. The present writer has elsewhere dealt in some detail with English patterns (Abe, 1954). To cite a few examples: ˉ*Give me the* ˋ*knife.*/ˉ*Think what you are* ˋ*saying.*/ ˉ*Don't be so par*ˋ*ticular.* (fall)//ˊ*Please bring me the* ˊ*water, Tom.*/ˉ*Do sit* ˊ*down.*/ ˉ*Don't trouble to* ˊ*answer it.* /ˉ*Don't* ˊ*worry.* (rise).

Finally a word about intonational patterns of exclamatory expressions. The term 'exclamatory' is vague and loosely defined; but here we merely follow the conventional classification. We limit ourselves to a citation of a few examples: *Nanto kiree-nandaroo!* 'How lovely!' /*Maa!* 'Oh dear!' (fall). It will be observed that the English expressions like the above end with a falling pitch, too.

We shall now pass to the final and non-final aspects of Japanese intonation.

In an unemphatic 'statement' the voice usually goes down to the bottom of the speaker's pitch range as he concludes the statement. However, there is a point that must be borne in mind here: e.g. ('What's started to fall?') *Ame.* 'Rain.'/ ('What do you like to eat?') *Ame.* 'Candy.' The first example offers no knotty problem, since the tone of *ame* (as we have observed) follows the direction of the falling intonation. In the second example, on the other hand, the tone of *ame* is the exact reverse of the falling intonation of finality. In Japanese it is not customary to terminate this 'rising' tone by superimposing upon it a too decided falling intonation. (Too much 'fallingness' would indeed cause the utterance to sound exceptionally emphatic.) Instrumentally, there is a slight down-glide immediately following the element *me*, but perceptually its fall is not conspicuous. So the impression is that of a sustained pitch, but this is different from the rise indicative of a rising intonation. Thus, 'ideologically', *ame* (candy) has a falling intonation despite the fact that this does not necessarily correspond to the expected low sentence-final fall.[3] In this particular respect, Japanese appears to resemble East Norwegian (see pp. 432–3).

In sentence-medial position either a high (or raised) pitch or a rising pitch, or a suspended level pitch might be employed to signal non-finality and/or attention. In impersonal, dispassionate speech – be it the type often heard in narrative reading style or in normal conversation – the latter

3. Likewise, the utterance *Soreo mimasu.* ('[I] see it.') would end in a suspended pitch (in a statement) if the final vowel *u* is not pronounced. But if this vowel happens to retain its full vowel quality, as in careful speech, we have the regular fall (low) on *u*.

device (i.e. suspended level pitch) appears to be more prevalent either as an ordinary 'suspensive' pattern or as a 'hesitation' contour. Unless some manneristic 'particles' of an emotional nature are used phrase-finally, a rising pattern is apparently not used in this position so frequently. *Mimashilaga kiniirimasendeshita.* 'I saw it, but I didn't like it.' / *Solonidete sampoo shimashitayo.* 'I went out, and took a walk.'

We have, of course, a rising or a raised pitch occurring sentence medially. This 'positive' intonational pattern contrasts with the 'negative' one just mentioned. In fact, this intonation is actually used when the speaker wishes particularly to call for the auditor's attention, or to imply that something is still to come, or even to indicate the location of emphasis. This pattern is typical of a pompous, oratorical style – a pattern by means of which the speaker usually endeavors to influence his audience. It is also suggestive of an 'advertising' voice. This positive intonation is particularly noteworthy in such a case as the following: *Arutokoroni onnanokoga sundeimashita.* (Lit.) 'Certain-place-at [rise] girl [rise] living-was' = 'There lived at a certain place a little girl.' This example may be matched with English *'Arthur 'stood and 'watched them 'hurry a`way.* This example is from Mrs Uldall's work. She says that rising unstressed syllables add surprise or interest to statements on the falling tune and calls the above intonation 'fairy-tale' intonation (Uldall, 1939). In English we see that either a suspended or a rising intonation occurs with slightly different implications. We even have a complete fall. For detailed accounts of this point see, for example, Pike's analysis of various contours (e.g. 2–4, 2–3, 2–3–2, 2–4–3) in American English (Pike, 1949).

We shall finally attempt to compare, in some details, the intonation of the so-called Special Questions in English (i.e. questions beginning with interrogative words such as *what, when, why, who,* etc.) and their (near) equivalents in Japanese. This would enable us to have a fairly good panoramic view of some of the typical Japanese intonational patterns and their implications.

First, there exists what might conveniently be termed a gradually falling intonation. This features normal questions of information-seeking type. *Itsu yukuno?* '`When are you `going?' / *Dokoni atta?* 'Where was that?'. It will be noticed that both Japanese and English employ a similar pattern on such occasions. Sweet remarks that 'questions which are begun with an interrogative word have the falling tone because they can be regarded as commands.' Elsewhere, he says: 'The brevity and imperativeness of special interrogative sentences such as *what is his name?* is often avoided by substituting a longer general interrogative form: *can you tell me what his name is?*' (Sweet, 1890, p. 32; 1922, pt 2, p. 39). This falling intonation is often quite perfunctory, and will be taken as such. It is interesting that similar patterns are employed in many other languages: e.g. *Waar, kind?* / *Quién ha venido?* / *Wann soll ich kommen?* / *Quel âge avez-vous?* / *Gde oni?*

If a slight rise, instead of a fall, is added to the utterance, it would impart an effect of curiosity or cordiality. Try this on the examples just given. And compare these with English ⁻*How's your 'mother?* / ⁻*What's the 'time?* where we note not infrequently a rising intonation. This rise would sound, depending upon the situation in which it is used, either pleading, wheedling, or even importunate. We often hear people say *Doo?* 'How do you like this?'/*Daare?* 'Who's this?' (May be said to a visitor at the door who cannot be identified).

A heightened tune is suggestive of intensified feelings – animation, anger, irony, exultation, and what not. Superimposed upon an interrogative word – upon the 'accented' element which is as often as not elongated to carry the intonation – such a raised or rising pitch gives, in consequence, what we might term a convex or 'surgy' intonation. *Na(a)nio miteirund-desu(ka)?* 'Whatever are you looking at?' / *Do(o)koni itteta?* 'Where on earth have you been?' / *Na(a)ze naiteiruno?* 'What on earth are you crying for?' Either a rising or a falling intonation may be added to these utterances sentence-finally. The general effect given is that of curiosity, the tail rise imparting a greater degree of that feeling. Cf. '*Who could `that 'be?*

If the interrogative word is pronounced with a rapid decrescendo of voice – that presupposes the existence of a high pitch and stress – and with a falling sentence-final intonation, a note of accusation would be introduced into the utterance. *Nandesuka!* 'What a thing to say!' / *Nanio mile-rundesu(ka)?* (Possible implication:) 'What are you looking at? Don't look off!' Mori remarks that *Nanio-suruka* may be uttered in a falling tone as a threat. I presume that *Nanio* will be heavily stressed. Referring to the example *Who wrote this* (where *Who* is high and *wrote this* is low), Bush observes that if an American speaks this way, he is expressing disapproval of whoever wrote it (Bush, 1952).

A conspicuous rise of pitch at the end would indicate that the speaker is surprised or is highly incredulous. Utterances upon which such an intonation is superimposed would range from a mere request for repetition of the preceding remark, either in its entirety or in part, to a kind of retort or challenge. In other words, this pattern is likely to become rhetorical in nature.

*Nanio watashiga shiteru?* 'What am I doing?' / *Nandatte?* 'What?' Compare (Hanako's coming.) *Dare?* 'Who?' (rise) ('Who did you say was coming?') with ('Somebody's coming.') *Dare(ga)?* (fall or possibly rise) = 'Tell me who this somebody is.' It appears that English usage corresponds roughly to ours.

We shall, by way of experiment, try some of these intonations on the utterance *Nanio yatteruno?* ('What you are doing?'). A gradual fall is a normal colorless question asking for a piece of information. A slight rise at the end would make this expression sound cordial – or it might mean that the speaker is curious. A 'gentle' convex intonation on *Nanio* or *Naanio* would turn the expression into an intensely curious question. The sentence-final intonation may be either falling or rising with a slight difference in the degree of interest shown by the speaker. Heavily stressed *na* plus a rapid glide down to the low pitch of *nio* and the sentence-final fall would suggest that the speaker has lost his temper. If a convex intonation (actually a raised pitch) is superimposed on the element -*ter*- (with the result that the peak in the group *yatteruno* is higher than the peak in the group *nanio*) the expression might be taken as a sarcastic comment on the behavior of the person addressed. Compare this last example with English *'What are you do`ing?* mentioned by Bolinger (1948).

The above observations are confined to a few typical expressions, and I conjecture that other intonational patterns – and consequently other interpretations – might be possible, too. I hope this brief sketch of mine is free from too subjective impressions. A more comprehensive investigation yet remains to be attempted of Japanese intonational patterns which are likely to sound UN-English. This brief sketch is a tentative attempt to verify to what extent intonations – that is, psychological pitch curves as they are usually called – may be declared international. And limited though this article is in scope, there would appear in many points rather striking similarities in the way intonation curves are employed in English and Japanese. (This gives a promising hint for our further studies.) This does not, of course, imply that parallel expressions in these languages would sound quite alike if actually pronounced. I don't think they would; details differ, and various other linguistic factors add to melodic composition as a whole. The present writer merely wishes to emphasize that the psychological channeling of voice in English and Japanese seems to have much in common – particularly with reference to such crucial points as 'question' and 'statement' tunes. And these, we presume, constitute the very kernel of human speech.

### References

ABE, I. (1954), 'Intonation of "request–command" expressions in English', *Bull. Phonetic Society of Japan*, no. 85.

ARISAKA, H. (1940), *The Theory of Phonology*.

BALLY, C. (1935), *Le Langage et la vie, Romanica Helvetica*, vol. 1, Zurich, M. Niehans.

BOLINGER, D. L. (1947), 'Comments on Pike's American English intonation', *Studies in Linguistics*, vol. 5, no. 3, pp. 69–78.

BOLINGER, D. L. (1948), 'Intonation of accosting questions', *English Studies*, vol. 29, no. 4, pp. 109–14.

BOLINGER, D. L. (1949), 'Intonation and analysis', *Word*, vol. 5, no. 3, pp. 248–54.

BUSH, H. C. (1952), 'Connotations of the stressed interrogatives in English', *The Rising Generation*, vol. 48, no. 2.

CHAO, Y. R. (1933), 'Tone and intonation in Chinese', *Bull. National Research Institute of History and Philosophy*.

GARDINER, A. H. (1932), *The Theory of Speech and Language*, Clarendon Press.

HATTORI, S. (1954), 'Japanese accent from a phonemic point of view', *Inquiries into the Japanese Language*, no. 2.

JIMBO, K. (1925), 'The word tone of the standard Japanese language', *Bull. School of Oriental Studies*, vol. 3, no. 4.

KURATH, H. (1930), 'A specimen of Ohio speech', *Curme Volume of Linguistic Studies*, Waverly Press.

MARTIN, S. E. (1952), 'Morphonemics of standard colloquial Japanese', *Language Supplement to Language Dissertation*, no. 97.

MIYATA, K. (1927), 'My view of Japanese accent', *Study of Sounds*, nos 1, 2 and 3.

PIKE, K. L. (1949), *The Intonation of American English*, University of Michigan Press, 2nd edn.

SWEET, H. (1890), *A Primer of Spoken English*, Clarendon Press.

SWEET, H. (1922), *A New English Grammar*, Clarendon Press.

TERAKAWA, K. (1945), *A Study of East-Asiatic Japanese*.

TOKIEDA, M. (1950), *The Theory of Japanese Philology*.

ULDALL, E. T. (1939), 'The Intonation of American English', unpublished thesis.

# 20 Kerstin Hadding and Michael Studdert-Kennedy

An Experimental Study of Some Intonation Contours

Kerstin Hadding and Michael Studdert-Kennedy, 'An experimental study of some intonation contours', *Phonetica*, vol. 11, 1964, pp. 175–85, published by S. Karger, Basel.

## Introduction

Questions[1] are often said to be distinguished from statements by a terminal rise in fundamental frequency ($f_o$) as against a terminal fall. However, questions may also be distinguished by a comparatively high $f_o$ throughout the utterance (Hermann, 1942). Spectrographic analyses of Swedish speech have shown that, in this language, questions tend to be spoken on a higher $f_o$ than statements, usually ending in a moderate rise (Hadding-Koch, 1961).

In the description we postulate four $f_o$ levels, numbered 1 (lowest) to 4 (highest).[2] Thus the sequence $3\ 42\uparrow^3$ represents the typical intonation curve of a Swedish question. The arrow at the end shows the direction of the terminal glide and the superscript following it indicates at what level the glide ends. The first of the three numbers stands for the precontour (the portion of the utterance before the stress); the second and third numbers, which are clustered together, stand for the stress – the level at which it begins and the level it reaches at the point where the terminal glide begins. Other examples: $2\ 32\uparrow^3$, a 'less interested' Swedish question; $2\ 31\downarrow$ or $2\ 21\downarrow$, typical statements.

Similarly, a typical American-English question is said to display a continuously rising contour that may be notated, for example, $2\ 23\uparrow$ or $2\ 23\uparrow^4$ (Pike, 1945; Bronstein, 1960). A typical American-English statement may be notated exactly as in Swedish, $2\ 31\downarrow$.

However, polite statements in Swedish, though spoken on a lower frequency level than questions, quite often end with a rise. In American English also, terminal rises are reported to occur in statements (Uldall,

---

1. 'Question' refers throughout to so-called Yes–No questions.

2. The acoustic correlates of intonation are said to be changes in one or more of three variables: fundamental frequency, intensity, duration, with fundamental frequency being the strongest single cue (Bolinger, 1958; Denes, 1959; Denes and Milton-Williams, 1962). The present study is concerned with only one of these variables, fundamental frequency, and the term 'intonation contour' refers to contours of fundamental frequency.

1962). In fact, Uldall, using synthetic speech, demonstrated that an utterance could have quite a large terminal rise and still be heard as a statement, if the rise was preceded by a high fall. If there was no pitch higher than the end point of the terminal rise, the utterance tended to be heard as a question.

These facts concerning both Swedish and American English suggest that not only the direction and range of the terminal glide, but the shape and level of the entire contour affect listeners' judgements (Gårding and Abramson, 1960; Hadding-Koch, 1961). The present experiment was designed to explore this notion in more detail by means of synthetic intonation contours, and to compare for Swedish and American listeners their preferred question and statement contours. In addition, as a partial check on the degree to which listeners could actually hear the detailed tonal movements involved, some purely psychophysical data were collected.

## Method

The utterance *För Jane* [foe ′Jein] = *for Jane*, spoken on a monotone and in such a way as to be acceptable as Swedish to Swedes, as American to Americans was recorded on magnetic tape. From this recording forty-two different fundamental frequency contours, simulating Swedish intonation, were prepared by a procedure described below. The $f_o$ values were based on detailed spectrographic analyses of a long sample of the Swedish speaker's natural speech. The correspondences between level notation and fundamental frequency derived from this analysis are given in Table 1.

Table 1 **Correspondences between level notation and fundamental frequency in hertz** (from Hadding-Koch, 1961)

| Level | Fundamental frequency in hertz |
|---|---|
| 4 | 370 and above |
| 3 | 260–370 |
| 2 | 175–260 |
| 1 | 175 and below |

As poles, a Swedish question contour, $2\ 42\uparrow^4$, and statement contour, $2\ 31\downarrow$, were used. In the present experiment the first number represents the level of the precontour on *För*, the second number the level of the intonation 'peak', the third number the level of the 'turning point' (Gårding, 1960) before the terminal glide. Between the poles of ideal question and statement, various $f_o$ values at peak, turning point and end point were introduced. Diagrams of the contours are reproduced above Figures 1 and 2. All contours started at a fundamental frequency of 250 Hz, sustained for 140 ms over *För*. They then rose to a peak of either 370 Hz (the *S*, or superhigh series of contours) or 310 Hz (the *H*, or high, series), dropped to one of three turning points: 130 Hz (*S1* and *H1* series), 175 Hz (*S2* and *H2* series), or 220 Hz (*S3* and *H3* series), and then proceeded to one of seven end points between 130 Hz and 370 Hz. The rise and fall on either side of the peak lasted for 300 ms, the terminal rise or fall, from turning point to end point, lasted 200 ms. The actual contours were rounded at peak and turning point rather than pointed as in the schematic contours above the figures.

The intonation was varied by means of the Intonator connected with the Vocoder at Haskins Laboratories, New York. The Vocoder first analyses a speech sample in a bank of filters and then reconstitutes it in simplified form on the basis of information obtained from the analysis (Dudley, 1939; Borst and Cooper, 1957). The fundamental frequency of the output is controlled by the Intonator, and may be varied independently of other characteristics of the speech sample. Thus, the same utterance may be given any desired number of different fundamental frequency patterns. Instructions to the Intonator are transmitted through photo-electric tubes responding to light reflected from a contour painted on an acetate loop. Also attached to the loop is a strip of adhesive magnetic tape bearing the speech sample to be processed. The loop is reeled past the photoelectric tubes of the Intonator and the magnetic input heads of the Vocoder. The outputs of the synthesizer in the present experiment were the forty-two stimuli previously described. These were recorded on magnetic tape and spliced into five different random orders, with a five-second interval between stimuli and a ten-second pause after every tenth stimulus. They were presented to twenty-five Swedish and twenty-four American undergraduates in two counterbalanced sessions. In each session all five test orders were presented with a short pause between orders. In one session subjects were instructed to indicate for each stimulus whether it would be better characterized as a statement or a question (semantic judgement). In another session subjects were instructed to indicate for each stimulus whether it ended with a rising or a falling pitch (psycho-physical judgement). Approximately half the subjects in each group (Swedish and American) made their psychophysical judgements first.

### Results

In the semantic test, responses varied as a function of the fundamental frequency at all three of the variable points of the contours: peak, turning point and end point.

two-category semantic judgements

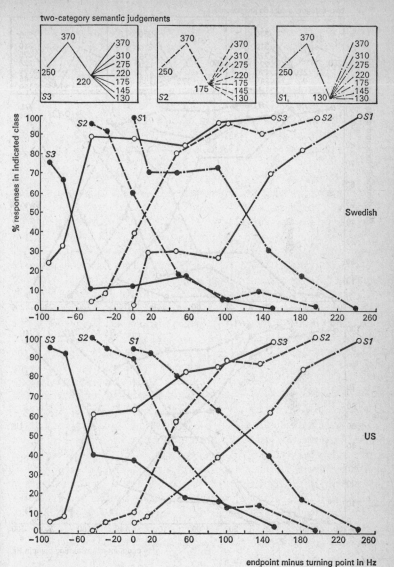

O question
● statement

Figure 1 Peak $f_o$ at 370 hertz: percentage of statement and question responses as a function of the terminal rise (positive) or fall (negative) in hertz of $f_o$ (endpoint $f_o$ minus turning point $f_o$). Parameters of the curves are turning point $f_o$: 130 Hz (S1), 175 Hz (S2) and 220 Hz (S3). The Swedish data are plotted above, the US data below.

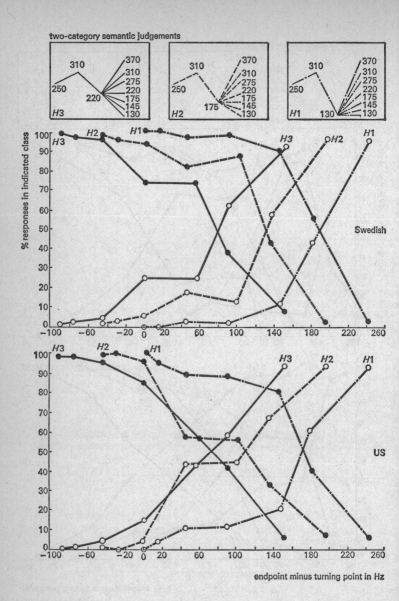

two-category semantic judgements

Figure 2 Peak $f_o$ at 310 hertz: percentage of statement and question responses as a function of the terminal rise (positive) or fall (negative) in Hz of $f_o$ (endpoint $f_o$ minus turning point $f_o$). Parameters of the curves are turning point $f_o$: 130 Hz (*H1*), 175 Hz (*H2*) and 220 Hz (*H3*). The Swedish data are plotted above, and US data below.

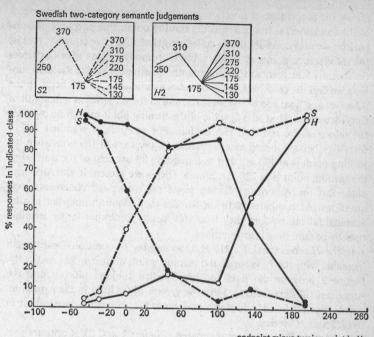

Swedish two-category semantic judgements

○ question
● statement

Figure 3 Percentage of statement and question responses as a function of the terminal rise (positive) or fall (negative) in hertz of $f_o$ for Swedish subjects. The curves for two values of peak $f_o$ [370 Hz ($S$) and 310 Hz ($H$)], with turning point $f_o$ constant at 175 hertz, are compared. The crosses indicate the points of subjective equality for the US subjects in the $S2$ (left) and $H2$ (right) series.

Figure 1 presents the semantic data for the Swedish subjects (above) and American subjects (below) on the $S$ series of contours (peak at 370 Hz). Against the ordinate are plotted the percentages of question and statement responses. Against the abscissa are plotted the values of the terminal rise or fall in hertz of fundamental frequency (end point minus turning point): a negative value indicates a terminal fall, a positive value a terminal rise. Parameters of the curves are peak $f_o$ (370 Hz) and turning point $f_o$ (130 Hz for $S1$, 175 Hz for $S2$, 220 Hz for $S3$).

The effect of the terminal rise or fall is immediately obvious and very much as expected: for all three series the higher the terminal rise, the higher the percentage of question responses. Equally obvious is the effect of the fundamental frequency at the turning point. For purposes of comparison we may consider the so-called points of subjective equality, that is, the indifference points at which subjects' responses cross over from predominantly statements to predominantly questions. For the Swedish subjects we find the crossover in the $S1$ series at a final rise of 120 hertz, in the $S2$ series at a final rise of twelve hertz, and in the $S3$ series at a final fall of sixty-five hertz. Thus, the $f_o$ value of the turning point may quite override the effect of the terminal rise or fall. For example, a terminal fall of forty-five hertz is heard as a statement 96 per cent of the time when the turning point is at 175 Hz, but as a question 89 per cent of the time when the turning point is at 220 Hz. Similar effects are present in the American data. But the Americans display some preference for statements over questions. As compared with the Swedes they require somewhat smaller terminal falls to be sure they hear statements, somewhat larger terminal rises to be sure they hear questions.

In the $H$ series (peak $f_o$: 310 Hz) the number of questions heard again increases with the $f_o$ value at the turning point, although less markedly. Figure 2 presents the data for the Swedish subjects (above) and the American subjects (below). Here the groups differ little in their question curves. But the Swedes display a preference for statements, particularly in the $H2$ and $H3$ series.

If the $S$ and $H$ series are compared (Figures 1 and 2), it appears that more questions are heard in the $S$ series and more statements in the $H$ series. In other words, a rise in $f_o$ at the peak – exactly as a rise in $f_o$ at the turning point – is accompanied by an increase in the number of questions heard. Figure 3 facilitates this comparison by displaying the Swedish data for the $S2$ and $H3$ series on the same axes. For example, a stimulus with a final rise of 100 hertz is heard as a question 96 per cent of the time when the peak is at 370 Hz ($S$), but as a statement 89 per cent of the time when the peak is at 310 Hz ($H$). In other words, the lowered peak overrides the effects of a substantial final rise, and induces a virtual reversal of the response distributions.

Turning, finally, to the results of the psychophysical tests, in which subjects were asked to indicate whether the contours ended with a rising or a falling pitch, we find greater subject uncertainty but the same general effects as have been described for the semantic tests. Figure 4 compares the American psychophysical and semantic data for the $H1$ series of contours: the two sets of data are nearly identical. Contours identified as statements tend to be heard as having a terminal fall (even when, in fact, the final contour is rising), while contours identified as questions tend to be heard as having a terminal rise. On other series, the agreement is not always so

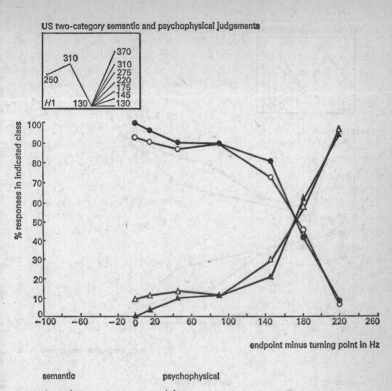

Figure 4 Percentage of statement and question responses (semantic: solid circle or triangle) and of rise and fall responses (psychophysical: empty circle or triangle) as a function of terminal rise (positive) or fall (negative) in hertz of $f_o$. Data from US subjects on the $H1$ stimulus series.

marked. For example, Figure 5 displays the American psychophysical and semantic data from the $S3$ series. Here, as is generally true, the psychophysical judgements are more uncertain than the semantic – particularly for the contours displaying terminal falls. None the less, there is still remarkable agreement between the two sets of curves.

## Discussion

The results confirm what naturalistic observation and some previous experiments have already suggested: that listeners may make use of the entire $f_o$ contour in identifying questions and statements. Not only terminal rise

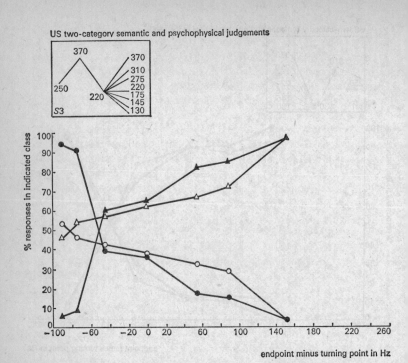

Figure 5 Percentage of statement and question responses (semantic: solid circle or triangle) and of rise and fall responses (psychophysical: empty circle or triangle) as a function of terminal rise (positive) or fall (negative) in hertz of $f_o$. Data from US subjects on the S3 stimulus series.

or fall, but also preceding peak and turning point are relevant. These three variables interact in a manner that cannot be easily described. But, in general, for a given $f_o$ at the other two points, an increase in $f_o$ at the third point leads to an increase in the number of questions heard.

As to the actual $f_o$ values preferred by listeners for the question and statement contours, the Swedish results agree with the predictions based on spectrographic analysis. The contours yielding the greatest proportion of question responses (S3) had a peak at 370 Hz and a turning point at 220 Hz. This contour yielded a high proportion of question responses even when there was a moderate terminal fall. But the preferred question contour was

2 42 plus a final rise. Similarly, the contours yielding the greatest proportion of statements (*H1*) had a peak at 310 Hz and a turning point at 130 Hz. Here, a large proportion of statement responses occurred even when there was a considerable terminal rise (cf. Introduction). But the preferred statement contour was 2 31. Since the turning point $f_o$ (130 Hz) was the lowest $f_o$ in the experiment, no final fall could occur with the *H1* contour.

As was stated earlier, Swedish and American English are said to have similar typical statement contours, but different typical question contours. As to questions, the data of the present experiment do not contradict this. For, although both groups selected a typical Swedish question (*S3*, 2 42↑) as their preferred question contour, the Americans did require a higher terminal rise to reach complete agreement on their question responses than the Swedes: lacking the typical continuously rising question of American English (2 23↑), they gave more weight to the terminal glides than did the Swedes. However, they also gave more weight to the terminal glides in the preferred statement series (*H1*). This suggests that the two groups may differ in their preferred statement as well as in their preferred question contours.

Finally, the psychophysical data perhaps throw some light on the process by which the $f_o$ values at peak and turning point exert their influence on listeners' semantic judgements. These data show that listeners were unable to follow the terminal glide with anything like the precision that might have been predicted from simple pure tone pitch discrimination (Stevens and Davis, 1938): psychophysical judgements were influenced by peak and turning point $f_o$ very much as semantic judgements. In so far as semantic and psychophysical judgements agree (as in Figure 4), it would seem that listeners may have been using the *perceived* direction of the terminal glide rather than its physically measured direction to make their semantic decisions. The role of peak and turning point $f_o$ would then seem to lie in their effect on the perception of the terminal glide. On the other hand, in so far as the psychophysical data display greater uncertainty than the semantic (as in Figure 5), the peak and turning point $f_o$ values would seem to exert an independent influence on the semantic judgement, presumably in some weighted combination with the perceived terminal glide.[3]

3. A follow-up of the experiments reported here appears as 'Further experimental studies of fundamental frequency contours', in *Status Report on Speech Research*, Haskins Laboratories, New York, 1965.

*References*

BOLINGER, D. L. (1958), 'A theory of pitch accent in English', *Word*, vol. 14, pp. 109–49.
BORST, J. M., and COOPER, F. S. (1957), 'Speech research devices based on a channel vocoder (abstract)', *J. Acoust. Soc. Amer.*, vol. 29, p. 777.

Bronstein, A. J. (1960), *The Pronunciation of American English: An Introduction to Phonetics*, Appleton-Century-Crofts.

Denes, P. (1959), 'A preliminary investigation of certain aspects of intonation', *Language and Speech*, vol. 2, pp. 106–22.

Denes, P., and Milton-Williams, J. (1962), 'Further studies in intonation', *Language and Speech*, vol. 5, pp. 1–14.

Dudley, H. (1939), 'Remaking speech', *J. Acoust. Soc. Amer.*, vol. 11, pp. 169–75.

Gårding, E. (1960), 'A study of the perception of some American English intonation contours', Paper read before 75th Meeting Mod. Lang. Ass. Amer., Philadelphia, 28 December.

Gårding, E., and Abramson, A. S. (1960), 'A study of the perception of some American English intonation contours', Haskins Labs. Quarterly Progress Report no. 34, New York, June.

Hadding-Koch, K. (1961), *Acoustico-Phonetic Studies in the Intonation of Southern Swedish*, Gleerups, Lund.

Hermann, E. (1942), *Probleme der Frage*, Nachrichten von der Akademie der Wissenschaften in Göttingen, vol. 3–4.

Pike, K. L. (1945), *The Intonation of American English*, University of Michigan Press.

Stevens, S. S., and Davis, H. (1938), *Hearing, its Psychology and Physiology*, Wiley.

Uldall, E. T. (1960), 'Attitudinal meanings conveyed by intonation contours', *Language and Speech*, vol. 3, pp. 223–34.

Uldall, E. T. (1962), 'Ambiguity: question or statement? or "Are you asking me or telling me?",' Proc. IV Int. Congr. Phon. Sciences, pp. 779–83, Mouton.

# 21 Marguerite Chapallaz

## Notes on the Intonation of Questions in Italian

Marguerite Chapallaz, 'Notes on the intonation of questions in Italian', from
*In Honour of Daniel Jones*, edited by David Abercrombie, D. B. Fry, P. A. D.
MacCarthy, N. C. Scott and J. L. M. Trim. Longman, 1964, pp. 306–12.

Short interrogative sentences have the intonation of one or other of two
basic intonation patterns of Italian, viz. the falling and the falling–rising,
referred to respectively as Basic Pattern 1 (BP 1) and Basic Pattern 2 (BP 2).

### Basic pattern 1

This is similar to Tune 1 of English described by Armstrong and Ward
(1950, pp. 4, 19–20),[1] except that the last stressed syllable has only a very
slight fall of pitch to a low level. If unstressed syllables, or a short group
of a parenthetical nature follow, these syllables are on a low level pitch.
Any initial unstressed syllables form an ascending scale going up to the
first stressed syllable.

BP 1 is the most usual pattern for X-questions, that is, questions
beginning with a specific interrogative word, in their simplest form; as, for
instance in:

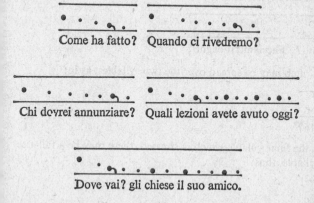

Come ha fatto?  Quando ci rivedremo?

Chi dovrei annunziare?  Quali lezioni avete avuto oggi?

Dove vai? gli chiese il suo amico.

1. Tune 1 is defined: 'The stressed syllables form a descending scale. Within the last
stressed syllable the pitch of the voice falls to a low level' (p. 4).

## Basic pattern 2

Similarly, Italian BP 2 is like English Tune 2 described by Armstrong and Ward.[2] It is the common pattern for Yes–No questions, that is, for questions expecting the answer 'Yes' or 'No', as in the questions:

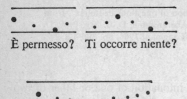

È permesso?   Ti occorre niente?

Non ti andava il lavoro?

There is, however, a great deal of variety in the treatment of the final part of a BP 2 question group especially when the final word has penultimate stress. I have noted the following examples:

1. The last stressed syllable may be on low level pitch with a rise of pitch in the following unstressed syllable, as in:

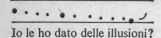

Io le ho dato delle illusioni?

2. There may be a fall of pitch in the last stressed syllable and a rise in the following unstressed syllable, as in:

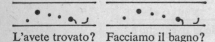

L'avete trovato?   Facciamo il bagno?

3. The rise in pitch may be spread over the two syllables, as in:

Ho indovinato?

4. When it is the final syllable which is stressed, there may be a fall–rise within that syllable, thus:

Va bene così?

2. Defined: 'The outline of [Tune 1] is followed until the last stressed syllable ... This is on a low note, and any syllables that follow, rise from this point' (p. 20).

5. A high pitch for the final syllable in the group creates the impression of heightened curiosity. Thus:

La proviamo?  Pensi di potei giocare?

A parenthetical group following a BP 2 question, as for instance in reported speech, often has a BP 1 intonation, but with a narrower pitch range than that of the main group. An example is:

Sei contento? disse la mamma.

**Longer groups**

In the gradually descending scale of syllables in a long BP 1 or BP 2 question, one, or sometimes more than one stressed syllable, is pronounced higher than the preceding syllable, the descent continuing after this raised syllable as before. There is thus a break in the gradual descent, the raised syllable forming a 'peak'. (In the text of the examples below an arrow shows the raised syllable.)

A che dis↑tanza è Londra? chiese.

È questo lo spor↑tello per i telegrammi?

Io la↑devo intervistare?

**X-questions with basic pattern 2**

Where an answer is courteously requested rather than insisted upon, an X-question is commonly spoken with BP 2, as in these examples:

Quando potete farlo?  Da che paese viene?

## Yes–no questions with basic pattern 1

Italian has no special grammatical written forms corresponding to *est-ce que* or to the inversion of the subject in French, nor to the anomalous finites[3] in question forms in English; so that a yes–no question must be spoken with BP 2 or it will have the intonation as well as the grammatical form of a statement.

The following examples with BP 2 are yes–no questions:

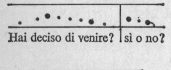

Non è vero?    Io la ↑devo intervistare?

With BP 1 the same examples are turned into statements, thus:

Non è vero    Io la ↑devo intervistare.

Under certain circumstances, however, yes–no questions can be heard spoken with BP 1. This is when either the context is sufficient to indicate that the group is an interrogative one, or a short phrase or 'tag' preceding or following the main group gives the clue. Examples:

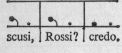

Hai deciso di venire? | sì o no?

scusi, | Rossi? | credo.

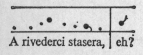

A rivederci stasera, | eh?

## Alternative questions

Basic Pattern 2 is general for alternative questions, as in the examples below, but if these are spoken in a more peremptory manner then BP 1 may be heard.

3. The forms *do, did,* as in *He went, Did he go?*

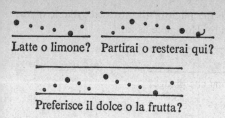

Latte o limone?  Partirai o resterai qui?

Preferisce il dolce o la frutta?

## A common modification in BP 1 and BP 2

Some degree of liveliness and interest is added to a question if there is a wide pitch interval between the last stressed syllable and the syllable which precedes it and which is at the same time higher than any other syllable in the group. Thus:

Che cos' è?    Dove vai?

L'ha portata tu?

## Emphatic intonation

Apart from the modifications to BP 1 and BP 2 already mentioned in the preceding notes and which add a certain degree of liveliness or interest, ways of giving extra emphasis to questions resemble those used in English. To illustrate this I conclude with a few examples of:

1. *Emphasis for intensity* where the pitch range is widened and the stressed syllables are pronounced with increased stress. (In the text the marks " show intensity stress and ″ contrast stress.) Thus:

Che "cosa me ne im"porta

"Cosa in"tendi "dire?

"C'era qual"cuno?

2. *Emphasis for contrast,* where the pitch of the stressed syllable of the contrast word falls from a high to a low note as in:

"Che "gridi?        È la "donna che piange?

Ma "Lei sarebbe il giornalista lo"cale,    vero?

*Reference*

ARMSTRONG, L. E., and WARD, I. C. (1950), *A Handbook of English Intonation,* Cambridge University Press.

# Part Seven
## Perturbations

The study of intonation is complicated by the fact that many things
which happen when we speak cause changes in pitch that may be
accidental or at least unrelated to intonation. For example, when we
'intend' a particular intonation level are there nevertheless irregular
ups and downs associated with individual vowels and consonants?
In the first Reading, Lehiste and Peterson demonstrate that such
perturbations not only occur but are rather highly predictable.
Vowels differ in their tendencies to raise or lower pitch, and so do
consonants. A further question that always comes up when the
melody of speech is compared with the melody of song is how exact
the parallel is. Two specific answers are given here on whether exact
intervals are used, as in music, and, if not, whether all speakers at least
make jumps in pitch of approximately the same size when they
produce an intonation pattern. (The reader unaccustomed to phonetic
terms may find it helpful to remember that 'syllable nucleus' is, in
effect, the vowel, or diphthong, contained in a syllable.)

In the second Reading we find the reverse of the perturbations noted
in the Lehiste–Peterson study. There it was the interference of vowels
(and consonants) with intonation. Here it is the interference of
intonation with vowels. If intonation is a melodic line, how is it
possible to tell one contour from another – a question from a
statement, for example – when someone whispers? If there is no voice,
there is no fundamental pitch and no melody. Nevertheless listeners
can detect intonation contours in whispered speech, and apparently do
so by cues unconsciously supplied by the whisperer, which include
certain distortions of the vowel sounds. Meyer-Eppler's study deals
with German, but the same phenomenon can be observed in English.

The sharpest clash of all occurs when the pitch of the voice is
required to convey distinctive tone as well as intonation. Tone
languages use contrasting levels or movements of pitch as part of the
structure of syllables, just as they use consonant and vowel sounds for
the same purpose: the two syllables /ba/ and /ma/ are different by

reason of their consonants; the two syllables /bá/ and /bà/ differ by reason of the pitch of the vowel, the first high and the second low – and this serves as well as anything else to distinguish one word from another. But when languages using pitch in this way also find it necessary to add another layer of pitch to show moods and attitudes (as most if not all do), certain adjustments are necessary. The best known of all tone languages is Chinese, because of its long cultural history. In her study of the Chengtu dialect, the third Reading in this section, Nien-Chuang T. Chang shows first the interaction among the tones themselves – the changes or 'tone sandhi' that occur when two or more are combined – and then the changes, now referred to as 'perturbations', that occur on just one syllable, the final one, to distinguish what is essentially a rising tune from a falling one.

Languages that distinguish words from one another by differences in tone are not all outside the Indo-European family that includes English. Some, notably the languages of Scandinavia, are part of that family and indeed closely related to English. It has been debated whether Norwegian, for example, should be called a 'tone language', defining the latter as a language in which each syllable is assigned a distinctive tone. With such a rigorous definition, the Scandinavian languages do not qualify. Nevertheless the 'accents' of Swedish and Norwegian have an inner distinction that is directly tied to pitch. The same question therefore comes up again, as with Chinese: how are tone and intonation adjusted to each other? In the fourth Reading, Haugen and Joos describe the differences in pitch that set one accent off from the other in East Norwegian, and the differences of placement that affect the domains of tone and intonation.

# 22 Ilse Lehiste and Gordon E. Peterson

## Some Basic Considerations in the Analysis of Intonation

Ilse Lehiste and Gordon E. Peterson, 'Some basic considerations in the analysis of intonation', *Journal of the Acoustical Society of America*, vol. 33, no. 4, April 1961, pp. 419–25.

## Introduction

In most languages, the fundamental frequency of the voice has a distinctive function. In so-called 'tone languages', pitch level or movement may contribute to lexical and morphological distinctions. In languages where pitch has no such function, levels or contours of pitch may in part determine the meaning of the message in which the contour appears. Some analyses of English postulate suprasegmental morphemes, consisting of pitches and terminal junctures, with differential meaning (Trager and Smith, 1957, pp. 41–52, 65–77). According to two widely accepted analyses, American English has a system of four intonation levels (Pike, 1945; Wells, 1945). Both of these systems were formulated without the benefit of instrumental analysis. The present paper represents an attempt to analyse acoustically one intonation contour in American English, and to determine some of the factors that influence the phonetic realization of the intonation contour.

## Material and method

The material analysed consists of two sets of utterances, a large set of 1263 utterances by one speaker, and a smaller set of 350 utterances by five speakers (see Peterson and Lehiste, 1960, for further details on this corpus). It is assumed that a reasonable correspondence between the two sets of data indicates that the larger set may be considered representative, even though every item included in the larger set was not actually compared with data from several different speakers. The sets consist of the frame 'Say the word ... again.' Primary stress and a change from highest to lowest intonation level occurred on the word that was in the commutation position. The speaker for the large corpus used 1263 CNC words[1] with the frame; the five speakers of the control group all read an identical set of

---

1. The term 'CNC word' refers to monosyllabic words consisting of an initial consonant phoneme, one of the fifteen stressed syllable nuclei of American English, and a final consonant phoneme. Both the consonant phonemes and the syllable nuclei may be phonetically complex. The set of 1263 words is described in more detail by Lehiste and Peterson (1959a).

seventy words in the same frame. All speakers used approximately the same stress and pitch pattern.

Various acoustic analyses were made of the recorded data; the measurements most relevant for the present paper were from four-inch narrow-band spectrograms. The fundamental frequency could be determined from these spectrograms with an accuracy of approximately $\pm 1$ Hz.[2]

## Intrinsic fundamental frequency

The average fundamental frequency that was associated with each stressed syllable nucleus was computed for both sets of data. The results appear in Table 1 and Figure 1. The fundamental frequency measures for the speaker of the CNC list are appreciably higher than those for the male speakers of the Peterson and Barney data. This is probably the result of the fact that

**Table 1 Average fundamental frequency associated with syllable nuclei**

| SN | Average for five speakers | GEP | Peterson–Barney |
|----|---------------------------|-----|-----------------|
| i | 129 | 183 | 136 |
| ɪ | 130 | 173 | 135 |
| eᴵ | 130 | 169 | |
| ɛ | 127 | 166 | 130 |
| æ | 125 | 162 | 127 |
| ə | 127 | 164 | 130 |
| ɑ | 120 | 163 | 124 |
| ɔ | 116 | 165 | 129 |
| oᵁ | 122 | 170 | |
| ʊ | 133 | 171 | 137 |
| u | 134 | 182 | 141 |
| ɑᵁ | 119 | 159 | |
| ɑɪ | 124 | 160 | |
| ɔɪ | 123 | 163 | |
| ɝ | 130 | 170 | 133 |

2. The fundamental frequency was derived by measuring the center frequency of selected higher harmonics on a four-inch narrow-band spectrogram; the measured frequency was divided by the order number of the respective harmonic to obtain the fundamental frequency. Usually, both the tenth and the twentieth harmonics were measured. On these spectrograms 0·1 inch represents about 88 Hz, and the individual harmonics are appreciably narrower. Calibration tones and repeated measurements show the accuracy to be within $\pm 20$ Hz, and in the region of the twentieth harmonic this represents an accuracy of $\pm 1$ Hz. Rapid cycle-to-cycle fluctuations in fundamental frequency are smoothed by the analysing filter, of course, and are not represented in such measurements.

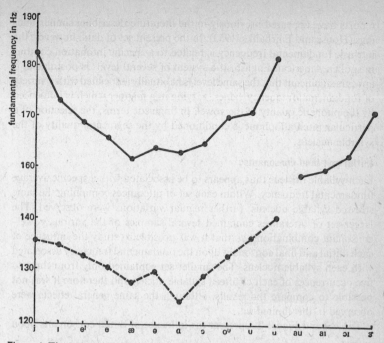

Figure 1 The points connected by the solid lines represent the average fundamental frequencies, arranged according to syllable nuclei, that occurred at the peak of the intonation contour in the 1263 CNC words uttered by GEP; the points connected by the dashed lines represent average values from Peterson and Barney (1952)

the measurements presented in Figure 1 were taken at the peak of the intonation contour, and that the speaker employed a relatively wide range of fundamental voice frequency. A different intonation pattern was associated with the utterances measured in the course of the Peterson–Barney study. It will be noted further from both Table 1 and Figure 1 that for any given speaker an intrinsic fundamental frequency is associated with each vowel. The two curves of Figure 1 resemble an acoustical vowel diagram, in which /i/ and /u/ are associated with the highest intrinsic fundamental voice frequencies, the open vowels (in articulatory terms) are associated with the lowest fundamental frequencies, and the central vowels (such as /ə/ and /ɝ/) occur approximately in the middle of the frequency range. With the dipthongs, the peak of the intonation contour occurred on the first element, and the fundamental frequency associated with it was similar to that occurring on /ɑ/ and /ɔ/. This is not a new observation;

Ilse Lehiste and Gordon E. Peterson  369

reports have appeared previously in the literature describing similar findings (House and Fairbanks, 1953). In the present set of data, however, the intrinsic fundamental frequency is related to a specific intonation contour in spoken American English. If a system of several levels is postulated, it appears significant that the same level is habitually associated with a variety of fundamental frequency values, varying in a manner which is influenced by the phonetic quality of the vowel. In linguistic terms, the selection of a particular pitch allophone is conditioned by the segmental quality of the syllable nucleus.

## Initial and final consonants

Each syllable nucleus thus appears to be associated with a specific average fundamental frequency. Within each set of utterances containing the same stressed syllable nucleus, further regular variations were observed. The larger set of utterances contained several samples of the various vowel–consonant combinations, so that it was possible to study the influence of each initial and final consonant upon the fundamental frequency associated with each syllable nucleus. The smaller set contained only from three to five occurrences of each of fifteen syllable nuclei, and therefore it was not possible to compare the results, although the same general effects were observed in this limited set.

Table 2 and Figure 2 represent the influence of initial consonants upon

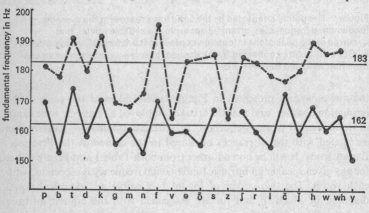

initial consonants

Figure 2 The fundamental frequency is of two vowels from the CNC set uttered by GEP, presented as a function of the initial consonant. The points connected by the dashed line represent the values associated with /i/; the points connected by the solid line represent the respective values for /æ/. The top straight line shows the average for all occurrences of /i/; the bottom straight line presents the average value of /æ/

Table 2 Fundamental frequency of the peak of the intonation contour, in Hz, as influenced by the initial consonant of the test word

| Syllable nucleus: | i | ɪ | eᴵ | ɜ | æ | e | ɑ | ɔ | oᵘ | ʊ | u | ʊə | ɪə | ɪc | ɜ |
|---|---|---|---|---|---|---|---|---|---|---|---|---|---|---|---|
| **Average peak:** | 183 | 173 | 169 | 166 | 162 | 164 | 163 | 165 | 170 | 171 | 182 | 159 | 160 | 163 | 170 |
| **Preceding consonant** | | | | | | | | | | | | | | | |
| p | 182 | 176 | 180 | 174 | 170 | 169 | 166 | 175 | 181 | 178 | 198 | 168 | 166 | 175 | 173 |
| b | 178 | 165 | 161 | 163 | 153 | 159 | 164 | 161 | 164 | 173 | 178 | 160 | 160 | 160 | 169 |
| t | 191 | 180 | 175 | 170 | 175 | 169 | 175 | 171 | 173 | 170 | 194 | 165 | 169 | 170 | 180 |
| d | 180 | 167 | 166 | 158 | 158 | 157 | 160 | 158 | 166 |  | 190 | 148 | 157 |  | 164 |
| k | 192 | 176 | 178 | 175 | 171 | 173 | 172 | 175 | 176 | 178 | 196 | 168 | 178 | 170 | 164 |
| g | 170 | 172 | 167 | 163 | 156 | 166 | 159 | 159 | 170 | 160 | 196 | 152 | 152 | 145 | 174 |
| m | 169 | 168 | 158 | 164 | 161 | 156 | 153 | 162 | 163 | 175 | 160 | 163 | 163 | 165 | 167 |
| n | 173 | 164 | 164 | 163 | 153 | 151 | 156 | 164 | 163 | 160 | 173 | 130 | 158 | 145 | 156 |
| f | 196 | 181 | 170 | 173 | 171 | 169 | 170 | 172 | 171 | 175 | 173 | 163 | 165 | 165 | 169 |
| v | 165 | 165 | 154 |  | 160 | 165 | 173 | 173 | 158 | 165 | 178 | 160 | 150 | 165 | 165 |
| θ | 184 | 177 | 170 | 156 | 160 | 150 | 160 | 173 | 155 |  | 183 | 148 | 160 |  | 158 |
| ð | 185 | 170 |  | 173 | 168 | 175 | 168 | 168 | 175 | 155 | 190 |  | 165 | 165 | 180 |
| s | 165 | 177 | 175 | 165 | 167 | 171 | 156 | 156 | 175 | 165 | 185 | 148 | 164 | 150 | 170 |
| z | 185 |  | 173 | 159 | 160 | 162 | 152 | 160 | 168 | 180 | 181 | 158 | 160 | 185 | 175 |
| ʃ | 183 | 180 | 173 | 165 | 155 | 157 | 173 | 166 | 164 | 165 | 173 | 155 | 164 | 150 | 170 |
| r | 179 | 167 | 168 | 179 | 173 | 173 | 160 | 165 | 178 |  | 188 | 145 | 170 |  | 158 |
| l | 177 | 174 | 161 | 164 | 159 | 162 | 164 | 171 | 174 | 165 | 172 | 173 | 164 | 130 | 173 |
| tʃ | 180 | 185 | 185 | 172 | 168 | 170 | 149 | 158 | 170 | 165 | 189 |  | 160 |  | 158 |
| dʒ | 190 | 169 | 163 | 151 | 160 | 168 | 158 |  | 174 |  | 180 |  | 159 |  | 173 |
| h | 186 | 182 | 182 | 176 | 165 | 170 | 152 | 158 | 170 |  | 172 |  | 160 |  | 169 |
| w | 187 | 176 | 171 | 164 | 160 | 168 | 149 | 158 | 170 | 165 | 185 |  | 159 |  | 170 |
| wh |  | 174 | 180 | 169 | 165 |  | 158 |  |  |  |  |  | 172 |  | 170 |
| y | 175 | 170 | 170 | 166 | 150 | 145 | 152 | 145 | 170 | 170 | 185 | 173 |  |  |  |

the fundamental frequency associated with syllable nuclei. The table presents the average fundamental frequency for all occurrences of the syllable nucleus preceded by each of the consonants listed.[3] Figure 2 presents two curves, showing the fundamental frequency of two vowels /i/ and /æ/ as a function of the initial consonant; these two vowels have the highest and the lowest intrinsic fundamental frequencies respectively in this set of data. The straight lines in Figure 2 represent the average fundamental frequencies for /i/ and /æ/, computed for 105 occurrences of /i/ and 131 occurrences for /æ/. In general, higher fundamental frequencies occur after a voiceless consonant and considerably lower fundamental frequencies occur after a voiced consonant. This distinction is accompanied by a different distribution of the fundamental frequency movement over the test word: after a voiceless consonant, and particularly after a voiceless fricative, the highest peak occurs immediately after the consonant; whereas after a voiced consonant, especially a voiced resonant, the fundamental frequency rises slowly, and the peak occurs approximately in the middle of the test word.[4]

In these data, the final consonants have no such regular influence on the preceding syllable nuclei. Table 3 presents average values associated with each final consonant and syllable nucleus; Figure 3 shows the same material graphically for the two vowels /i/ and /æ/. As in Figure 2, the straight lines represent the average fundamental frequencies for /i/ and /æ/, computed for 105 occurrences of /i/ and 131 occurrences for /æ/. It appears that the distance of the points from the straight lines is related to the number of occurrences of a particular syllable-nucleus, final-consonant sequence. The greater the number of occurrences, the closer is the value for a particular final consonant to the average value, and thus the smaller the distance of the point from the line representing the average value. The position of points representing single occurrences of a particular sequence may be influenced by the initial consonant, and may fall anywhere within the limits of fluctuation possible for a given syllable nucleus. It seems probable that in English the voiceless–voiced contrast of the final consonant has no significant influence on the fundamental frequency appearing on a preceding syllable nucleus. The two instances of greatest divergence from the average are the values associated with the sequences /ig/ and /iʒ/. Both points represent only one word each, *league*

3. The number of occurrences from which the value for each entry was computed may be found from the distribution charts of initial and final consonants and syllable nuclei in the CNC words. Lehiste and Peterson, (1959b).

4. This effect has been described in more detail elsewhere (Peterson and Lehiste, 1960).

Table 3 Fundamental frequency of the peak of the intonation contour, in Hz, as influenced by the final consonant of the test word

| Syllable nucleus: | i | ɪ | eᴵ | ɛ | æ | e | ɒ | ɔ | oᵁ | ᵁ | u | aᵁ | ɪɒ | ɔɪ | ɜ |
|---|---|---|---|---|---|---|---|---|---|---|---|---|---|---|---|
| Average peak: | 183 | 173 | 169 | 166 | 162 | 164 | 163 | 165 | 170 | 171 | 182 | 159 | 160 | 163 | 170 |
| Following consonant | | | | | | | | | | | | | | | |
| p | 191 | 179 | 173 | 169 | 164 | 176 | 167 | 165 | 177 | 180 | 183 | | 154 | 163 | 175 |
| b | | 166 | | 170 | 165 | 167 | 161 | 155 | 160 | | 188 | | 165 | | 165 |
| t | 185 | 172 | 166 | 163 | 163 | 164 | 160 | 168 | 164 | 162 | 184 | 157 | 164 | | 172 |
| d | 180 | 172 | 168 | 167 | 163 | 165 | 160 | 153 | 168 | 167 | 178 | 160 | 165 | 160 | 168 |
| k | 174 | 177 | 177 | 163 | 165 | 166 | 160 | 167 | 171 | 172 | 175 | | 168 | | 172 |
| g | 160 | 173 | 160 | 171 | 160 | 162 | 165 | 157 | 159 | | | | | | 170 |
| m | 185 | 171 | 169 | 157 | 160 | 164 | 172 | 161 | 167 | | 183 | | 159 | | 163 |
| n | 181 | 176 | 167 | 169 | 165 | 168 | 163 | 162 | 165 | | 178 | 145 | 162 | 150 | 169 |
| ŋ | | 171 | | | 166 | 159 | | | | | | | | | |
| f | 181 | 170 | 175 | 154 | 166 | 163 | | 165 | 170 | | 182 | 160 | 160 | 180 | 175 |
| v | 184 | 182 | 168 | | 165 | 162 | | 170 | 169 | | 180 | 156 | 156 | | 171 |
| θ | 187 | 173 | 160 | 167 | 160 | 155 | | 151 | 165 | | 184 | 170 | | | 172 |
| ð | 182 | 175 | 168 | | | | | | 170 | | 185 | | 156 | | |
| s | 184 | 172 | 176 | 164 | 156 | 163 | 160 | 163 | 174 | 180 | 176 | 161 | 160 | 175 | 172 |
| z | 184 | 193 | 168 | | 153 | 155 | 158 | 164 | 174 | | 179 | 160 | 160 | 160 | 160 |
| ʃ | 190 | 178 | | 165 | 161 | 157 | | 145 | | 173 | | | | | |
| ʒ | 165 | | 155 | | | | | | | | 175 | | | | |
| r | | 173 | 153 | 170 | | | 166 | 169 | 169 | 174 | 172 | 165 | 156 | | 174 |
| l | 181 | 170 | 169 | 161 | 165 | 165 | 165 | 170 | 175 | 170 | 194 | 158 | 160 | 165 | |
| tʃ | 181 | 175 | | 175 | 167 | 172 | 153 | | 175 | | 205 | 167 | | | 178 |
| j | 180 | 173 | 173 | 173 | 162 | 170 | 170 | | 170 | | | 160 | | | 158 |

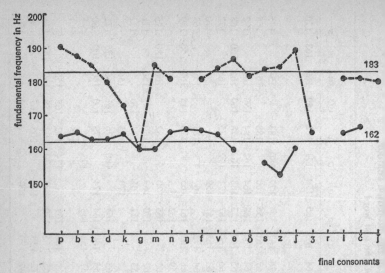

Figure 3 The fundamental frequencies for /i/ (dashed curve) and /æ/ (solid curve) for GEP as a function of the final consonant of the CNC sequence. The top straight line shows the average for all occurrences of /i/; the bottom straight line presents the average value of /æ/.

and *liege*, and it is likely that the initial /l/ has caused the low fundamental frequency on both words.

Table 4 and Figure 4 present the combined data for GEP for all initial and final consonants and all syllable nuclei. The solid curve presents the average values for all syllable nuclei associated with an initial consonant, and the dashed curve shows the corresponding fundamental frequencies associated with each final consonant phoneme. The straight line represents the average fundamental frequency that occurred at the peak of the intonation contour in all 1263 utterances. It appears that the initial consonant influences the frequency associated with the syllable nucleus, and that voiceless initial consonants are associated with a higher fundamental frequency than are voiced initial consonants.

### Test-word intonation contours

The foregoing analysis has shown that the phonetic quality of the syllable nucleus is one of the factors that determine the fundamental frequency at which the peak intonation level is realized. The next consideration is whether the lower level at which the downward movement terminates in a given CNC word also depends upon the phonetic quality of the syllable

Table 4 Influence of initial and final consonants on the fundamental voice frequency at the peak of the intonation contour in CNC words

| Consonant | Average for all vowels after initial consonant | Average for all vowels before final consonant |
|---|---|---|
| p | 175 | 174 |
| b | 165 | 166 |
| t | 176 | 168 |
| d | 163 | 168 |
| k | 176 | 170 |
| g | 163 | 164 |
| m | 162 | 168 |
| n | 161 | 167 |
| ŋ | | 165 |
| f | 173 | 169 |
| v | 155 | 169 |
| θ | 173 | 170 |
| ð | 161 | 171 |
| s | 175 | 169 |
| z | 169 | 171 |
| ʃ | 173 | 163 |
| ʒ | | 165 |
| r | 166 | 168 |
| l | 164 | 169 |
| č | 177 | 174 |
| ǰ | 161 | 168 |
| h | 174 | |
| w | 167 | |
| wh | 174 | |
| y | 164 | |
| Average | 169 | 169 |

nucleus. If the lower intonation level shows fluctuations similar to those of the peak, the further implication should be considered that the movement from one intonation level to the next may involve a fixed ratio of frequencies, possibly corresponding to some musical interval. If this holds true, it is necessary to investigate whether different speakers use the same intervals when producing the same intonation contour.

The fundamental frequency on the final part of the test word, as well as the fundamental frequencies associated with the precontour 'say the word' and with the final word in the sentence, 'again', were measured for both sets of data. Table 5 presents these data for GEP, and Table 6 for the five

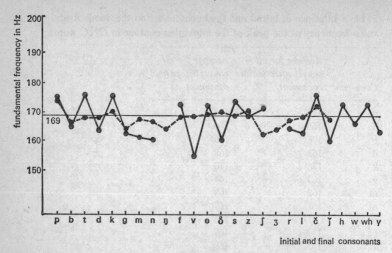

Figure 4 Average peak values of all fifteen syllable nuclei as functions of initial and final consonants. The averages were computed from the 1263 CNC words recorded by GEP. The solid curve represents the influence of the initial consonant on the combined average of the syllable nuclei, the dashed curve the influence of the final consonant. The straight line represents the average for all syllable nuclei in the total set

speakers of the smaller set of utterances. The first and second columns in these tables indicate the syllable nuclei and the number of occurrences of each in the two sets of material. The third column presents the average fundamental frequency of the first part of the frame sentence, 'say the word'. The following two columns show the average values of the peak that occurred during the test word, and the average values of the frequency at the end of the test word. The last three columns present three measurements taken during the final word of the frame, 'again'; the measurements present the fundamental frequency that occurred on the unstressed first syllable, on the highest peak of the stressed second syllable, and at the end of the utterance. It appears that there is no significant connection between the average fundamental frequency of the peak, as determined by the phonetic value of the syllable nucleus, and the fundamental frequency pattern of the rest of the contour. The average values for the lower intonation levels on the test words show only negligible fluctuations. This indicates that no fixed ratios of frequencies are involved. As may be seen from Table 7, the interval range differs considerably with each speaker. The same intonation contour was habitually pronounced by one speaker with a downward movement in frequency with a frequency ratio between a

Table 5 Average fundamental frequencies at specified points within the sentences uttered by GEP

| SN | Number of occurrences | Fundamental frequency | | | | | |
| | | Precontour ('word') End | Test word | | End of frame ('again') | | |
| | | | Peak | End | Beg. | Peak | End |
| --- | --- | --- | --- | --- | --- | --- | --- |
| i | 105 | 129 | 183 | 94 | 115 | 132 | 87 |
| ɪ | 141 | 126 | 173 | 98 | 114 | 131 | 87 |
| eᴵ | 119 | 130 | 169 | 98 | 116 | 131 | 91 |
| ɛ | 94 | 129 | 166 | 95 | 115 | 132 | 88 |
| æ | 131 | 126 | 162 | 92 | 112 | 130 | 87 |
| ə | 109 | 124 | 164 | 98 | 111 | 128 | 85 |
| ɑ | 75 | 127 | 163 | 93 | 113 | 128 | 88 |
| ɔ | 79 | 125 | 165 | 92 | 111 | 130 | 84 |
| oᵁ | 93 | 126 | 170 | 93 | 113 | 130 | 84 |
| ʊ | 28 | 125 | 171 | 91 | 109 | 127 | 81 |
| u | 74 | 127 | 182 | 94 | 113 | 133 | 87 |
| ɑᵁ | 35 | 127 | 159 | 93 | 113 | 127 | 86 |
| ɑɪ | 93 | 125 | 160 | 91 | 111 | 129 | 85 |
| ɔɪ | 16 | 128 | 163 | 93 | 111 | 129 | 84 |
| ɝ | 71 | 126 | 171 | 94 | 113 | 131 | 85 |
| Average | | 127 | 169 | 94 | 113 | 130 | 86 |
| Total | 1263 | | | | | | |

major third and a pure fourth, whereas the speaker with the greatest voice inflection used a downward movement in frequency approximately equivalent to a major seventh. It may perhaps be concluded that the actual interval range is irrelevant in this intonation contour.

Table 7 also contains statistical information about the percentage of musically 'pure' intervals used by the different speakers.[5] The calculation is based on comparing the frequency ratios used by the different speakers with the ratios of successive harmonics of a complex tone. Several factors make this part of the table tentative. The accuracy of measurement is approximately $\pm 1$ Hz. This limitation of measurement accuracy affects the ratio in a different manner, depending on the ranges in which the measurements are taken. Little is known, however, about the fluctuation

5. For the purposes of this study, a musically 'pure' interval was defined as the difference between two fundamental frequencies that can be expressed as a simple numerical ratio: 2/1 for an octave, 3/2 for a pure fifth, 4/3 for a pure fourth, 5/4 for a major third, 6/5 for a minor third, etc. We considered an intonation pattern to represent a 'pure' interval when the ratio between the two frequency values did not differ from that of a 'pure' interval by more than 1/100.

Table 6 Average fundamental frequencies at specified points within
the sentences uttered by five speakers

| SN | Number of occurrences | Precontour ('word') End | Fundamental frequency | | | | |
| | | | Test word | | End of frame ('again') | | |
| | | | Peak | End | Beg. | Peak | End |
|---|---|---|---|---|---|---|---|
| i | 25 | 102 | 129 | 90 | 92 | 100 | 77 |
| ɪ | 20 | 104 | 130 | 91 | 93 | 99 | 78 |
| eᴵ | 20 | 102 | 130 | 87 | 92 | 97 | 78 |
| ɛ | 20 | 105 | 127 | 91 | 95 | 101 | 81 |
| æ | 20 | 103 | 125 | 87 | 92 | 98 | 78 |
| ə | 20 | 105 | 127 | 90 | 92 | 99 | 77 |
| ɑ | 25 | 104 | 120 | 89 | 90 | 100 | 80 |
| ɔ | 20 | 100 | 116 | 83 | 90 | 96 | 77 |
| oᵁ | 20 | 104 | 122 | 88 | 90 | 96 | 78 |
| ʊ | 15 | 101 | 133 | 90 | 96 | 97 | 78 |
| u | 20 | 103 | 134 | 88 | 93 | 97 | 77 |
| ɑʊ | 20 | 103 | 119 | 84 | 91 | 98 | 79 |
| ɑɪ | 20 | 101 | 124 | 85 | 89 | 96 | 79 |
| ɔɪ | 15 | 103 | 123 | 88 | 89 | 96 | 77 |
| ɜˑ | 20 | 104 | 130 | 86 | 92 | 96 | 78 |
| Average | | 103 | 126 | 88 | 92 | 98 | 78 |
| Total | 300 | | | | | | |

Table 7 Fundamental frequency ratios on the test words
expressed as musical intervals

| Speaker | Average frequency ratio on test word | Corresponding musical interval | Percentage of 'pure' intervals (3,4,5,6,8) |
|---|---|---|---|
| Bi | 136/83 | 1·64 m6-M6 | 25 |
| Br | 126/99 | 1·27 M3-P4 | 27 |
| Ch | 120/82 | 1·46 D5-P5 | 22 |
| He | 136/97 | 1·40 P4-D5 | 30 |
| Re | 113/78 | 1·45 D5-P5 | 32 |
| GEP (total set) | 169/94 | 1·79 m7-M7 | 14 |
| GEP /i/ | 183/94 | 1·95 M7-P8 | 14 |
| GEP /æ/ | 162/92 | 1·76 m7-M7 | 14 |

in fundamental frequency within which a listener may identify a pitch movement with a specific musical interval, particularly when this interval occurs in speech. It is at least a possibility that the fluctuation in fundamental frequency due to vowel quality has no corresponding effect on the perception of the pitch interval.

### Word and frame contours

In the spectrographic analysis, the test word and the final word of the frame, 'again', were always included. This often did not leave room for the complete frame preceding the test word, but a selected set of analyses showed that the contour preceding the frame was approximately level for the various informants. Thus, only the average fundamental frequency on the part of the precontour immediately preceding the test word (i.e. on 'word') appears in column 3 of Tables 5 and 6. Both perceptually and physically (in terms of Hz) the precontour appears to form a middle intonation level compared to the highest and lowest levels that were observed on the test word. Since the segmental structure of the part of the utterance on which this middle intonation level occurred remained identical for all utterances, the data provide some information about the range of variations within one phonemic intonation level, unconditioned by differences in phonetic quality.

Table 8 shows that the syllable nucleus of the following test word has

Table 8 **Fundamental frequency ranges for 'word' in utterances preceding syllable nuclei /i/ and /ɑ/**

| Fundamental frequency ranges for 'word' in Hz | Number of occurrences of 'word' preceding SN | |
|---|---|---|
| | i | ɑ |
| 106–110 | | 3 |
| 111–115 | 2 | 6 |
| 116–120 | 17 | 12 |
| 121–125 | 33 | 20 |
| 126–130 | 37 | 16 |
| 131–135 | 7 | 11 |
| 136–140 | 8 | 7 |
| 141–145 | 1 | |

no essential influence on the fundamental frequency used on the last word of the precontour. The table presents the number of instances in which the fundamental frequency on 'word' fell within a particular frequency range preceding test words containing the syllable nuclei /i/ and /ɑ/. The frequency ranges are approximately the same for the fundamental frequency on 'word' preceding 105 occurrences of test words containing /i/ and 75 occurrences of test words containing /ɑ/ as syllable nucleus. Since the intrinsic fundamental frequency on /i/ is appreciably higher than that on /ɑ/, the rise in frequency from the precontour to the peak of the intonation contour is correspondingly different. The fundamental frequency on words with /i/ rises approximately 55 Hz from the end of the precontour, but only 36 Hz from the end of the precontour for /ɑ/. Table 9 shows the number of instances in which the rise in fundamental frequency from the

Table 9 Ranges of the rise of fundamental frequency from the end of the precontour to the peak occurring on syllable nuclei /i/ and /ɑ/

| Difference between precontour and peak of SN in Hz | Number of occurrences of SN | |
|---|---|---|
| | i | ɑ |
| 11–15 | | 2 |
| 16–20 | | 1 |
| 21–25 | | 8 |
| 26–30 | 2 | 12 |
| 31–35 | 2 | 20 |
| 36–40 | 8 | 16 |
| 41–45 | 11 | 9 |
| 46–50 | 20 | 5 |
| 51–55 | 20 | 1 |
| 56–60 | 17 | 1 |
| 61–65 | 18 | |
| 66–70 | 3 | |
| 71–75 | 3 | |
| 76–80 | 1 | |

end of the precontour to the peak of the test word fell within a particular range. Since the values on the precontour remained relatively constant, a greater rise was associated with /i/ than /ɑ/.

The actual value reached by the syllable nucleus depends partly on the initial consonant, as has been shown. Considerable overlap between the ranges of fundamental frequency for the different vowels may be expected; for example, the fundamental frequency of a vowel with high intrinsic fundamental frequency occurring in a word beginning with a consonant that has a lowering influence may overlap that of a vowel with a low intrinsic fundamental frequency preceded by a consonant that has a raising influence. Table 10 presents both the ranges for /i/ and /ɑ/ and the area of overlap between the two.

**Table 10 Fundamental frequency ranges for test words containing syllable nuclei /i/ and /ā/**

| Fundamental frequency ranges for test word in Hz | Number of occurrences of SN | |
|---|---|---|
| | i | ɑ |
| 136–140 | | 3 |
| 141–145 | | 5 |
| 146–150 | 1 | 3 |
| 151–155 | 1 | 8 |
| 156–160 | 2 | 19 |
| 161–165 | 8 | 10 |
| 166–170 | 8 | 14 |
| 171–175 | 10 | 7 |
| 176–180 | 20 | 5 |
| 181–185 | 17 | 1 |
| 186–190 | 24 | |
| 191–195 | 6 | |
| 196–200 | 4 | |
| 201–205 | 3 | |
| 206–210 | | |
| 211–215 | 1 | |

In addition, the fundamental frequency occurring on a syllable nucleus may vary over a certain range in successive repetitions of the same word. Table 11 shows the percentage of instances in which the fundamental fre-

**Table 11 Percentages of instances in which the fundamental frequencies associated with the 1263 utterances of 'word' fell within various ranges**

| Fundamental frequency ranges in Hz | Percentage of occurrences |
|---|---|
| 105–110 | 2·6 |
| 111–115 | 4·2 |
| 116–120 | 21·2 |
| 121–125 | 25·1 |
| 126–130 | 30·5 |
| 131–135 | 9·2 |
| 136–140 | 6·6 |
| 141–145 | 0·6 |

quency on the 1263 occurrences of 'word' at the end of the precontour fell within a specified frequency range. Approximately 75 per cent of all occurrences were between 116 and 130 Hz, but the total range was from 105 to 145 Hz.

The contour applied to the last word in the frame is, in a sense, a smaller-scale repetition of the sequence of three levels that appeared on 'Say the word . . .' Here, too, we found three levels; from the point of view of the item 'again' alone, these might be described as a sequence of middle, high and low intonation levels. However, the actual values that appeared as a manifestation of these three levels differed considerably from those appearing on the first part of the contour. For GEP the *high* level on 'again' was consistently slightly higher than the *middle* level of the first part, but was very considerably lower than the *high* of the first part of the contour ('Say the word . . .'). For the five speakers of the smaller set, the *high* of the sequence of intonation levels on 'again' was lower than the *middle* of the first part of the contour. The *low* of 'again' was noticeably lower than the *low* that occurred on the test word. The drop from *high* to *low* in the contour on 'again' was always smaller than the comparable drop on the test word; expressed in musical intervals, the average drop was approximately equal to a pure fifth (v. a major seventh) for GEP and equal to a major third (v. a diminished fifth) for the five speakers. The physical data do not suggest any immediate technique for identifying the levels as they appeared on the word 'again' with any of the levels that occurred on the first part of the contour preceding the word 'again'.

We considered the hypothesis that the pitch peak on the word 'again' might be conditioned by the presence of secondary stress at the beginning of the second syllable, and that the intonation pattern on 'again' might thus involve only a sequence of *middle* intonation level followed by *low* intonation level. In the case of GEP this appears plausible, as the average value of the fundamental frequency of the peak that appeared on 'again' was slightly higher than that occurring on the precontour. In the case of the five speakers, however, this hypothesis appears untenable. The peak on 'again' is lower than the level used on the precontour; there were actually a considerable number of instances where the fundamental frequency on the word 'again' was consistently falling, so that the frequency on the syllable with secondary stress was lower than the frequency on the unstressed first syllable. In Table 6, it may be seen that the average difference between the values that were measured on the unstressed and stressed syllables may differ by as little as 1 Hz (when 'again' followed words with the syllable nucleus /ʊ/), with a maximum average difference of 10 Hz (on 'again' following /ɑ/). The difference between the averages on the unstressed and stressed syllables in 'again' is approximately 6 Hz, which may be compared with the differences that occurred on different repetitions of the last word in the precontour, where the differences between the averages amounted to a maximum of 5 Hz. In all instances, however, subjective listening made it possible to identify the stress on the second syllable of 'again'. It appears from the analysis of this part of the intonation contour that differences in stress are not necessarily represented by conditioned differences in the phonetic realization of intonation levels.

## Conclusion

The investigation reported in this paper indicates a number of problems involved in the instrumental analysis of intonation. A linguistically significant intonation level may have a wide range of phonetic manifestations. Some factors that influence the selection of a particular pitch allophone have been described. It appears that the phonetic quality of the syllabic sound has an influence on the fundamental frequency at which the intonation level is produced. Further, the initial consonant in a consonant–vowel sequence may influence the fundamental frequency appearing on the vowel following the consonant. The variations in fundamental frequency, however, that may occur when the same intonation level is repeatedly produced on the same word, may be greater than the variations associated with changes in segmental quality; the differences can only be established when a sufficient number of utterances are compared. The influence of stress upon the manifestation of a particular intonation level needs to be explored more fully; the data reported here suggest that, at least in some instances, lower fundamental frequency may occur on a stressed syllable than on a preceding unstressed syllable. The problem of relating contourlike movements to musical intervals seems to be less relevant for a study of English than for a study of tone languages; it appears from our data that the intonation contours of American English are not based on recurring musical intervals. Most of the data presented illustrate the realization of a single intonation level occurring under sentence-maximum stress; the question of contrastive intonation levels and their relation to contrastive degrees of stress remains to be considered. The instrumental analysis of intonation emerges as a problem of great complexity.

## References

HOUSE, A. S., and FAIRBANKS, G. (1953), 'The influence of consonant environment upon the secondary acoustical characteristics of vowels', *J. Acoust. Soc. Amer.*, vol. 25, pp. 105–13.

LEHISTE, I., and PETERSON, G. E. (1959a), 'Linguistic considerations in the study of speech intelligibility', *J. Acoust. Soc. Amer.*, vol. 31, pp. 280–86.

LEHISTE, I., and PETERSON, G. E. (1959b), Speech Laboratory Report No. 3, University of Michigan.

PETERSON. G. E., and BARNEY, H. L. (1952), 'Control methods used in a study of the vowels', *J. Acoust. Soc. Amer.*, vol. 24, pp. 175–84.

PETERSON, G. E., and LEHISTE, I. (1960), 'Duration of syllable nuclei in English', *J. Acoust. Soc. Amer.*, vol. 32, pp. 693–703.

PIKE, K. L. (1945), *The Intonation of American English*, University of Michigan Press.

TRAGER, G. L., and SMITH, H. L., Jr (1957), *An Outline of English Structure*, *Studies in Linguistics:* Occasional papers no. 3, American Council of Learned Societies, Washington D.C.

WELLS, R. S. (1945), 'The pitch phonemes of English', *Language*, vol. 21, pp. 27–39.

# 23 Werner Meyer-Eppler

Realization of Prosodic Features in Whispered Speech

Werner Meyer-Eppler, 'Realization of prosodic features in whispered speech',
*Journal of the Acoustical Society of America*, vol. 29, no. 1, 1957, pp. 104–6.

### Author's summary

Experiments utilizing a visible-speech analyser showed that changes of pitch in normal (voiced) speech are replaced in whispered speech by shifts of some formant regions accompanied by added noise between the higher formants.

### Introduction

It is a well-known fact that people can be understood without any difficulty when they whisper instead of speaking normally. This fact is not very strange if the formant frequencies of the vowels and the envelopes and spectra of the fricative and plosive sounds are considered to be the information-carrying elements of speech. It must be doubtful, however, whether full information can be carried by whispered speech in tonal languages like Chinese or many West-African languages where pitch is used to differentiate the meaning of various lexical items consisting of otherwise identical groups of phons.

Recently, Panconcelli-Calzia (1955) and Giet (1950) have dealt with the problem of whispering in tone languages. Whereas Panconcelli-Calzia found that it was difficult for Chinese-born subjects to understand whispered Chinese, Giet, who had lived in China for many years as a missionary, states that whispering in Chinese is as effective a means of verbal communication as normally spoken speech. According to Giet's arguments (1956) there must exist some substitute for the missing pitch quality in whispered speech within the acoustical range. As Giet has already pointed out, there is no need to use tone languages for investigating substitutes in whispered speech. Similar results would be achieved by using any language where intonation belongs not to the *phonemic* but to the *prosodic* level, which term refers to features belonging to a sentence as a whole that are expressed by pitch and stress patterns. Intonation e.g. may differentiate between a question and a statement.

## Vowels 'sung' without voice

Some orienting investigations were undertaken with German vowels 'sung' without voice. It is not difficult to produce the same whispered vowel on different pitch levels within a range of about a musical fifth (i.e. a frequency ratio of 2:3). Obviously this can only be done by changing the spectral structure of the vowels within the limits of recognizability. The subjects were asked to 'sing' the first five tones of a diatonic scale (e.g.: *c*, *d*, *e*, *f* and *g*) maintaining the quality of a given vowel as well as possible. The sounds were recorded on magnetic tape and analysed by means of a visible-speech analyser (Sona-Graph). The spectrograms of a test series using the German vowels [a] (as in *Tal*), [e] (as in *See*), [i] (as in *viel*), [o] (as in *Sohn*), and [u] (as in *Schuh*) are shown in Figure 1. Whereas in the case of [a], [e], [i] and [o] the position of the first two formants remains unchanged, the third formant of [a] is shifted from its position near 2·5 kc to about 3 kc if higher pitch is intended; a similar shift is found at a weak fifth formant near 5 kc. In the case of [u] the main formant itself is raised from 600 Hz to 700 Hz. This can be seen more easily in Figure 2

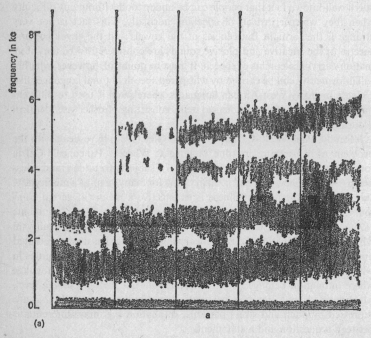

(a)

Figure 1 German vowels, whispered in a diatonic scale

where an enlarged frequency scale together with better spectral resolution is used. The spectrogram of Figure 2 was achieved by playing back the magnetic tape upon which the vowels had been recorded at a higher than normal speed. The higher formants of [u], however, remain unaffected (Figure 1). Since in the case of [e], [i] and [o] no very clear shift of formant positions can be observed, the apparent change of pitch must be caused by other spectral properties. Pike already had supposed that differences in intensity might serve as substitute for pitch (Pike, 1948, p. 34), and his expectation is confirmed by the spectrograms of Figure 1. Raising the 'pitch' of [e], [i] and [o] means increasing their intensity, thus filling the gaps in the higher spectral regions with noisy components and eventually broadening the formants above 2 kc to a less-sharply profiled, fricative-like spectrum. The same happens with [a] and [u] in addition to the shift

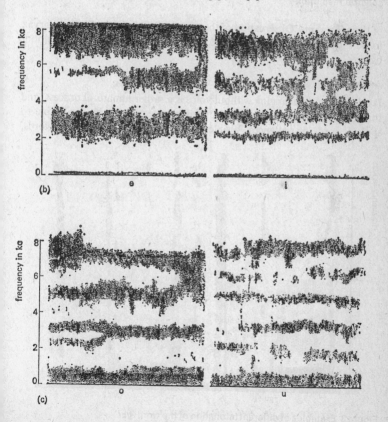

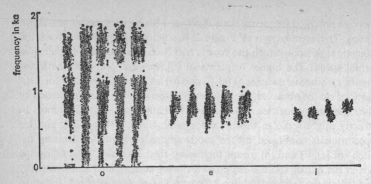

Figure 2 Three vowels of Figure 1 with enlarged frequency scale and improved spectral resolution

of their formants. Observation of the 'singing' subjects reveals their larynx to be raised at the 'higher' vowels, indicating a narrowing of the glottal fissure.

### Analysis of spoken sentences

It might seem that singing without voice is a rather unnatural process, and that results obtained in this case need not necessarily be applicable to spoken words or sentences. Visible-speech diagrams of whispered words,

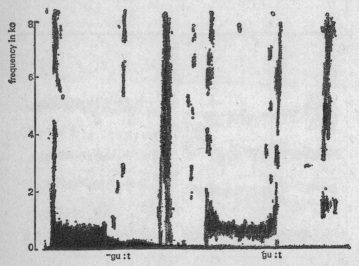

Figure 3 Examples of different intonation of the word 'gut'

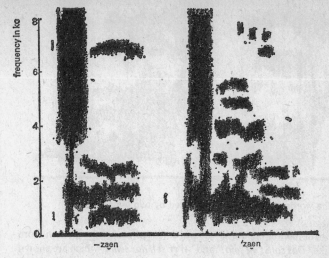

Figure 4 The whispered words '...*sein*!' and '...*sein*?'

however, show that the same effects as with sung vowels occur. Since [u] is an exceptionally good vowel for investigating the influence of intonation, sentences like '*Das ist aber nicht gut*' and '*Ist das etwa nicht gut?*' were whispered by different speakers and analysed. Figure 3 gives an example of the word '*gut*' spoken with the level tone (-) and with rising tone ('). In the latter case the shift of the formant of [u] towards the likewise raised formant region of [t] is very impressive.

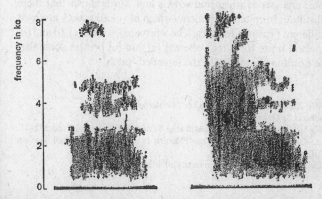

Figure 5 The words '*ja*?' and '*ja*!' whispered by two male subjects

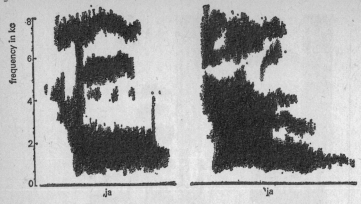

Figure 5 The words 'ja?' and 'ja!' whispered by two male subjects

A new phenomenon occurs in the words [-zaen] and ['zaen], taken from sentences like '*Das sollst du sein!*' and '*Wer soll das sein?*' which are shown in Figure 4. The interrogative intonation causes a new formant to originate at 2 kc belonging to the considerably reinforced [n], whereas the diphthong [ae] shows no clear differences.

Figure 5 was chosen to give an impression of the reliability of our conclusions concerning the shift of formant positions. The same pair of words having different intonations ('*ja?*' and '*ja!*'), as spoken by two male subjects, shows, despite the unequal length of the individual vowels, the same type of evolution of the third formant.

### Summary

Spectrographic analysis of whispered vowels and words shows that there exist two substitutes for pitch movements which in voiced speech are used to indicate different prosodic features. The whispered vowels [e], [i] and [o] substitute spectral noise for pitch, whereas [a] and [u] possess some formants whose position changes with the intended 'pitch'.

### References

GIET, F. (1950), *Zur Tonität nordchinesischer Mundarten*, Verlag der Missiondruckerei St Gabriel, Vienna.

GIET, F. (1956), 'Kann mann in einer Tronsprache flüstern?', *Lingua*, vol. 5, pp. 372–81.

PANCONCELLI-CALZIA, G. (1955), 'Das Flüstern in seiner physio-pathologischen Bedeutung', *Lingua*, vol. 4, pp. 369–78.

PIKE, K. L. (1948), *Tone Languages*, University of Michigan Press.

# 24 Nien-Chuang T. Chang

## Tones and Intonation in the Chengtu Dialect (Szechuan, China)[1]

Nien-Chuang T. Chang, 'Tones and intonation in the Chengtu dialect (Szechuan, China)', *Phonetica*, vol. 2, nos. 1/2, 1958, pp. 59–84.

### Notes on the transcriptions

p, t, k, ts, tʃ = aspirated

b, d, g, dz, dʒ = unaspirated p, t, k, ts and tʃ respectively

ʃ, ʒ, tʃ, dʒ before i and y = prepalatal

n before i = ɲ

r = əʳ when syllabic; when it is after ʃ, ʒ, tʃ, dʒ, it is a fricative with strong
    friction

i = ɪ in ai and ei, otherwise = i

e = e˕ in ei

  = ɛ in ien and yen, otherwise = e

a = a˕ in au, ai and when before n

  = ɑ when before ŋ or when final

o = o˕ when before ŋ

  = ɔ when final

u = ʊ in au and əu, otherwise = u

ə = ə– in əu

  = ʌ when before ŋ, otherwise = ə

The quality of vowels varies to some extent with the tones; opener varieties are generally used with the second, third and fourth tones.

### Introduction

In the Chinese language there are many dialects. Each dialect has its separate set of tones. In order to make a careful study of tones and intonation I chose to work on the Chengtu dialect of Szechuan, this being the

1. Author's note: This is the summary of a Ph.D. dissertation entitled 'A descriptive study of the tones in the Chengtu dialects (Szechuan, China) and the intonation of certain types of sentences' presented to the University of Edinburgh. A large number of examples as well as the sonograms, kymograms and graphs plotted from their tracings have been omitted, and the discussion has been shortened. This study I took up at the suggestion of Mr David Abercrombie, Head of the Department of Phonetics, University of Edinburgh, and throughout my research I received invaluable advice from him and Mrs Elizabeth Uldall, which I here gratefully acknowledge. I wish also to thank

dialect I was brought up on. It is also the mother tongue of the informant, my father, who was born and brought up in Chengtu. He speaks no other dialects.

In this study I am trying to find out (1) whether intonation exists in the Chengtu dialect; (2) if it does exist what then becomes of the individual tone, which is one of the basic elements in the word; (3) whether the individual tone always remains exactly the same no matter if it is spoken in isolation or in succession, i.e. whether the tone changes if it follows or is followed by the same or another tone; (4) if it does change when spoken in succession, if it no longer retains the value which it has when pronounced by itself, then what the change is like.

In Part I of this study I shall deal with tones, in answer to questions (3) and (4). In Part II I shall study their relationship to intonation, trying to answer questions (1) and (2). In studying intonation I first recorded eight hours of conversation with my father. From the recordings I picked out sentences whose intonation could be grouped under various emotional states or attitudes. With the help of a swanee whistle and a tape-repeater I noted down the intonation. Finally I checked the results on the spectrograph. In observing the tones and their changes, I first wrote down words of one syllable, and then phrases containing two or three syllables in all the possible combinations of tones. They were read aloud and the tones noted down. The results were then checked on the kymograph and the spectrograph.

## Part 1 Tones and their changes

When a Chinese character is read aloud the sound produced consists of not only the consonants and the vowels but also a tone. This tone, which is used in reading aloud a character in isolation, may be called the Naming Tone (NT), since it is the tone by which that character is known. It is used when the character is uttered by itself, not in conjunction with other characters.

But for a character occurring in a phrase or a sentence the naming tone is often replaced by another tone. The naming tone and those which take its place are allotones of one toneme. This replacement of one tone by another, i.e. the interchange of allotones, is called perturbation or tone-sandhi in this study.

Each tone has its Shape or Feature. This consists of two elements, pitch and course. By 'pitch' I mean whether the tone is high or low or mid. By 'course' I mean whether it rises or falls or remains level. The pitch dis-

Professor Y. R. Chao of the University of California, who gave me many important suggestions through correspondence and private conversations. Without the cooperation of my father this study would not have been possible.)

cussed here is relative and not absolute. It is relative in the sense that every individual has his or her range of voice.

*Monosyllables*

If we divide the pitch of an individual's voice-range into (1) high, (2) mid-high, (3) mid, (4) mid-low and (5) low, the four naming tones in the Chengtu dialect may be described as follows:

**1.** Tone I, high-rising – – – it starts between mid-high and mid and rises to high, e.g. [tʃin] ˧ (clear).

**2.** Tone II, low-falling – – – it starts somewhere lower than mid and ends between mid-low and low, e.g. [tʃin] ˩ (fine, when referring to weather).

**3.** Tone III, high-falling – – – it starts about mid-high and falls to somewhere a little higher than low, e.g. [tʃin] ˥ (to invite).

**4.** Tone IV, low-falling-rising – – – it starts about mid-low and falls to low and then rises ending at about mid or higher, e.g. [tʃin] ˧ (to celebrate). Often the fall reaches so low a point that the voice is almost creaky.

Using Professor Y. R. Chao's method of showing Mandarin tones (1948), we may represent the four naming tones of the Chengtu dialect as follows:

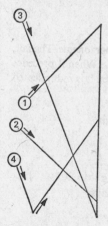

*Two-syllabled group*

In the two-syllabled group the tone-sandhi is as follows:

**1.** Toneme I becomes a mid-level tone when it follows Tonemes I or II or III. But it remains high-rising when it follows Toneme IV or when it precedes another toneme.

e.g. T. I + T. I 　　⌐⌐→⌐⌐　　[goŋ fu] time
　　T. II + T. I 　⌐→⌐　　[gue dʒia] nation
　　T. III + T. I 　⌐→⌐　[tsau gu] mushroom
　　T. IV + T. I 　⌐→⌐　[mien bau] bread
　　T. I + T. II 　⌐→⌐　[tʃin tʃi] relatives
　　T. I + T. III 　⌐→⌐　[ʃiaŋ gaŋ] Hong Kong
　　T. I + T. IV 　⌐→⌐　[dʒoŋ dʒiau] religion

2. Toneme II remains low-falling no matter whether it precedes or follows another toneme. But when it is reduplicated as a form of address or as in baby talk then the second syllable becomes a mid-level tone.

e.g. T. I + T. II 　⌐→⌐　[dʒr ʃr] knowledge
　　T. II + T. II 　⌐→⌐　[fa dʒia] hair clip
　　T. III + T. II 　⌐→⌐　[ie man] savage
　　T. IV + T. II 　⌐→⌐　[di tʃiəu] the globe
　　T. II + T. I 　⌐→⌐　[li ba] fence
　　T. II + T. II 　⌐→⌐　[tʃiəu pe] racket
　　T. II + T. III 　⌐→⌐　[taŋ go] sweets
　　T. II + T. IV 　⌐→⌐　[fei dzau] soap
　　T. II (same 　⌐→⌐　[ba ba] father
　　syllable re-
　　duplicated)

3. Toneme III remains high-falling when it follows another toneme. The fall, however, often reaches only to mid-low instead of low. When it precedes another toneme then it becomes a high-level tone. When it is reduplicated then the second syllable becomes a low-falling tone.

e.g. T. I + T. III 　⌐→⌐　[gən bən] the origin
　　T. II + T. III 　⌐→⌐　[poŋ iəu] friends
　　T. III + T. III 　⌐→⌐　[ʃiau tʃəu] clown
　　T. IV + T. III 　⌐→⌐　[fu mu] parents
　　T. III + T. I 　⌐→⌐　[tʃin i] pyjamas
　　T. III + T. II 　⌐→⌐　[ʃiau tʃi] small flags
　　T. III + T. IV 　⌐→⌐　[ʃiau tʃi] stingy
　　T. III 　　⌐→⌐　[bau bau] baby
　　(reduplicated)

4. Toneme IV becomes a very low-falling tone arrested by a glottal stop when it follows another toneme. It remains low-falling-rising when it precedes another toneme. When it is reduplicated the second syllable becomes a mid-level tone.

e.g. T. I + T. IV   ⌐⌐→⌐⌐   [tʃiŋ dʒoŋ]   weight
T. II + T. IV   ⌐⌐→⌐⌐   [ʃi guan]   habit
T. III + T. IV   ⌐⌐→⌐⌐   [koŋ pa]   perhaps
T. IV + T. IV   ⌐⌐→⌐⌐   [yin tʃi]   luck
T. IV + T. I   ⌐⌐→⌐⌐   [di faŋ]   place
T. IV + T. II   ⌐⌐→⌐⌐   [ʃiaŋ pi]   rubber
T. IV + T. III   ⌐⌐→⌐⌐   [ʃaŋ xai]   Shanghai
T. IV
(reduplicated)   ⌐⌐→⌐⌐   [di di]   younger brother

5. When a syllable is not stressed as often happens with the particles, it is pronounced so short that we cannot distinguish whether it is going up or down. In such cases it is called a neutral tone, represented by a dot. The pitch level of the neutral tone is decided by the toneme preceding it. It is high when preceded by Toneme I and Toneme III but is mid when preceded by Toneme II or Toneme IV.

e.g. T. I   ⌐ ·   [ta di]   his
T. II   ⌐ ·   [be di]   white
T. III   ⌐ · → ⌐ ·   [guei di]   ghost's
T. IV   ⌐ ·   [guai di]   ugly

The following chart shows the combinations of the two-syllabled group and their tone-sandhi.

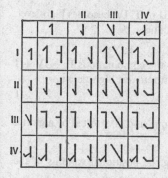

*Three-syllabled group*

In the three-syllabled group the tone-sandhi is as follows:

1. Toneme I remains high-rising when it is in the initial position. It becomes mid-level when final except in the combinations II + IV + I and III + IV + I in which cases it remains high-rising.

When it is in the middle position, then if the first syllable is T. I or T. III, it becomes a mid-level tone; but if the first syllable is T. II or T. IV, then it remains high-rising.

2. Toneme II has no change whatever. It remains a low-falling tone in whichever position it occurs.

3. Toneme III remains high-falling when final and becomes high-level when initial.

When it is in the middle, then if the first syllable is T. I or T. III it remains high-falling, though ending at about mid-high; but if the first syllable is T. II or T. IV, then it becomes high-level.

4. Toneme IV remains low-falling-rising when initial.
It becomes low-low-falling and is checked by a glottal stop when final.
When it is in the middle position then it becomes low-level.

5. The following positional variants occur:

Initial: T. I remains high-rising.
       T. II remains low-falling.
       T. III becomes high-level.
       T. IV remains low-falling-rising.

Medial: T. I, when the first syllable is T. I or T. III, becomes a mid-level tone. Otherwise it remains high-rising.
       T. II remains low-falling.
       T. III, when the first syllable is T. II or T. IV, becomes high-level. Otherwise it becomes half-high-falling.
       T. IV becomes low-level.

Final: T. I becomes mid-level except in the combinations II + IV + I and III + IV + I in which cases it remains high-rising.
       T. II remains low-falling.
       T. III remains high-falling.
       T. IV becomes a low-low-falling tone and is arrested by a glottal stop.

The following figure is a chart showing the positional variants of the three-syllabled group.

| toneme | naming tone | initial | medial | final |
|---|---|---|---|---|
| I | ˥ | ˥ | ˥[ I/III +I+X ] <br> ˥[ II/IV +I+X ] | ˥[ III/II +IV+I ] |
| II | ˩ | ˩ | ˩ | ˩ |
| III | ˥˩˥ | ˥˩ | ˥˩[ I/III +III+X ] <br> ˥˩[ II/IV +III+X ] | ˥˩˥ |
| IV | ˩˥˩ | ˩˥˩ | ˩˥ | ˩˥ |

*Examples of three-syllabled group*

| | | | |
|---|---|---|---|
| I + I + I | ˥˥˥ → ˥˥˥ | [san ʃyen taŋ] | soup made of three ingredients |
| I + I + II | ˥˥˩ → ˥˥˩ | [ʃu dʒuaŋ tai] | dressing-table |
| I + I + III | ˥˥˅ → ˥˥˅ | [xua sən mi] | peanuts |
| I + I + IV | ˥˥˄ → ˥˥˩ | [tʃuan i dʒin] | a long mirror |
| I + II + I | ˥˩˥ → ˥˥˥ | [dʒiau ma dʒi] | peppered chicken |
| I + II + II | ˥˩˩ → ˥˥˩ | [iŋ li nien] | lunar year |
| I + II + III | ˥˩˅ → ˥˥˅ | [tsan məu dʒaŋ] | chief of staff |
| I + II + IV | ˥˩˄ → ˥˥˩ | [dʒi du dʒiau] | Christianity |
| I + III + I | ˥˅˥ → ˥˥˥ | [dzz bən dʒia] | capitalist |
| I + III + II | ˥˅˩ → ˥˥˩ | [dʒin r xuan] | golden earrings |
| I + III + III | ˥˅˅ → ˥˥˅ | [tʃuei gu ʃəu] | bandman |
| I + III + IV | ˥˅˄ → ˥˥˩ | [tʃien li dʒin] | binoculars |
| I + IV + I | ˥˄˥ → ˥˩˥ | [san dzz dʒin] | the Trimetrical Classic |
| I + IV + II | ˥˄˩ → ˥˩˩ | [goŋ bu dʒy] | the municipal council |
| I + IV + III | ˥˄˅ → ˥˩˅ | [xua lu ʃuei] | eau-de-Cologne |
| I + IV + IV | ˥˄˄ → ˥˩˩ | [dʒau dai xuei] | reception party |
| II + I + I | ˩˥˥ → ˩˥˥ | [liəu ʃən dʒi] | gramophone |
| II + I + II | ˩˥˩ → ˩˥˩ | [y gan iəu] | cod-liver-oil |
| II + I + III | ˩˥˅ → ˩˥˅ | [tu ʃu guan] | library |
| II + I + IV | ˩˥˄ → ˩˥˩ | [ʃən dʒin biŋ] | mental disease |

| | | | |
|---|---|---|---|
| II + II + I | ⌐⌐↑→⌐⌐↑ | [dʒyo ta tʃe] | bicycle |
| II + II + II | ⌐⌐⌐→⌐⌐⌐ | [tie so tʃiau] | iron-chained bridge |
| II + II + III | ⌐⌐∨→⌐⌐∨ | [xan i li] | the name of a lane |
| II + II + IV | ⌐⌐↘→⌐⌐↘ | [be ʃe dʒuan] | the Story of the White Snake, name of a play |
| | | | |
| II + III + I | ⌐∨↑→⌐⌐↑ | [fu li dʒin] | the fox spirit |
| II + III + II | ⌐∨⌐→⌐⌐⌐ | [iŋ xo tʃoŋ] | firefly |
| II + III + III | ⌐∨∨→⌐⌐∨ | [xan ʃu biau] | thermometer |
| II + III + IV | ⌐∨↘→⌐⌐↘ | [piŋ go ʃu] | apple tree |
| | | | |
| II + IV + I | ⌐⌐↑→⌐⌐↑ | [ʒoŋ ʃien ʃan] | knitwear |
| II + IV + II | ⌐↘⌐→⌐⌐⌐ | [fan bu tʃuan] | canvas bed |
| II + IV + III | ⌐↘∨→⌐⌐∨ | [xuaŋ dəu fən] | yellow bean powder |
| II + IV + IV | ⌐↘↘→⌐⌐↘ | [dza xo dien] | a general store |
| | | | |
| III + I + I | ∨↑↑→↑⌐⌐ | [ʃuei ʃien xua] | narcissus |
| III + I + II | ∨↑⌐→↑⌐⌐ | [ʃəu foŋ tʃin] | accordion |
| III + I + III | ∨↑∨→↑⌐∨ | [dʒoŋ dʒin li] | general manager |
| III + I + IV | ∨↑↘→↑⌐↘ | [ʃuei ien dai] | waterpipe |
| | | | |
| III + II + I | ∨⌐↑→↑⌐↑ | [dʒuei ʃuən gau] | lipstick |
| III + II + II | ∨⌐⌐→↑⌐⌐ | [ʃuei loŋ təu] | water tap |
| III + II + III | ∨⌐∨→↑⌐∨ | [li tie guai] | Cripple Lee, a legendary character |
| III + II + IV | ∨⌐↘→↑⌐↘ | [ʃien uei dʒin] | microscope |
| | | | |
| III + III + I | ∨∨↑→↑↑↑ | [bau ʃien ʃiaŋ] | safe-box |
| III + III + II | ∨∨⌐→↑↑⌐ | [pau ma tʃaŋ] | race course |
| III + III + III | ∨∨∨→↑↑∨ | [bau ʃəu daŋ] | the Conservative Party |
| III + III + IV | ∨∨↘→↑↑↘ | [ʃuei go dien] | fruit shop |
| | | | |
| III + IV + I | ∨↘↑→↑↓↑ | [da dzz dʒi] | typewriter |
| III + IV + II | ∨↘⌐→↑↓⌐ | [ʃiau tsai tʃaŋ] | vegetable market |
| III + IV + III | ∨↘∨→↑↓∨ | [li bai u] | Friday |
| III + IV + IV | ∨↘↘→↑↓↘ | [gan mien dʒaŋ] | rolling pin |
| | | | |
| IV + I + I | ↘↑↑→↓↑↑ | [dien dən pau] | bulb for lamp |
| IV + I + II | ↘↑⌐→↓↑⌐ | [dʒiau xua po] | beggar woman |
| IV + I + III | ↘↑∨→↓↑∨ | [ʃuən foŋ r] | an ancient kind of megaphone |
| IV + I + IV | ↘↑↘→↓↑↘ | [uai dʒiau bu] | Foreign Ministry |
| | | | |
| IV + II + I | ↘⌐↑→↓↑↑ | [ʃiaŋ pi dʒin] | rubber band |
| IV + II + II | ↘⌐⌐→↓↑↑ | [ʃiaŋ ia tʃuan] | ivory bed |
| IV + II + III | ↘⌐∨→↓↑∨ | [dzz iəu daŋ] | the Free Party |
| IV + II + IV | ↘⌐↘→↓↑↘ | [ti təu dʒiaŋ] | barber |

| IV + III + I | ⌁ [da la ba] | trumpet |
| IV + III + II | ⌁ [dien xo lu] | electric fire |
| IV + III + III | ⌁ [dzau dʒiəu tʃaŋ] | brewery |
| IV + III + IV | ⌁ [dʒau dʒu dʒiau] | Bishop Chao |
| | | |
| IV + IV + I | ⌁ [kuai dʒi ss] | accountant |
| IV + IV + II | ⌁ [ʃən dan dʒie] | Christmas |
| IV + IV + III | ⌁ [da ʃaŋ xai] | Greater Shanghai |
| IV + IV + IV | ⌁ [da dʒiau ʃəu] | professor |

The results of this investigation may now be summarized:

1. There are ten principal allotones for the four tonemes.

They are: Toneme I { (1) high-rising
                     (2) mid-level
          Toneme II    (3) low-falling
          Toneme III { (4) high-falling
                       (5) high-level
                       (6) half-high-falling
          Toneme IV { (7) low-falling-rising
                      (8) low-low-falling
                      (9) low-level
                     (10) neutral tone

2. Toneme II always remains low-falling.

3. Toneme I and Toneme IV remain unchanged when they are in the initial position.

4. When Toneme I goes through perturbation the naming tone is always replaced by a mid-level tone.

5. Toneme III remains unchanged when it is in the final position.

6. The naming tone of Toneme III is replaced by a high-level tone when it is initial in a three-syllabled group. It is replaced by a half-high-falling tone when it is the middle syllable.

7. The naming tone of Toneme IV is replaced by a low-level tone when it is in the middle of a three-syllabled group. It is replaced by a low-low-falling tone checked by a glottal stop when it is the final syllable.[1]

1. In a three-syllabled group the first syllable has the strongest stress, the last syllable the secondary, and the middle syllable has the least stress.

I also worked on the four-syllabled group though without the help of the spectrograph. A total of 256 four-syllable combinations were studied and the results are as follows:

1. Toneme I remains high-rising when it is in the initial position. When it is the second or third or fourth syllable then it becomes mid-level.

2. Toneme II remains low-falling in whatever position it occurs.

3. Toneme III remains high-falling when final. It becomes high-level in any other position.

4. Toneme IV remains low-falling-rising when it is in the initial position, but becomes low-level when it is the second or third syllable, and becomes low-low-falling when it is in the final position.

5. The following positional variants occur:

Initial: T. I    remains high-rising.
         T. II   remains low-falling.
         T. III  becomes high-level.
         T. IV   remains low-falling-rising.
Medial:  T. I    becomes mid-level.
         T. II   remains low-falling.
         T. III  becomes high-level.
         T. IV   becomes low-level.
Final:   T. I    becomes mid-level.
         T. II   remains low-falling.
         T. III  remains high-falling.
         T. IV   becomes low-low-falling and is arrested by a glottal stop.

The following figure is a chart showing the positional variants of the four-syllabled group.

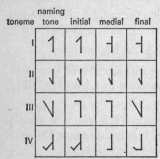

As in the three-syllabled group, the first syllable in the four-syllabled group has the strongest stress, the last syllable the secondary and the middle ones have the least stress.

## Part 2 Intonation and its relationship to tones

Intonation is the fluctuation of the voice pitch as applied to the whole sentence. It is the sentence melody and is superimposed on the sentence as a whole. Tones apply to individual syllables whereas intonation covers the whole sentence. Unlike tones, furthermore, a change of intonation does not affect the lexical value of words. It only adds shades of meaning to the sentence spoken and brings out the attitude of the speaker and the emotional state he is in.

Every community has its own intonation pattern, i.e. its own rules of changing the voice pitch when uttering the sentence. The fluctuation of the voice pitch of the individual follows, consciously as well as unconsciously, these patterns. Those whose intonation does not coincide with these patterns are considered foreign speakers. ('Foreign' in the broad sense, meaning 'strange' or 'peculiar' or 'alien'.) Those who are not familiar with these patterns naturally miss the subtle 'overtones' of the sentence spoken.

One would imagine the pitch of each syllable in a tonal language to be fixed beforehand, and therefore that it would be difficult for a tonal language to have intonation. But on closer examination we find pitch phenomena which we can only regard as 'intonation' superimposed upon the tonal system. Apart from the change due to tonal environment as shown above, there remain characteristics and modulations of the voice pitch which bring out different shades of meaning. The fact is that the sentence may be spoken in different 'keys' when representing different attitudes, and that the syllables go through perturbation (see under 'perturbation' below), thus giving the whole sentence a rising or falling tune.

I shall now try to describe the intonation of some types of sentences in the Chengtu dialect, the circumstances under which they are used and the shades of meaning they convey. According to the data which I have assembled, intonation in the Chengtu dialect may be regarded as consisting of three factors:

1. The pitch level on which the sentence is spoken - - -. This may be divided into high, mid-high, mid, mid-low and low.

2. The range of pitch the sentence covers - - -. The range may be divided into wide, medium and narrow.

3. Perturbation of the final syllable - - -. In connected speech, syllables often form groups of two, three or four and their perturbation follows the patterns discussed in Part I. It is the final syllable alone, however, which gives the clue to the listener whether the sentence is a question or a statement, whether it has a rising or falling tune. I must here explain that this

rising or falling has no reference to the pitch of the preceding syllables, but only to the pitch of the final syllable itself. Thus whether I regard a sentence as having a rising or a falling tune depends on whether, after undergoing perturbation, its final syllable is a rising or falling tone. In the case of a rising naming tone of the final syllable being replaced by its level allotone, I classify the sentence as having a 'falling' tune; and in the case of a falling naming tone being replaced by a level allotone I classify the sentence as having a 'rising' tune.

The examples are put on music manuscript paper. The four spaces and the blank above the top line of each staff represent the pitch levels. (High, mid-high, mid, mid-low, and low.) The intonation of the sentence is marked above the phonetic transcription. The mark ['] represents rising, ['] represents falling and [–] represents level. The difference in length of the marks represents roughly the relative time taken over the syllable uttered. In rapid conversation many words are unstressed and become neutral tones. These are marked with dots. The Arabic numerals under each syllable represent the toneme to which it belongs.

The examples given are all picked out from the eight hours' conversation I recorded. Unfortunately there is scarcely one single sentence among them that is spoken with two different types of intonation. But against this disadvantage may be set the fact that all the examples are from real life situations; none of them have been spoken with 'simulated emotions' or read aloud, or made up for the purpose of illustrating intonation.

Rhythm, stress, tempo and voice quality also help to indicate the mood or the emotional state of the speaker. Where these elements seem significant, I have also touched on them in a very general way.

*Ordinary statements*

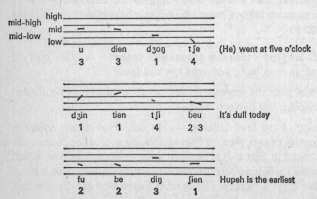

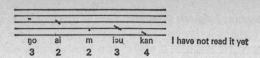

ŋo   ai   m   iəu   kan    I have not read it yet
3    2    2   3     4

## Ordinary questions

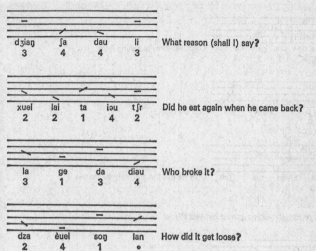

dʒiaŋ   ʃa   dau   li    What reason (shall I) say?
3       4    4     3

xuei   lai   ta   iəu   tʃr    Did he eat again when he came back?
2      2     1    4     2

la   ge   da   diau    Who broke it?
3    1    3    4

dza   èuei   soŋ   lan    How did it get loose?
2     4      1     °

## Emphatic sentences

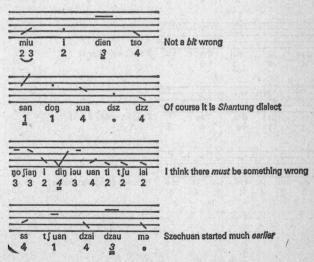

miu   i   dien   tso    Not a *bit* wrong
2 3   2   3      4

san   doŋ   xua   dsz   dzz    Of course it is *Shan*tung dialect
1     1     4     °     4

ŋo ʃiaŋ   i   diŋ   iəu   uan   ti   tʃu   lai    I think there *must* be something wrong
3  3      2   4     3     4     2    2     2

ss   tʃuan   dzai   dzau   mə    Szechuan started much *earlier*
4    1       4      3      °

## Sentences expressing emphatic approval

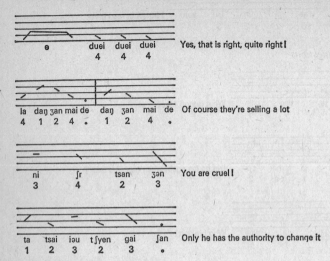

| | e | | duei | duei | duei | Yes, that is right, quite right! |
| | | | 4 | 4 | 4 | |

| la | daŋ | ʒan | mai | de | daŋ | ʒan | mai | de | Of course they're selling a lot |
| 4 | 1 | 2 | 4 | . | 1 | 2 | 4 | . | |

| | ni | | ʃr | | tsan | | ʒən | You are cruel! |
| | 3 | | 4 | | 2 | | 3 | |

| ta | tsai | iəu | t ʃyen | | gai | | ʃan | Only he has the authority to change it |
| 1 | 2 | 3 | 2 | | 3 | | . | |

## Sentences expressing annoyance or vexation

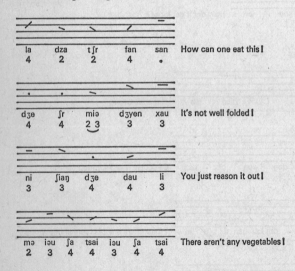

| la | | dza | t ʃr | | fan | san | How can one eat this! |
| 4 | | 2 | 2 | | 4 | . | |

| dʒe | ʃr | miə | | dʒyen | xau | It's not well folded! |
| 4 | 4 | 2 3 | | 3 | 3 | |

| ni | ʃiaŋ | dʒe | | dau | li | You just reason it out! |
| 3 | 3 | 4 | | 4 | 3 | |

| mə | iəu | ʃa | tsai | iəu | ʃa | tsai | There aren't any vegetables! |
| 2 | 3 | 4 | 4 | 3 | 4 | 4 | |

## Sentences expressing awe

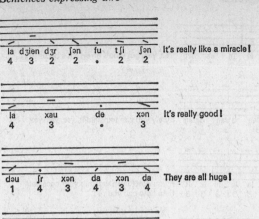

| la | dʒien | dʒr | ʃən | fu | tʃi | ʃən | It's really like a miracle! |
|----|-------|-----|-----|-----|-----|-----|
| 4 | 3 | 2 | 2 | • | 2 | 2 |

| la | xau | de | xən | It's really good! |
|----|-----|-----|-----|
| 4 | 3 | • | 3 |

| dəu | ʃr | xən | da | xən | da | They are all huge! |
|-----|-----|-----|-----|-----|-----|
| 1 | 4 | 3 | 4 | 3 | 4 |

| dʒe | ʃr | dʒye | da | li | tso | u | This is a great mistake! |
|-----|-----|------|-----|-----|-----|-----|
| 4 | 4 | 2 | 4 | • | 4 | 4 |

## Sentences expressing contempt

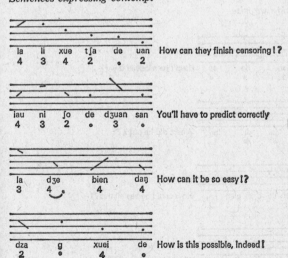

| la | li | xue | tʃa | de | uan | How can they finish censoring!? |
|----|-----|-----|-----|-----|-----|
| 4 | 3 | 4 | 2 | • | 2 |

| iau | ni | ʃo | de | dʒuan | san | You'll have to predict correctly |
|-----|-----|-----|-----|-------|-----|
| 4 | 3 | 2 | • | 3 | • |

| la | dʒe | bien | daŋ | How can it be so easy!? |
|----|-----|------|-----|
| 3 | 4 | 4 | 4 |

| dza | g | xuei | de | How is this possible, indeed! |
|-----|-----|------|-----|
| 2 | • | 4 | • |

## Sentences containing a protest

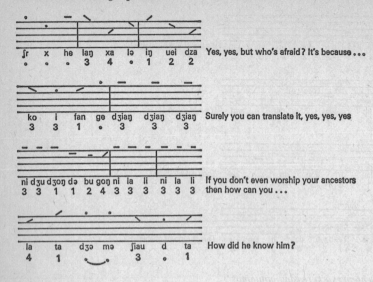

| ʃr | x | he | laŋ | xa | lə | iŋ | uei | dza | Yes, yes, but who's afraid? It's because ... |
| • | • | • | 3 | 4 | • | 1 | 2 | 2 | |

| ko | i | fan | ge | dʒiaŋ | dʒiaŋ | dʒiaŋ | Surely you can translate it, yes, yes, yes |
| 3 | 3 | 1 | • | 3 | 3 | 3 | |

| ni | dʒu | dʒoŋ | də | bu | goŋ | ni | la | li | ni | la | li | If you don't even worship your ancestors then how can you ... |
| 3 | 3 | 1 | 1 | 2 | 4 | 3 | 3 | 3 | 3 | 3 | 3 | |

| la | ta | dʒə | mə | ʃiau | d | ta | How did he know him? |
| 4 | 1 | | • | 3 | • | 1 | |

## Sentences expressing surprise

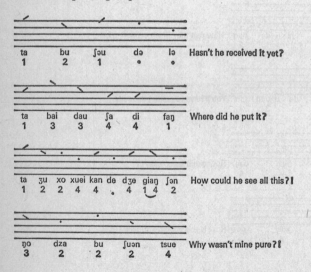

| ta | bu | ʃəu | də | lə | Hasn't he received it yet? |
| 1 | 2 | 1 | • | • | |

| ta | bai | dau | ʃa | di | faŋ | Where did he put it? |
| 1 | 3 | 3 | 4 | 4 | 1 | |

| ta | ʒu | xo | xuei | kan | de | dʒe | giaŋ | ʃən | How could he see all this?! |
| 1 | 2 | 2 | 4 | 4 | • | 4 | 1 4 | 2 | |

| ŋo | dza | bu | ʃuən | tsue | Why wasn't mine pure?! |
| 3 | 2 | 2 | 2 | 4 | |

## Sentences implying a dismissal of the topic

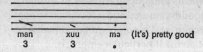

man    xuu    mə    (It's) pretty good
3        3     •

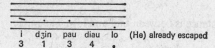

i    dʒin   pau  diau  lo    (He) already escaped
3    1     3    4    •

dʒi    bu    dau    (I) can't remember
4      2      3

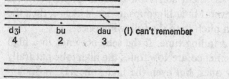

i    dzr   ʃia   tʃe  a    Walk straight down
2    2     4     2   •

## Unfinished sentences

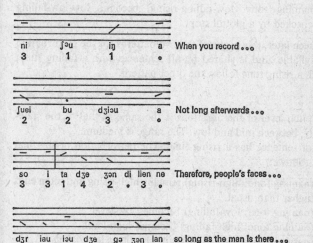

ni    ʃəu    iŋ    a    When you record ...
3    1     1    •

ʃuei   bu   dʒiəu  a    Not long afterwards ...
2    2     3     •

so  i  ta  dʒe  ʒən  di  lien  ne    Therefore, people's faces ...
3  3  1   4    2   •   3   •

dʒr  iau  iəu  dʒe  gə  ʒən  lan    so long as the man is there ...
2   4   4   4   •  2   •

## Ordinary sentences

By ordinary sentences I mean statements and questions used in ordinary polite conversation. The speaker is good-humoured and in a conversational mood. He is emotionally placid and calm, and is non-committal in what he says. He is merely stating a fact, not giving it particular emphasis.

### Statements

The pitch level of this type of sentence is between mid and low. The range is medium.

If the statement consists of several high tones, i.e. high-rising or high-falling, then each one of them starts on a lower pitch than the preceding one. If there are several breath groups in one sentence, then the first breath group is higher in pitch than the following ones.

This type of sentence has a falling tune. If the sentence ends in a high tone while the rest of the sentence are low tones the high tone naturally remains higher than the low ones, but even the high tone has an inclination to fall. The perturbation of the final syllable is as follows:

Toneme I (naming tone: high-rising) becomes mid-level.
Toneme II (naming tone: low-falling) remains low-falling.
Toneme III (naming tone: high-falling) remains high-falling.
Toneme IV (naming tone: low-falling-rising) becomes low-low-falling checked by a glottal stop.

As will be seen later, this is one of the two patterns for the perturbation of the final syllable, and is shared by all sentences with a falling tune; sentences with a rising tune follow the other pattern.

### Questions

The general pitch level of the questions is the same as that of the statements, namely, between mid and low. The range is medium.

This type of sentence has a rising tune. The perturbation of the final syllable is as follows:

Toneme I (naming tone: high-rising) remains high-rising and often ends higher than usual.
Toneme II (naming tone: low-falling) becomes low-level.
Toneme III (naming tone: high-falling) becomes high-level.
Toneme IV (naming tone: low-falling-rising) becomes low-rising.

This is the pattern for the perturbation of the final syllable in sentences with a rising tune.

In spoken Chinese, sentences often end with particles like [a], [san], [mə], [le], [lo]. These particles are meaningless by themselves, but they play an important part in bringing out the intonation of the sentence and thus denote whether the sentence is a question or a statement. If the particle is pronounced on a high pitch level or with a rising tone, then the sentence is a question. If on the other hand the particle is pronounced with a falling tone, then the sentence is a statement. It may be asked whether it is these particles that fix the intonation of the sentence or whether they merely bring out the intonation more clearly to the listener by indicating whether the sentence has a rising or a falling tune. The latter explanation seems a more plausible one since the same particle can be used in different types of sentences and it is then pronounced with different tones.

These particles are often also used with unfinished sentences, in which case they are pronounced with a rising tone, and give a sense of suspense to the listener.

On the other hand, questions containing Verb–*no*–Verb (e.g. 'go or not go?') or Adjective–*no*–Adjective (e.g. 'good or not good?') constructions have a falling tune like that of the ordinary statement.

## Emphatic sentences

By emphatic sentences I mean statements in which the speaker gives emphasis or prominence to some specific point. He is concerned to bring it into contrast with other points or to intensify its significance. But emotionally he is not agitated. In ordinary speech, Chinese syllables are more or less evenly stressed. But in this type of sentence there is often one particular word or syllable which receives an extra stress, the word being the point emphasized. This stress on the part of the speaker seems to imply: '*This* is what I mean.'

The pitch level is between mid-high and low.

The range is wide.

The perturbation of the syllable receiving extra stress is as follows:

Toneme I  (naming tone: high-rising) remains high-rising and ends yet higher than its normal pitch in an ordinary statement.

Toneme II  (naming tone: low-falling) falls yet lower.

Toneme III (naming tone: high-falling) becomes high-level.

Toneme IV (naming tone: low-falling-rising) remains low-falling-rising but ends in a higher pitch than usual.

This type of sentence has a falling tune. The perturbation of the final syllable is the same as that in the ordinary statement.

## Sentences expressing certain attitudes or emotional states

When we speak, we may merely be stating a fact or giving special emphasis to certain points. But sometimes we may want to do more; we want also to convey our personal reactions or attitudes to our listener or to express our feelings as well. Under these circumstances our emotion is a predominant element; therefore the intonation we use is different from that we use when speaking under unemotional circumstances.

In this section I shall describe the intonation of several types of sentences which express different attitudes or emotions. The seven types of sentences that I choose are:

1. Sentences expressing emphatic approval.
2. Sentences expressing vexation.
3. Sentences expressing awe.
4. Sentences expressing contempt.
5. Sentences containing a protest.
6. Sentences expressing surprise.
7. Sentences implying dismissal of the topic.

1. Sentences expressing emphatic approval:

By these I mean statements in which the speaker is very sure of himself and at the same time is in perfect accord with the last speaker. There is a sort of finality in his sentence. It implies 'that's that' or 'I know it is so'. In showing approval the sense involved is 'Quite right!' or 'That's just it.'

The pitch level of this type of sentence is between mid-high and low. The range is wide. The tune used is a falling one. The perturbation of the final syllable is the same as that of the ordinary statement.

2. Sentences expressing vexation or annoyance:

This type of sentence is used when the speaker is in a bad mood. He is trying to start an argument. What is implied seems to be 'Now I ask you...' or 'It's all your own fault, so ...' or 'How can you ask such a stupid question?'

The pitch level of this type of sentence is between high and mid. The range is medium. It has a rising tune. The perturbation of the final syllable is the same as that in the ordinary question.

3. Sentences expressing awe:

This type of sentence is used when the speaker wants to show that what he is talking about is something of great importance. He wants to impress his listener and at the same time to convey the idea that he himself is impressed by what he is trying to tell. He aims to create awe among his listeners. What is implied is 'This is something wonderful!' or 'That is terrific!'

This type of sentence is spoken on a low pitch, varying between mid-low and low. The range is narrow and all the tones seem to be compressed together; therefore there is a tendency for all the tones to become level. Both the rising and the falling are very slight. The sentence has a falling tune. The perturbation of the final syllable is the same as that of the ordinary statement.

The voice quality in this type of sentence is often 'breathy' or 'husky'.

## 4. Sentences expressing contempt:

This type of sentence is used when the speaker is in a contemptuous frame of mind. He is ready to snap at the person spoken to and close the conversation as soon as possible. The sentence implies 'This is impossible', or 'What nonsense you are talking' or 'Let's proceed no more.'

The pitch level is between mid-high and low. The range is wide. The sentence has a falling tune and the perturbation of the final syllable is the same as that of the ordinary statement.

The characteristic feature of this type of sentence is that one syllable in the sentence is always lengthened. The syllables coming before or after the lengthened one are usually huddled together and spoken quickly; thus they often become neutral tones.

## 5. Sentences containing a protest:

This type of sentence is used when the speaker is greatly agitated or excited. It is often used in argument when the speaker hopes to shout his opponent down. Unlike sentences expressing vexation, the speaker is not deliberately starting an argument. On the contrary, he is the victim; he is being provoked. He is anxious to make himself understood. Under these circumstances, the listener is often also trying to talk at the same time; the result therefore is that this type of sentence is usually spoken throughout on a high pitch level, between high and mid-high. Sometimes the sentence may start on a high pitch level and then fall to low, but one feels it is the high-pitched part of the sentence that contains the protest, because by the time the voice pitch falls to low, the speaker's emotional state has returned to normal. Also it is not infrequent that the sentence is left unfinished.

The range of this type of sentence is narrow. It has a rising tune and the perturbation of the final syllable is the same as that of the ordinary question.

## 6. Sentences expressing surprise:

This type of sentence is used when the speaker is taken by surprise or is puzzled. It implies incredulity as well. It means 'Really?' or 'Can this be true?'

The pitch level is between high and mid-low. The sentence usually starts on a high pitch and gradually falls. The range is wide. It has a falling tune. The perturbation of the final syllable is the same as that of the ordinary statement.

## 7. Sentences implying a dismissal of the topic:

This type of sentence is used when the speaker is preoccupied with something else. This does not mean that the speaker wants to put a stop to the conversation, nor is this type of sentence as forbidding as those expressing contempt and vexation. In this case, the speaker merely wants to pass on to another topic. It is used to dismiss the subject matter but not the person spoken to. It implies 'Never mind this, it's not important.'

The pitch level is between mid-low and low. The range is narrow; therefore the rising and falling of the tones are very slight. This type of sentence has a falling tune and the perturbation of the final syllable is the same as that of the ordinary statement.

From the results given above, we may draw the following conclusions:

1. There is a definite relationship between pitch level and the type of sentence. For instance, sentences containing a protest are spoken on a high pitch level whereas sentences implying dismissal of the topic are spoken on a low pitch level. But it is difficult to make any general statements on this relationship.

2. (a) The range of the pitch varies with the type of sentence. Sentences containing a protest and sentences implying dismissal of the topic have completely different pitch levels, yet both have a narrow range. On the other hand, emphatic sentences and sentences expressing contempt, for example, both have a wide range. Ordinary statements and questions have a medium range. Thus, the range is at least a clue to the emotional state of the speaker.

(b) When the range of a sentence is narrow, there is a tendency for all the tones to become level, i.e. the rise and fall of the tones are very slight.

3.(a) The perturbation of the tones of the final syllable in the sentence follows two distinct patterns. In sentences with a 'rising' tune, the perturbation of the final syllable is as follows:

Toneme I   (N.T. high-rising) remains high-rising.
Toneme II  (N.T. low-falling) becomes low-level.
Toneme III (N.T. high-falling) becomes high-level.
Toneme IV (N.T. low-falling-rising) becomes low-rising.

In sentences with a 'falling' tune, the perturbation of the final syllable is as follows:

Toneme I    becomes mid-level.
Toneme II   remains low-falling.
Toneme III remains high-falling.
Toneme IV becomes low-low-falling.

(b) The two tunes are used for different types of sentences. The rising tune is used for

1. Questions other than those containing Verb–*no*–Verb and Adjective–*no*–Adjective constructions.
2. Sentences expressing vexation.
3. Sentences containing a protest.
4. Unfinished sentences.

The falling tune is used for

1. Ordinary and emphatic statements and questions containing the Verb–*no*–Verb and Adjective–*no*–Adjective constructions.
2. Sentences expressing emphatic approval.
3. Sentences expressing awe.
4. Sentences expressing contempt.
5. Sentences expressing surprise.
6. Sentences implying dismissal of the topic.

Tone-sandhi has already been studied in many Chinese dialects. It would be desirable for similar work to be done on intonation. A very interesting question is whether in other dialects intonation is also indicated by the perturbation of one particular syllable, which in the case of the Chengtu dialect is the final syllable. It would also be interesting to know if the resulting tunes could be divided into two or more patterns. If a number of other dialects could be studied along similar lines to the present inquiry, we could perhaps come to a general explanation of tonal behaviour and intonation in the Chinese dialects.

## Summary

From the above we conclude that

1. Tones pronounced in isolation behave differently from those pronounced in connected speech. In connected speech they go through perturbation. This is usually governed by the position they occupy in the phrase or by the tonal environment. It may also be governed by grammatical structure, though this does not form part of my present inquiry.
2. Besides the four naming tones in the Chengtu dialect, the author found six other tones which, together with these naming tones, could be grouped into four tonemes.
3. Intonation does exist in the Chengtu dialect. It is superimposed on the sentence as a whole. And it is this superimposed intonation that modifies the individual tones and not the tones themselves that decide the intonation of the sentence.

*Reference*

CHAO, Y. R. (1948), *Mandarin Primer*, Harvard University Press.

# 25 Einar Haugen and Martin Joos

## Tone and Intonation in East Norwegian

Einar Haugen and Martin Joos, 'Tone and intonation in East Norwegian',
*Acta Philologica Scandinavica*, vol. 22, 1952, pp. 41–64.

### Authors' note

The purpose of this study was to provide (for the first time) spectrographic
evidence on the tonal patterns of a Scandinavian dialect, in order to illustrate my contention that the so-called 'word tones' could only be understood in relation to the linguistically significant stressed syllables. As I had
written in 1949, 'the difference between two significantly contrastive tones
may consist of nothing more than a different timing of the tonal curve in
relation to the syllabic stress'. In the absence of any satisfying definition of
stress, I took it to be located in those syllables which in Norwegian have
either a long vowel or a short vowel followed by a long consonant: $\bar{V}(C)$,
$VC(C)$. I called this minimally necessary portion of the stressed syllable,
i.e. $\bar{V}$ or $VC$, its 'core' (p. 430) and showed that the two tones contrasted
in the timing of their highs and lows in relation to this core. Much more is
now known about the nature of the tones in various Scandinavian dialects,
and questions have been raised about the very existence of what I called
'stress' (e.g. by Fintoft, 1970, esp. p. 37). Regardless of what the acoustical
correlates of stress will turn out to be, it cannot be questioned that the
(usually) initial syllable of a Germanic language like Norwegian is linguistically primary. Tone can hardly be the sole determinant of stress, since
there are two different tones in syllables which native speakers perceive as
being identically stressed.

Our article was also intended to clear up the common confusion of
(word) tone with (sentence) intonation. Every word in the language has an
inherent tone (which is non-contrastive in monosyllables). In native words
the tone is generally determined by its grammatical function (for the rules
see my article 1967). As pointed out in the 1952 article, tone 1 is generally
identical with primary stress and may be regarded as unmarked. The
marked tone, peculiar to Scandinavian, is tone 2, because of the failure of
its peak (low or high) to coincide with the syllabic core (being normally
delayed). It is, accordingly, the most difficult for non-natives to learn and
by them often misheard as delayed stress. For discussion of this aspect see
also my article (1963) and my Norwegian–English Dictionary (1965), introduction.

A few small corrections have been made in the text of the present article, including the addition of some more recent bibliographical references. 'Satellite' has replaced 'contour' where this is contrasted with 'nucleus', and the measures have been marked in the transcription, after being redefined as juncturally bounded.

E.H., 1971.

The purpose of the present study is to analyse the function of pitch in a Norwegian utterance. This topic has a particular interest for general linguistic theory because of the so-called 'word tones', which have been compared with the tones of various African, Indian and Oriental languages.[1] In the literature the tones bear various names, but we shall here call them 'accents' in order not to prejudge their nature. The simpler of the two, which is closest to the pitch patterns of other Germanic languages, will be called accent 1; the more complex, which is peculiarly Scandinavian, will be called accent 2. As early as 1860 the Norwegian phonetician Johan Storm succeeded in identifying and describing the musical difference between such otherwise identical words as *bønder* 'farmers' (accent 1) and *bønner* 'beans' (accent 2). He elaborated his descriptions in later publications, but never went beyond an auditory determination expressed in musical notes. Instrumental evidence was brought to bear in the 1920s in a series of studies by Ernst W. Selmer, who used a kymograph to analyse the word tones of the dialects spoken in Oslo, Bergen, Stavanger, Sunnmøre and the Faroe Islands. Selmer was not greatly interested in the relation between these tones and the intonation of the whole utterance, but this was the chief topic of Ivar Alnæs, whose book *Norsk Sætningsmelodi* of 1916 is still the only one devoted to the study of Norwegian sentence intonation.[2] Important additions to our knowledge concerning the function of the tones have been made in a series of articles by Olaf Broch (e.g. 1935, 1937, 1939, 1944), in which the relation between tonal and rhythmic patterns is clarified. We will not here be concerned with the large body of literature that discusses the historical origin of the tones (e.g. Oftedal, 1952), or their distribution in the present-day vocabulary. But it should be pointed out that parallel phenomena are to be found in Sweden and Denmark, where a number of important descriptions have made their appearance in recent years (Bo, 1933; Hansen, 1943; Smith, 1944; Bjerrum, 1948; Meyer, 1937; Ekblom, 1933; Stalling, 1935).[3]

1. Cf. Pike (1948), where Norwegian and Swedish are excluded by definition.
2. Cf. also his *De levende ord* (1932). For the local studies by Selmer, see the original of this Reading, p. 41, footnote 3.
3. See now especially the researches of Bertil Malmberg and Kerstin Hadding on South Swedish, Carl Borgstrøm, Martin Kloster Jensen and Arne Vanvik on Norwegian and the mathematical models of Sven Öhman, all listed in the comprehensive bibliography of Fintoft (1970).

The method adopted in this study will be a combined phonetic and phonemic analysis. New, precise data derived from instrumental analysis will be presented, and then analysed by structural methods to derive the relevant units of Norwegian pitch. Wherever they are pertinent, the views of earlier scholars will be discussed and either accepted or rejected. Some of the views here presented are only tentative, since the material available is still small, and the methods of structural linguistics are still far from adequate for the solution of such difficult problems as those offered by pitch. But it is hoped that some steps forward may be made toward a revised approach to these problems.[4]

One of the difficulties facing the investigator of intonation has been that of gaining an objective picture of the tonal movement, particularly in longer utterances. Much of this has been eliminated by the invention of the spectrograph, which makes it possible to determine the melodic movement with less effort than earlier (Joos, 1948). At the same time it must be recognized that from a linguistic point of view the impressions registered by the ear alone are of the highest importance and cannot be eliminated in favor of mechanical recordings, no matter how perfect. For the present investigation a text was chosen which should render natural Norwegian speech, a phonograph recording by the actor Hauk Aabel.[5] The passage analysed is spoken in a rapid, conversational manner, with great variations of emotional expression, including examples of questioning and exclamations. The dialect is standard colloquial Oslo speech, with a lapse into substandard in his imitation of the chauffeurs.

The first step was to prepare a phonetic transcription, marking the tones and stresses. The passage was then analysed by means of the spectrograph, and the intonational information transferred from the spectrograms to semi-logarithmic paper. Photographs of the six charts resulting from this analysis accompany the present article. A new phonetic analysis was then made from the spectrograms, which is here presented along with the standard Norwegian spelling of the text. Only those sounds are shown that could be positively identified in the spectrograms. Stress is marked by accents preceding the syllables affected: ['] primary stress with accent 1, ["] primary stress with accent 2, [ᵢ] secondary stress; these are auditorily determined. Quantity is marked by a colon after the sound affected: [:]. The sound values of the vowel symbols are those of East Norwegian, [a] low back, [å] mid back over-rounded, [o] high back over-rounded, [u]

4. Martin Joos is responsible for the spectrographic analysis and the preparation of the six plates with their phonetic and intonational analysis; Einar Haugen has written the text and made the linguistic interpretations presented in the article.

5. Hauk Aabel, b. 1869 at Søndfjord, moved to Valdres in 1876, lived in Oslo thereafter, according to *Hvem er Hvem? 1948* (Oslo, 1948) and Johan B. Halvorsen, *Norsk Forfatter-Lexicon 1.1* (Kristiania, 1885).

high central over-rounded, [y] high front half-rounded. Word division is
included for convenience in reading; the numbers in parentheses represent
the pause groups. Contour junctures (see below) are marked by perpendicular bars.


Et Hekseskudd
Hauk Aabel

(1) En dag som jeg går og spaserer på Karl Johan, så får jeg et hekseskudd.
　　en ˈda:g|sm æ ˈgå:r|å spaˈse:rər|på kaṛḷ jåˈhan:|så ˈfå: jæ t|"hekseˌskud:

(2) Ganske plutselig, (3) uten noen slags forutgående fornemmelser
　　"ganskə| "plutsli　　"u:tn|"nåən sjlaks| ˈfårutˌgåənə|fåṛ ˈ ṇemlsər

(4) Og der stod jeg uten å kunne røre meg av flekken. (5) Først tenkte
　　å ˈdæ:ṛ|ˈṣto: jæ|"u:tn å kunə|"rø:rə mæ|a　ˈflek:ən　　føṛṣt "tengt

jeg: (6) Ryggen må være gått av. (7) Du får vente litt, så kanskje den
jæ　　ˈryg:ən må værə|"gåt: ˌa:　　du få "vent ˌlit:|så "kåsjə　　n|

gror i sammen igjen. (8) Jeg stod midt i verste trafikken. (9) Rett imot
"gro:ər i samn　jen　　jæ ˈsto:|ˈmit:|i "værṣtə|raˈfik:ən　　ˈret:|iˈmo:t

meg kom det en bil, og rett bak meg en. (10) Så tenkte jeg: (11) Du får
mæ|kåm　dæ n ˌbi:l| å ret ˈba:k mæ ˌe:n　　så "tengt jæ　　du få

rekke høyre armen i været, så stanser de kanskje. (12) Ja, jeg så gjorde,
"rek:ə|ˈhøyərə|ˈarmən|i :ˈvæ:rə|så "stansər i kansjə　　ˈjaæ|ˈjæə|ˈså| "jo:rə

(13) og bilene stanset ganske riktig. (14) Sjåførene skrek og bar seg:
　　å "bi:lnə|"stansət| "ganskə|"rikti　sjåˈfø:rnə|ˈskərə:k|å ˈba:æṛ ṣæ

(15) «Se til å komme unna der din idiot!» (16) Men det var meg ikke
　　"sje tə|å kåmə "un:a　ræ| in "id:jot　　mn　də ˈva: mæi ke|

mulig å gå. (17) Den høyre armen min var nesten lam. Så tenkte jeg:
"muli| å ˈgå　　dən|ˈhøyərə|ˈarmən min|vaṛ "nestn|ˈlam:|så "tengt jæ

(18) Nå gjelder det å få opp den venstre (19) før de begynner å kjøre.
　　ˈnå:|ˈjel:ər|　å "få ˌop:| n　ˈvenstrə　　ˈfø:r|i ˈbjyn:ər|ə "çø:rə

(20) Men jeg rakk det ikke. (21) Begge bilene kjørte over meg.
　　me jæ ˈrak: d ikə　　"beg:ə|"bi:lnə| "ço:ṛṭ ˌå: mə

(22) Trafikken stanset og en av sjåførene kom bort til meg. (23) «Lever
　　traˈfik:ən|"stansət|å ˈe:n|a sjaˈfø:ṛnə|kåm "boṛṭ: ə mæ　　ˈle:vər

De?» sa han. (24) «Ja-a, jeg tror det,» sa jeg. (25) «Men De får endelig
i　sa n　　ˈja: | jə ˈtro:r ə　sa jæ　　mn　di får "endli

ikke bry Dem noe om meg. Jeg har – (26) hekseskudd, jeg!» (27) Den
kə|"bryd:əm　no| om ˈmæi | jə ˈha:r　　"heksəˌskud: jæ　　den

ene av sjåførene – han så riktig så snill ut – (28) han la meg pent oppi
"*e:n a|sja*'*fø:ṛṇə* | *an* '*så:*|"*rikti|så* '*snil:*|'*u:t*      *han* '*la: mæ*|'*pe:ənt|opi*

bilen sin og (29) kjørte meg (30) like hjem.[6]
'*bi:ln sin|å* –      "*çø:ṛṭ mæ*      "*li:k* '*jem:*

We shall now turn to the six plates which depict the tonal movement of
this passage. The abscissa is calibrated into centiseconds (cs.) and the
ordinate into vibrations per second. The scale on the left-hand side trans-
lates these into musical notes, while the scale on the right-hand side shows
the actual number of vibrations. Small perpendicular lines crossing the
main curve show the approximate boundaries between neighboring segments. The whole text is divided into pause groups from one to thirty;
these will here be called utterances and references to them will be by number
and centisecond, e.g. the *d* of *en dag* begins at U 1.18. The utterances will
be convenient divisions from which to start our analysis, but it will be
evident that they correspond only in part to the units that would result
from a grammatical-semantic analysis. In some cases the speaker's rapid
speech has carried him over from one grammatical unit to another without
pause (1, 7, 9, 11, 17, 22, 25); in others an accidental or deliberate hesitation has broken up an obvious unit (2, 3, 26, 29, 30). But the great majority
of the utterances do coincide with grammatical units, and the intonation
contours do not run over from one to the next. For our purposes we may
thus consider them as autonomous utterances, and study their characteristics with a view to further reduction of their extent.

An inspection of the curves shows that most of the musical movement
is confined to a band from about d (150 ∼) to b (250 ∼), or a musical sixth;
near the end, however, it sinks to B–g (125 ∼–200 ∼). This may be
regarded as the normal speech range of this speaker, and will of course
vary greatly from speaker to speaker. The interval of a sixth corresponds

6. Translation: (1) One day as I am out walking on Karl Johan (street), I get an
attack of lumbago. (2) Quite suddenly, (3) without any kind of previous sensations. (4)
There I stood without being able to stir from the spot. (5) First I thought: (6) My back
must have cracked in two. (7) You better wait a little, and maybe it will grow together
again. (8) I stood right in the worst of the traffic. (9) Straight toward me came a car,
and right behind me one. (10) Then I thought: (11) You better put your right arm up,
and maybe they'll stop. (12) Well, I did so, (13) and sure enough, the cars stopped. (14)
The chauffeurs screamed and yelled: (15) 'See that you get out of there, you idiot!'
(16) But I just could not move. (17) My right arm was almost paralysed. Then I thought:
(18) If I can only get my left one up (19) before they start to drive. (20) But I didn't
make it. (21) Both the cars ran over me. (22) The traffic stopped and one of the
chauffeurs came over to me. (23) 'Are you alive?' he said. (24) 'Ye-es, I think so,' I said.
(25) 'But whatever you do, don't bother about me. I have – – (26) a touch of lumbago!' (27) One of the chauffeurs – he looked really very kind – – (28) he laid me nicely
in his car and (29) drove me (30) straight home.

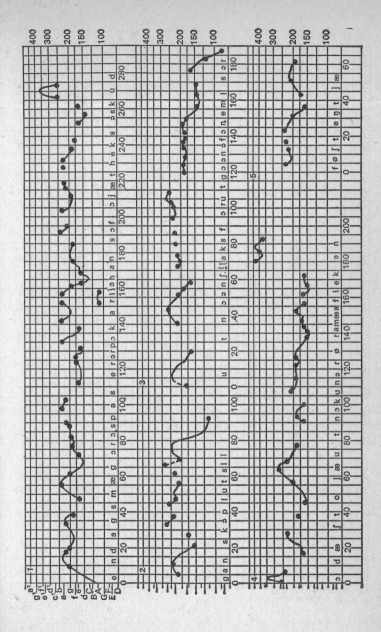

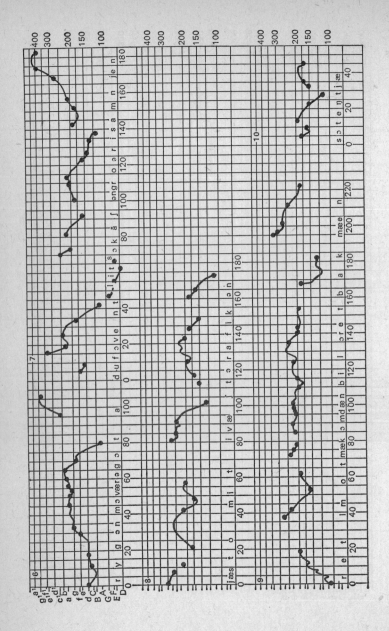

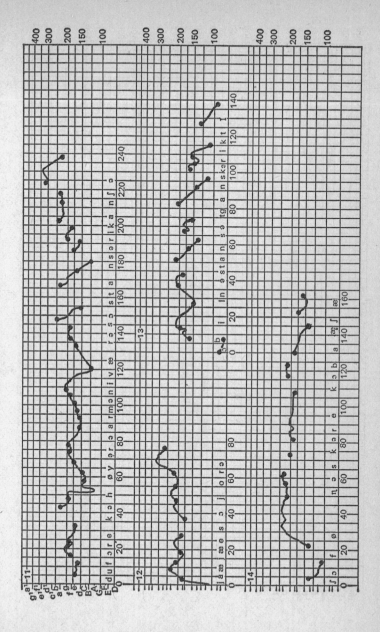

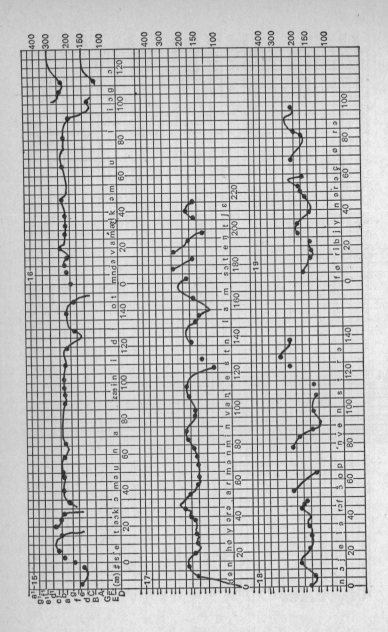

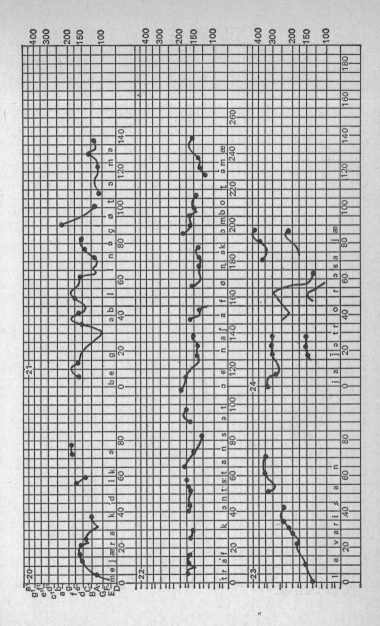

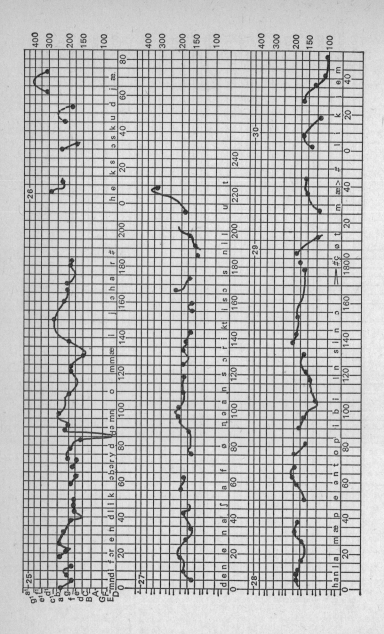

well with the descriptions given in the literature of the normal rise expected for the two musical tones. For each such rise there is also a corresponding fall, so that in an average utterance the successive high points will be approximately equal. Storm described accent 1 as rising a musical fourth; accent 2 as falling a third and rising a fourth (Storm, 1884, p. 44). Alnæs estimated the rise in both cases to be a sixth, the fall in accent 2 to be a third (Alnæs, 1925, p. 27). Selmer found an average rise of a fifth, though it could exceed the octave in some cases, with a slightly smaller fall in accent 2 (1920, pp. 65, 74). We may thus expect that the intervals between Aabel's high and low points in the curve are those of the rising and falling accents, or word tones. We expect to find an accent 1 which is rising, and an accent 2 which is falling-rising.

But the curves as they appear on the spectrograms are not clearly divided into such units. The movement is everywhere continuous, with an up-and-down alternation, if we disregard the unvoiced intervals. It appears that if one did not know (by auditory means) where the stresses are located, it would not be possible to detect the characteristic word tones. If we compare the tonal movement of *spaserer på* 1.98–135 with that of *hekseskudd* 1.238–272, we find that the two first syllables of each have almost identical appearance; for the moment we may disregard the high tone on the third syllable of the latter, noting only that in both there is a rise at the end. Yet we know that the first has accent 1 on the second syllable, while the second has accent 2 on the first, with light stress on the second. Similarly if we compare *jeg går og spa-* 1.55–98 with *ganske* 2.11–33 or *i bilen* 28.96 with *bilene* 21.40. Only if we locate the stresses, does a difference appear between the two tones, and then only in relation to the location of the stress. Wherever we have an accent 1, its stress falls near the low point of the curve; in accent 2, the stress comes earlier, and usually includes the preceding high point, while the low point follows the main stress.[7]

The up-and-down melody of East Norwegian may thus be regarded as a kind of carrier wave for the accentual contours. When non-Norwegians or speakers of other Norwegian dialects say that the East Norwegian 'sings', this billowing movement is what they hear. Conversely, when East Norwegians say that the others sing, it is because they hear a melody different from their own. In the words of Thomas Carlyle, 'Accent is a kind of chanting; all men have accent of their own, – though they only notice that of others' (Alnæs, 1916). The melody is not in itself distinctive,

7. An interesting consequence of this fact is that when an uneducated East Norwegian speaker shifts the stress backward from the second to the first syllable of a word like *spaserer*, there is no change in melody, and we would be unable to see the difference in a melodic chart like the present one. Cf. *sjafførene* 27.45; *bilene* 21.40 and *bilen* 28.96.

but acquires distinctive value when it is associated with stress in a particular way. The opinion that dynamic facts were more important than musical in creating the distinction between Accent 1 and 2 has already been advanced by Selmer (1928). But he was not willing to carry this reasoning further because of the impossibility of precisely measuring the factor of stress. Although the nature of stress thus remains something of a mystery, its auditory reality is unquestioned.

Once we have located our primary stresses, we will have no difficulty in identifying most of them as associated with either accent 1 or 2, as these have been described in the literature. The falling–rising melody of 2 is especially conspicuous, e.g. in *hekseskudd* 1.238, *tenkte jeg* 5.24, *gror i sammen igjen* 7.110. Accent 1 is less uniform; it rises in *stod jeg* 4.0, *flekken* 4.162, falls in *fornemmelser* 3.140, *en* 9.200, falls and rises in *imot* 10.40, *været* 11.20. The fact that accent 1 can fall instead of rising was observed already by Selmer, but he drew no further conclusions concerning the essential features of the melodic contrast (1920). This fall is calculated to cast doubt on the traditional description of accent 1 as rising and its relation to 2, the falling–rising tone. But in order to arrive at a new conception of the contrast, we have to clear away another common error concerning the two accents, namely that they are 'word tones'. It is true that when words are spoken in isolation and are stressed on the first syllable, they show two kinds of melodic contours, accent 1 most often rising, 2 most often falling-rising. But if we consider words as they occur in utterances, we find that there is no basis whatever for identifying words with these melodic contours. If we eliminate the notion of 'word' entirely from our description of the tones, we may then be able to isolate the real contrast between them.

The idea that the accents are word tones arose from the fact that each word, when pronounced as a whole utterance, has one or the other of the two accents traditionally associated with its stressed syllable. But in context the word may either have or not have this accent, depending on whether it still contains a stressed syllable; and under certain circumstances, it may even acquire a different accent (changing from 1 to 2 or vice versa).[8] Furthermore, as we have shown above, the extent of the tonal contour is quite independent of the number of words. The contours move without break from stress to stress, so that together they constitute the tonal movement of the entire utterance. We need only cast an eye on the text before us to see evidence of this. In utterance 6 the five words *ryggen må være / gått av* are divided into two tonal contours. Nearly everywhere the contours cover anywhere from two to five words; in utterance 23 the melody includes a whole sentence of four words.

8. For the rules see Alnæs (1925, pp. 30, 34).

The use of 'word' in this connection has troubled previous investigators. Broch writes that 'the idea of a "word" in relation to the two tonic accents is to be taken in a wider sense than the usual grammatical one' (1935, p. 86). Elsewhere he says, 'Der rhythmische Abschnitt hat somit in der unbefangenen ungekünstelten Sprechweise gewissermassen die Funktion des "Wortes" übergenommen' (1939). The fact itself has been well-known, and Alnæs has created the word *tonelagsgruppe* to describe a group of words held together by a single tonal contour. 'The word melody', he writes, 'can include more than a single word' (1916, p. 92). This is equivalent to saying that the word melody is not a word melody, and has led to an unfortunate terminological situation.

The difficulty has arisen because previous investigators have not always distinguished between the structural or word-differentiating function of the accents and their contextual or syntactic function. In the lexicon, where each word appears in a full form as distinct from all other words as its pronunciation in isolation permits, the accent appears as a word tone. But in context, the accent is a property of the utterance as a whole, and its function must be seen in relation to the stresses which form the rhythmic movement of the utterance. Here we cannot say that 'the word tone is extended to include many words', but that each measure has its melodic contour, and that the word has the melodic contour of a measure or even of a whole utterance whenever it constitutes a measure or an utterance by itself. In any case, the 'word' is a semantic-grammatical unit, and as such is irrelevant to our analysis of the tonal movement of the utterance; we do not at this stage of our analysis have any way of determining what is a 'word'. Instead of speaking of *words*, we shall therefore speak of *measures*, and divide our text into measures, each one of which contains a stressed syllable and includes a complete tonal contour. The beginning and end of a contour will be considered as constituting a tonal juncture, usually coinciding with a syntactic break.[9]

We now find that we have two kinds of measures, according to the accents which characterize the stressed syllables. But is the entire contour of these contrasting accents really relevant to the difference? If we compare two final measures like *flekken* 4.160, with accent 1, and *hekseskudd* 1.235, with accent 2, we see that the difference between them is localized in the early part of the measure, preceding the low point. If we compare two non-final measures like *sto jæ* 4.40, with accent 1, and *ganske* 2.0, with accent 2, we find the same thing. In each case there is a rise from the low point around d which appears to be independent of the preceding parts

9. The word 'takt' has been used by Olaf Broch (1935; 1939); cf. his statement (1935, p. 104) '. . . the basic norm may be defined as a tendency to produce stress-waves of a certain size, i.e. *length-units*, or in musical terms *measures*. . . .'

of the curve. A study of the measurements made by Selmer of words in isolation confirms the hypothesis that the melody which follows the low point is independent of the part that precedes. We can thus divide the contour of the measure into two parts, calling the first, which contains the tonal distinction, the (tonal) *nucleus*, and the second, which follows the low point, the (tonal) *satellite*. The nucleus is not necessarily identical with the stressed syllable, but it must include some or all of it.

If we now compare the nuclei of all accent 1's, we find that they have in common nothing more than the presence of a relatively lower note somewhere in the stressed syllable. In contrast, the accent 2's may have a preceding high, which is regularly followed by a fall to a low point that often comes in the following syllable. But, it may be objected, what about monosyllables like *ut* 27.210 or whole utterances like 23 with a steep rise from beginning to end? Here, too, we propose to find a nucleus consisting of a low, followed by a rising satellite; the contrast with a corresponding accent 2 would only make itself felt in the opening part of the contour. Some have been tempted to regard monosyllabic utterances as lacking in distinctive tone because of the inability of these to take accent 2. But when we divide each measure into tonal nucleus and satellite, it is seen that monosyllables fall into the same pattern as other utterances with accent 1. But the greatest advantage of this distinction is that it makes room for those instances where the contour of utterances is falling or level. This is especially common with accent 1, as Selmer found when five of his thirty-two words failed to rise at the end; but even in accent 2 there were two which showed no rise.[10] In none of these cases were the two accents confused; their distinctive features were still present, as we are defining them here. But Selmer assumed that he had secured 'lexical pronunciations' and that these were therefore pure examples of 'word tone'. But every utterance, even of a word in isolation, must have a tonal satellite, and the examples measured by Selmer show that while the accentual difference is localized to the nucleus of the measure, the rest of the contour is dependent on other factors which we shall analyse later.

We must now consider the formulation of our contrast between accent 1 and 2. If we consider only the point in the tonal curve at which stress sets in (the beginning of the ballistic stroke), we could describe 1 as 'low', 2 as 'high'. This was the solution of Carl Borgstrøm (1937) when he made the only previous attempt to apply structural points of view to this problem.[11] But in view of the fact that a low is just as essential to 2 as to 1, this

10. Accent 1: N2 dag, N12 hus, N20 været, N22 søndag, N27 gårdsgutttjeneste. Accent 2: N44 stuepikene, N59 selskapene. For a discussion between Selmer and the author see Selmer (1954) and Haugen (1955).

11. A somewhat different interpretation was advanced in his article (1947). [See now

is not entirely satisfactory. Accent 2 is quite different from the usual German or English *hochton*, and even in Norwegian it contrasts with an expressive high tone, as we shall see. The most adequate musical description is one which characterizes 1 as low, 2 as falling, or high-low. The fall always implies a preceding high and a following low, even when these are not actually present.

But we need to push this analysis a step further. By our definition accent 1 and 2 have a low in common; the low is thus not distinctive. But this leaves us without any relevant feature in accent 1, contrasting with a preceding high in accent 2; in Prague school terminology, one would then have to say that in this contrast 1 is unmarked (merkmallos), 2 is marked (merkmalhaft). The low is relevant to primary stress only, or in other words: East Norwegian stress is normally accompanied by a low tone. This has nothing to do with the presence of the two tonal accents; the same is found, for example, in South German. Accent 1 is therefore the accent which is accompanied only by the typical tonal quality of a stressed syllable; for this reason Norwegians generally identify it with the stress accents of other languages, even when these have the opposite kind of tone. In accent 1 the melodic nucleus coincides with the stressed syllable. But in accent 2 the melodic nucleus has a tendency to spread into the following, unstressed syllable as well. We must turn back to our earlier consideration of the melodic movement in East Norwegian. In both accents there is a potential melodic curve of high-low-high; in accent 1 the stress falls on the low, in 2 it falls between the first high and the low, so that the difference between them is one of phase. It is often said that accent 2 is felt to be incomplete at the end of the stressed syllable; this is because the melody has not yet reached its low point. A new syllable is essential for its completion; such a syllable is heard by the ear in many cases where it is not actually pronounced (e.g. 5.40, 7.50, 10.30 etc.).

But if this is true, we glimpse the possibility of defining the accents, not so much in terms of tonal movement, as in terms of the extent of their nuclei. Accent 1 is characterized as a short nucleus, concentrating the relevant tonal movement within the stressed syllable, 2 as a long nucleus, in which the tonal movement runs over into the next. The accents are often called 'monosyllabic' and 'dissyllabic' because they are derived historically from respectively mono- and polysyllables; but if our definition is correct, this would also be an accurate synchronic description of them.

Since this definition is independent of the specific tonal movement of

---

his paper 1962.] A popular book entitled *Korrekt Dagligtale* (1949) by Inger Bugge uses the terms *mørk* 'dark' for accent 1 and *lys* 'light' for accent 2, obviously to express the difference in initial tone (the writer has found that these terms are immediately understandable to speakers of Oslo Norwegian).

East Norwegian, it should be possible to test it by trying it out on other Norwegian dialects having relevant tonal accents. A study of the measurements made by Selmer of the Norwegian spoken in Bergen, Sunnmøre and Stavanger shows that this is not only possible, but provides for the first time a common formula for these various melodic types. An impression of the analysis that could be made will be given by placing side by side the schematic tonal patterns which Selmer has drawn to sum up his results. In order to make them comparable in terms of our formula, we have here drawn dotted lines to show approximately the borders of the stressed syllables (including only the core consisting of the long vowel or the short vowel plus voiced consonant).

All three of the West Norwegian tonal patterns differ from the East Norwegian in having a high tone within the nucleus of both accents. On this point they stand closer to the other Germanic languages. But otherwise there is a great contrast between North-west Norwegian (Bergen and Sunnmøre) on the one hand, and South-west Norwegian (Stavanger) on the other. In the North-west the nucleus includes a low as well, in both accents, while in the South-west it does not. The two North-west dialects have a steep fall in accent 1, a more leisurely one in accent 2 extending into the following syllable. The common high-low melody of the nucleus is in one case concentrated in the stressed syllable, in the other spread out into the next. In the South-west the nucleus of accent 1 is high (the peak of a movement low-high-low, in which the second low is contour). The nucleus of accent 2 is high-low-high (with a following low which is contour); the second peak may simply be regarded as a repetition of the first, whereby the nucleus is marked as extending over into the second syllable. It should be noted that the second high is not a new stress; in a compound like the place name Ystervåg the second syllable has the second high, while the third has the secondary stress (Selmer, 1927, p. 53). The second high of the nucleus gives rather an auditory effect of a carry-over of stress. There is a parallelism with Swedish stress conditions which suggests that the South-west Norwegian may reflect an older Scandinavian situation than the East Norwegian.[12]

An interesting consequence of the views here advanced is that they make it possible to draw parallels with the hypotheses concerning accentual conditions in Danish recently advanced by the Danish phonetician Svend Smith (1944; 1938). He has brought forward evidence to show that the glottal catch found in many Danish words is not the main difference between accent 1 and 2. Even when the glottal catch is missing, there is a difference in the innervation of accent 1 and 2. In the former it is short and intense, in the latter it is long and relatively weak. A comparison with a Danish dialect which has preserved the tonal distinctions lost in most Danish speech shows similar conditions to those of South-west Norwegian. In the Felsted dialect, as investigated by Marie Bjerrum (1948, p. 53), accent 1 has one high and is relatively short, while accent 2 has two highs and is relatively long. It seems very probable that the contrast between a relatively short, dynamically (and therefore musically) intense nucleus and a relatively long, but weak nucleus is the essence of the accentual contrast throughout Scandinavia.

After this digression, we shall now return to the text and study the examples of abnormal and emphatic speech contained in it. In utterances 14, 15 and 16 we have a series of nuclei which contain no lows whatever. The tonal curve is here practically level, with only occasional lapses into the usual melody. The speaker is shouting in 14 and 15, whimpering in 16; in both cases the average level is about the same as the high which else-where is characteristic of unstressed syllables.[13] Alnæs describes this as 'dvælende betoning' (drawn-out tone), which occurs in 'strongly emotional speech' (1916, p. 89; 1932, pp. 55, 68). He says it is characteristic of shouting, of exclamations like *fy*! or *skam*! 'shame', and of dramatic declamation. It may even be used by a man who is trying to make himself heard on the telephone: Det er *Lund*! (1916, p. 113). We see that in this kind of speech the distinction between accent 1 and 2 disappears; cf. *hva* 16.15 and *mulig* 16.50, *sjåførene* 14.0 and *unna* 15.50.

12. Cf. the measurements of N. C. Stalling, which are not unlike those of Stavanger. He defines (p. 173) accent 1 as high (with falling contour), 2 as falling-rising (i.e. high-low-high).

13. The double line in utterances 16 and 24 is due to uncertainty concerning the interpretation of the spectrograms; the two octaves may be due to some special kind of voice, like the *knarrstimme* of some writers on the subject; the effect is similar to falsetto.

Within the nucleus of a Norwegian measure we may therefore find three possible tonal accompaniments. But we cannot set up an accent 3 to account for the last of these. Its high tone is not in contrast to either one of the two accents, but to the normal low tone of both. The low tone is the normal accompaniment of primary stress; high tone is expressive.

Having determined the essential contrasts of the nucleus, we shall now turn to the satellite. Some satellites are non-final in the utterance, others are final. Since it is generally agreed that most of what is usually called 'sentence intonation' is concentrated at the end of the utterance, we may expect that the study of the satellites will lead us to some conclusions about sentence intonation. In this study, however, we shall not use this expression, since it does not appear from our material that there is any special sentence intonation, any more than there is a word intonation. Like the word, the sentence is a grammatical unit which does not coincide with any particular intonational contour, and can only be determined, if at all, at a later stage of analysis.

If we study the satellites, e.g. in utterance 11, we find a series of non-final contours which rise from the usual low of Aabel's speech to the usual high, about g. These reach a point which is also the beginning of the following measure. While this is the usual non-final contour, it is rather less common in final position. But it does occur, for example, in the utterances 5, 10 and 17 which end with the words *tenkte jeg*, also in utterances 20, 22, 28 and 29. As will be seen, all of these involve the expectation of a continuation. But this is not strictly necessary, since one can easily change an expression like *så tenkte jeg* 'then I thought' into *det tenkte jeg* 'I thought so', or even *hva tenkte jeg* 'what did I think', without changing the tonal satellite. There is a neutral quality in this satellite, common to non-final and final positions, which makes it usable for incomplete statements, but also for questions or complete statements if these are spoken in an unemphatic and unemotional way. Its function is to fill out and complete the measure, and its final high note is in contrast with the low note of the stressed nucleus. In dialects like those of South-west Norway, where the nucleus is high, the normal satellite ends low. Even in Eastern Norway, the expressive change to high tone in the stressed nucleus brings with it a falling satellite.

Most of the utterances in our material, however, end either on a much higher or lower note than that of the normal satellite. Aabel's finals in this selection are characteristically very high, so that twelve of the thirty utterances end on a note that is nearly a whole octave above the normal high (falsetto in 16 and 24). They are not all equally high, and in ordinary undramatic speech the difference would be much less. The function of these high finals is clearly one of animation; the high notes express the speaker's interest in what he is saying. Lower notes in the same utterances would have reduced the excitement of the narrative. Alnæs has pointed out this function of the rising final contour; anyone who has heard East Norwegians speaking, especially young girls, will have noticed the so-called 'Oslo tone', with its cheerful, almost twittering quality (1916, pp. 107–8). A comparison of the question in utterance 23 with the other high finals shows that, as Alnæs has maintained, there is no special tone for questions. But it is the usual thing for questions to be spoken with a high final, at least when the speaker is interested in the answer. The effect of the extra high final is one of appeal to the listener, and it is therefore usually avoided in reading, especially in serious or impersonal material. The high final, with a pitch only slightly raised over that of the normal, is the one we find in most of Selmer's recorded examples and in Storm's and Alnæs's notation. Here it is not one of expressive appeal, but of ordinary finality with sustained interest.

The interest is not always thus sustained to the end of the utterance. In our material we have low final tone at the end of utterances 3, 8, 13, 15, 21 and 30. Of these, 15 must be eliminated at once as exemplifying the low final after an exclamatory stress, discussed above.[14] There is not much difference in finality between these and most of the rising satellites. The general rule of low tone for finality applies only in part to ordinary East Norwegian speech, even though it is often taught in Norwegian schools and shows its effects in a typical 'reading tone' which good teachers attempt to discourage. This international, or at least west European tradition, is in conflict with the movement of natural speech in Norwegian; it may go back to a medieval practice.[15] Yet low final is also a part of Norwegian speech. Alnæs has formulated the rule that 'if the emphatic stress comes at the end of the sentence or word combination, the melody ends rising; if the emphasis is placed at the beginning of the phrase or sentence, the sentence melody is falling' (1932, pp. 7, 56, 65, 75). He shows that if two or more equal stresses are combined into one phrase, the last receives the main stress unless there is some reason to stress an earlier one. In *smør og brød* 'bread and butter' the second stress is stronger than the first and gets rising tone, while in *mine damer og herrer* 'ladies and gentlemen', the second is weaker (because of the formularistic nature of the combination) and gets low final tone. This theory appears to be borne out by our materials, since we find that in several of the utterances with low

14. Alnæs makes the error of discussing this kind of falling final together with the others, though they have clearly different functions.

15. Cf. the medieval melody used for teaching the proper intonation at commas (small rise), questions (large rise), periods (fall), cited in Alnæs (1916, p. 152).

final, the main stress comes early; e.g. in 3 the stress is on *noen* 3.45, in 8 on *verste* 8.90.

The contrast between high and low final thus seems to be associated with the distribution of stress among the measures of the utterance. If we assume that each utterance (or perhaps we should say 'phrase') has one primary stress which is emphasized beyond the others, we may say that the high final may mark the last stress as emphatic, while low final points back to some previous stress as the emphatic one. Alnæs gives many examples of utterances which must be read with emphasis on a preceding stress to make sense, e.g. *Øyvind* het han '*Øyvind* was his name' or han var som en *ungdom* frisk 'he was as chipper as a *youth*'. The utterance stress has a function which points beyond the utterance to other utterances before or after as well as unifying the structure of the utterance itself. It makes it possible for the speaker to indicate what is new and important in his statement. In utterance 1 our actor holds the whole statement together and marks the final word as emphatic by the sharp rise at the end. In utterance 2 there is less novelty and therefore normal tone (disregarding the dragging tail). In utterance 3 he simply repeats in other words the contents of 2, so that there is additional reason for allowing it to sink at the end. In utterance 4 comes a new and surprising item of information, which accordingly ends far up in the clouds. Whatever finality the low tone has in Norwegian is due to this tendency to slacken interest near the end of a predictable sequence. Its use in reading and lecturing is understandable in view of the speaker's awareness of each approaching end. By de-emphasizing the end one also avoids putting too much of one's own personality into an impersonal statement.

We are now ready to generalize our results by expressing them in terms of the basic contrasts discovered.

1. The utterance can be divided into one or more tonal *measures*, each characterized by containing one primary stress, and the measures into tonal *nucleus* containing the contrast between accent 1 and 2 and a tonal *satellite* which fills out the rest of the measure.

2. The nucleus is normally accompanied by a *low* tone, but may have expressive *high* tone; this contrast is *morphemic*, since it conveys meaning directly.

3. The low tone of the normal nucleus may come within the stressed core of the syllable, resulting in *accent 1*, or shortly after it, resulting in *accent 2*; this contrast between a *short* and a *long* nucleus may be regarded as *phonemic*, since it distinguishes otherwise identical words and has no semantic function of its own.

4. The *normal* satellite rises from a low point at the end of the nucleus to a high that may be approximately the same in final or non-final position; this high contrasts with the low of the nucleus, but has a neutral significance in relation to the statement as a whole.

5. The final pitch may be either *higher* or *lower* than that of the normal satellite if some special emphasis within the utterance is to be expressed; a high final lends emphasis to the last measure, a low final de-emphasizes it, so that these can be said to have a *syntactic* function.

6. A high final may be augmented as a dramatic device to show the speaker's interest in the statement and appeal to the listener's attention; like the high tone in the nucleus, this may be regarded as an *expressive* morphemic variant.

7. If it were desired to set up levels of Norwegian pitch similar to those often used in describing American English, three would probably be sufficient (low, high, extra high), though one might want to add a plus to the extra high for the expressive morphemic variant and a minus to the low in some cases of extra low finals; if one numbers them from below, accent 1 would be 1, 2 would be 2–1, a normal satellite would be 1–2, high final 1–3, low final 1–1.

The difference between (East) Norwegian and other Germanic languages should now be clear. Norwegian has a second (tonal) stress accent where the non-Scandinavian languages (plus Icelandic, Faroese and Finnish Swedish) have only one. East Norwegian has low tone with stress where English and North German normally have high tone. The unstressed syllables of the satellite rise in East Norwegian more often than in the other languages, and the contrast of high-low final is used in a special way.

Otto Jespersen, the Danish linguist, once suggested that the Norwegian and Swedish 'word melodies' might make it more difficult to express the nuances of thought and feeling than in other languages (1897–9, p. 606). This opinion can hardly be maintained in view of the analysis made in our study. It has been shown that the two accents are irrelevant to the tonal contour of the utterance as a whole, constituting as they do together the equivalent of the high stress tone of other Germanic languages. Beyond this, Norwegian has means of tonal variation within the measure and the utterance which correspond to those of other, related languages. Jespersen's reaction is probably due to the non-native's difficulty in hearing nuances in systems markedly different from his own. Though this has not been the theme of the present study, further variation of expression can of course be produced by changing the location of the stresses and altering the tempo, so that the pauses will fall differently and thereby create new utterance groupings. The size of the intervals between high and low can also be altered for expressive purposes. Every linguistic structure possesses infinite possibilities of variation if its speakers have the need and the desire to make use of them.

## References

ALNÆS, I. (1916), *Norsk Saetningsmelodi*, Oslo.

ALNÆS, I. (1925), *Norsk Uttaleordbok*, Oslo.

ALNÆS, I. (1932), *De Levende Ord*, Oslo.

BJERRUM, M. (1948), *Felstedmaalets Tonale Akcenter*, Aarhus.

Bo, A. (1933), *Tonegangen i Dansk Rigsmaal*, Copenhagen.

BORGSTRØM, C. (1937), *Norsk Tidsskrift for Sprogvidenskap*, vol. 9, pp. 260–63, Oslo.

BORGSTRØM, C. (1947), 'De prosodiske elementer i norsk', *Festskrift Broch*, Oslo, pp. 41–8.

BORGSTRØM, C. (1962), 'Tonemes and phrase intonation in South-Eastern standard Norwegian', *Studia Linguistica*, vol. 16, pp. 34–7.

BROCH, O. (1935), *Transactions of the Philological Society*, pp. 80–112.

BROCH, O. (1937), 'Begriffsunterschied auch Intonationsunterschied in dem Ostnorwegischen', Mélanges Holger Pedersen, *Acta Jutlandica*, vol. 9, no. 1, pp. 308–22.

BROCH, O. (1939), 'Numerusunterschied durch Intonationsunterschied in Ostnorwegischen', *Travaux du Cercle Linguistique de Prague*, vol. 8, pp. 116–29.

BROCH, O. (1944), 'Tonelag bestemmende for lydutvikling', *Maal og Minne*, pp. 145–61.

BUGGE, I. (1949), *Korrekt Dagligtale*, Oslo.

EKBLOM, R. (1933), *Om de danska Accentarterna*, Uppsala.

FINTOFT, K. (1970), *Acoustical Analysis and Perception of Tonemes in some Norwegian Dialects*, Oslo.

HANSEN, A. (1943), *Stødet i Dansk*, Copenhagen.

HAUGEN, E. (1949), 'Phoneme or prosodeme?', *Language*, vol. 25, pp. 278–82.

HAUGEN, E. (1955), 'Tonelagsanalyse', *Maal og Minne*, pp. 70–80.

HAUGEN, E. (1963), 'Pitch accent and tonemic juncture in Scandinavian', *Monatshefte*, vol. 55, pp. 157–61.

HAUGEN, E. (1965), *Norwegian–English Dictionary*, University of Wisconsin Press.

HAUGEN, E. (1967), 'On the rules of Norwegian tonality', *Language*, vol. 43, pp. 185–202.

JESPERSEN, O. (1897–9), *Fonetik*, Copenhagen.

JOOS, M. (1948), *Acoustic Phonetics*, Language Monograph no. 23.

MEYER, E. A. (1937), *Die Intonation im Schwedischen*, Stockholm.

OFTEDAL, M. (1952), *Norsk Tidsskrift for Sprogrindenskap*, vol. 16, pp. 201–25.

PIKE, K. L. (1948), *Tone Languages*, University of Michigan Press.

SELMER, E. W. (1920), 'Enkelt og dobbelt tonelag i Kristianiasprog', *Maal og Minne*, pp. 55–75.

SELMER, E. W. (1927), *Den musikalske aksent i Stavangersmålet*, Oslo.

SELMER, E. W. (1928), 'Noen bemerkninger om den musikalske aksent i dens forhold til den sterkt og svakt skårne aksent', *Festskr. Quigstad*, pp. 250–62.

SELMER, E. W. (1954), 'Tonelagsproblemer', *Maal og Minne*, pp. 180–88.

SMITH, S. (1938), 'Zur Physiologie des Stosses', *A.Ph.Sc.*, vol. 12, pp. 33–9.

SMITH, S. (1944), *Stødet i dansk Rigssprog*, Copenhagen.

STALLING, N. C. (1935), *Das phonologische System des Schwedischen* I, Nijmegen.

STORM, J. (1860), *Illustreret Nyhedsblad*, no. 40, p. 42.

STORM, J. (1884), 'Norsk lydskrift', *Norvegia*, vol. 1, pp. 40–56.

STORM, J. (1892), *Englische Philologie*, 2nd edn, vol. 1, Leipzig.

# Part Eight
## Varieties of English

Of all the influences that languages in contact wield upon one another, those of the prosody are most subtle and resistant to attempts to regulate them according to some standard. An intonation may persist long after the other remnants of a language have vanished, as happened with the Cacana language in South America. As English has expanded around the globe, or as large groups of speakers of other languages have formed enclaves in English-speaking territory, the varieties of English that have resulted from the amalgam carry a residue of other accents – the English of India has its characteristic intonations, as does that of Hawaii and that of American Blacks. A sample of each of the latter two is offered. The first, by Vanderslice and Pierson, has been slightly expanded by the principal author from its original version. The second is taken from Lorenzo Turner's pioneering study of Gullah, a dialect spoken on the Sea Islands of Georgia and South Carolina and the mainland coast nearby. What distinguished Turner's work was its break from a kind of dialectology based largely on geography that American linguists inherited from Europe, where geography has always been the most powerful factor in separating one dialect from another. He showed that Gullah, in its intonation and in other features, resembled certain West African languages in ways that could not be put down to co-incidence. The significance of this – that the Gullah dialect is not merely another variant of English as it was transported from England and developed into a regional form of speech in America – for several years escaped American dialectologists. But it has finally caught on, helped by the vigorous concern with social groupings, particularly urban classes and ethnic minorities and specifically Black English. That intonation should be singled out by Turner bears witness to its persistence, its tendency to live on when other features are submerged.

# 26 Ralph Vanderslice and Laura Shun Pierson

## Prosodic Features of Hawaiian English

Ralph Vanderslice and Laura Shun Pierson, 'Prosodic features of Hawaiian English', *Quarterly Journal of Speech*, vol. 53, no. 2, April 1967, pp. 156–66.

'A hateful jargon', 'a lingo of lesser breeds' (Carr, 1961), 'an unintelligible gibberish which passes for English' (Lind, 1960), 'a desecration of the greatest language on earth, and an abomination in the sight of the Lord' (*Honolulu Star Bulletin*, 13 February 1962). These are some of the epithets which have been hurled at Hawaii's Pidgin English.

The Fiftieth State has had a unique linguistic history. Captain Cook's discovery in 1778 of the 'Sandwich Islands' with their indigenous Polynesian culture; the arrival of New England missionaries in 1820 to counteract the immoral influence of the whaling fleets and, incidentally, teach English; the growth of the sugar industry after 1860, with massive immigration of contract laborers from various parts of the world to work the sugar and (after 1900) pineapple plantations; the overthrow of the monarchy (with American connivance) in 1893, leading to US annexation in 1898 and ultimately to statehood in 1959; all have influenced the development of the English dialect spoken in Hawaii and known locally as 'Pidgin'.

Although an English-based pidgin – in the technical sense of a highly simplified lingua franca used in a contact situation where it is native to neither side (Hall, 1966, p. xii) – arose during the first century of the Hawaiians' contact with the outside world (while internecine warfare and 'western' diseases reduced their numbers from 300,000 to 44,000) it was the 400,000 contract laborers imported between the 1860s and 1932 from China, Portugal, Japan, Puerto Rico, Korea and the Philippines who chiefly shaped the plantation pidgin from which the currently de-creolizing dialect is descended. *Pidgin* is the usual term for this dialect in Hawaii and will be so used here.

Today this dialect is socially embedded and fraught with connotations of race, class and group loyalty. Scathing censure by schools and newspapers has not discouraged use of Pidgin by the youth of the non-Caucasian majority (Shun, 1961, pp. 1–9).

There has been a dearth of descriptive study amid the vigorous but unsuccessful efforts to 'stamp out Island Dialect'. Pidgin has been treated as 'careless speech' or 'bad English'. Even supposedly scholarly studies often turn out to be merely classifications of 'most commonly encountered errors' (see, e.g. Kasdon and Smith, 1960).

The most neglected aspect of Pidgin has been its suprasegmental or prosodic features, and it is the purpose of this paper to describe the salient prosodic features of Hawaiian English. By prosodic features we mean what Abercrombie calls features of voice dynamics; in particular rhythm, pitch fluctuation (intonation), tessitura and register (1967, p. 89). By salient features we mean those in which Pidgin contrasts with General American English.[1] We use *GAE* to refer to the set of American English dialects which share the features under discussion in contrast with *Hawaiian American English* (*HAE*),[2] which we define as the English spoken in the state of Hawaii by native or long-term residents whose speech is marked by typical regional characteristics. The latter term thus covers a dialect continuum from standard *HAE* to broad Pidgin; except after such attributives we use *Pidgin* and *HAE* coterminously.

Hawaiian Pidgin differs conspicuously from *GAE* not only in features of voice dynamics but also in segmental sounds, grammar and vocabulary.[3] Certain of these correlated attributes appear in the examples below.

### Rhythm, tessitura and register

*Isosyllabism*. The rhythm of Pidgin is basically a syllable-timed rather than, as in most dialects of English, a stress-timed one. Syllables tend to have equal prominence in terms of loudness and duration, and to succeed each other at regular intervals with an effect 'like the steady tapping of a typewriter' (Linn, n.d., p. 7). The opposition between weak- and strong-stressed syllables is largely leveled, especially that between content and function words:

(1)

He said it was personal, and he couldn't release it without a requisition.

This is a sample of Standard *HAE* which differs only phonetically from a comparable *GAE* utterance:

(2)

He said it was personal, and he couldn't release it without a requisition.

1. The contrasts are in particular with the North Midland dialect of the senior author, but we believe they hold for a rather wide range of dialects spoken on the mainland.

2. The redundancy of this term seems worth tolerating to forestall a misleading contrast between *Hawaiian* and *American*. *Hawaiian* is used in its regional, not its ethnic nor its linguistic sense; of course *GAE* is also widely spoken in Hawaii.

3. For a good (but dated) study of the syntactic and lexical peculiarities, see Reinecke and Tokimasa (1934). See now also Reinecke (1969 – revised version of 1935 thesis).

The most noticeable prosodic feature of (1) is its isosyllabism. The terminal pitch pattern is also characteristic of Pidgin and will be discussed under *scoop*.

It should be noted that the impressionistic term *choppy* as used in local 'speech improvement' training subsumes both this syllable-timed rhythm and the frequent occurrence of intrusive glottal stops before syllable-initial vowels in Pidgin.

*Drawl*. Although Pidgin syllables tend to have equal duration, *ceteris paribus*, words of special semantic importance are often extended or drawled to an extreme degree:

(3)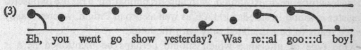
Eh, you went go show yesterday? Was re::al goo:::d boy!

The falling intonation on *yesterday* exemplifies the Pidgin pattern for general questions discussed below.[4] What is to be noted here is the lengthening for emphasis of *real* and *good*, the latter lasting on the order of a second. We may summarize the rhythm of HAE, then, as basically syllable-timed but with marked drawling of occasional syllables for emphasis.

*Tessitura*. The 'characteristic range of notes, or compass, within which the pitch fluctuation . . . falls' (Abercrombie, 1967, p. 99) is generally wider in HAE than in GAE, and more frequent use is made of the higher pitches within that tessitura. The wide tessitura tends to be interpreted as an affective index by GAE speakers, to whom Pidgin therefore often sounds markedly enthusiastic or excited.

*Register*. Registers are transitory 'voice quality' modifications arising from changes in the complex of adjustments of the laryngeal structures affecting phonation. These modifications are transitory by comparison with the quasi-permanent features of an individual's voice quality norm, but their time domain is usually long with respect to the same or similar adjustments employed as segmental features, e.g., in languages where creaky voice or breathy voice are criterial features of certain phonemic distinctions (see Ladefoged, 1964; Catford, 1964). Two such registers which play a significant role in HAE are raspy voice and falsetto.

4. The sentence means 'Did you go to the show yesterday?' This citation should be read with the typically monophthongal [e] and [o]. *Went* is one of the Pidgin auxiliaries which form compound tenses with the unmarked infinitive. The vocative *boy* is here used by one girl speaking to another; *man, guys* as vocatives are similarly ungendered in HAE.

Raspy voice is technically a voiced ary-epiglottic trill. The vocal cords vibrate in the usual way, and in addition the collar of the larynx constricts in a sphincter-like closure and vibrates at a lower frequency. This produces a rough quality which is apparently a permanent feature of voice quality for some speakers – notably Louis Armstrong – but in Pidgin is employed as a register which is brought into play for short periods, especially on drawled syllables, as a sort of intensifier. Its use is more common among, but not restricted to, male speakers.

Falsetto on the other hand is a register restricted to female speakers, except for jocular use by males comparable to that in GAE. Many female HAE speakers regularly produce their upper levels of pitch, within the wide tessitura previously noted, with falsetto phonation. This use of falsetto register is found in standard HAE as well as broad Pidgin, whereas raspy voice tends to be associated only with the latter.

One type of utterance which should perhaps be mentioned here is the reduplication of certain monosyllabic interjections, particularly [ʔoʔoʔoʔoʔoʔoʔo] 'oh' (in the sense of 'now I understand') and [jɛjɛjɛjɛjɛ] 'yes' (in much the same sense). With respect to both their high falling intonation and the frequent presence of raspy voice, these utterances are closely comparable to the drawled syllables noted above.

### Intonation

*Pitch accent.* Word stress is but loosely fixed in isosyllabic HAE and is often identifiable only by the occurrence of an accent or pitch obtrusion (see Bolinger, 1958), which is more regularly at the end of intonation clauses in Pidgin than in GAE; usually on the penult or ultima. Thus arise such pronunciations as: *hospital* [hɑsˈpɪtəl], *operate* [ɑpəˈɹeːt], *catalog* [kʰætʰəˈlɔg]. This is particularly noticeable in compound nouns which have falling stress in GAE: *snack bar* [snækˈbɑː], *crewcut* [kɹuˈkʰɑt], *summertime* [sɑmɑ ˈtɑɪm], *Volkswagen* [voksˈwægən].

However, accent placement is not entirely predictable. Ordinary adjective-noun phrases are often forestressed (even in quite noncontrastive contexts) as if they were compound nouns: *a pretty kitten* [ə ˈpɹɪtʰi kʰɪtʰɛn]. There is, in short, a certain randomness in the location of accent in Pidgin but a strong tendency for it to occur at the ends of clauses. In any case, accent location does not perform an information-pointing function in Pidgin as it does in GAE, where it is usually associated with the point of least redundancy (Bolinger, 1958; Hultzén, 1959). In Pidgin the accent location, usually clause-final, is independent of redundancy or contrast:

(4)
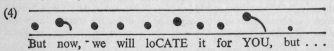
But now, we will loCATE it for YOU, but . . .

The speaker of (4), from the Honolulu Board of Water Supply, was explaining a policy under which his department could no longer *repair* a break in the pipe serving a private house, although they would still *locate* it. In a comparable GAE statement, contrastive accent would be obligatory:

(5)
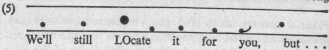

We'll still LOcate it for you, but . . .

Another example of insensitivity of Pidgin accent-location to implied contrast is a male student's reply (7) to his friend's contention (6):

(6)
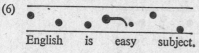

English is easy subject.

(7)
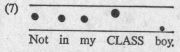

Not in my CLASS boy.

Even where there is explicit contrast within the immediate context, a redundant reiterative element will usually be accented if it is clause-final (speaking of land in Hawaii):

(8) (i)
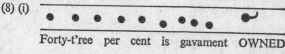

Forty-t'ree per cent is gavament OWNED

(ii)
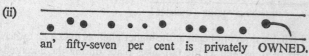

an' fifty-seven per cent is privately OWNED.

A shift of accent would be obligatory in GAE at least in (ii), not only because *privately* contrasts with *government*, but also because *owned* has already occurred in the context. It would be optional in (i) – i.e., the contrast can be anticipated or not. Such an anticipatory accent-shift in a Pidgin utterance is shown in (9i) on THIS *semester* but (ii) the Pidgin pattern reasserts itself to obliterate the expected (by GAE speakers) parallel emphasis on *nine* and *next*:

(9) (i)
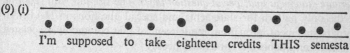

I'm supposed to take eighteen credits THIS semesta

(ii)
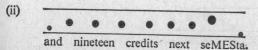

and nineteen credits next seMESta.

Thus at the same time that word stress in HAE is both less conspicuous and less stable than in GAE, accent is less context-sensitive, being more regularly at clause ends rather than correlated with information point even in contrastive contexts.

*Scoop.* Pidgin statements usually (and special or interrogative-word questions sometimes) take a rise-fall intonation which is very like the corresponding contour of GAE except for the phonetic shape of the pitch accent:

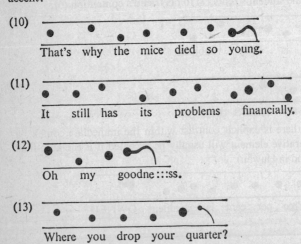

(10) That's why the mice died so young.

(11) It still has its problems financially.

(12) Oh my goodne:::ss.

(13) Where you drop your quarter?

The accented syllable does not begin at the higher pitch as in GAE; rather the rise, or part of it, as well as the fall takes place during the accented syllable or succeeding ones. For this phenomenon we borrow Hockett's term *scoop*, extending it to include pitch rise after as well as on the accented syllable. (Pittenger, Hockett and Danehy, 1960, pp. 193–4). A closely similar intonation is described by Jones as used sometimes in Southern England and especially in Wales (1966, pp. 159, 161–2).

*Alternate statement and special-question tunes.* The rise-fall with scoop is not the only pattern for statements and special questions in HAE. An alternate statement intonation, reminiscent of that commonly associated with Mexican Spanish, is sometimes heard:

(14) Let's hope it's this buggah.

(15)

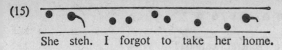

She steh. I forgot to take her home.

Interrogative-word questions (exclusive of reclamatory and echo questions, etc.) have basically the same two patterns in both Pidgin and GAE. One is identical with the rise-fall statement tune (sans scoop in GAE); the other, which has been curiously neglected in descriptions of GAE, is very common in HAE:

(16)

Where can I get some cups?

(17)

What room is Doctor Boyer?

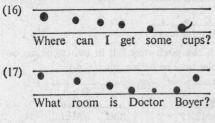

(18) (i)

To where you going Richard?

(ii)

To the wedding?

Note in (18) that the terminal pitch rise of the special question (i) is taken over by the vocative, as it would be also in GAE.

*General questions.* The Pidgin pattern for yes–no questions is a very conspicuous feature of the dialect, being markedly different from the GAE pattern of rising or high pitch with rising terminal. The usual form of HAE general questions starts at or quickly rises to high pitch level which lasts until just before the accented ultima or penult, on which there is low pitch with terminal steadying or slight rise:

(19)

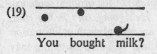

You bought milk?

(20)

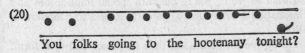

You folks going to the hootenany tonight?

(21)

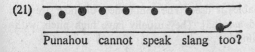

Punahou cannot speak slang too?

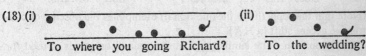

(22)

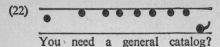

You need a general catalog?

Note that the accented syllable is the one after the pitch drop; such a downward pitch obtrusion is rare in GAE and mainlanders often have difficulty hearing it as a question-marker. A variant with fall-by-glide on the ultima is sometimes used (the vocative here being of course a separate clause):

(23)

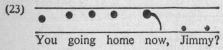

You going home now, Jimmy?

When the penult is accented, the pitch may fall in two steps, as on *wedding* in (18ii), or both syllables may be on low pitch (24i):

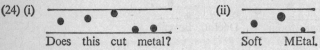

(24) (i) Does this cut metal?  (ii) Soft MEtal.

(Note that the reply (ii) to the question (i) exemplifies the absence of contrastive accent shift in HAE.)

An intonation quite similar to that for general questions is used for prepositive dependent clauses; it is especially noticeable when the clause is longer than the conversational norm, as in this example from a university debate:

(25) Until the gavament realizes that there is a problem here . . .

*Tag questions.* A question tag is a special form which when appended to a statement or command converts it into a question. The commonest GAE tag form repeats the subject (with obligatory pronominalization) and the verb (with obligatory reduction to auxiliary or *do*) of the original sentence, with verb inversion and negative-switching: *He's going, isn't he? It runs, doesn't it? They can't come, can they?* There are several distinct intonation choices, e.g. low-rising, high-falling, high-rising. Negative-switching may be deleted (*You want to go, do you?*), but with special implications and syntactic and intonational constraints apparently subject to considerable dialectal variation.

Pidgin tags are of interest because of their frequency and their form. The GAE type just discussed is seldom encountered; rather a special set of questioning monosyllables is used. The commonest of these are *yeh* [jɛ], *no* [no], *eh* [ʔe], and *huh* [hã]. They usually have high pitch, with terminal rise if sentence final:

(26)

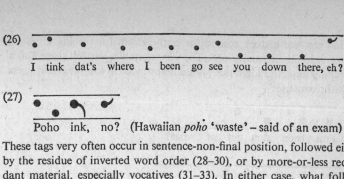

I tink dat's where I been go see you down there, eh?

(27)

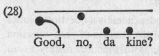

Poho ink, no? (Hawaiian *poho* 'waste' – said of an exam)

These tags very often occur in sentence-non-final position, followed either by the residue of inverted word order (28–30), or by more-or-less redundant material, especially vocatives (31–33). In either case, what follows the tag is at low pitch:

(28)

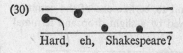

Good, no, da kine?

(29)

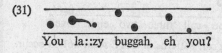

T'ree-credit course, eh was?

(30)

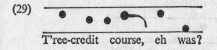

Hard, eh, Shakespeare?

(31)

You la::zy buggah, eh you?

(32)

You fema::le, eh Joyce?

(33)

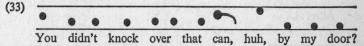

You didn't knock over that can, huh, by my door?

Besides these monosyllabic tags there are two others which should be noted. The question tag *you know?* has very wide currency among the younger speakers of HAE, but its distribution and intonation do not contrast with GAE usage except for a sharper pitch rise on the second syllable (a correlate of wide tessitura). The use of the tag-like phrase *or what?* on the other hand contrasts markedly. In GAE this is not a true question tag, but a stock second (or last) element for turning a yes–no question into an alternative one. The *what* normally has full stress and a high-falling tune. In Pidgin this phrase is appended at low pitch and stress and without pause:

(34)
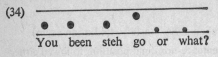
You been steh go or what?

(35)
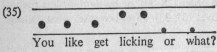
You like get licking or what?

Whether the material preceding the tag is independently a question is moot in these citations (and typically) because of the absence of verb inversion in Pidgin. Sometimes the tag *or what* seems to function merely as an expletive comparable to GAE 'or anything':

(36)
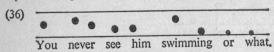
You never see him swimming or what.

*Vocatives.* Pidgin calling vocatives tend to be like one of the common GAE patterns, with high pitch followed by a slight drop and terminal rise:

(37)
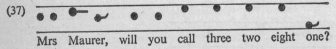
Mrs Maurer, will you call three two eight one?

The mid-rising and high-falling call patterns of GAE seem not to occur.

Conversational utterance-initial vocatives in Pidgin usually have a falling intonation with very conspicuous scoop, as opposed to the rising of fall–rise patterns typical of GAE:

(38)

Alfre::d . .

(39)
William . . .

(40)
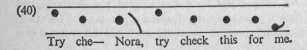
Try che— Nora, try check this for me.

Parenthetic medial vocatives follow the GAE pattern, e.g. (18), but final ones are regularly at low pitch with falling contour. They do not as in GAE follow the pitch of high preceding material, e.g. (32), and the contrast between low-rising and low-falling vocatives (see Pittenger, 1957, p. 45) is absent.

## Summary and outlook

Hawaiian American English is a unique dialect, of which the most salient prosodic features are:

1. Syllable-timed rhythm, modified by emphatic drawl.
2. Wide tessitura.
3. Special registers: raspy voice, falsetto.
4. Scoop on the rise-fall statement (and special-question) tune.
5. Fluid word-stress and non-information-pointing accent placement.
6. Specific characteristic intonations: especially a general-question pattern with sharp pitch drop contrasting with GAE rise.

None of these features is a serious barrier to mutual intelligibility with other Englishes, although of course these features function as indices of provenience – social and racial as well as geographical.

Dialect leveling proceeds apace in Hawaii as elsewhere under the impact of television, talkies and travel. But 'Haole talk' (GAE) is not the sole alternative to monodialectal broad Pidgin; nor, to many Island youth, an acceptable one. Arthur Bronstein has wisely stated that in this country one's speech is considered standard '*if it reflects the speech patterns of the educated persons in your community*' (1960, p. 6). Standard Hawaiian American English, regionally marked and distinct from GAE particularly in the prosodic features herein described, is spoken by many educated Islanders including community leaders, especially those of non-Caucasian descent.

Every language, and every dialect of a language, is a structured system which should be studied as such and which cannot be fruitfully regarded as mere careless speech or as a haphazard amalgam of mistakes and deviations from the norm. Hawaii's Pidgin, as a dialect of American English, is a particularly interesting case in point.

*References*

ABERCROMBIE, D. (1967), *Elements of General Phonetics*, University of Edinburgh Press.
BOLINGER, D. L. (1958a), 'A theory of pitch accent in English', *Word*, vol. 14, pp. 109–49.
BOLINGER, D. L. (1958b), 'Stress and information', *American Speech*, vol. 33, pp. 5–20.

BRONSTEIN, A. J. (1960), *The Pronunciation of American English*, New York.

CARR, E. (1961), 'Bilingual speakers in Hawaii today', *Social Process*, vol. 25, p. 54.

CATFORD, J. C. (1964), 'Phonation types: the classification of some laryngeal components of speech production', in D. Abercrombie *et al.* (eds.), *In Honour of Daniel Jones*, Longman.

HALL, R. A. Jr. (1966), *Pidgin and Creole Languages*, Ithaca, N.Y.

HULTZÉN, L. S. (1959), 'Information points in intonation', *Phonetica*, vol. 4, pp. 107–20.

JONES, D. (1966), *The Pronunciation of English*, Cambridge University Press, 4th edn.

KASDON, L. A., and SMITH, M. E. (1960), 'Pidgin usage of some pre-school children in Hawaii', *Social Process*, vol. 24, pp. 63–72.

LADEFOGED, P. (1964), *A Phonetic Study of West African Languages*, Cambridge University Press.

LIND, A. (1960), 'Communication, a problem of island youth', *Social Progress*, vol. 24, p. 46.

LINN, J. (n.d.), 'Speech improvement in Hawaii', mimeo no. 5855, Department of Speech, University of Hawaii.

PITTENGER, R. E. (1957), 'Linguistic analysis of tone of voice in communication of affect', *Psychiatric Research Reports*, vol. 8, p. 45.

PITTENGER, R. E., HOCKETT, C. F., and DANEHY, J. J. (1960), *The First Five Minutes*, Ithaca, N.Y.

REINECKE, J. E. (1969), *Language and Dialect in Hawaii: A Sociolinguistic History to 1935*, Honolulu.

REINECKE, J. E., and TOKIMASA, A. (1934), 'The English dialect of Hawaii', *American Speech*, vol. 9, pp. 48–58, 122–31.

SHUN, L. L. (1961), 'A study of selected bilingual speakers of English in the Hawaiian Islands', unpublished thesis, University of Hawaii.

# 27 Lorenzo Turner

## Gullah Intonation

Lorenzo Turner, 'Gullah intonation', *Africanisms in the Gullah Dialect,*
Chicago University Press, 1949.

Probably no characteristic of the Gullah Negro's speech appears so strange
to one who hears this dialect for the first time as its intonation. To understand fully the intonation of Gullah one will have to turn to those West
African tone languages spoken by the slaves who were being brought to
South Carolina and Georgia continually until practically the beginning of
the Civil War. Among these tone languages are Mende, Vai, Twi, Fante,
Gã, Ewe, Yoruba, Ibo, Bini, Efik, and a few others. In the discussion that
will follow, an effort has been made merely to reveal some of the more
striking similarities between certain tonal patterns of Gullah and those of
a few of the West African tone languages.

So far as my own observation is concerned, features of tone in Gullah
are not used as primary phonemes, i.e. the tones of Gullah words do not
distinguish meanings as do tones in the African tone languages. There are
in Gullah, however, several intonation patterns, used in sentences, phrases
and words, that are quite common in the African languages but are not
used in cultivated English under similar conditions. These tonal patterns
will be grouped under eight headings.

### The use of a high or mid tone at the end of a declarative sentence

In an English declarative sentence in which no implication or special
meaning is intended, the final syllable takes a falling tone if it is stressed
and a low tone if it is unstressed. In a similar Gullah declarative sentence,
however, the final syllable frequently takes a high or mid tone, and the
syllable may be stressed heavily, or weakly, or not at all.

$de_2$ 'tɒ$k_3$ ɒ$n_2$ h$\text{DU}_2$ h$i_2$ 'k$\Lambda s_3$ d$\varepsilon m_2$ 'They talked about how he cursed them'
$d$ə$_1$ 'g$\text{D}d_3$ 'w$\Lambda k_2$ 'It is God's work'

In many West African languages the final syllable of a declarative
sentence frequently takes a high or mid tone when no implication or
special meaning is intended:

Ewe:   $o_1 ve_1 ko_1 me_1 kp$ɔ$_3$ 'No, I saw only two'
       $de_1 vi_3 la_3 va_3$ 'The child came'
       $e_3 ts$ɔ$_{3-1} tu_3$ 'He took the gun'

Ibo:  ɔ$_3$ de$_1$ n$_1$sö$_3$ 'It is near'
  ɔ$_3$ de$_1$ n$_2$sɔ$_2$ 'It is forbidden'

Yoruba: mo$_2$ro$_3$hũ$_2$ke$_3$Ɉi$_1$ lo$_2$ru$_3$kɔ$_2$ mi$_2$ 'mo$_2$ro$_3$hũ$_2$ke$_3$ Ɉi$_1$ is my name'
  mo$_2$ sɔ$_2$ ɔ$_2$ 'I told it'
  nwɔ̃$_3$ wa$_3$ ni$_3$ ɔ$_2$mɔ̃$_2$de$_3$ 'They came as children'
  o$_3$ da:$_2$ 'It is good'

## The use of a rising tone at the end of a declarative sentence

On the final stressed syllable of an English declarative sentence, as already indicated, only a falling tone would be used unless some special meaning is intended. In Gullah, on the other hand, as in several West African languages, the rising tone is common in this position:

Gullah:  DI$_1$ 'tɛl$_3$ əm$_3$ 'so$_{1-3}$ 'I tell them so'
  'dat$_1$ 'flat$_2$ 'flDU$_{2-3}$ 'That's flat flour'
  'man$_3$ n$_1$ 'wɛɪf$_3$ n$_1$ 'cɪl$_3$ən$_1$ də$_1$ 'wʌk$_3$ fə$_1$ 'dɛm$_{2-3}$ '[The] man and wife and children are working for them'

Ewe:  e$_3$kpɔ$_3$ ho$_{1-3}$ 'He possesses money,' lit. 'He saw, received money'
  gɛ:$_{1-3}$ 'It is money'
  et$_3$sɔ$_3$ a$_1$ti$_3$ ɖe$_3$ a$_1$bɔ$_3$ta$_{1-3}$ 'He carries a tree on his shoulder'

Efik:  e$_3$fe$_{1-3}$ 'It flies'
  e$_3$be$_{1-3}$ 'He passes'
  a$_1$mi$_1$ ŋ$_3$ka$_{1-3}$ 'I go'

Yoruba: mo$_2$ mɔ̃:$_{1-2}$ 'I knew her'

## The use of level tones – mid, high or low – throughout a statement

Gullah: yu$_2$ 'go$_3$ dɛ$_3$ ən$_3$ 'mit$_3$ səm$_3$ 'man$_3$ 'brʌk$_2$ 'You go there and meet some man broken'
  'ol$_3$ 'le$_3$ɾɪ$_3$, yu$_2$ 'bɛ$_2$tə$_3$ go$_3$ 'hom$_3$ go$_3$ 'si$_3$ bɐu$_3$cɔ$_3$ 'cɪl$_3$ən$_2$ 'Old lady, you'd better go home and see about your children'
  'dɛm$_3$ 'gal$_3$ 'kʌm$_3$ 'hom$_3$; 'de$_3$ 'tɒk$_3$ ɒn$_2$ hɒu$_2$ hi$_2$ 'kʌs$_3$ dɛm$_2$ 'Those girls came home; they talked about how he cursed them'

The occurrence of many level tones in words, phrases and sentences is a common phenomenon in West African languages.

Ibo:  ö$_3$nyɛ$_3$ a$_3$nya$_3$ u$_3$ku$_3$ 'covetous person'
  ö$_3$gö$_3$nö$_3$gö$_3$ ö$_3$si$_3$si$_3$ 'tall tree'
  a$_3$kwa$_2$la$_2$ a$_2$kwa$_2$ 'Do not cry'
  e$_3$kwu$_2$ze$_2$na$_2$ ɔ$_2$kwu$_2$ 'Stop speaking'
  mu$_3$ lɛ$_3$ma$_3$ a$_3$na$_3$ 'Let me be looking'
  mu$_1$fan$_1$ mi$_1$, n$_1$ɲin$_1$ i$_1$sa$_3$ŋa$_1$ ɔ$_1$tɔ$_1$ kiet$_1$ 'My friend, let us walk together'

Yoruba: ba$_2$ba$_2$ ba$_2$ba$_2$ mi$_2$ 'my grandfather,' lit. 'the father of my father'

mo$_2$ mɔ̃$_2$ ba$_2$ba$_2$ rɛ$_2$ 'I knew your father'

kai$_3$ye$_3$ o$_3$ gũ$_3$ 'May the world be straight'

Ewe: nu$_3$ la$_3$ tsɔ$_3$tsɔ$_3$ 'the carrying of the thing'

to$_3$ɖo$_3$ɖo$_3$ nu$_3$fi$_3$a$_3$la$_3$ 'obedience to the teacher'

me$_1$ga$_1$yi$_1$ 'I went again'

Vai: goŋ$_1$go$_1$lo:$_1$goŋ$_1$go$_1$lo:$_1$goŋ$_1$go$_1$lo$_1$ 'anything very large or ponderous'

## The alternation of low and mid or low and high tones throughout a statement

Gullah: 'de$_3$ nə$_2$ 'en$_2$ 'nʌn$_2$ ə$_2$ dɛm$_2$ 'bɪn$_3$ dɛ$_2$ 'tɒk$_3$ 'lɒŋ$_2$ 'tɒɪm$_2$ 'There haven't been any of them there to talk in a long time'

'tʌk$_1$ 'ca$_1$ ə$_1$ 'mɒɪ$_3$ 'hɐʊs$_1$ 'wɒɪls$_3$ 'dɪ, 'liw$_{2-3-1}$ 'Take care of my house while I leave'

'dɛm$_2$ də$_1$ 'ca$_2$ əm$_1$ də$_1$ 'ʃi$_2$ əm$_1$ dɪ$_1$ 'pi$_2$pl$_1$ wɒt$_1$ haw$_1$ 'man$_2$ n$_1$ 'wɛɪf$_2$ n$_1$ 'cɪl$_3$ən$_1$ də$_1$ 'wʌk$_3$ fə$_1$ 'dɛm$_{2-3}$ 'They carry them and give them to the people who have man and wife and children to work for them'

Ibo: ɔ$_3$kɔ$_1$ ɛ$_2$dɛɪ 'He planted coco yam'

ɛ$_3$ bum$_1$ a$_1$kwa$_2$ na$_1$ dʒi$_2$ 'I have brought eggs and yam'

Efik: n$_3$sin$_1$ i$_2$sɔŋ$_1$ 'I am laying the floor'

e$_1$di$_3$wak$_1$ o$_2$wo$_1$ 'a crowd of people'

Ewe: a$_1$ti$_3$zɔ$_1$ti$_3$ 'walking-stick'

e$_3$ɖe$_1$ e$_3$me$_1$ 'He took its inside out'

a$_1$ti$_3$ la$_1$ kɔ$_3$ 'The tree is high'

Yoruba: i$_1$ya$_3$ mi$_2$ n$_3$ʃɛ$_3$ ʃaŋ$_1$go$_3$bũ$_1$mi$_2$ 'My mother had the name of? ʃaŋ$_1$go$_3$bũ$_1$mi$_2$'

ni$_3$gba$_1$ti$_3$ nwɔ̃$_3$ si$_1$ de$_3$ ɔ$_1$hũ$_3$ nwɔ̃$_3$ ʃe$_1$re$_3$ kpu$_3$kpɔ$_1$ 'When they arrived there, they played a great deal'

## The use of tones that fall from high to mid

Gullah: dɪ$_2$ gɒn$_2$ dɛ$_2$, gɒɪn$_1$ 'wɪz$_2$ɪt$_2$ 'hɪm$_{3-2}$ 'I went there to visit him'

i$_1$ 'bʌnt$_2$ 'ʌm$_{3-2}$ 'He burned them'

'ʌ$_2$'ɲʌn$_{3-2}$ 'onion'

Efik: a$_1$ma$_{3-2}$ ɔ$_2$fɔn$_2$, ɲe$_2$kop$_2$ 'If it is good, I will consider it'

Ibo: ɛ$_1$bɛ:$_{3-2}$ ka$_1$ i$_2$ dʒɛ$_1$kɔ$_1$ 'Where are you going?'

Yoruba: o$_1$ũ$_2$ da:$_{3-2}$ 'He is good'

o$_2$ ba:$_{3-2}$ lai$_3$ye$_1$ ? 'You met her alive?'

# The use of tones that rise from low or mid to high or from low to mid

In English this tone might occur when some special meaning is implied, or it might occur at the end of an unfinished tonal group – for example, at the end of a subordinate clause that does not end the sentence; but it does not occur under such conditions as obtain in the following Gullah sentences:

$de_1$ $'aks_3$ $'ples_2fə_2$ $sɪt_2$ $'dɒʊn_{2-1}$ $'af_3tə_2$ $u_2nə_2$ $'gɒn_{2-3}$ 'They asked for a place to sit down after you left'

$di_1$ $ol_1$ $le_1di_1$ $'dɒɪ_{1-3}$ $nɒʊ_1$ 'The old lady is dead now'

Efik:     $e_1ɲe_3$ $a_3ka_{1-2}$ $i_1ŋwaŋ_2$ 'He goes to the farm'
          $a_1mi_1$ $ŋ_3ka_{1-3}$ 'I go'

Ewe:     $ɲa_{1-3}ti_3$ 'my tree'
          $a_1ŋu_1ti_3$ $gbo_3gbo_{1-3}$ 'unripe lime'

Yoruba: $mo_2mɔ̃:_{1-2}$ 'I knew her'
          $ɔ_1rɔ_1$ $kpu_3opɔ_1$ $ki:_{1-2}$ $kũ_3$ $a_2gbɔ̃_1$ 'Many words do not fill a basket'

# The use of non-English tones in Gullah words and short phrases

Gullah:    $bʌ_1krʌ_3$ 'white man'
          $hʌz_1bʌn_3$ 'husband'
          $o_1kra_3$ 'okra'
          $be_1bi_3$ 'baby'
          $bʌnt_2$ $ʌm_{3-2}$ 'Burn them'

Ibo:     $a_1la_1$ 'ground'
          $n_1nɛ_3$ 'mother'
          $u_1do_3$ $o_3bi_1$ 'peace of heart'

Efik:     $u_1di_1$ 'grave'
          $u_3di_1$ 'a town in Nigeria'
          $e_1fe_2$ 'shed'
          $e_3fe_1$ 'which'?
          $o_3du_3du_3$ 'hole'

Twi:     $ɔ_1kra_3$ 'soul'

Ewe:     $ka_1$ 'to scatter'
          $ka_3$ 'to touch'
          $a_1tsu_3$ 'male'

Yoruba: $i_1fe_2$ 'a small bird'
          $i_1fe_3$ 'whistling'
          $i_2fe_2$ 'cup'

### The use of a level tone at the end of a question

In English at the end of a question when no special meaning is implied, a rising tone is the usual one if *yes* or *no* is required for an answer, and a falling tone if it is not. In Gullah, on the other hand, a level tone is quite common at the end of a question whether or not *yes* or *no* is required for an answer.

Gullah: $w\text{ɒ}t_3$ 'd$\varepsilon m_{2-1}$ d$\text{ə}_1$ 'ʃ$i_2$ $yu_2$ 'What do they give you?'

'$yu_3$ $no_3$ $w\text{ɒ}t_3$ d$\varepsilon m_3$ 'p$e_3$ f$\text{ə}_2$ 'bi$n_3$? 'Do you know what they pay for beans?'

'$\varepsilon n_2 ti_3$'r $\varepsilon_2 bl_2$ t$\text{ɒ}$ɪ$m_2$ $k\text{ʌ}m_2$ɪ$n_2$ 'ba$k_2$? 'Isn't slavery coming back?'

In the West African languages a level tone is frequently heard at the conclusion of both types of questions.

Efik: $m_1 m\text{ɔ}_3$ŋ$\text{ɔ}_1$ $e_1 nye_2$ $\text{ɔ}_2 kp\text{ɔ}_2 b\text{ɔ}_1$? 'Do you think he would have taken it?'

$n_1 si_3 di_3$ $n_3 tak_3$ $m_3 m\text{ɔ}_1$ $i_1 mi_{3-1}$ $ka_1$ $ha_2$ $e_2 k\text{ɔ}$ŋ$_2$? 'Why didn't they go to war?'

Ibo: $k\varepsilon_1 do_3$ ö$_3 tu_3$ ö$_3$ $si_1$ $ti_3$ $ge_2$? 'How did he hit you?'

Yoruba: $ta_2 lo_3$ $k\text{ɔ}_2$ $ku_3$, $i_1 ya_3$ $r\varepsilon_2$ $ta_1 bi_3$ $ba_2 ba_2$ $r\varepsilon$? 'Who was it that died first, your mother or your father?'

$kp\varepsilon_1 lu_3$ $ta_2 ni_2$? 'With whom?'

$o_3$ ŋ$_3 gbe_3$ $kp\varepsilon_1 lu_3$ $r\varepsilon_2$? 'He is living with you?'

Ewe: $mi_1 a_3 va_3 a_1$? 'Are you coming?'

$ma_3 kpe_3$ ɖ$e_3$ ŋ$u_1 wo_3 a_1$? 'Am I to help you?'

# Acknowledgements

First thanks go to the authors who have permitted their works to be republished and cooperated in the alterations necessary to make them fit into a coherent whole, in several cases revising extensively; and no less to the two whose articles appear here for the first time.

The editor is grateful also to those who made suggestions about what to include: Isamu Abe, David Crystal, Fred W. Householder Jr, and William S.-Y. Wang.

Permission to reproduce the following readings in this volume is acknowledged to the following sources:

1 Harvard Educational Review
2 Marcel Didier (Canada) Ltd
3 University of Michigan Press
4 Longman Group Ltd
5 Robert P. Stockwell
6 Cambridge University Press
7 Marcel Didier (Canada) Ltd
8 United States Office of Education
9 *Phonetica* S. Karger, Basel
10 Richard Gunter
11 Mouton & Co
12 *Journal of the Acoustical Society of America*
13 Longman Group Ltd
14 *Ethnomusicology*
15 General Gramphone Publications Ltd
16 *Zeitschrift für Phonetik Sprachwissenschaft und Kommunikationsforschung*
17 Linguistic Society of America
18 *Pacific Linguistics*
19 *Word*
20 *Phonetica* S. Karger, Basel
21 Longman Group Ltd
22 *Journal of the Acoustical Society of America*
23 *Journal of the Acoustical Society of America*
24 *Phonetica* S. Karger, Basel
25 *Acta Philologica Scandinavica*
26 *Quarterly Journal of Speech*
27 Arno Press and Lorenzo Turner

# Author Index

# Subject Index